T0051646

Stalin and the Fate of Europe

STALIN
and the
FATE of
EUROPE

THE POSTWAR STRUGGLE
FOR SOVEREIGNTY

Norman M. Naimark

The Belknap Press of Harvard University Press

CAMBRIDGE, MASSACHUSETTS

LONDON, ENGLAND

2019

In memory of Selma Naimark Carra, 1921–2017

First printing

Library of Congress Cataloging-in-Publication Data
Name: Naimark, Norman M., author.
Title: Stalin and the fate of Europe : the postwar struggle for sovereignty /
Norman M. Naimark.
Description: Cambridge, Massachusetts : The Belknap Press of Harvard University Press,
2019. | Includes bibliographical references and index.
Identifiers: LCCN 2019012559 | ISBN 9780674238770 (alk. paper)
Subjects: LCSH: Stalin, Joseph, 1878-1953. | Cold War. | Communist countries—
Boundaries. | Europe—History—1945- | Europe—Politics and
government—1945- | Soviet Union—Foreign relations—1945-1991. |
North Atlantic Treaty Organization.
Classification: LCC D843 .N266 2019 | DDC 940.55/4—dc23 LC record available at
https://lccn.loc.gov/2019012559

Book design by Dean Bornstein

CONTENTS

INTRODUCTION

We forget, perhaps, how much of the world is not controlled by the
Great Powers and how many people have a will of their own.
—A. J. P. TAYLOR

The European continent was utterly devastated by World War II. Everywhere were destroyed cities and sad throngs of hungry faces. Whatever differences there might have been between eastern and western Europe in the interwar period—mostly deriving from economic underdevelopment over significant stretches of eastern Europe—were leveled by the horrendous costs of the war in human lives and materiel. The continent as a whole was beset by hunger, apathy, unemployment, and, especially during the winter of 1946–1947, fierce cold—the worst in three centuries. Food and coal were in desperately short supply. Food production sank to two-thirds of the prewar level in part because of the shortage of fertilizer, livestock, and labor. Kerosene was found in some localities for light and cooking. Wood, charcoal, and peat—when available—served as the main sources of heat. Europeans were destitute, malnourished, and weakened by the low caloric intake. This in turn prompted the frequent appearance of pneumonia, diphtheria, tuberculosis, and typhus. Given the widespread shortages of drugs—in particular penicillin, sulpha drugs, and antibiotics—disease, epidemics, and high rates of death from illness were inevitable. Not surprisingly, the elderly and very young were the most susceptible.

Tens of millions of people were on the move in 1944–1945: demobilized soldiers, returning POWs and forced laborers, expellees, settlers, deserters, and drifters in search of booty, work, and something to eat. Up to forty million people were displaced during the war.[1] After having survived the wartime years of highly restrictive and punitive labor laws (including the threat of mobilization), factory workers in Łódź, Milan, Paris, and elsewhere went on strike for higher wages, better working conditions, and, frequently, increased workers' control. Frightful anti-Semitism was rampant in many European societies, despite—indeed one could argue because of—what the Nazis had done to the Jews. Instead of stamping out anti-Semitism, knowledge of what happened to the Jews seemed only to exacerbate it. Few locals wanted the Jews back in their communities, east or west, and those Jews who returned to their homes and workplaces tended to face the hostility bred, in many cases, by guilt and indifference.[2] Avaricious and sometimes simply needy neighbors had seized Jewish homes and shops during the war. Few were ready to return them afterward.[3]

Europeans in all parts of the continent resented ethnic minorities. During the war and after, the ruling nationalities carried out generally popular policies of ethnic cleansing. The Nazi leaders were the primary perpetrators of the violent deportations of peoples, but they also forcibly resettled Germans from the east to return to the Reich (*Heim ins Reich*) to take over the farms and properties of deported minorities. Once the war was lost, Germans themselves were driven from their former homes in eastern and central Europe in the millions, as the combination of changing borders and attacks by nationalist vigilante and militia groups exposed German communities to extreme danger.[4] Hungarians, Ukrainians, Italians, Poles, and others faced the same fate in territories where they once held sway and were now no longer welcome. The victorious Soviets joined the act, both by approving the deportation of minority peoples and by cleansing their own territory of Poles and Germans.

Many targeted peoples tried to adopt new national identities to avoid expulsions, whether Italians in Dalmatia, Ukrainians in Poland, or Hungarians in Slovakia. German Silesians and Mazurians claimed that they were Poles. In the newly constituted Czechoslovakia, Yugoslavia, and Poland, judicial processes decided who was a "native" and who was not.[5] The nationalist principle reigned supreme. Keeping in mind the elimination of the vast majority of European Jews, Poland was never so Polish as after the war, Ukraine never so Ukrainian, Germany never so German, Denmark never so Danish, and Italy never so Italian.[6]

Yet everywhere, too, people sought solace in the latest dances and music, jazz and swing, and did what they could to come up with fashionable outfits to wear among the ruins, using the black markets that sprang up all over Europe to obtain occasional luxuries to distract themselves from poverty and want.[7] Sexual mores were upended as women were sometimes forced to seek sustenance through semi-prostitution with occupation soldiers. Roving groups of weary trekkers, men and women, found some comfort in sex and coupling. In the displaced persons (DP) camps set up by the Allies for Jews in Germany after liberation, many of whom had fled postwar hostility and persecution in Poland, there were a striking number of marriages and births, as refugee Jews, just like other Europeans, sought to put the past behind them and embark on a new life.[8]

The psychological state of Europeans was complex and difficult. One Polish historian describes what he calls "the great fear" (*wielka trwoga*) experienced by the vast majority of Poles, a deep unease about what would become of them given the horrors they had endured, the extreme want that surrounded them, the political uncertainty of incipient communist rule, and the incessant rumors of a new world war.[9] In German-language memoirs, one encounters repeatedly the words for anxiety (*Verzweiflung* and *Angst*), which characterized the mood of the Germans. There was also hope, but it tended to be overwhelmed by fear and anxiety.[10] At the end of the war and beginning of the peace, suicide rates jumped to record numbers. Especially Germans and Austrians were terrified of the onslaught of Soviet troops and the impending occupation. But even after the war was over the challenges of staying alive and safe were too much for many Europeans.

Women were in a particularly psychologically challenging position at the end of the war. Their husbands, brothers, sons, and fathers were often absent, killed in the war, languishing in POW camps, or simply missing. Not only were they the primary "workhorses" of reconstruction, but for every surviving male there were 1.6 women of marriageable age.[11] The insecurity of not knowing whether their loved ones were alive or dead, or where they were interned—and not being able to communicate with them if they were in POW camps or on labor details in the USSR—was extremely trying. This became a major political issue in Soviet-occupied Germany and Austria, as well as in Italy and Hungary. Men who returned from camps were often physically or emotionally broken, and turned out to pose a greater burden for the household economy than when they were absent. Divorce rates skyrocketed.[12]

Women and girls had their own traumas to bear, starting with humiliating accusations of and social punishment for "horizontal collaboration" in Norway, France, Poland, Italy, and elsewhere. There was also the ever-present threat and reality of rape and sexual violence by Allied soldiers, which continued even after the end of the war in all the occupation zones of Germany and Austria (though far worse in the Soviet zones), in France and Italy, and in east central Europe, especially in Hungary.[13] Informal prostitution was known wherever Allied soldiers were billeted. The spread of syphilis and gonorrhea became a major issue for Allied commanders and for local health officials, especially given the shortages (or complete absence in the east) of penicillin. If infected, Soviet soldiers were forced to endure excruciating applications of mercury.

The occupations imposed burdens beyond those of threats to and violence against women. The Allies confiscated housing for their troops and villas for their officers, while many locals had to find shelter in barns and garages. They requisitioned food and coal, which were in desperately short supply. The Soviets took reparations from Germany and Austria, and removed supposedly German assets from eastern Europe, as well. The political officers of the victorious armies, east and west, often behaved with arrogant superiority toward the indigenous populations, which in turn aroused considerable resentment and anger. With some bitterness, Europeans noted that they would be glad to be "liberated from the liberators." In all of the war-ravaged countries of Europe, planning for reconstruction was at the heart of government and policy planning. East and west, the desires of the extreme left and extreme right quickly made themselves known at the end of the war but faded quickly in comparison to the need for governments to take the lead in clearing rubble, rebuilding cities, and getting basic infrastructure—water, sewage, transportation—back in place.[14] The centralization of economic life during the war in many parts of the continent contributed to the "etatization" of Europe's economies in the postwar period.[15]

Postwar Europe was no place for utopian fantasies. The political catastrophes that engulfed the countries of Europe during the war—the murderous attacks on the left, the collaboration of the right, and the demonstrable fecklessness of the liberals—had intensified rather than gutted the desire for the reconstitution of political parties after the peace, albeit in the new framework of anti-fascism and democratic institutions. The lust for revenge and retribution after the war certainly took its toll in victims and political uncertainty. The demand for justice quickly gave way in most of Europe to scapegoating and then to selective memory as Belgians, French, Dutch, Poles, Czechs, and others eagerly pursued the return to normalcy and regularity in their lives.[16]

The "shadow of the past" would never quite elude postwar European culture and politics, haunting those years (and even up to today) in unpredictable ways.[17] The tasks at hand of feeding, housing, and heating the dwellings of a desperate population quickly took precedence throughout Europe. Besides, so many people were implicated in one fashion or another in the crimes of the wartime regimes that few were interested in a thorough cleansing of the administrations or political parties that had survived as forces of order in postwar society.[18] Continuities between the wartime and postwar periods were as notable as the elements of starting afresh at the so-called zero hour, *Stunde Null*.

The Soviet Union had won the war on the ground in Europe. Its troops were present in many parts of the continent, from the Danish island of Bornholm to the Bulgarian littoral of the Black Sea. The Red Army had liberated the capitals of central Europe—Warsaw, Prague, Berlin, Vienna, and Budapest—sometimes at enormous cost to their soldiers and with disastrous results for the local populations. The Soviet people themselves suffered desperately from the consequences of the war. The sheer grief and mourning of losing twenty-seven million soldiers and civilians—more than sixty-five times the American losses during the war—weighed heavily on the society.[19] The fierce fighting on and German occupation of the western part of the Soviet Union created untold misery for the peoples of the region. As a result of the destruction, tens of millions lived in utter poverty, many finding shelter in hovels, earthen dugouts, and bombed-out apartment blocks. Yet the Soviet state was intact, its army—some six and a half million strong—was an intimidating presence on the continent. Thus was Stalin poised to lead the Allied efforts to construct a postwar settlement in Europe.

At Cecilienhof, the German royal residence in Potsdam, Stalin gave every appearance of being in control during the Allied conference of July 17 to August 2, 1945. Franklin Roosevelt had fallen ill earlier that spring and died on April 12. He was replaced by Harry S. Truman, who had little experience in foreign affairs and only reluctantly attended the Potsdam summit at all. That Winston Churchill lost the British election of July 25, 1945, and was replaced at Potsdam by the Labor leader Clement Attlee only raised Stalin's status in Europe and the world as the senior leader of the victorious wartime coalition. Truman was reportedly buoyed by the information that he received in Potsdam of the successful testing on July 16, 1945, of the atomic bomb in Alamogordo, New Mexico. But Stalin himself seemed little intimidated by this news, which Truman whispered in his ear at a conference reception.[20] Stalin already knew about the nuclear weapons project through his intelligence. Much more important for the Soviet dictator was the actual explosion of the bomb on August 6 at Hiroshima, which prompted him to order his secret police chief, Lavrentii Beria, to launch an all-out Soviet project to build a bomb.[21]

There is very little evidence that Stalin had a preconceived plan for creating a bloc of countries in Europe with a common Soviet-style system. Given his proclivity to see the world through ideological lenses, his long-term goals included the communization of Europe (and the world). But in the short term, he was most concerned that Germany not be rearmed or rendered capable of carrying out another invasion of the Soviet Union through Poland, and that the countries of east central Europe not serve as willing helpmates in such a war. Stalin frequently noted after 1945 that war with Germany was likely in fifteen or twenty years. He also was worried about the West's possession of the atomic bomb and its potential use against the Soviet Union militarily, in a direct conflict between Moscow and the West, but also politically, as a way to deprive him of his territorial gains in Europe.[22] Stalin's growing interest after the war in spreading Soviet influence into east central Europe may well have been related to the idea that increased Soviet "space" would compensate him for the postwar asymmetry in

1. Postwar Europe

nuclear weaponry with the West.[23] (The first Soviet bomb was successfully tested only in August 1949.)

The immediate postwar years, the chronological period of greatest concern in this work, were characterized by the emergence of legitimate conflicts between the security interests of the Soviet Union on one side and the United States and Great Britain on the other. These conflicts were palpable already before the end of World War II and grew more salient as the fighting came to an end and joint efforts to construct a peaceful postwar world failed to satisfy the victors. But diplomacy still was able to resolve some testy questions and provide long-term solutions. A few of the cases I present necessarily reach beyond the 1948–1949 outer limit, when conflicts of great power interest were frequently overwhelmed by ideological hostility. But most of the discussion in this book is centered on the early years of the peace, when, I would suggest, there was greater fluidity and openness to postwar settlement in Europe than is often assumed both in the historiography and in public memory.[24]

As a way to understand the development of the uneasy peace and, within several years, the division of the continent that followed, I have conceived this study along three primary vectors, the first of which is Stalin and his policies toward Europe. From the time of the Russian Civil War (1917–1922) and the Polish-Soviet War (1919–1921) up through the tense period of the Nazi-Soviet Pact (1939–1941) and especially war with the Third Reich (1941–1945), Stalin had garnered considerable experience in dealing with the outside world. This he brought to bear in his flexible and probing approach to the problems in Europe during the postwar years. The second vector of this study involves the challenges, goals, and accomplishments of the European nations themselves and their politics after World War II. I am as interested in the political development and reconstruction of postwar Europe as its governments confronted the power, prestige, and influence of Stalin and the Soviet Union as I am in the shifting contours of Moscow's policies and actions. The third and final vector at play here is the coming of the Cold War, in particular the growing Soviet-American rivalry and the mutual hostility that exacerbated it. This hostility inevitably influenced events in the nations of Europe, but an important goal of this study is to foreground European considerations and keep Cold War politics, as important as they later become, in appropriate perspective. Most of the events in the book take place at the intersection of these three vectors— Stalin's policies, European politics, and the coming of the Cold War— where they influence one another and to some extent merge, making it difficult to talk about one without the others.

Stalin

There is something to John Gaddis's statement that "as long as Stalin was running the Soviet Union a cold war was unavoidable."[25] In any analysis of the dictator's policies, foreign or domestic, one has to factor in his pathological predisposition to create enemies internally and externally, to focus on the ideologically determined hostility between capitalism and socialism, and to see the Soviet Union involved in a worldwide class war. To deprive Stalin of his ideological lenses and Bolshevik mentality would be to miss important dimensions of his motivations. When, at the end of World War II, the Soviet Union absorbed new territories and fighting erupted in a series of civil wars on the USSR's new western borders and in its freshly incorporated lands, Stalin sense of insecurity only seemed to increase.[26]

Stalin's views are important to Europe because he sat at the very epicenter of Soviet foreign policy making after the war. There is no question that the input of Foreign Minister Viacheslav Molotov was important and that a variety of party officials, higher officials in the foreign ministry, and even military officers—"bold subordinates" as one historian characterized them—played important roles here and there in decision making.[27] But Stalin not only oversaw the entire process, stepping in when he thought it was time for him to take a decisive role; he was also a micromanager, watching his deputies like a hawk as they handled a myriad of issues over which he had supreme control. He was hardworking, focused, and capable of absorbing vast amounts of information regarding international developments. Despite his frequent absences from the Kremlin in Sochi to revive his flagging health in the postwar years, Stalin remained in command and, as was noted in the propaganda of the time, "always at his post" (*Stalin vsegda na postu*), using the telephone, telegraph, and visits from senior officials to maintain his reins of power. One is quickly convinced in reading his editorial remarks on proposed newspaper articles, analyses of foreign policy, annotations in the margins of books, or his rewriting of party statements that Stalin was smart and knowledgeable, with a penchant for lively and direct prose.[28] He was determined to remain in charge in particular of foreign affairs, despite a full agenda of domestic problems, and his underlings knew that.

Although he was trying to minimize his responsibility for the crimes of the Stalin era, Nikita Khrushchev was essentially correct about the role of the Soviet leadership when he wrote in his memoirs, "The rest of us were just errand boys."²⁹ Molotov said something very similar when he noted that the decisive figure in the making of Soviet foreign policy was Stalin and not some diplomat.³⁰

Stalin sometimes even abused Molotov as a way to make sure that he did not exceed his mandate as foreign minister. In one notable incident in early December 1945, Stalin pointedly criticized Molotov in a letter to the other three of his chief deputies, Georgi Malenkov, Lavrentii Beria, and Anastas Mikoyan. (Molotov was the fourth in the ruling "four," the *chetverka*). Molotov had made such serious errors in judgment as foreign minister, wrote Stalin to the three, that "I can no longer consider such a comrade my first deputy." Stalin added that he was not at all sure that Molotov had a "clear conscience." When read Stalin's recriminations by the deputies in person, Molotov broke down in tears. He then wrote a pathetic letter of self-criticism to Stalin (December 7) that was more a demonstration of total subservience than an explanation for his misdeeds. He expressed deep sorrow at the expression of Stalin's unhappiness with him and his work and promised that he would "earn back the trust of Stalin and the party."³¹

Stalin never mentioned this incident again, and Molotov was allowed to continue as foreign minister until 1949, and as an important, if distrusted, member of the ruling party elite until 1952, when he was dropped from the presidium elected at the Nineteenth Party Congress. There is still a lot we do not know about the way Stalin made and implemented decisions: relatively few documents emanated from Stalin himself and from those around him at the time, and a significant portion of the Stalin papers remains classified.³² But we can be sure that Stalin himself was responsible for the conception and implementation of Soviet policies abroad.

Stalin no doubt read and shared many of the suppositions of two of the major policy-planning documents to emerge from the Ministry of Foreign Affairs during World War II, Ivan Maiskii's "Note" of January 10, 1944, and Maxim Litvinov's "Memorandum" of January 11, 1945. According to the Maiskii note, continental Europe would be inevitably transformed into a series of socialist states. Barring armed conflict, which could speed the process, this would take somewhere between thirty and fifty years. Meanwhile, Soviet cooperation with the United

States and Great Britain was critical for setting up democratic regimes and functioning economies in formerly fascist and fascist-occupied countries.[33]

The Litvinov document was prepared in association with the upcoming Yalta Conference and explored the possibility of establishing an agreement between the Allies about three spheres of influence on the continent: one zone in the east and north, including Finland, Sweden, Poland, Hungary, Czechoslovakia, Romania, Yugoslavia, Bulgaria, and Turkey, that would be linked to the Soviet Union. A second zone would be dominated by Great Britain and include Holland, Belgium, France, Spain, Portugal, and Greece. Most interesting was the so-called "neutral sphere," which included Germany, as well as Denmark and Norway, Austria, and Italy. In this zone, the great powers would share responsibility for the security of the area, cooperating on issues of reparations and trade.[34]

There is no indication in these documents or even in the immediate postwar period that Stalin intended to get into a worldwide shoving match with the United States, nor did he anticipate that one would emerge from the circumstances of the settlement following World War II. Great Britain was always identified as the Soviet Union's primary rival, its policies seen as deeply contradictory with those of the United States. Stalin had no firm plan for postwar Europe, nor even what we would call today a road map for the development of a socialist continent. He was too tactically inclined for that. It is likely that he looked at the future of countries as diverse as Great Britain, Spain, Norway, Czechoslovakia and Greece with the idea that they would develop into different constellations of people's democratic governments, ruled by coalitions of the left and center, including communist parties, that would gradually stabilize their respective societies and rebuild their economies, based primarily on the model of state-controlled industries. Eventually, these countries might move by stages to more socialist-oriented governments, but not precipitously and not in the near future. As we know from the examples of Greece and Yugoslavia, as well as from Stalin's treatment of leftist revolutionaries all over the continent, he was not interested in fomenting socialist revolutions in Europe; nor was he anxious to alienate the Americans and British by assisting in the elimination of noncommunist parties of the left and center.[35]

Arguments among historians about whether Stalin was motivated primarily by Leninist internationalism or by foreign policy realism do not make a lot of sense in the context of postwar Europe. Stalin was by all accounts the ultimate realist. In fact, one might best think of him as a hyperrealist, which constituted, as he himself understood it, the essential meaning of Marxist-Leninist-Stalinist teaching when it came to foreign affairs, which he firmly believed advanced the thinking of Lenin to a new level. During the war, he noted to the Croatian communist leader Andrija Hebrang, "Lenin did not think you could conclude an alliance with one wing of the bourgeoisie against the other. We have done that: we are not led by emotions but by *rational analysis calculation*."[36] This kind of super pragmatism in foreign affairs was embedded, to be sure, in Stalin's own sharp awareness of the geopolitical interests of the Soviet Union and his sensitivities to the vulnerability of the Soviet Union—and before that Imperial Russia—to invasion from external powers.[37]

This does not mean that Stalin did not sometimes make mistakes in his foreign policy calculations. In the course of this book, the reader will see that he made quite a few such errors of judgment. But he made every effort to weigh carefully ends against means and assess without wearing any blinders the "correlation of forces," a factor in foreign policy making that constantly informed his decisions. After the Second World War, he was convinced—absolutely correctly—that he could not fight a war against Great Britain and the United States. Thus he would push, demand, and bully, short of provoking warlike reactions on the part of his former Allies. He would try to defuse conflict situations, like the Greek Civil War or the Azerbaijan dispute in Iran, which had the potential of breaking out into a wider conflict. His policies in China and Korea were especially cautious and moderate. Not even President Truman's refusal on August 18, 1945, to allow the Soviets to land in Hokkaido according to their plans—and thus participate in the occupation of Japan—deflected Stalin from his course of accommodation with the United States in Asia and Europe.[38]

Above all Stalin sought security for the Soviet Union, while looking to expand Soviet influence in Europe. Defending the interests of the Soviet Union was, in essence, what it meant to be a good communist anywhere in Europe—or the world. Excessive ideological enthusiasm, frequently known derogatorily in party circles as "sectarianism," was for naïfs. Unwavering obedience and thoroughgoing understanding of Moscow's priorities were the crucial markers of a good communist. Among the best Stalinists, foreign and domestic, was an unspoken code of rigid hierarchy that needed no articulation or discussion. In a conversation of November 19, 1944, the head of the French Communist Party, Maurice Thorez, profusely thanked Stalin for his advice and counsel. Stalin replied that there was no need for thanks. These matters, he said, are perfectly understood between communists.[39]

Stalin's goals on the continent were geostrategic in the narrowest sense of the term; he was desirous of exerting influence in all of Europe but above all in the bordering lands of eastern Europe. At the same time, he showed remarkable lack of interest in the colonies both of his wartime enemies and of his postwar rivals and was relatively indifferent to China, despite the successes of the Chinese Communist Party. Instead, he expressed regrets that Soviet soldiers had not marched into Paris as the Russians did in the Napoleonic Wars. "We [in Moscow] toyed with idea of reaching Paris," he told Thorez. The ever-obsequious French communist leader opined "The French people would have enthusiastically received the Red Army."[40]

But if by the fall of 1947 the vision of Soviet troops marching into Paris was a vain fantasy, Stalin's insistence on extending the Soviet Union's borders to the west, as he had by dint of the Nazi-Soviet Pact of August 23, 1939 (specifically the secret protocols that accompanied it), and the Red Army invasion of Poland on September 17, 1939, was not. At the minimum, he sought a sphere of influence in eastern Europe and direct influence on the future development of Germany and Austria. He was determined not to allow foreign powers to gain a foothold in postwar Poland, with its borders shifted westward, in Finland (now without Karelia), and in Romania (without Bessarabia). Beyond these consistent and overlapping military and political interests, coinciding with tsarist foreign policy aims, was enormous variation and flexibility in Stalin's short and medium-term goals, whether the objects were Czechoslovakia and Hungary, Germany and Austria, or France and Italy. One of Stalin's overriding priorities was that Europe *not* be divided into strict eastern and western zones of influence. Certainly at the outset, Stalin did not want an Iron Curtain. One sees that in his policies toward Germany and Austria, which demanded that the unity of these countries be preserved, even when the Western Allies had decided that division was the most advantageous way for them to deal with the "German Question," if not that of Austria.[41] He was also anxious to receive reparations in the form of coal from the Ruhr and exert influence in France and Italy.

At the same time, Stalin wanted to see the creation of a Europe of discrete national units that he could control through bilateral relations. One observes this in his negative reaction to the formation of the West European Union or Brussels Treaty Organization of March 17, 1947, which was the anti-German security agreement between France, Great Britain and the Low Countries.[42] There was some hope in Moscow that the organization would demonstrate anti-American sentiments, but more important was the potential to oppose Soviet interests. He showed the same hostility toward attempts at a Balkan Union, proposed at different times by Marshal Tito in Yugoslavia and Georgi Dimitrov in Bulgaria. Stalin was deeply interested in Europe, but just not in one that was joined in units larger than individual countries and as such could offer resistance to his blandishments and bullying.

Stalin and the party ideologues who followed his lead designated the immediate postwar period in Europe as one of the development of "new," "popular," or "people's" democracies. His idea, derived primarily from Comintern thinking during the Popular Front period of the mid-1930s, was for Europe's communist parties to ally with socialist and other anti-fascist parties, including those of the "center," to complete the bourgeois revolution and begin the long process—sometimes articulated as twenty-five to thirty years—of a gradual transition to socialism. The idea had also been employed in 1940–1941 as a way to soften Stalin's policies in the Baltic countries as they were gradually incorporated into the Soviet Union during the period of the Nazi-Soviet Pact.

Repeatedly Stalin reminded his interlocutors that in Europe, in contrast to Russia, there was no need for "the dictatorship of the proletariat," no need for a violent revolution, and no need for bloodshed. The revolutionary dictatorship was particular to Russia because of the revolutionaries' need to overthrow tsarism and autocracy and seize control of the country during a world war and civil war. Even the British parliamentary system had the potential to evolve slowly and surely to socialism, in Stalin's view.[43] The two major countries in Europe that historically embarked on the path toward socialism, he told the leaders of the British Labour Party in a meeting of July 8, 1946, were the Soviet Union and Great Britain. The former was forced to endure a violent and at times bloody revolution; the latter could achieve socialism by peaceful means.[44]

European communist leaders at the end of the war and the beginning of the peace were granted the opportunity—indeed given the mandate—from Moscow to represent the sovereign interests of their respective peoples. They were to carry out the "anti-fascist democratic revolution" and begin the process of increasing their power and influence in society. They were to lead the fight for expropriating large landowners and industrialists but not collectivizing agriculture or imposing a dictatorship of the party in place of a parliamentary system.[45] Private property was to be respected, and national front programs, which were to appear "impeccably democratic," were to be implemented.[46] Of course, this was not always observed in practice, but Stalin's views, at least until the first meeting of the Cominform (Information Bureau of the Communist and Workers' Parties) in September 1947, and even after, provided a powerful impetus for the development of mass communist parties in Europe based on thoroughgoing patriotic impulses.

Even in a country like Poland that seemed destined to fall under Soviet control, Stalin indicated to Polish interlocutors that they would be free to choose their allies, among them, of course, the Soviet Union, and develop in the direction of a "new democracy." He told Stanisław Mikołajczyk in Moscow (August 2, 1944) that "between Poland and the Soviet Union there should be trust and friendship" but that "Poland should also have ties with England, France, and the United States." "Poland will be a big and strong country," Stalin announced during a

June 1945 discussion about the formation of the Polish Provisional Government of National Unity. "For such a Poland it is not sufficient to have ties with only one country. . . . Poland is in need of ties with Western states, with Great Britain, France, and friendly relations with America. . . . Poland should conclude new alliances."[47]

Free to form alliances where it wished, Poland would, however, follow the template of a "people's democracy." There was no need for the dictatorship of the proletariat, Stalin explained to Jakub Berman and Eduard Osóbka-Morawski in May 1946. Poland's government would be a "new type of democracy," which could go about the business of nationalizing industry and mustering the resources of the country for the benefit of the working people better than could the more retrograde forms of government presently ruling France and Britain. "Therefore," Stalin concluded, "there is no need for you to copy Western democracy. Let them copy you."[48]

Just how genuine Stalin's commitment was to these ideas is an important historical question—that is, whether the propaganda about the new democracies was not simply a ruse created to deceive the Western powers and European voters and politicians.[49] One historian calls Stalin's statements about "new democracy" nothing but a "regular performance [spektakl']."[50]

The evidence cuts both ways, depending both on the time and place Stalin indicated what he would like done and the chronology of his growing disgruntlement with the West. In some cases, he seemed determined to seize power one way or another, using the "new democracy" as a smoke screen. He upbraided the East German communists for being excessively "Teutonic" about achieving their socialist goals; instead they needed to learn to "mask" their aims.[51] Walter Ulbricht, the East German communist leader, took Stalin's message to heart when he told a group of party activists that their policies and actions "should look democratic but we must keep everything in our hands."[52] But there were other times, especially when Stalin was dealing with the Italian or Austrian communists, or even the Polish comrades in the immediate postwar period, that the "boss" indicated a genuine commitment to the idea of "new democracy."

Eventually, of course, the new democracies in eastern Europe, under increasing Soviet control, evolved into Stalinist entities, though maintaining the democratic facade of multiparty elections, "democratic blocs," and parliaments. But right after the war, many East European noncommunist leaders, especially in Hungary and Czechoslovakia, continued to believe that they were competing for electoral support in genuine, if new, democracies. Since most of them were not fools—in fact, just the contrary, most were capable and perspicacious politicians—either Stalin used extremely clever deception to draw them into his devious postwar political game or he was, at least for the time being, sincere enough in his convictions about this new and innovative transitional stage to socialism to convince them of his integrity.[53]

The latter explanation is the more likely, at least until the fallout over the Truman Doctrine in March 1947 and the Marshall Plan in June of that year convinced the already suspicious Soviet dictator that he could not trust the Americans. Those noncommunist politicians who remained behind in eastern Europe frequently ended up behind bars, put on trial, and executed by judicial order. The lucky ones narrowly managed to escape to the West with the help of American or British embassy officials.[54]

The Cold War

The history of the origins of the Cold War weaves its way in and out of any consideration of the development of immediate postwar Europe. But the history of Europe in this period should begin, at least, with the proposition that the antagonistic Soviet-American rivalry about the European settlement was not necessarily always the dominant, and certainly not the only, factor of interest in determining the ultimate fate of the continent. Even if there were signs of the coming of the Cold War, the Iron Curtain did not descend across Europe when Winston Churchill spoke of it in his famous Fulton, Missouri, speech of May 5, 1946. As Churchill's most recent biographer writes, Churchill was looking into the future rather than describing the present in his Iron Curtain speech, where "he delivered a warning just as grave, and just as prescient as any made about the Nazis in the appeasement period."[55] People, goods, ideas, and even military personnel continued to move in both directions across this "border" until well into the late 1940s and early 1950s.[56] Stalin's famous election speech of February 9, 1946, spoke of the progressive character of "the anti-fascist war," "a war of liberation, one of the tasks of which was to restore democratic liberties." In this war, Stalin emphasized, the alliance of the United States, Great Britain, and the Soviet Union played the decisive role in defeating the Nazis.[57]

We know that Stalin was ready to deal with the Allies constructively on a number of issues, ranging from the settlements in Germany and Austria to the internationalization of Ruhr coal and the Danube.[58] We will never really know for certain whether a consistent and forceful policy of engagement on the part of the United States and Great Britain, one that would have brought unrestricted aid and loans for Soviet rebuilding, not to mention access to the reparations promised at Yalta, would have made any difference in avoiding the kinds of clashes that ended up dividing Europe. There is also the question whether the counterfactual of Western willingness to accede to Soviet postwar demands for a demilitarized and neutral Germany (though, of course with Soviet troops on its eastern borders in Poland, in effect, therefore, under indirect Soviet influence) would have produced a more palatable result for all Europeans.[59]

Given Stalin's predilections it is unlikely that a settlement between the Soviet Union and the United States could have been reached that would have satisfied both sides. But that is a conclusion that one can only reach in retrospect, when we know that it never came about. At the time, an alternative history was not impossible. To state the problem a little differently, one cannot write the history of Soviet involvement in Europe without including the growing Soviet rivalry with the Americans and the unexpected and utterly novel involvement of Washington in postwar European affairs. Still it would be a distortion to blanket postwar European developments and Stalin's initiatives on the continent with the well-honed dark images and paradigms of traditional Cold War history.

The international context of European history in the years 1944–1949 has an extraordinarily rich historiography, given its integral role in the origins of the Cold War.[60] Cold War historiography grew by leaps and bounds in the Gorbachev period and after the fall of communist governments in eastern Europe and the Soviet Union. With newly available documents from the Soviet archives, in particular, a series of landmark books and articles were published that increased our understanding of Stalin's motivations, U.S. interactions with Soviet initiatives, and the escalation of conflict between Washington and Moscow.[61] Likewise seeing publication were a number of important studies of specific European countries and their participation in the dynamics of the growing rivalry between the Soviet Union and the United States.[62] But few of these studies look at Europe as a whole, and most tend to keep their periscopes leveled on Washington and Moscow, much as analogous studies of Russian and American objectives in Europe do today.[63] The realities and sometimes the pretensions of Great Powers are reflected in the works of their historians, whether approving or sometimes critical in their points of view.

The Cominform meeting of late September 1947 in Szklarska Poręba in Poland represented both a serious retreat from the ideas of new democracy and separate roads to socialism and a strong signal of Soviet dissatisfaction with the political development of Europe. This was the moment when Andrei Zhdanov, representing Stalin at the meeting, gave his famous "two camps" speech, which portrayed the world divided between socialist and capitalist powers in ways that intensified the rhetorical hostility of the Soviets to the West—a shift from the more accommodating tone of Stalin's election speech of more than a year-and-a-half earlier.[64]

Stalin was upset by the removal of the French and Italian parties from their governments in the late spring of 1947, and during the summer he sought to impose his views regarding the rejection of the Marshall Plan on the European communist parties. The Czechoslovak leaders were summoned in early July 1947 to Moscow, where Stalin insisted that the Prague government rescind its decision to participate in the Marshall Plan. Czechoslovak statesman Jan Masaryk noted, "I went to Moscow as a Foreign Minister of an independent sovereign state. I returned as a lackey of a foreign country."[65] On March 10, 1948, Masaryk died when he either jumped (or was thrown) from a window after the Czechoslovak communist coup d'état of February 1948.

The real division of Europe began in the aftermath of the Cominform meeting, as Stalin and his allies in the East European parties began to impose uniformity and hierarchical discipline on their members. In western Europe, Stalin demanded the same allegiance from party members but continued to encourage their participation in their respective parliamentary institutions. The "two camps" paradigm sketched out by Zhdanov now also meant that the communist-dominated societies in the East and their respective parties would develop along different lines than those in the West. The Czechoslovak coup of February 1948 and the Berlin blockade from June 1948 to May 1949 completed the process whereby Soviet geostrategic and political interests in claiming a sphere of influence and domination in eastern Europe trumped earlier ideas of developing an all-European zone of interest.

The communist takeover in Czechoslovakia delineated a particularly important moment in postwar European history and had profound effects on political developments in Italy, Finland, and Austria, among other parliamentary governments that feared a communist seizure of power. Despite their widespread influence, the leaders of the Communist Party of Czechoslovakia had grown increasingly frustrated by their inability to control the parliamentary democracy led by President Eduard Beneš. The communist authorities in Prague purged the state's police force, provoking the resignation from the government on February 21, 1948, of twelve noncommunist ministers who counted on the president to dissolve the government and call for new elections. Instead, the communists, allied with the Social Democrats, were able to outmaneuver the noncommunists and appointed new ministers from their own ranks. With major demonstrations in Prague of pro-communist workers' groups and the purges of democrats from government institutions around the country by communist-led action committees, Beneš felt he had no choice but to accede to the forces on the street. The new communist-dominated government was sworn in on February 25, formally ending the last genuine parliamentary democracy in east central Europe. Beneš resigned in June.[66]

European Politics

The history of politics in interwar Europe and even more so during World War II was depressing and grim. Therefore, it is surprising in many ways that a talented and remarkably adept generation of European politicians emerged from the war to skillfully lead countries out of the war into the uncertain early tribulations of the peace. They were a motley mix of the old—sometimes very old, and experienced—who had spent the war in hiding, confinement, exile, internment, or isolation of one form or another, and of the young and ambitious, who had managed to avoid military service, fought in the underground, and found ways to emerge unscathed from the chaos of Nazi defeat and Allied victory. These younger politicians were ready to throw all of their energies into rebuilding political lives in their respective countries. Some had been in government prisons or concentration camps. Others had to struggle with Allied occupation authorities to gain reentry into their countries from exile abroad.

Against the backdrop of the war, the new leaders of Europe shared a commitment to the sovereignty and independence of their countries as well as to the rebuilding of their nations' economies and societies. For some, sovereignty meant a struggle against Soviet dominance. For others, it meant resisting American and British influence. There were also cases where political leaders saw their countries' futures inextricably linked to the policies of the dominant powers. But even in the communist world this was rare. Most European politicians were deeply worried about the reconstitution of German power on the continent. But all, even the vast majority of the communists who had entered politics during the anti-German partisan movement or in the campaign for the "new democracies" after the war, were committed to ensuring their country's ability to make its own decisions about the future, despite the constraints foisted upon them by foreign occupation forces.

Not only were there numbers of supremely competent and inspirational political leaders dedicated to the reconstitution of "democratic" governments across Europe, however variably the term was sometimes defined, but Europeans themselves seemed remarkably willing to participate in genuine political competition after six years or more of authoritarianism, Nazism, fascism, and wartime occupation regimes. The elections held after the war were characterized by extraordinarily high levels of participation, genuine political engagement, and the mobilization of interest groups. The elections' results mattered, though they were sometimes manipulated or influenced by non-democratic forces, especially in the East. Elections had important effects not just on democratic politics in Europe but on the ways Stalin and the Soviets viewed their policies on the continent and subsequently behaved in areas under their influence and control. Soviet officials carefully analyzed election results and came up with political and propaganda initiatives as a result.

Case Studies

This book was conceived and is organized according to a series of seven case studies of individual European countries and the issues they faced during the crucial postwar period of political reconstitution, including how those nations dealt with shifting Soviet objectives. Each chapter comprises a separate case study. Some are better known than others, and some cover longer periods than others. They are, in the order in which they appear: the Soviet occupation of the Danish island of Bornholm, 1945; Albania and the Yugoslavs, 1944–1948; Zhdanov and Finland, 1944–1948; the Italian elections of 1948; Hoxha and the Yugoslavs, 1944–1948; the Berlin blockade, 1948–1949; the struggle between Gomułka and Stalin, 1944–1949; and the Austrian settlement, 1945–1949. Different aspects of the relationship between the Soviet Union, a Europe in flux, and the emerging Cold War are examined in each case study.

The purpose of using cases studies confined in time and space and thematically is in part to be able to dig deeper into the stories of the individual countries and crises in order to give the reader a better understanding of the political processes at work in the postwar world. Given the documentary evidence I have been able to use in each, the case study method also allows me to tell each of these stories in a way that might make a contribution to the historiography of each as well as to that of postwar Europe as a whole. These particular cases were chosen because I thought they would provide a diverse set of interesting, enlightening, and even provocative examples. Some are from what could be considered western Europe (Italy and Bornholm); some from central Europe (Germany and Austria); and one each from Soviet-dominated eastern Europe (Poland), from the Balkans (Albania), and from northern Scandinavia (Finland.) The Soviets occupied at least for a time parts of several of the locales under study—Poland, Germany, Bornholm, Finland, and Austria—but not others such as Italy and Albania. In some of the areas (Italy, Austria, and Finland), Stalin weighed the possibility of supporting a communist takeover but decided against it. In eastern Germany and Poland, Soviet troops were part of the landscape of the country until the collapse of communism. Each chapter here explores the goals of Stalin and the Soviet Union while demonstrating the agency of the Europeans, communists and noncommunists alike, as they struggled for sovereignty on a continent increasingly dominated by the Cold War.

Although the chapters of this book tell discrete stories of political struggle, the narratives are embedded in a common context that emerges at the end of the war and the onset of the recasting of Europe: the tragedy of poverty and social chaos; the weakness of political institutions; Soviet influence on the continent; and increasing American attention to European issues. The announcements of the Truman Doctrine and the Marshall Plan in March and June 1947—and especially their actual implementation over the months and years to follow—served as important stimuli to events on the ground in almost all of the case studies. The first Cominform meeting (September 1947) and particularly the second (June 1948), when the Yugoslavs were expelled, influenced political movements throughout the continent but especially in eastern Europe. Developments in Albania and in Poland were particularly impacted by Stalin's shocking treatment of the Yugoslav comrades, which few European communist leaders approved of. The Czechoslovak coup d'état in February 1948 had profound reverberations in Italy, which held crucial elections in April of that year in the shadow of a potential coup by the Italian communists. After the assassination attempt on Palmiro Togliatti in June of 1948, the threat of a communist takeover again seemed possible.

The Czechoslovak coup was very much on the mind of Mayor Ernst Reuter and General Lucius Clay when both, in their own way, sought to overcome the dire effects of the nearly year-long blockade of Berlin (June 1948–May 1949). The Western powers and the Austrian government were caught off guard by the Berlin blockade and worried themselves about how they could survive a similar set of Soviet actions regarding Vienna. When negotiating the friendship treaty with the Soviets in early 1948, the Finnish government similarly did so against the background of a potential communist takeover.

Examined together, these seven case studies point to the diversity and complexity of Stalin's aims on the continent. They demonstrate that postwar Europe was in a state of flux: Allied armies evacuated occupied territories; alliances were redefined; local politics mattered. Elections were crucial and political leadership meant a lot. These case studies point to the openness of outcomes and alternative trajectories, recognizing that the Soviet Union increasingly—and brutally—shut down possibilities of genuinely democratic politics in eastern Europe while seeking to increase its leverage over communist parties and the broader societies they sought to influence in the West. The general historiographical portrait of a continent divided from the end of the war, with the predetermined outcome of the Cold War, is much more blurred and uncertain when looked at from the perspective of the immediate postwar history of Europe.

CHAPTER ONE

THE BORNHOLM INTERLUDE

1945–1946

One of the most widely quoted statements by Stalin cited in Cold War historiography comes from Milovan Djilas's *Conversations with Stalin,* when the Soviet leader reportedly declared in April 1945 that "whoever occupies a territory also imposes on it his own social system. Everyone imposes his own system as far as his army can reach. It cannot be otherwise."[1]

There is no certainty that Djilas accurately reported Stalin's views, though it is certainly the case that one can find other similar pronouncements about the nature of postwar occupation by the Soviet dictator. Whether he said it or not, the quotation is frequently used to demonstrate that Stalin understood both that the Soviet system would be extended as far as the Red Army was able to march, and that the Anglo-American powers would impose their own form of democracy on the territories that they liberated from the Nazis.[2]

Yet the facts of Soviet occupation history at the end of World War II do not conform to the essence of Stalin's statement. The presence of Red Army forces in various parts of Europe after the war did not assure the development of a Soviet-style system. Austria is a good example, as is the Danish island of Bornholm. Albania and Yugoslavia developed socialist systems independent of Soviet occupation. Soviet troops quickly withdrew from Czechoslovakia, leaving behind a democratic political system, including an influential communist party, which then seized power in a coup d'état in February 1948. At the end of the "Continuation War" in 1944, Soviet troops also withdrew from parts of Finland that they had invaded. Finland developed its own methods of dealing with overwhelming Soviet power and

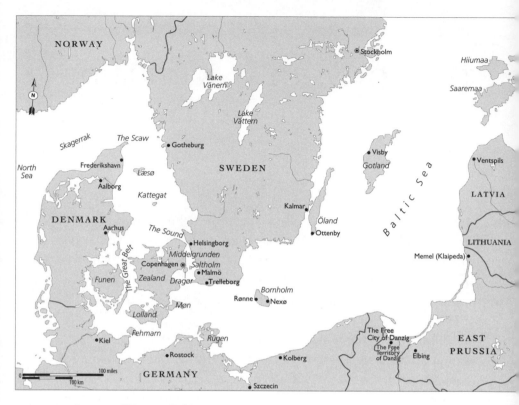

2. Interwar Western Baltic

influence in its neighborhood, without losing its sovereignty or democratic system.

The Soviet occupation of Bornholm from May 9, 1945, to April 5, 1946, is an episode of the postwar history of occupation that is little known outside of Denmark, in good measure because the Red Army contingent was withdrawn after eleven months and the bucolic island returned to Danish control. The long-term effects of the occupation on Denmark and the island were minimal, especially since Denmark joined NATO in 1949 as a founding member and became a part of the Western alliance system.[3] Yet the Bornholm interlude between war and peace provides important insights into the Soviet calculus of strategic thinking, occupation, and political intentions, as well as into Danish politics and society.

Why Occupy Bornholm?

The island of Bornholm today is a quiet tourist haven, with picturesque fishing villages and a pastoral landscape, crisscrossed by flat country lanes perfect for recreational bike riding and strolling in the countryside. During World War II, Denmark and Bornholm survived reasonably well under the relatively benign protectorate of Nazi Germany, with the Danish king, Christian X, serving as an important symbol of national unity. Until the summer of 1943, the Allies looked at Denmark as collaborating with the Third Reich. But during that summer, the combination of strikes among Danish workers and the Nazi plenipotentiary's insistence that the Danish government crack down harder on society led to the ouster of the democratically elected government and the replacement of the recalcitrant Danish police by the German overlords. Resistance groups, represented in a "Freedom Council," launched a serious campaign of sabotage, linked up to and supplied by the Allies. These at times spectacular acts of sabotage rescued the Danes' reputation among the Allies and made it possible for them to establish their own government after liberation (on May 5) and to become a founding member of the United Nations. The new Danish government represented a combination of leading members of the Freedom Council and Danish politicians from the dissolved parliament of the summer of 1943, a number of whom had made their way to England.[4]

Some prominent Danish civil society and resistance figures connived with sympathetic Nazi administrators to evacuate the bulk of the country's Jews to Sweden, an important story of humanitarianism and survival of the Jews in an otherwise bleak landscape of death and destruction.[5] Denmark cannot be said to have suffered terribly much during the war, though the majority of the Danes certainty resented their loss of sovereignty to the Nazi overlords. They also were embarrassed by the "short war" that saw them succumb to the Nazis within a matter of days. As in Denmark proper, the German presence in Bornholm did not oppress the islanders, though there were groups of Danish resisters, who emerged at the end of the war to help the Soviets clear the island of the Wehrmacht soldiers. The German navy used Bornholm's ports to patrol the western Baltic and make sure the British would not penetrate the strategic waters guarding the Nazi empire. The island was also a convenient "listening post" to intercept communications of enemy ships and submarines.

The island of Bornholm is located some 250 kilometers northeast of Lübeck and centered between the southern tip of Sweden and Kołobrzeg (then Kolberg) on the Polish (at that point Pomeranian German) coastline. Though located considerably to the east, Bornholm could be considered as a stepping-stone to the entrance to the Belts (Great Belt and Little Belt) and Sound of Denmark, the entrance and egress from the Baltic Sea to the North Sea. The island could also be seen as ensuring access to the Kiel Canal, linking the North Sea to the Baltic through German territory. No doubt, the strategic location of the island, described by a number of commentators, both Soviet and Western, as a potential "Gibraltar of the Baltic," was a serious factor in the Soviet decision to occupy the island. The official reason for the ongoing occupation provided by the Kremlin, and announced to the Danish public, was that Bornholm was essential to resolving issues that had emerged from the defeat and occupation of Germany. German troops and naval units fled from the Soviet armies to the island and, after the capitulation, hoped to surrender to the Western Allies. The Soviets explained to the Danish people that the island would be occupied "until the military question in Germany had been solved."[6] Some historians believe that the goal of the Soviet occupation was to put pressure on the Danes to make concessions about allowing Soviet access to the Belts and Sound rather than military considerations tied to the German occupation.[7]

There are several reasons that the argument about the control of the Belts and Sound as the paramount cause of the Bornholm occupation is unconvincing. First, the Soviets generally showed much more interest in the Mediterranean than the Baltic at the wartime conferences and in meetings with their Western Allies. During the Moscow meeting between Churchill and Stalin in October 1944, for example, the subject of the Kiel Canal came up, if only to mention the principle of internationalization of the canal. There were no details and no mention of the Belts and Sound.[8] At Potsdam, the Soviets showed keen interest in bases in the Mediterranean and control of the Straits, but neither the Baltic nor Bornholm were subjects of discussion.[9] Generally, Stalin pursued a decidedly defensive posture when it came to naval matters.[10] In this connection the fairly consistent British and American policy of the "internationalization" of the Kiel Canal and the Belts and Sound with ultimate control in the hands of the riparian powers suited the needs both of the Soviets in the Baltic and of the Western Allies.[11] British intelligence speculated in addition that the Soviets wanted Bornholm as a way "to control sea routes in the Baltic which would enable her to deny to Germany and Western Europe a large proportion of Swedish iron ore supplies."[12]

There had been some thinking in the Soviet foreign ministry during the war about sharing the occupation of all of Denmark itself with the British, and along with that establishing a base in Bornholm, as a way to extend more direct influence over Danish society and politics.[13] Denmark's own strategic position between the Baltic and the North Seas interested the Soviets, and they frequently noted the friendly relations between Russia and Denmark that went back even before the time of Peter the Great. But there were also considerable differences of opinion in the Soviet foreign ministry about how to deal with Denmark and Bornholm after the war. The Danes had broken off relations with Moscow in 1941 and, under pressure from the Germans, joined the anti-Comintern Pact. As a result, the Soviets were in no mood to treat Denmark as an ally, even if the two countries were not in a state of war. Certainly, this generally hostile attitude regarding Danish wartime behavior affected their readiness to occupy the Danish island. In Ivan Maiskii's memorandum to Foreign Minister Molotov of January 11, 1944, outlining Soviet interests in Europe and the world, Denmark and Scandinavia, with the exception of Finland, played a relatively minor role. It was important, wrote Maiskii, that there be no Scandinavian federation, no way for the countries of the region to balance the Soviets' overwhelming military preponderance in the Baltic that would emerge after the war. There also should be no "Anglo-American" bases in the region. Although Bornholm was not mentioned in the memorandum itself, Maiskii was clear on the issue of the Belts and Sound: Soviet access to and egress from the Baltic Sea should be guaranteed in the postwar order.[14]

The commission on the postwar world, chaired by Deputy Foreign Minister Maxim Litvinov, wanted to deny the Baltic to any and all military vessels, but was aware that Great Britain and the Scandinavian countries would be opposed, since this would leave the Baltic under effective Soviet military control.[15] Already during the summer of 1944, Deputy Foreign Minister Solomon Lozovskii talked about a Soviet presence in Bornholm in connection with his argument that it was critical for the Soviets to have a military base between the Åland Islands, off the Finnish coast, which guarded the entry to the Gulf of Finland, and the Kiel Canal that ran between the North Sea and the Baltic Sea, as a crucial defense point against foreign naval vessels. Litvinov responded that the Soviet Union was not at war with Denmark and therefore would have no legal claim to the island. Lozovskii noted that one could claim that Bornholm was necessary for the strategic defense of the Soviet Union against Germany, the argument that was eventually used to justify occupation.[16]

Meanwhile, Deputy Foreign Minister V. G. Dekanozov and his aides M. S. Vetrov and V. S. Semenov came to the conclusion that Denmark would be an essential object of Soviet postwar security policy, precisely because of the issues of access to the Baltic, as well as the Schleswig problem, and therefore the Soviets should join in the liberation of Denmark in order to protect its postwar interests. Once again, Bornholm was specifically mentioned as a potential Soviet objective, while the foreign ministry officials seemed to agree that the Soviets could leave the liberation of Copenhagen to the Western Allies and what the Soviets called "Fighting Denmark" (the Danish Freedom Council), an alliance of the Danish resistance movements.[17]

In a memorandum of January 11, 1945, Litvinov suggested to Molotov and Dekanozov that Denmark should be part of a "neutral zone" of influence (along with Germany, Austria, Switzerland and Italy), with Finland, Sweden, and Norway being in the Soviet sphere of influence and Holland, Belgium, and France in the British. Litvinov did not mention Bornholm, though, in a second memo of January 12, he suggested that the island of Helgoland on the North Sea side of the Belts and Sound be given to England or Denmark and that the island of Rügen (eventually included in the Soviet zone of occupation in Germany) be made available for Soviet use.[18]

Not a great deal is known about the Soviet military's position on the question of Denmark and Bornholm. There was some speculation in the military press in early 1945 that the Belts and Sound could well be the site of the last big battles of World War II with the Germans. Meanwhile, the foreign ministry officials Semenov, Dekanozov, and Molotov were convinced that the Soviets needed to liberate Bornholm as a way to ensure Soviet interests in the resolution of Danish issues. On March 12, they thus urged Nikolai Bulganin in the People's Commissariat of Defense to "seize and occupy this small piece of the Kingdom. . . ." Bulganin replied in the affirmative on April 9, and on April 23 the People's Commissar of the Navy, N. G. Kuznetsov, suggested to the general staff that Bornholm (and Rügen) be taken by Soviet naval forces. On May 4, the same day that the German Wehrmacht surrendered to Field Marshall Montgomery in Denmark proper, Kuznetsov instructed the commander of the Baltic fleet, V. F. Tributs, to seize the islands of Bornholm and Rügen.[19]

The role of Danish politicians in the Soviet calculations about Bornholm was minimal. A prominent Social Democrat (and later communist), Thomas Døssing, more radical in his critical stance toward the Danish government than either the Soviets or the Danish communists liked, tried to convince Moscow during his repeated visits to Kremlin leaders that cooperation with the prewar political leadership would do harm to Soviet interests. Even the Danish communists found him excessively subservient to Moscow.[20] Danish foreign minister Christmas Møller tended to think of Døssing "as more of a representative of the Kremlin in Denmark than as a representative of the Danish government in Moscow."[21]

No one in Denmark was quite sure what Døssing was up to in his negotiations and his relations with the Danish Freedom Council were complicated, since many of its members represented to him the "old Denmark." Still Døssing seemed to have good connections to Moscow, and his views were respected by his interlocutors there. (He became the first postwar Danish ambassador to the Soviet Union.) But, as elsewhere in Europe, Stalin had already decided on a program that emphasized a broad anti-fascist coalition and looked to working with middle-class parties and the Social Democrats, like Vilhelm Buhl, associated with the Danish Freedom Council and "Fighting Denmark," who became the first prime minister of the postwar government. For the Danes, the main issue was how to make sure that there were firm agreements with the Allies about who would occupy Denmark and for how long, in the case that the Soviets played a major role in driving out the Germans. In this spirit, the Freedom Council used Døssing to establish a concrete arrangement with the Soviets about their intentions in postwar Denmark, but to no avail. The lack of progress in these discussions and the Soviet advance in the German Baltic region prompted the British to speed up their military operations in Jutland and to march into Copenhagen.[22]

With good reason, Churchill worried that Stalin would be tempted to seize Lübeck and then Denmark from his advanced position in Stettin (Szczecin).[23] As late as May 5, 1945, Orme Sargent of the British Foreign Office wrote to General Hastings Ismay, chief of the War Office:

> We have the thought that after the capitulation of Denmark, there might be a request that the Russians be given the task to cleanse a part of the country, that they actually were to have a "zone" in this country. It is not at all impossible that the Russians themselves will demand it. It would of course be political desirable that this is hindered at any cost and would like to make sure that Eisenhower knows this.[24]

General Dwight D. Eisenhower, commander-in-chief of SHAEF, the Supreme Headquarters of the Allied Expeditionary Forces, agreed with Churchill that Denmark should belong to the British sphere of influence. But neither the supreme command nor the British seemed overly concerned about Bornholm itself, though the Foreign Office was clear that it wanted the British forces to accept the German surrender on the island.[25] Apparently Montgomery's deputy, Major-General Richard Henry Dewing, had prepared some troops to move on to Bornholm from Jutland, but the orders never came.[26] Because the island was considered east of the so-called bomb line drawn up by the Allies to make sure that neither the Soviets bombed west of the line nor the British and Americans to the east, Bornholm was designated to the Soviet operational sphere.[27]

There is some argument among statesmen and military leaders from the period whether such a bomb line actually existed. But the argument was mooted, since the Soviets moved more quickly and decisively to take Bornholm before the British could or at least did act. Still, there is a plethora of evidence that British political and military leaders believed that at least an informal agreement existed about spheres of aerial bombing that left Bornholm in the Soviet sphere and therefore the island should be left to them despite the liberation of Denmark by Montgomery.[28]

There are also questions regarding the possibility of the Danish resistance taking action to seize the island at the beginning of May before the Germans capitulated. Some Bornholmers argued that a Danish resistance battalion in Sweden, disguised as a police unit, could have joined with the resistance on the island to defeat the Germans and accept their surrender. Also, after May 5, when the Nazis in Denmark itself surrendered to the British, some Bornholm islanders thought that a detachment from the mainland could have been outfitted with boats to invade the island and begin its liberation. Certainly, this was the fervent hope of the resistance fighters on Bornholm. But, as the former resistance leader Arne Sørensen pointed out, the Danish Freedom Council, which was formally head of the Danish resistance, had put its forces "at the disposal of the 'Western alliance'" and therefore was under the command of General Eisenhower at SHAEF and General R. H. Dewing, commander of the British forces in Copenhagen.[29] There had been some vague plans in early May mentioned by the Admiralty to "send a small British navy" to Copenhagen and then dispatch a naval detachment on to Bornholm, once minesweepers had cleared Danish waters.[30] The British also showed some interest in the German submarines that were harbored at Rønne on Bornholm, as no doubt did the Soviets.[31]

The Germans on Bornholm, the Bornholmers, the British, the Americans, and the Danes would have all preferred in early May 1945 that the Germans on the island surrender to the British. But this did not happen. As General Dewing explained in an interview with Copenhagen's *Berlingske Tindende* twenty years later, the situation was "confusing," and he had arrived in the Danish capital with only one hundred men. "We could have sent a symbolic force to Bornholm," he explained, but in those days "Bornholm was only a detail," and, one might add, only a minor one at that. He claimed that there was no talk of Bornholm before he arrived in Denmark and that "my knowledge of the country's geography was probably not so good that I became aware of the situation on my own."[32] No doubt, a more straightforward assessment of the situation was reported by the resistance member Arne Sørenson when he remembered General Dewing's words at a dinner for the Danish Freedom Council, "right after his arrival on May 5."

> You will most likely be sad that I say this but it is nevertheless the case that England cannot be as interested in Bornholm as you obviously are. I have instructions not to take over Bornholm and in general not to get close to the island until we have seen what the Russians wanted to do. . . . It had to be left to the Russians to do as they pleased. And they did.[33]

If the British had been further along in their occupation of Denmark, they might have tried to take Bornholm. "It was a question of who could reach the island first," Anthony Eden reported, somewhat disingenuously, to parliament on May 30.[34] The fact is that the British were not interested enough in the island to preempt any Soviet moves.

Occupying Bornholm

Originally, there were no more than one thousand German soldiers garrisoning on the island. But this situation quickly changed as the Germans increasingly used Bornholm as a refuge for German soldiers evacuated from the mainland, primarily from Libava (Liepāja), Vindava (Ventspils), and the Hel Peninsula (today in Poland). On January 25, 1945, the German general staff ordered the strengthening of the defense of the island and the construction of defensive fortifications in the ports. In March, new coastal artillery emplacements were brought in from Kurland, and in April the Germans gave the orders to quickly expand the ability of the airport to serve as a base for fighter planes that could protect troop ships in the Baltic.[35]

By the time the Soviets seized control of Bornholm, there were an additional 19,000 military and civilian refugees, the majority of them hungry and demoralized.[36] The Germans on the island made ready to surrender to the British; they were in touch in that connection with the British 21st Army (soon renamed the Army of the Rhein), commanded by Field Marshal Montgomery. Just one British soldier, the German commander pleaded to the Danish leadership on the island, would have been sufficient for the Germans to capitulate.[37]

Marshall Konstantin Rokossovskii claimed that the German presence on Bornholm presented a serious tactical military problem for the Soviet forces.[38] In order to interdict the evacuation of further Wehrmacht soldiers from the German coast to the island, Soviet torpedo boats were launched from Kolberg (Kołobrzeg) on May 5.[39] The Soviet command issued an ultimatum for the Germans on Bornholm to surrender at 23:00 on May 7, which was refused by the German commander of the garrison, naval Captain Gerhard von Kamptz, a thoroughgoing Nazi and a deputy to Admiral of the Fleet Karl Dönitz.[40] His orders stated that he should surrender only to the British. Also on May 7, the Soviets flew missions over the island, dropping scattered munitions in response to German fire from the ground. That evening Soviet airplanes dropped leaflets around the island demanding that the commander of the garrison come to Soviet headquarters in Kolberg to sign the capitulation. They buzzed the port towns of Rønne and Nexø, with the idea of frightening the citizens to take shelter elsewhere. Radio transmissions starting on May 5 had also warned the Bornholm residents that the ports would be bombed.

The next day, May 8, with no response from the Germans, the Soviets heavily bombed the harbors of Nexø and Rønne, inflicting considerable damage on housing and public buildings in both towns, and destroying both German and Danish ships and smaller craft. The bombing was imprecise, thus hitting civilian quarters of both cities.[41]

In Rønne alone, some three thousand islanders were made homeless by the bombing. In Nexø, 111 houses were destroyed, 700 damaged to some extent, and only 147 remained whole.[42] Governor Poul Christian von Stemann later assessed the damage of the bombing at approximately one hundred thousand Danish kroner.[43] Fortunately, only ten Danes were killed and thirty-five wounded, since most had been evacuated to shelters outside or on the outskirts of the towns before the worst raids hit. Meanwhile hundreds of German ships and boats of all sorts and sizes, loaded down with troops and refugees, were on their way to the island. According to the commander of a Soviet air squadron: "There remained nothing else for us to do but to renew the attack"—one of the last bombing raids of the Second World War in Europe:

> [A]t 11:20 [on May 8], under the protection of our jet fighters we carried out a powerful bombing attack against the ships and port facilities of Rønne. Our munitions consisted of two thousand-kilogram bombs on each airplane. Around the central pier some twenty large fires burned, clouds of black smoke enveloped the entire port.

After a brief respite for the aircraft and crew, the attack was renewed at 16:30 on Nexø at "an unusual height for us of 2300 meters we delivered our blow to the port and the ships in its harbor. The anti-aircraft fire of the defenders was very dense, but apparently had little effect, since we departed with no losses.—The explosions were very powerful, and the smoke almost reached to the height of our planes."[44]

At 6:15 in the morning on May 9—when "the rest of the world was celebrating the victory over Nazi Germany"—a squadron of six torpedo boats loaded with Soviet soldiers was sent to Bornholm to seize the island. They had to deal with an intercepted German barge and motorboats and were caught in the fog before proceeding. But they finally landed at Rønne at 15:30 without encountering any resistance.[45] Only eight or nine Soviet soldiers were killed in the Bornholm action, all of them in the process of eliminating German resistance at various points on the island and at sea, rather than in the taking of the island itself. There was almost no resistance from the thousands of hungry and demoralized Germans, who knew, in any case, that the war was over. The German officers were taken immediately to Kolberg, where they signed the formal surrender of the Bornholm garrison. Even some Russian historians have criticized the May 8 bombing and destruction of Rønne and Nexø as senseless and unnecessary.[46]

Colonel Pavel Strebkov, head of the three battalions of landing forces, noted, "The local [Danish] authorities politely received the Soviet armed forces, but did not conceal their fear about whether we would be here for a long time."[47] Following the departure of the Germans, and of the clearing of the island by Soviet forces joined by local Danish resistance groups, Major General F. F. Korotkov, accompanied by some eight thousand Red Army soldiers, arrived from the mainland on May 13 to take control of the island. Given his successful experience with military action in northern Norway against the Germans, while demonstrating considerable skill dealing with the locals, he was considered the best person for the job.[48]

On May 10, the chief of the Soviet general staff Aleksei Antonov answered the inquiries from the SHAEF on May 8 and 9 about the situation on Bornholm. There had been no communications from the Soviets up until that point. Antonov wrote to Eisenhower,

> Arriving from Stettin, Danzig, and Kurland, German soldiers gathered on the island of Bornholm, which, as is known, is located 250 km to the east of the sphere of operations of the Soviet forces. As a result of this, Soviet forces seized the island, taking into account the request of the commander of the German garrison on the island to help with food products and to surrender the island to our forces.[49]

After the end of the war, Maxim Litvinov, working out of the foreign ministry, pushed hard for the control of the Belts and Sound by the countries bordering on the Baltic, excluding Norway, which technically was not a Baltic country. But he also made sure to include Poland, which could be counted on to support Soviet initiatives. The Danes should not have exclusive control of the passage, because it would be too easy for them to fall under the influence of the great powers (meaning, of course, Great Britain and the United States). If Soviet wishes were not respected with regard to the entry to and egress from the Baltic Sea, Litvinov suggested, then Moscow could guarantee its security interests by creating "its own type of Baltic Gibraltar" by fortifying its bases on Rügen and Bornholm.[50]

Not surprisingly, the British were firmly committed to a policy of the free passage of international shipping, both merchant and military, in the Belts and Sound, to which the United States agreed.[51] Eventually, the Soviets went along with this policy as well. In his long telegram of February 22, 1946, George Kennan suggested—like Litvinov—that the Soviet presence on Bornholm was part of larger picture of ensuring Soviet security interests, though Kennan, we know, thought of these as the product of the Soviets' "neurotic view of world affairs" founded in "the traditional and instinctive Russian sense of insecurity."[52]

Bornholm under Soviet Occupation

After having accepted the surrender of the German forces on the island, the Soviet detachments returned to Rønne, where they met with the Danish resistance force on the island in the city hall and came to an agreement about sharing responsibility for clearing the island of the remaining Germans. Together they immediately went about the task of disarming and interning more than eleven thousand German soldiers, with the Danes accepting major responsibility of guarding the Germans until they could be transferred to the mainland.[53]

Members of the resistance also went about the business, typical of occupied Europe, of identifying Danish collaborators and of shaving the heads of Bornholm women who had allegedly consorted with German soldiers. Female islanders who wore kerchiefs all the time were known to be those who were shamed in this way.[54] A report from a Danish intelligence office in Rønne from May 14, 1945, emphasized the strong relationship between the Soviet forces and the Danish resistance units.

> The Russians have no qualms about handing over arms to the resistance fighters. The weapons that the resistance fighters find on the island are not to be handed in to the Russians but they can dispose of them as they see fit. In all respects, there's intimate collaboration between the Russians and the resistance forces. For example, there is no Russian on sentry duty without a resistance fighter serving as a sentry as well. The resistance fighters have the right to arrest Russian soldiers.[55]

The Danish governor of the island under the Germans, Poul Christian von Stemann, was kept in his administrative position by the Soviets, and the governor in turn made every effort to be accommodating to their wishes, while sending desperate private notes to Copenhagen begging his superiors to find a way to get the Soviets to leave. On the surface of things, Soviet soldiers and Bornholm islanders seemed to get along well.[56] Von Stemann reportedly had very good relations with Col. Strebkov, the initial Red Army commander.[57] A Soviet band played at the funeral of the Danish victims of the bombardment arranged by the resistance committee.[58] There were some soccer matches and chess tournaments that involved both Bornholmers and Red Army personnel. Although the Soviets refused Copenhagen's requests to send Danish soldiers to the island, everyone on the island and in Denmark thought the Soviet soldiers would be gone in a matter of weeks. Von Stemann mobilized the remaining Danish shipping on the island to evacuate the remaining Germans, with the idea that this would speed up the Soviet desire to leave. But the same boats that took German soldiers to the mainland arrived back with more Soviet soldiers and equipment, as well as artillery pieces and livestock, making the Bornholm authorities all the more nervous.[59]

Positive reports of good relations between the islanders and the Soviet soldiers were balanced by harsh criticism of Soviet behavior, familiar, though not as extreme, as in those parts of eastern and central Europe that had experienced direct Soviet occupation. Governor von Stemann complained in a note to the Danish foreign ministry (May 14, 1945) that the occupation was becoming extremely burdensome for the island's population. From the locals the Soviets demanded increasing amounts of firewood (for cooking and heating) and gas (for fueling their trucks and jeeps).

The bitterness among the Bornholmians hasn't decreased. I heard remarks like: "If we had known this it would have been better not to have shot *Printzenskiöld!!*" [the Swedish commander in 1658, the year Bornholm became part of Denmark[60]]. . . . The tragedy is endlessly major, especially taking into account the partying mood in the rest of the country. [The Russian guards] at our house were

1.1 Two Soviet officers, Col. Petr Strebkov and Capt. E. Osetskii (?) with Danish governor P. Chr. Von Stemann, on the right, and his daughter Regitze and his wife Helga on the far left. THE ROYAL LIBRARY, DENMARK.

thoroughly drunk. . . . You would have not believed how it looked. They had taken everything from my wine cellar: brandy, champagne, liquor, burgundy, schnapps, all had been finished. . . . Everywhere there are complaints that the Soviets are stealing like ravens. Now they are also taking horses and bikes. . . . They have plundered widely in all the gardens around here.[61]

In a telephone conversation with the Danish foreign minister Møller the following day, May 15, von Stemann described the mood of the islanders as "apocalyptic." The Soviets showed no signs of withdrawing as a result of the capitulation. Just the opposite; it was starting to look like they were staying for a good long while. The talk of permanent Soviet bases on Bornholm became all the more realistic given the import of building materials from the mainland for constructing barracks on the island for Soviet troops, who had been housed up to that point mostly in tents. The construction accelerated in the late fall of 1945 in preparation for the winter.[62] The reason the Soviets gave the Bornholmers for staying for the time being was that the Germans were preparing a new war and Bornholm was of "great strategic importance" in countering those plans."[63]

Soviet officers on Bornholm gave the locals mixed signals about whether they were staying, and for how long. It became increasingly obvious that they themselves did not know. They also could not have been aware of the secret directive, signed by Stalin on May 15, that indicated that Bornholm was unquestionably part of Denmark and that Soviet troops were there only because of its proximity to the Soviet occupied zone of Germany and because there were still "many German agents" there. The Soviets would remain in Bornholm, the order stated, "until the military situation in Germany was resolved," and this should be explained to the Danes.[64] The promise to leave the island combined with an open-ended formula about precisely when this would happen was of little solace to the islanders or to their governor, who constantly inveighed on the Copenhagen government to find out when the Soviets intended to leave.

The premier historian of the occupation criticizes the Danish government (press and political parties) for hushing up, even ignoring, the difficult fate of the Bornholm islanders.[65] Not wishing to offend the Soviets, the authorities in Copenhagen kept everything about the life of the island under occupation quiet and out of view of the average Danish citizen. Little mention was made of the bombing of Bornholm on May 7 and May 8 in order not to disturb the festivities in Copenhagen celebrating the end of the war.[66]

The prime minister of Denmark, Vilhelm Buhl, inveighed upon Governor von Stemann to prevent any form of demonstrations on the part of the islanders against the Soviet presence.[67] The Danish government also claimed the right to censor all press articles about Bornholm, as a way to ensure that the Soviets would not be offended and thus be tempted to extend their stay on the island.[68] Still, the Danish daily newspapers carried "factual stories" about the bombing of Bornholm, the destruction of property, the presence of the Russians on the island, and the need for relief.[69] There was also little discussion in the press or in public of the fact that the Danes had agreed to pay for the substantial occupation costs of the unwanted "guests." Both the amount and nature of the payments were unknown to all but a few government insiders.[70] At the same time, the Danes' claims for compensation for their property in the Baltic states, which had been incorporated into the Soviet Union, were rejected by Molotov.[71]

Despite Danish efforts to keep negative publicity about Bornholm out of the newspapers and parliamentary debates, the Soviets constantly complained about their press coverage in Denmark, which they found intemperate and insufficiently appreciative of the role the Soviet Union played in the war. The TASS correspondent—and Soviet intelligence agent—in Copenhagen, Mikhail Kosov, told the Danish press attaché that "Danish suspicion with regards to the question of Bornholm was unfounded and that he very much hoped that the newspapers would make sure that the public was informed in the right way. . . ."[72]

When von Stemann was finally allowed to travel to Copenhagen and meet with the Danish ministers about Bornholm on May 18, he expressed the islanders' frustration and disappointment that none of the Danish officials had even mentioned Bornholm in their speeches to the parliament. The ministers responded that there was a statement about Bornholm but that it was too "delicate" to publish.[73] No doubt, the Danes acted like they were walking on eggshells dealing with the Soviets on the Bornholm issue. They were hesitant to send their foreign minister to Bornholm in fear of having the Soviets think the island would be a subject of bilateral negotiations.[74] They urged the Americans to develop a model for establishing bases on Iceland that would involve the United Nations, so that the Soviets would be discouraged from setting up bases in Bornholm, or, at the least, be persuaded to involve the United Nations as well.[75] The Danish Foreign Office was "horrified" at hearing about a "potential" American request for bases in Greenland on Danish territory, fearing that this would be "immediately followed by Soviet demand for bases on Bornholm."[76]

Von Stemann convinced the Danish authorities that conditions for the islanders might improve if a delegation of Soviet officers and men from Bornholm could be received in Copenhagen. The invitation was extended to General Korotkov on behalf of the Danish government, and the Soviets accepted. The visit was scheduled for July 1, 1945, and for two days beforehand the leading political officers trained the participants in the delegation on how to conduct themselves at the table using proper etiquette. The soldiers were given enough kroner to buy what they needed, and after an hour's plane ride the delegation landed in Copenhagen. They were met by a high-ranking Danish and Allied delegation; even a small group of Danish communists greeted them on the street. The highlight of the visit was the reception of General Korotkov and Colonel Strebkov by the Danish king, Christian X, and the queen. A Soviet political officer, Lieutenant G. F. Khromushina, described the meeting as follows: "The king carried himself very simply, was attentive, and did not ask any political questions at all. He asked that we pass on greetings to Comrade Stalin." There was a grand reception afterward, attended by leading Danish and Allied officials. All in all, the Soviets were deeply impressed by the friendliness and warmth of their Danish hosts. The visit was a great "triumph," Khromushina wrote, and relations between the Danes and the Russians notably improved thereafter.[77]

The Danish foreign minister, Christmas Møller, was also pleased with the visit. His basic tactic in dealing with the Soviets was to flatter them, to sugarcoat any differences of opinion, to praise their wartime contributions to the Allied cause, and to build confidence in Moscow that the Danes would remain in the future on friendly terms with the Soviets and neutral between East and West. The payoff, he reckoned, would be Moscow's voluntary evacuation of the island. Though a member of the conservative party, Møller genuinely believed that the Soviet Union, given its sacrifices and victories in the war, had earned the right to play a major role in European and Danish affairs.[78]

In this connection, Møller was convinced that if the British evacuated their troops from Denmark, the Soviets would do the same in Bornholm. The British were ready to go along with Møller's efforts and began the process of reducing their contingent in the Faroe Islands (at the meteorological station there) and in Denmark proper. But they resented Møller's public statements that seemed to equate the unwanted Soviet presence in Bornholm with the requested help of the British military in defusing bombs, sweeping mines in Danish waters, and training Danish troops.[79] At the same time, the small American contingent withdrew from Denmark without any problems.

If the Soviets were interested in setting up bases in Bornholm, as von Stemann and his fellow islanders feared, the occupiers made little effort to impose their system on the civilian residents. There were some modest attempts to support the political interests of the small resistance movement that had formed on the island during the later stages of the German occupation, but there were no efforts made to "Sovietize" the island or interfere excessively with its governance beyond what was necessary to support the military's needs. Here and there von Stemann complained that his prerogatives were violated by the Soviets, but on the whole he ran the administration of the island as he saw fit. There was some encouragement of local communists by Soviet political officers who could speak a bit of Danish or find another common language with the locals. But nothing really came of this. (In percentage terms, there were fewer votes for communists in Bornholm in the October 1945 elections than in the rest of Denmark.)[80]

Initially, there was quite a bit of contact between the Soviet soldiers and the locals, and everything seemed to go well. There were even dances and merrymaking. The Copenhagen communist newspaper wrote on May 26, 1945, "The Russian military band plays and people are dancing on the square at Ronne. Danish girls are dancing with Russian soldiers and female Russian soldiers are dancing with young Danish men."[81] But the inevitable drunken brawls and instances of thievery and mayhem prompted von Stemann to ask Korotkov for remedial measures, which he took.[82] Korotkov himself had a severe drinking problem, and was replaced by General A. V. Iakushev, who instituted a non-fraternization order.[83] Officers and soldiers were forbidden to have any social contacts with the local population, except at controlled formal occasions, when concerts and cultural performances provided entertainment for both the troops and civilians on the island.[84] There were even a number of reports from Bornholmers that they missed the contacts with their Russian friends.

Crown Prince Frederick and his wife, Ingrid, came to Bornholm on June 18, 1945, to bolster the islanders' spirits. General Korotkov, who had been demoted to colonel because of excessive drinking, was again promoted to general for the occasion; the rank of colonel was not enough for the commander of the garrison to greet members of the

1.2 Soviet soldiers and Bornholm civilians at a dance, 1945. BORNHOLM MUSEUM, RØNNE, DENMARK.

royal family.[85] Korotkov remembered later that he worried at the time about the appropriateness of his dress and manners and was enormously impressed by the young Danish couple, who were friendly and open to the Russians.[86] The visit went well by all reports, and the Bornholmers, who generally felt ignored by Copenhagen, were encouraged by the royal couple's stay. Governor von Stemann made a point of encouraging a raft of visitors to come to Bornholm from the Danish mainland. Journalists, schoolchildren, military representatives, parliamentary delegations—all were invited and feted by von Stemann (and sometimes the Soviets)—for the purposes of demonstrating that Bornholm was an integral part of Denmark.

The Soviets Leave Bornholm

The question arises, why did the Soviets stay on Bornholm as long as they did, especially given the initial promises to evacuate once the Germans had been cleared off the island? (A similar promise regarding the Soviet evacuation of the Finnmark in northern Norway was honored in September 1945.) Along with this question comes the follow-up question: why did they leave when they did, eleven months after they arrived? Clearly, once the Red Army had seized control of the island, some Soviet officials thought that Moscow could gain some leverage over the Danish government if their military stayed. For example, T. Zhdanova in the Soviet foreign ministry wrote a note to M. S. Vetrov, head of the 5th European Department (June 27, 1945), suggesting that a permanent Soviet base (or bases) on Bornholm would bolster Soviet influence in the Belts and Sound and Kiel Canal. Bornholm and Rügen could also serve as the two major strategic military installations that would protect the Soviet Union against potential German revanchism. "This will be all the more just," wrote Zhdanova, "since England will demand control over the island of Helgoland in the North Sea."[87]

In another internal foreign ministry memorandum addressed to Molotov, dated July 9, 1945, the author suggested taking up Danish Foreign Minister Christmas Møller's suggestion of closer Soviet-Danish cooperation by putting on the table joint Soviet-Danish naval and air force bases on Bornholm to ensure common security in the region. This kind of military cooperation would "serve as an important factor in our influence on Danish foreign policy," and, implicitly, reduce that of the British. In order to make the Danes more cooperative in this venture, the author suggested that the joint bases be agreed upon before Red Army troops were evacuated from the island.[88] Moscow looked to the occupation of Bornholm to make the Danes even more compliant than they already were, even perhaps to have them loosen their ties with the West and join the ranks of the "new democracies."

Soviet plans in this connection were frustrated by the fact that the Danes were decidedly uninterested in a pro-Soviet government. Especially when the anti-socialist liberals from the Venstre party made significant gains in the October 30, 1945, elections, Deputy Foreign Minister Dekanozov complained, "We didn't expect this [the election of so many 'right-wing parties' to power] of Denmark."[89] Although the Communist Party notably gained eighteen seats in the parliament, the Social Democrats continued to dominate the voting habits of Danish citizens and refused any blandishments to join in a bloc with the communists. Instead, the elections demonstrated remarkable continuity between those of 1939, 1943, and 1945. Danish political leaders were ready to grant Moscow an important role in constructing the postwar European order, but they were unwilling to alter the form and content of their government and monarchy.[90]

The British made no serious efforts to convince the Soviets to leave the island. In fact, from the beginning of the occupation, they told the Danes repeatedly that they thought it was best that the withdrawal of Soviet forces be negotiated directly between Copenhagen and Moscow.[91] The United States government made even less effort to pressure the Soviets to leave.[92] The signaling of American intentions to turn temporary bases on Greenland and the Faroe Islands into permanent ones may have encouraged the Soviets to withdraw, not wishing to give the Americans the excuse to remain in Danish territories. One specialist on the history of Soviet security policy writes, "The delay in the otherwise smooth return of Bornholm to Denmark was revealing of what was foremost on Stalin's mind—the network of U.S. military bases around the world that he could not possibly hope to match. By giving up on seeking such bases for himself in the Baltic, he was inviting American reciprocity there and also elsewhere, particularly Iceland and Greenland."[93]

The Svalbard (*Spitsbergen*) archipelago and Bear Island in the Norwegian far north, both of which had been ceded to the Soviets, may have provided Moscow with security support points in Scandinavia that made Bornholm seem less important.[94] Moscow also gained crucial territorial concessions from the Finns as a result of the Armistice of September 19, 1944, concluding the "Continuation War" between the Soviet Union and Finland. Moscow received Petsamo in the north of Finland on the Arctic Sea, which gave Moscow a common border with Norway. The Finns also turned over to the Soviets a major naval installation at Porkkala on the Gulf of Finland that not only guaranteed the defense of Leningrad but was close enough to Helsinki to insure a compliant Finland. Soviet security in the eastern Baltic was also guaranteed by the incorporation of the Baltic states and of the northern part of East Prussia (*Kaliningrad oblast*) after the war. Along with the generally acceptable internationalization of the Kiel Canal and the Belts and Sound, as well as the establishment of Soviet naval strongholds in Rostock in eastern Germany and Świnoujście (*Swinemünde*) in Poland, the

Soviet presence in the center of the Baltic Sea was guaranteed without Bornholm. Besides, as British intelligence noted after the withdrawal from Bornholm, the Soviets "primary consideration in the Baltic has, in fact, been the defence of Leningrad rather than access to open seas."[95] The argument that the Soviets needed Bornholm for security purposes was mooted by the combination of these territorial and strategic gains and guarantees. There was considerable goodwill in Denmark toward the Soviets; Moscow did not want to fritter it away on overstaying its welcome in Bornholm.

The issue of putting pressure on Denmark remained important to Moscow. The Americans and British made signs of building a western alliance; keeping Denmark neutral in these circumstances was, no doubt, an important Soviet objective. But in this question, the skill of Danish diplomats and the restraint of Danish society in face of the Soviet occupation of Bornholm served the Danes well.[96] The criticism of Danish passivity and indifference in face of the Soviet occupation of the island is misplaced; the Danes gave Moscow every reason to believe that they could be relied on not to seek advantages from the Soviets, denounce their actions once they had evacuated, or to engage in any kind of reprisals. On the contrary, Copenhagen strongly intimated that the Soviet evacuation of the island would have positive ramifications for Soviet-Danish relations. The Danes engaged in what the *Manchester Guardian* called "tactical silence" regarding the Bornholm question, fearful of offending the Soviets and prolonging the occupation.[97]

As mentioned earlier, despite considerable worry among Danish officials about the fate of Bornholm, the Copenhagen government convinced the Danish press to curtail critical articles about the Soviet occupation and not to raise publicly issues of the duration of the occupation.[98] There were sufficient reasons that Moscow might wish to establish a long-term position on Bornholm, given the proximity of the Western approaches to the Baltic Sea and the likelihood that they would have to be satisfied with less than control of the entrance to the Baltic Sea and the Kiel Canal because of their internationalization. Pressure on the Danes might yield some concessions in this regard.

In February and early March 1946, the Danish government, led by Foreign Minister Gustav Rasmussen and Ambassador Døssing, made a concerted diplomatic effort to convince the Soviets that their original promise to withdraw from Bornholm once the military situation in Germany was settled and German troops were no longer on the island should be honored. Rasmussen had gained British assent to withdraw the small contingent of British troops that remained in Denmark and the Faroe Islands. The Danes remained profoundly frightened of the Russian presence and worried that they would stay; thus, the Danish government would do anything it could, short of making concessions on the maintenance of their parliamentary system, to get the Soviets to withdraw.[99] They promised that the place of the Soviet troops would be taken by Danish military units, now ready to protect the island and contribute to Baltic security. The Danish military itself proved to be an active force for getting the Copenhagen government to approach the Soviets about leaving. Foreign Minister Rasmussen was convinced the deal would work, though American intelligence expressed some skepticism, noting—like the islanders—that the Soviets continued to construct an airfield and strengthen Bornholm's coastal defenses.[100]

The Danish legation in Moscow received positive signals from the Soviet Foreign Ministry that a deal for withdrawal was fully possible. But along with this, on March 5, Molotov raised the predictable question with the Danes of how long British troops would remain in Denmark. (There were a little more than a thousand British troops, mostly in training functions with the Danish army.) With this "obstacle" in mind, Molotov nevertheless stated,

> If Denmark's forces are now capable of taking possession of Bornholm and create its administration there without any participation from foreign troops or foreign administrators, then the Soviet government would withdraw its troops from Bornholm and release the island to the Danish government.[101]

On March 16, Foreign Minister Gustav Rasmussen announced, "On March 7, the Russian Minister in Copenhagen, Mr. Plakhin, called upon me to state that if the Danish government was able to send Danish troops to Bornholm immediately to take over its administration without any foreign participation, the Soviet government would immediately withdraw its troops from Bornholm and leave the island to the Danish government." Needless to say, the Danish government agreed to the terms; the result, added Rasmussen on March 16, "was that the evacuation has now begun."[102] Part of the deal was a substantial payment in exchange for the Soviet barracks and the costs of transfer. The Danes did not bargain; in fact, in the end the total cost of the Soviet occupation reached close to twenty million kroner.[103]

The Soviets immediately began the process of organizing the departure of their military forces, some 6,600 officers and troops, plus their military hardware and a good part of their infrastructure. On April 5, 1946, some five thousand Bornholm islanders turned out at the harbor in Rønne, waving paper Danish and Soviet flags, to send off the occupiers from the island. The Soviet national anthem was played and Governor von Stemann and General Iakushev exchanged greetings, praising Soviet-Danish friendship.[104] The last Soviet officers and men left Bornholm on board the minesweeper *Vladimir Polukhin,* closing out the relatively uneventful occupation that lasted nearly a full year.

What the Soviets pointedly asked for from the Danes was an agreement that once they removed their troops from Bornholm the Danes would not allow the presence of foreign troops—and here they had in mind specifically the Americans and the British—on Danish soil, including Greenland and the Faroes.[105] By their actions in Denmark, the Soviets hoped to keep this pivotal country from falling under the direct influence of the Western powers.[106] In particular, Moscow was interested in denying the Americans and British forward positions, like Bornholm, for basing their troops and aircraft in western and central Europe.[107] The Soviet strategy succeeded only in part. The Danes originally hoped to pursue a traditional neutralist policy by joining the proposed Scandinavian Defense Union. But when Finland signed the Treaty of Mutual Friendship with the Soviet Union in April 1948, Norway demonstrated increasing interest in the prospect of an Atlantic alliance, and Sweden's commitment to neutrality did not include alliances with Scandinavian neighbors, the pro-NATO voices in the Denmark, recalling the humiliation of the Nazi occupation, won the day.[108]

The occupation of Bornholm cut both ways in the NATO issue: some Danes used the experience as an argument for joining; others worried that the Soviets might return to the island if the Danes joined the

Western alliance. In the end, the Danes became founding members of NATO in 1949 and continued to participate fully in the alliance during the Cold War. Yet Danish restraint on the question of NATO bases and on other Western security issues vis-à-vis the Soviet Union can be dated, in some measure, from the time of the Soviet evacuation.[109]

Behind the positive Danish diplomatic efforts to encourage the Soviets to leave Bornholm was Soviet interest in healthy trading relations with the Danes. Foreign Ministers Møller and Rasmussen periodically dangled in front of the Soviets the possibilities of trade in Danish agricultural products, something that deeply interested Moscow. However, the Danes were unable to send a trade delegation to Moscow as long as Bornholm remained a potential bone of contention between Moscow and Copenhagen. (A low-level Soviet delegation did come to Copenhagen in December 1945 to negotiate about obtaining Danish bacon and butter; the Danes were interested in particular in feed grains from the Soviets.) The British demand for agricultural products prompted some protests in London about these negotiations, but the Danes stood by their need to deal on an equal basis with the Soviets.[110]

As soon as the Bornholm issue was settled, the Danes sent a high-level delegation to Moscow, which was received by Stalin himself. Stalin and Molotov's discussions with the Head of the Danish Trade Delegation Crown Prince Axel and Foreign Minister Rasmussen in early June 1946, after the evacuation had been completed, indicated that the Danes were ready to fulfill the promise of positive economic relations. Stalin opened the trade discussions with the observation that he had been in Copenhagen in 1906 and found it a "beautiful and fine city." Rasmussen urged him to visit again, but Stalin demurred, saying it was not possible given all he had to do. The trade talks focused on Danish bacon, described by Stalin as "pure gold," and Soviet grain and seed oil, which the Danes badly needed. Stalin tried to interest his Danish interlocutors in apatite, a mineral found in plentiful quantities in the North of Russia that can be used for fertilizers, but the Danes appeared to have little interest.

Much of the discussion between Stalin and the Danish trade delegation focused on the Danish desire to rid themselves of a large population of interned Germans, some two to three hundred thousand altogether. The Danes complained that the costs of their internment and feeding took up a substantial part of the Danish budget. Stalin sympathized, offering to take half of this population in the Soviet zone of Germany, if the Western Allies would take the rest in theirs. In any case, Stalin insisted, the Germans should pay, not the Danes. Even if the Germans were poor now they would quickly recover, he predicted. He even hinted, not too subtly, that the Germans stayed in camps in Denmark because they were so well taken care of by the Danes. "In Poland and Czechoslovakia . . . the Germans were left in such a position that the Germans were ready to scatter from these countries in various directions because of hunger."[111]

• •

Long after the Soviets evacuated the island, the Danes continued to give Moscow reasons for satisfaction, especially in connection with Bornholm. The islanders erected a typical Soviet-style obelisk monument dedicated to "[t]he eternal glory of the Russian heroes who died in the battle with the German occupiers!" with a nearby granite grave marker with the names of the thirty Soviet soldiers and officers who died or "disappeared" during the liberation of the island.[112] According to the Russian ambassador in Copenhagen (1999) the Danes and Soviets had made a gentlemen's agreement that there would be no "foreign troops" on Bornholm's soil after the evacuation. Although there is no evidence that any such agreement was reached, the Danes seemed to have accepted the Soviets interpretation of events. Thus, while welcoming Soviet and today Russian representatives to the island on "Victory Day," for the laying of a wreath at the Soviet war memorial, Copenhagen did not allow NATO troops, other than Danish soldiers, to use Bornholm for military purposes. The few random, sometimes unintended, violations of this policy routinely aroused the protests of Moscow.[113]

The issue came up during a major NATO operation, "Main Brace," in 1952, which demonstrated Denmark's vulnerability to Soviet pressure about Bornholm. On Copenhagen's insistence, the NATO alliance imposed geographical limitations on its plans for military exercises on or east of Bornholm. The Danes abandoned any military activities involving Bornholm convinced that "such activities were not of sufficient strategic importance to counter-balance the politico-military consequences of challenging the Soviet Union over Bornholm."[114] Bornholm and its waters were off-limits to NATO exercises and NATO presence. The Danes did not want to give the Soviets any excuses to return.

Stalin's readiness to compromise his strategic military advantages had a crucial impact on the outcome of the Bornholm question. His policies in Bornholm also demonstrated his desire to create a "neutral" zone of nonaligned countries in western Europe. At the same time, the Danes demonstrated an ability to employ diplomacy in effective ways to achieve their ends of Soviet evacuation. In the case of Bornholm, Soviet occupation did not mean Sovietization. Despite the many constraints and hardships forced on the Bornholm islanders by the occupation, they were able to resume their lives and occupations as full members of a free Danish polity.

CHAPTER TWO

THE ALBANIAN BACKFLIP

1944–1948

Josip Broz Tito and the Yugoslav partisan leadership exerted influence on their Albanian comrades almost from the very beginning of the war. Yugoslav advisors from the Communist Party of Yugoslavia (CPY) Miladin Popović and Dušan Mugoša were influential when the Albanian Communist Party (CPA) was founded on November 8, 1941, and when the Albanian National Liberation Front was formed under communist leadership in September 1942.[1] Some Yugoslav partisans fought together with Albanian partisan units in their successful struggle both against the noncommunist resistance—the *Balli Kombëtar*—and against the Italian and German occupations during the war. Especially from early 1944 on, when the Yugoslav partisans had regained at least nominal control of a good part of their country, the Albanians benefitted from Yugoslav partisan arms and munitions deliveries as well as military know-how.[2]

The Albanians prided themselves on the fact that they had sent, at the end of 1944, two divisions of their National Liberation Army to fight side by side with the Yugoslav partisans to help liberate Montenegro, southern Bosnia, and the Sanjak.[3] Enver Hoxha, head of the Albanian communist movement, recalled in his memoirs that the relationship between the Yugoslav and Albanian partisan forces had "a happy and promising start." Even after the liberation, he wrote, "we continued to retain a good, to some extent euphoric, opinion about the Yugoslav party."[4] Still Yugoslav help was rather limited, and the youthful and idealistic Albanian comrades—most of them in their early twenties— succeeded in assuming leadership of the national liberation struggle thanks to their ability to combine promises of social equality and national sovereignty.[5]

Stalin demonstrated little interest in Albania during the war. As he later reminded Hoxha, the general secretary of the Albanian party who now also headed the government, Albania remained a backward mountainous country whose socialist pretensions needed taming.[6] Befitting his background as a student of "nationalities," Stalin was curious about the origins of the Albanians, wondering whether they had any ties to the Slavs.[7] But as his postwar dealings with the Yugoslavs would demonstrate, he was not particularly committed to the reconstitution of an independent Albania. Some of his subordinates speculated that parts of the country might fall to Yugoslavia and other parts to Greece, whether it was a royalist Greece, dominated by the British, or a socialist Greece, which Stalin viewed with considerable skepticism. For example, in a February 1945 Soviet foreign ministry commission report on this "unsettled, dwarf country," Maxim Litvinov suggested that either the British would insist that Albania (along with Greece) be included in its camp or the Yugoslavs and royalist Greeks would partition the country between them. In exchange, the Greeks might be convinced to cede some of their territory to allow Bulgaria access to the Aegean Sea. Essentially, maintaining Albanian independence did not seem a particular focus of Soviet interests.[8] Moscow did not even object to the Italian proposal to send a military mission to Tirana after the war, to which the Western Allies had assented.[9] At that point, Stalin's highest priority regarding Albania was that no complications ensued with the Western Allies that might force his hand in the Mediterranean region. As a result, he seemed generally supportive of Belgrade's interests in Albanian affairs, as long as the Soviets were not implicated in any troublesome adventures. Albania was far away from Moscow, and it made sense for the Yugoslav party to continue its wartime efforts to help foster the development of the Albanian party and government. The Soviet party was circumspect regarding the Albanians and "cautious," Hoxha later wrote, "to the point of a certain 'neglect.'"[10]

Yugoslavia and Albania

The Yugoslavs, in contrast, treated Albania at the end of the war as their client state, much as the Soviets treated those countries of eastern Europe that they had occupied and whose destinies they controlled. The Yugoslavs already during the war had advisors in the Albanian military and in the economic units of the fledgling Albanian government. In the Albanian party, they also had a strong supporter in the person of Koçi Xoxe, a partner—yet a rival—of Enver Hoxha. The permanent representative of the Yugoslav Central Committee to the Albanian Central Committee, Velimir Stojnić, regularly met with and exerted considerable influence over the Albanian politburo. Once the war was over, Tito and his comrades assumed that Albania would quickly be absorbed into Yugoslavia as its seventh republic and then combined with mostly Albanian-inhabited Kosovo to form a separate Albanian republican entity. The Yugoslavs moved resolutely in that direction by eliminating tariff barriers between Albania and Yugoslavia and by creating, if not a common currency, then one that pegged the Albanian lek to the Yugoslav dinar in a one-to-one relationship.[11] They set up mixed Yugoslav-Albanian companies and took concrete steps toward the unification of the economic plans of the two countries. The treaty of February 20, 1945, was the first of several that were meant to seal the close partnership between Belgrade and Tirana. It guaranteed economic help to the Albanians, who suffered widespread food shortages and malnutrition.[12] Corn, grain, and sugar would be sent to Albania in exchange for oil, petroleum products, and coal.[13] It also included an agreement on mutual military help, ensuring Yugoslav military aid in the case of outside intervention. This agreement was followed up by the July 1946 Treaty of Friendship, Cooperation, and Mutual Assistance that cemented the economic and military arrangements, including measures to organize the Albanian army along Yugoslav lines and to begin the process of integration.

As for Soviet aid for Albania, the Yugoslavs insisted that all of it be funneled through Belgrade. The Soviets were willing to comply, as Stalin explained during his first meetings with Hoxha in late May and early June 1947, where munitions deliveries and other assistance for the Alba-

3. Postwar Balkans

nian army were discussed.[14] To be sure, this position had not kept the Soviets from sending their own advisors to Albania. The first had arrived already in August 1945 to help develop the oil and mining industries, and the Albanians had quickly grown dependent on this assistance.[15] At the same time, Stalin assured Tito in a meeting of May 1946 that the Soviet Union would have nothing against including Albania in the Yugoslav federation, although he also advised the Yugoslavs to be patient, since he feared that making such a move at that time might complicate the favorable resolution of the Trieste question.[16]

While the Soviets in Tirana carried on their modest relations with the Albanians, Tito and his comrades took charge of Albanian party, economic, and military matters, apparently with the blessing of Moscow. The Yugoslavs were especially interested in military issues: defense of the coastline against potential Allied incursions; defense of the southern border with Greece; and the construction of airports and railway lines in Albania for the purposes of responding to potential warlike situations.[17] Hoxha and the Albanians worried, no doubt excessively, that the royalist Greeks would try to hive off southeastern Albania, Northern Epirus, especially around the Korçë region of Albania, which they claimed, backed by the British, as their territory. In their quest for security, the Albanian comrades were determined to put their future entirely in the hands of the Yugoslav party and its Soviet sponsors.[18]

There were a few within the Albanian government who supported establishing relations with the Western powers, especially Sejfulla Malëshova, supported by former foreign minister Omer Nishani; but the opposition of Hoxha and Xoxe aside, the Yugoslav embrace was too tight for the Albanians to draw in the Americans or British.[19] By the beginning of 1946, the Albanian leadership refused to abide by American demands to recognize prewar treaties, thus effectively excluding the possibility of American and British recognition (and admission to the UN).[20] Joseph E. Jacobs, the U.S. representative in Albania, who claimed to have spent a considerable amount of time with Hoxha, cabled to Washington on February 28, 1946, "If at [the] next session [of] UNO [the United Nations] Albania [is] not admitted, Albania may become [a] unit [of the] Yugoslav federation."[21] The implication was that if the Western powers did not accord Albania a place at the table of nations, it might be more easily absorbed into Yugoslavia. Yet this was precisely where Albania and Yugoslavia appeared to be headed. With the signing of the Treaty of Friendship, Cooperation, and Mutual Assistance between the two countries during Hoxha's visit to Belgrade in July 1946, the stage was set for moving concretely in the direction of a federation at the first propitious moment. A CIA report to U.S. president Truman of January 6, 1947, exaggerated only slightly when it emphasized that "the political structure of Albania has already been assimilated to that of a state in the Yugoslav federation" and that "the Albanian army, trained and equipped by Yugoslavia, is virtually part of the Yugoslav military establishment."[22]

Notwithstanding these developments, the actual attitude of the Albanian political leadership toward what seemed to be the juggernaut for unifying with the Yugoslav federation is a subject of some dispute. Enver Hoxha claims in his memoirs that he was initially misled by the "devious" Yugoslavs into going along with their plans but quickly understood that they had only Belgrade's interests at heart and therefore started looking for ways to preserve Albanian independence.[23] The Albanian communists, like the Yugoslavs in their territory, saw themselves as liberators of their country and people, and, as Hoxha indicated, certainly chafed at times at the insistent "help" of their Yugoslav comrades. Even Tito recognized the Yugoslavs' "mistakes" in this connection, namely, their frequent playing the bossy "papa" in relations with the Albanian party.[24]

As one Albanian historian points out, the Albanian communists greatly appreciated the aid provided by the Yugoslavs because they understood that this helped them develop their industry, transportation infrastructure (especially railways), and financial institutions. But they nevertheless were at pains to maintain their own profile in what they considered a bilateral relationship.[25] At the same time, the Albanian party was rent by serious factional differences and personal political ambitions that were particularly notable in 1944–1945 but continued to influence Albanian party politics during the following years. A December 11, 1945, report to the Soviet Central Committee about the political situation of the Albanian party, probably authored by Koçi Xoxe, discussed at length the "sectarianism" of comrades who wanted to move immediately into socialism as well as the "right opportunism" and "liberalism" of others who were excessively focused on the recognition by the Americans and British and help from the Italians. The document's author added, "Under the influence of these opportunist tendencies, we did not orient our people towards the healthy brotherhood with Yugoslavia, as was needed."[26]

During the war and after, Koçi Xoxe, the minister of interior and a deputy head of the Albanian Council of Ministers, spent a great deal of time in Belgrade and with the Yugoslav comrades. This did not mean that he was any more closely dependent on the Yugoslavs than were, for example Hoxha or Nako Spiru. Nevertheless, he and the Albanian comrades grouped around him clearly pushed a pro-Yugoslav line as a way to advance their interests in the party. When formulating the new 1946 Albanian constitution, the Albanian comrades took many of its articles directly from the Yugoslav constitution.[27] Nako Spiru, the head of the Albanian State Planning Commission, a respected member of the Albanian politburo, and, like Xoxe, a deputy head of the Albanian Council of Ministers, seemed increasingly to be concerned about the all-encompassing Yugoslav embrace, even while he negotiated an economic package with Belgrade that presaged integration. But during and immediately after the war, Spiru got along just fine with the Yugoslav comrades, as did pretty much everyone in the leadership, including Hoxha. They all in some fashion were jockeying for power with one another while in the thrall of the Yugoslavs. Spiru is reported to have contacted the Yugoslavs during the plenum of the Albanian Central Committee at Berat in late November 1944, passing along a note of denunciation of Hoxha to the Yugoslavs, as a way to promote his own career.[28] At the same time, in 1945 and especially in 1946, Spiru developed contacts with the Soviet advisors and diplomats who came to Tirana. Spiru and his allies in the party were increasingly wary of what they perceived as the exploitation of Albanian resources—in particular mining and oil extraction—by the Yugoslavs.

Enver Hoxha's position in this central question of postwar Albanian politics is harder to characterize, though we know that these conflicts over the Yugoslav orientation overlapped with factional struggles within the party that surrounded Hoxha during the war.[29] He was aware of the weakness of the Albanian economy, the problems with the Albanian military, and the threats to Albanian security from the Greek royalist government and its territorial claims. He may also have learned of the various plans by Albanian émigrés—episodically supported by the British and American governments—to engage in military intervention in Albania.[30] As a consequence, he desperately needed the help and especially the military support of the Yugoslavs, in terms of both the arms and advice they provided to the weak and ineffectual Albanian military and the preparedness of Yugoslav troops stationed at Ohrid in

2.1 Entry of the government in Tirana, Albania, November 28, 1944 (?). *Left to right:* Koçi Xoxe, Baba Faja Martaneshi, Enver Hoxha, Myslim Pasha.
ROYAL GEOGRAPHICAL SOCIETY (UK).

Macedonia (near the border of the Korçë region in Northern Epirus) to intervene.

It is not impossible that Hoxha might also have entertained the idea of a larger political role for himself inside the Yugoslav federation, with the addition of the Kosovo Albanians to his national base. He later claimed that he informally requested that Kosovo be united with Albania and that Tito responded that this was unlikely at the time because of the inevitable opposition of the Serbs.[31] (Interestingly, the Americans believed that it was desirable that parts of Kosovo and Metohija be ceded to Albania.[32]) Tito held out to the Albanians the likelihood of the unification of Albania and Kosovo and Metohija in the potential formation of a federation of South Slavs, which he and the Bulgarian Georgi Dimitrov had discussed.[33]

Hoxha may well have believed that such a federation would rapidly advance the national and international horizons of Albania and Albanians. But he was also wary of the Yugoslavs, unhappy that they were both pushing Xoxe's role in the Albanian government and complaining about Spiru, who was dragging his feet on the integration issue. Hedging his bets, Hoxha therefore tried to develop his relationship with a reluctant Stalin and the Soviets, but his requests to go to Moscow, frowned on by the Yugoslavs, were turned down. When Hoxha was able to meet with Molotov on September 16, 1946, at the Paris Peace Conference, Molotov told the Albanian leader not to come to Moscow in the near future with a major Albanian delegation. It would be better, he advised Hoxha, if the Albanians first established "normal relations" with the Americans and British. Albania was neither recognized by the United States and Great Britain nor was it accepted in the United Nations, Molotov noted, leaving the country excessively vulnerable and unstable. Hoxha agreed, declaring that he had gotten everything he wanted from Moscow, though he also expressed the wish that Soviet advisors could be attached to every Albanian military brigade.[34]

During discussions with the Soviet envoy in Tirana, D. S. Chuvakhin, one week later, Hoxha complained about the increasingly intense sparring between Xoxe and Spiru, though without characterizing this conflict as one between pro-Yugoslav and pro-Soviet positions. As he described it, the two of them were at each other's throats so much that he even had to stop politburo meetings because of it. Hoxha focused most of his criticism on Xoxe, who no doubt wished to replace him: "[H]e completely overestimates his abilities and looks at things with excessive optimism." At the same time, Hoxha faulted Xoxe for having rushed to use force to crush the uprising that the remaining noncommunist opposition in Albania had staged in Shkodër on September 9, 1946.[35] All in all, Hoxha concluded, the Albanian politburo needed new people and fresh blood.

Stalin did not stay out of Albanian affairs for long. The powerful leader of the Soviet Union was a micromanager for whom control was the essence of politics; not for long would he leave Albanian affairs in the hands of the Yugoslavs, whose pretensions to pursue an independent foreign policy were beginning to grate on Moscow. As a result, Stalin intensified relations with the Albanian party, mainly through Chuvakhin, his envoy in Tirana. The Soviets also began to express their annoyance that Tito and the Yugoslavs seemed to keep all the Albanian cards in their own hands.[36] It was one thing to turn over the management of Albanian affairs to Belgrade; it was another that the Yugoslavs monopolized information about and control over the Albanian state.

When Stalin met with the Yugoslav party leader Edvard Kardelj in Moscow in April 1947, however, the Soviets did not yet openly oppose the Yugoslavs' plans. Judging by the Yugoslav transcript of this meeting, one might suggest that Kardelj pushed for the pro-Yugoslav Xoxe to replace Hoxha. Noted Kardelj, Hoxha "held up well during the war, and the people like him. But he does not have sufficient Marxist-Leninist training." Molotov, who was also present, seemed to concur. Hoxha was a cultivated and educated man, he indicated, "but in his education one notices the influence of the West."[37] From the Soviets, this was a damning indictment, which might well have indicated to Kardelj that Moscow was ready to see Xoxe replace Hoxha as general secretary of the Albanian party. Shortly thereafter, Stalin summoned Hoxha, Xoxe, and an Albanian party and state delegation to Moscow.

Hoxha was thrilled about his first visit with the Soviet leadership, which took place in July of 1947 and gave him the opportunity to talk to Stalin and Molotov about his analysis of repeated Greek incursions in the south of his country. In his discussions with Molotov, Hoxha used careful language to articulate his fears about possible repercussions of the substantial clandestine aid to the Greek communists that the Yugoslavs and Albanians were supplying through Albanian territory. Given that the Yugoslavs advised firing on Greek airplanes that violated Albanian airspace and were ready to muster their two air force squadrons based on Albanian soil to attack incoming aircraft, Hoxha expressed concern about drawing the Soviets into a larger conflagration. As he noted, the Albanians had already been chastised by the Soviets for mining their territorial waters. This had precipitated a major international incident when two British ships struck Albanian mines in the Corfu Channel in October 1946, which resulted in the death of forty-four British officers and men. This was exactly the kind of crisis situation that Stalin found completely unacceptable. Notably, at the end of his conversation with Molotov, Hoxha also complained about the terms of the economic agreements with the Yugoslavs and the poor performance of the joint stock companies.[38] Whatever his suspicions of the

2.2 The inauguration of construction work for the Durrës-Tiranë railway, April 11, 1948. Enver Hoxha's portrait hangs between those of Stalin and Tito. ALBANIAN TELEGRAPHIC AGENCY.

Yugoslavs at this point, Stalin remained firm with Hoxha and the Albanians. Even Soviet aid to the Albanians would continue to be forwarded through Yugoslav channels.[39]

Nonetheless, after Hoxha's and Xoxe's visit to Moscow, contacts between the Soviet economic advisors and members of the Albanian government intensified. This was not at all to Belgrade's liking.[40] It was no secret to the Yugoslavs that Nako Spiru regularly complained about them to his contacts in the Soviet legation in Tirana, while the Soviet advisors, and a group of technical specialists working in Albanian oil exploration and the refining industry in particular, sometimes worked at cross-purposes with the Yugoslav advisors who were assigned to the same areas. During Kardelj's visit to Moscow in April 1947, Stalin had brought up the conflicts between Yugoslav and Soviet advisors in Albania as well. Inter alia, he had mentioned that Hoxha had complained that the Yugoslav political advisors in the Albanian army weakened discipline among the troops. "That's new to us," was all Kardelj could answer; "they didn't say anything to us about it."[41]

The Spiru Affair

The low-level tug-of-war between the Yugoslav advisors and their sup porters around Xoxe in the Albanian party on the one hand and Nako Spiro, who had a modicum of support from a few Soviet advisors on the other, erupted into open conflict in the Albanian party in the fall of 1947. No doubt backed by the Yugoslavs and their representative in the Albanian party, Savo Zlatić, Xoxe, as minister of interior, initiated an investigation of Spiru, his wife, Liri Belishova, who was also a politburo member, and several associates, accusing the group of anti-party and anti-Yugoslav activity, tantamount to the subversive activities of alleged Western "imperialist agents" trying to undermine the Albanian state.[42] At the politburo meeting held on November 18–19, Zlatić and Xoxe charged Spiru and his allies with undermining Yugoslav-Albanian eco- nomic relations. On the next day, the shaken Spiru went to see his erst- while supporter Hoxha and begged for five days to organize his defense. Hoxha turned him down, stating that the matter was in the hands of the party and that Spiru would have to appear before the polit- buro that day.[43]

Spiru then sought support at the Soviet legation in Tirana, where he had contacts with the Soviet chargé, N. A. Gagarinov, who had been involved in following the Yugoslav initiatives to diminish the role of Spiru. Apparently, he had no luck with the Soviets, either, who still for- mally abided by the current arrangements. Rather than face the charges of his comrades in the Albanian politburo, and seemingly aban- doned by Hoxha, Spiru reportedly shot himself in the head and died as a result of his injuries on November 20, 1947.[44] Gagarinov related to the Albanians that Spiru had sent the Soviet legation a suicide note: "[A]fter the grave accusations which the Yugoslav leadership has made against me I am obliged to kill myself."[45] Shortly before his death, Spiru is said to have told his wife, Liri Belishova, about the Yugoslavs, "[T]hey are not looking for a self-critical statement, they want my head. They are not talking about mistakes; they are talking about an enemy."[46] He told Gagarinov pretty much the same: "This [denunciation of being anti- Yugoslav] threatens me with death. In the Albanian language, this means I am an enemy."[47] There have been intermittent claims over the decades since Spiru's death that the Sigurimi—the Albanian secret police—murdered Spiru on Hoxha's (or Xoxe's) orders. This is fully possible; Spiru knew himself that his condemnation as anti-Yugoslav was a virtual death sentence.[48]

The Yugoslavs were nervous about the Soviet reaction to the death of Spiru, whom Molotov would still recall as "a good worker and a friend of the USSR" almost one year later.[49] After thoroughly briefing the Yugoslav ambassador to the Soviet Union, Vladimir Popović, in Belgrade, Tito sent him back to Moscow to speak with Stalin about the Albanian situation. Upon his arrival, Popović learned that the Soviet leader was in the south at Sochi and could not receive him. Instead Popović met on December 4 with Andrei Zhdanov, who was in charge of relations with foreign parties in the Central Committee. Zhdanov promised to pass on Popović's messages to Stalin and also posed questions to Popović that Stalin might ask. In their conversation, Popović tried to convince Zhdanov that Spiru had interfered with the effective communications of Yugoslav advice and delivery of aid to the Albanians. As Popović told the story, with some grain of truth, Spiru had initially been pro-Yugoslav and anti-Hoxha. Later, driven by his rivalry with Koçi Xoxe, in Popović's words "the actual founder" of the Albanian Communist Party, Spiru had used his position as head of the economic planning office to undermine economic ties with Yugoslavia by keeping the Albanians from fulfilling their trading obligations. Unable to diminish Xoxe's or Hoxha's influence in the party, Spiru had then sought out Soviet advisors and embassy personnel, kept them isolated from the Yugoslav advisors, and engaged in anti-Yugoslav propaganda. In response, Popović told Zhdanov, Tito and the Yugoslavs had stepped up their activities within the Albanian party and helped the Albanian comrades overcome the negative influence exerted by Spiru. The death of Spiru could thus be used beneficially by Tito to "purge and consolidate" the Albanian party.[50]

The implication of Popović's message was that the Yugoslavs directly sought to mold the Albanian party in their own image, promoting the career of Xoxe in the process. Moreover, Popović indicated that Soviet specialists in Albania were sometimes working at cross-purposes with the Yugoslav ones and impeded Yugoslav plans for integration. Three days later, Stalin asked Popović (through Zhdanov) whether the Yugoslavs thought they could replace Soviet specialists in Albania, especially those in the oil industry. Popović replied that he could not get an answer until the Yugoslav leadership returned home from a trip to Hungary. He inferred from the question, however, that Stalin was ready to go along with the Yugoslavs' desire to assume complete control of Albanian matters.[51]

Meanwhile, the Yugoslavs were so confident in their position that they attempted to secure the Albanians' agreement to remove the Soviet advisors.[52] Hoxha, on his part, seemed pleased that the Albanian party had purged its "anti-Yugoslav" faction. Spiru had been a friendly rival in the party leadership since the end of the war.[53] The line of the Albanian party had been upheld: gradual integration with Yugoslavia to the point of a unified "state-confederation."[54] Yet Hoxha was also nervous that a political counterweight to Xoxe's (and the Yugoslavs') influence in the Albanian party had been removed. Xoxe, writes one historian of Albania, "lacked higher education, reveled in brutality, and despised intellectual types."[55] Hoxha had much to fear from him.

The Split

There are ways to read back into the Yugoslav-Albanian relationship of the winter and early spring of 1948 the formal split between Belgrade and Tirana that occurred as a result of the Stalin-inspired Cominform resolution on Yugoslavia of June 28, 1948. No doubt there were tensions beforehand, especially in relation to the Albanian inability to live up to their side of the trade agreement with Yugoslavia and Albanian complaints about Yugoslav deliveries. But until the actual split, there was every reason to assume these problems would be smoothed over in the process of eventual integration.[56] At the Eighth Plenum of the CPA's Central Committee (February 26–March 8, 1948), Xoxe led the charge to posthumously denounce Spiru and remove his widow, Liri Belishova, as well as Mehmet Shehu, head of the Albanian general staff, who had questioned the wisdom of the Yugoslavs' military policies, from the Central Committee. The same plenum declared the need for "even closer ties and cooperation with Yugoslavia."[57]

One could interpret the facts that the Albanian party was neither invited to the Cominform meeting in September 1947 nor held a party congress until after the Soviet-Yugoslav split as indicating that all parties—Belgrade, Moscow, and Tirana—saw the integration into the Yugoslav federation as the natural next step.[58] It could also be that Stalin simply did not want to antagonize the British and Americans by including the Albanian party in the Cominform group. Whatever Stalin's views, and they are hard to know exactly, the Yugoslavs were intent on going ahead with the incorporation of Albania. Reportedly, offices were already being prepared at the Yugoslav Federation Palace on the banks of the Sava in Belgrade for representatives of the Seventh (Albanian) Republic.[59]

Meanwhile, already by the end of 1947—as neither the Yugoslavs nor the Albanians seemed to realize yet—Stalin's confidence in Tito and the Yugoslavs had begun to wear thin. Well-placed informers in the Yugoslav party had been reporting about Tito's excessive pride and nationalism for quite a while, and in early fall, the Soviet Central Committee's Foreign Policy Department produced its own critical assessments of the Yugoslav leaders' "national narrowness" and their tendency to "over-estimate their achievements."[60] Stalin was also aware that there had been complaints in the Yugoslav politburo about Moscow's insufficient attention to Yugoslav needs for weapons and munitions, and that Popović's remarks about Soviet advisors in Albania (conveyed to him by Zhdanov) had echoes in the grumblings in the Yugoslav government about the activities of Soviet advisors in Yugoslavia itself. Stalin's purposeful maneuvers in December and January aimed at disrupting Tito's efforts in Albania and Greece were subtly carried out, while, in the words of one historian of the split, "simultaneously lulling the Yugoslavs into a false sense of security."[61] Still, when Stalin asked Tito in late December to send a high-ranking Yugoslav official—preferably Milovan Djilas—to Moscow to clarify the issues that had been broached in the Popović-Zhdanov exchanges, there was no indication yet that within only six months, tensions over Albania, among other significant issues, would erupt into a full-scale rift between the Soviet Union and Yugoslavia, until then, its most important and most loyal ally.

Djilas arrived in Moscow on January 17, 1948, along with a substantial Yugoslav military delegation tasked with renewing Belgrade's efforts to receive weapons, military technology, munitions, and, perhaps most importantly, industrial machinery for the construction of Yugoslav armaments factories. Djilas was immediately called to meet with Stalin, Molotov, and Zhdanov in a now famous late-night conversation. Once pleasantries were exchanged, Stalin blurted out, "So, members of the Central Committee in Albania are killing themselves over you [the Yugoslavs]. This is very inconvenient, very inconvenient." Djilas agreed but stated that Nako Spiru had isolated himself from the Albanian party by adopting an extreme anti-Yugoslav stance. Stalin did not seem to listen. "We have no special interest in Albania," he declared, and continued: "We agree to Yugoslavia swallowing Albania," making a gesture of swallowing his fingers. Djilas was clearly taken aback by Stalin's bluntness and tried to explain that this was a matter of working toward federation and unification, not annexation. "That is swallowing," Molotov chimed in. Stalin added: "Yes, yes. Swallowing! But we agree with you: you ought to swallow Albania—the sooner the better."[62]

It is very hard to say what Stalin was up to exactly in this conversation. But he was clearly annoyed by the Albanian issue and wanted the Yugoslavs to take it off the table for him. He asked Djilas, "And what about Hoxha? What is he like in your opinion?" Djilas tried to dodge the question, and Stalin provided his view, which was not unlike the Yugoslavs': was Hoxha not "a petit bourgeois, inclined towards nationalism? Yes, we think so too. Does it seem that the strongest man there is Xoxe?" Djilas agreed, reflecting the general Yugoslav position. Stalin then concluded that there were no differences between the Soviet and Yugoslav positions about Albania and told him to write a document to that effect to send on to Belgrade, which Djilas proceeded to do.[63]

To date no Soviet or Yugoslav transcript of this meeting has been found that would back up the veracity of the account in Djilas's memoirs. Two documents kept in the Yugoslav party archives, however, supplement Djilas's version. The first is a coded telegram from Djilas to Belgrade, sent from Moscow on January 19, which describes Stalin's injunctions to preserve the trappings of Albanian independence and self-determination and to keep up the appearance of the sovereign choice of Hoxha and the Albanian party leadership. The second is the draft resolution summarizing the principles agreed upon at the meeting that Djilas wrote on Stalin's suggestion. (The Soviets never sent it on to Belgrade.) According to it, Stalin and the Soviets agreed completely with the Yugoslav position that Albania's "future development should be tied to the development of Yugoslavia." Yet in contrast to all the talk about swallowing, it also reported that Stalin saw "no need to hurry" into unification. It should come at the appropriate moment, when "relations between the two countries are in accord with one another, avoiding meanwhile reasons for foreign intervention, and confirming such a decision through the Albanian parliament." In Djilas's rendition of the agreement, Stalin was conciliatory on the issue of Soviet military and economic advisors in Albania. They should report to their Soviet superiors in Belgrade, who would be responsible for "regulating" their activities with the Yugoslav authorities.[64]

Stalin's message as revealed in these documents was a deeply equivocal one. On the one hand, the Soviets had no objections to the Yugoslav plan to incorporate Albania into the Yugoslav federation as the seventh republic. On the other, Stalin insisted that appearances be maintained that this was above all the Albanians' choice. It was crucial that the United States and Great Britain not see this move as a justification to intervene. (This may well have been an excuse that Stalin used to delay incorporation.) Despite the Yugoslavs' clear preferences for Xoxe at the helm of the Albanian party, which the Soviets seemed to support, Stalin suggested that Hoxha be used to gather the political momentum for unification. Finally, as unpleasant as the whole issue must have been to him, Stalin signaled that the frictions between Soviet advisors and Yugoslav policies in Tirana could be ameliorated by tightening the link between the Soviets in Albania and the Soviet authorities in Belgrade.

So what caused this tenuous agreement between Stalin and the Yugoslavs about Albania to unravel? Most critically, Tito decided to send a division of troops to the southern Albanian border region of Korçë to supplement the Yugoslav air force squadron already stationed in Albania. Ostensibly, this division was intended to help defend Tito's Albanian protégés from the incursions of the "Greek monarcho-fascists."

On January 19 Aleksandar Ranković notified Hoxha about the transfer; on the following day Hoxha responded positively. He also issued a "state of war alert" for Korçë to prepare for the arrival of the Yugoslav troops.[65] When Lieutenant General Milan Kuprešanin, whom Tito had appointed to oversee the restationing of the Yugoslav unit, saw the shambolic character of the Albanian forces around Korçë, he began the process of organizing them as well.[66] The Yugoslavs found the Albanian army impossibly weak and incapable of defending the country and Belgrade's interests in the case of invasion. At the same time, there can be little doubt that Tito also intended to establish a strong military presence in order to consolidate his control of Albania, assuming that there would be no opposition from the Soviets.[67]

Tito erred. Stalin was livid at not having been told of the Yugoslav plans in advance. On January 28, Molotov sent the Yugoslavs a telegram via the Soviet ambassador in Belgrade, A. I. Lavrent'ev, stating that Moscow opposed the sending of troops.[68] At a critical February 10, 1948, meeting between the Soviets and the Yugoslav and Bulgarian party leaderships, Molotov broached the issue again by emphasizing that the Soviets had learned about these Yugoslav military plans only at the end of January 1948. "The Albanians said they were sure that this was done with our permission," Molotov stated.[69] (Enver Hoxha wrote in his memoirs that he decided to inform the Soviet legation in Tirana about the Yugoslav plan, while delaying presenting it to the Albanian politburo.[70])

The Yugoslav action made apparent, Molotov added, "that we assess the situation in Albania differently. It is unacceptable to pass by such differences in silence. We should speak openly about such questions. . . ." With typical sarcasm, Stalin added, no doubt correctly, "The Yugoslavs, apparently, are afraid that we will take Albania away from them. You must take Albania, but wisely." He also brought up a recent incident in which the Yugoslavs had essentially prevented the Albanians from buying grain from the Soviets. According to the Soviet record of the meeting, Stalin added that the Yugoslavs "believe that we are tearing away from them their union both with Bulgaria and with Albania and want to present us with a fait accompli."

Stalin demanded that no Yugoslav division be sent to Albania. It would only invite intervention from the United States, which had military bases and naval forces in the region. "They will begin to holler that Albania is occupied by Yugoslavia. . . . Of all the tangles in the struggle between reaction and democracy," Stalin noted, "the Albanian knot is our weakest link." He also stressed once again that Albania was neither a member of the United Nations nor recognized diplomatically by the United States or Great Britain, and he reiterated as he had done before in front of Djilas that disturbing the country's delicate sovereignty could easily prompt Western military intervention. Interestingly, Stalin presented the Soviet experience in China as an example of how the Yugoslavs should act in Albania. "Not one of our soldiers is in China," he said, "and look how well they [the Chinese communists] are doing against the imperialists. . . . Teach them [the Albanians], arm them, and they can fight themselves."[71] If the imperialists ended up invading Albania, then the Albanian parliament could still invite the Yugoslavs to help.[72]

Stalin was also peeved at Georgi Dimitrov, the Comintern veteran and leader of the Bulgarian Communist Party, for his recent candid talk about plans for a federation of the East European "people's democracies," which had had a direct impact on the Yugoslavs' desires to absorb Albania. In the beginning of August 1947, Dimitrov and Tito had agreed, without asking Stalin beforehand, on a treaty of Bulgarian and Yugoslav friendship, cooperation, and mutual help. At the time, Stalin had let both of them know in no uncertain terms that this was unacceptable until the peace treaty with Bulgaria had been signed. Both leaders accepted party discipline and fell in line.[73]

Yet on January 17, 1948, on the way home from signing the Treaty of Friendship, Cooperation, and Mutual Help between Bulgaria and Romania, Dimitrov gave an interview with journalists that broached the subject of the possibility of a federation or confederation of all the people's democracies in eastern Europe, including Albania and even Greece! In particular, Dimitrov had mentioned a potential customs union between these countries and declared that the views of "the imperialists" would not matter when the time came.[74]

Tito, to be sure, did not at all appreciate Dimitrov's grand ideas of an East European union. He preferred to work within the narrower Balkan context, no doubt in good measure because he felt he could control the Balkan communists. Tito wanted to incorporate Albania quickly and then turn to the project of federation with Bulgaria, with Yugoslavia as the senior partner. Stalin, on his part, was greatly upset with Dimitrov and wrote him (with a copy to Tito) that his loose talk was "injurious" to the cause.[75] At the February 10 meeting, Stalin went even further and accused Dimitrov of acting like a silly communist youth leader, boasting about his accomplishments and waving red flags to the imperialists. "You are either inexperienced or getting carried away, like the Komsomol activists who fly like moths right into the burning flames."[76] Molotov noted that the earlier premature attempt to conclude a Yugoslav-Bulgarian treaty had *"strengthened the position of reactionary elements in England and America, giving them a reason to bolster their intervention in Greece against Bulgaria and Yugoslavia."* The Soviet government, stated Molotov, *"cannot take responsibility for pacts of such enormous importance, concluded without the consultation of the USSR."*[77] For the Soviets, talk of a customs union was ridiculous and harmful. To make matters worse, Molotov added, everyone thought that Dimitrov and Tito spoke with Moscow's approval. "We consider that absolutely incorrect and unacceptable in the future."[78]

Stalin particularly harped on the need to avoid problems with the Americans, though it is hard to know how much of this was merely a way to get at Dimitrov (and, even more pointedly, the Yugoslavs) and how much he genuinely worried about American electoral politics. "You give the reactionary elements in America the material to convince public opinion that the Americans are not doing anything out of the ordinary by forming the Western bloc, because in the Balkans there is not only a bloc, but a customs union. Now there is a big election campaign in America. For us, it makes a big difference what kind of government there will be." If the "moneyed magnates" who "hate us" come to power, Stalin warned, then *"to a significant extent this will be our fault because of our conduct.* [. . .] Why do you provide succor to the position of our enemies in England, America, and France?" he snapped.[79]

Despite these criticisms of the past sins of the Bulgarians and Yugo-slavs, the Soviet leader indicated that the time was ripe to form a federation between the two countries, with Albania being added at the appropriate moment. Once the federation was formed, the Yugoslavs could move troops into Albania. The Soviets were not against federation, he said to the Bulgarian communist Traicho Kostov at the February 10 meeting. "[W]e are only against Komsomol methods."[80]

Tito and the Yugoslavs correctly understood that Stalin intended to delay Albania's incorporation into Yugoslavia by this tack, while using the more malleable Bulgarians to control Belgrade's growing sense of its own importance. Yet the Yugoslavs were by then less interested in a federation with the Bulgarians than they had been immediately after the war, when their hubris and revolutionary enthusiasm had driven their vision of Balkan unity. When Edvard Kardelj, who also attended the meeting, expressed reservations about the Soviets' call for federation, Stalin told him that he was "mistaken" and needed to initiate the process right away.[81] In the face of such patronizing directives, the Yugoslavs no doubt felt unappreciated and diminished by the Soviets; after all, they had begun the revolutionary transformation of a crucial Balkan country and reduced the threat of "capitalist encirclement" to the motherland of socialism.[82]

During the winter of 1947–1948, Stalin's attitudes toward Yugoslavia, Albania, and Bulgaria were also influenced by his pessimistic assessment of the chances of the Greek national liberation front winning the struggle against the royalist government. Stalin's Greek policies demonstrated remarkable consistency with those from the Second World War, when the Greek partisans controlled large swaths of territory in northern Greece, until February 1948, when the Soviet leader chastised Dimitrov for including Greece in his ideas of an East European Union. Stalin's attitudes also reflected the Moscow "percentages agreement" with Churchill from October 19, 1944, in which he had essentially acknowledged British predominance in Greece in exchange for the recognition of Soviet dominance in the rest of southeastern Europe, except for Yugoslavia, where the Soviets and the British were ostensibly to share a fifty-fifty interest.

Throughout the postwar years, the Bulgarians, Yugoslavs, and Albanians all sought to aid the Greek partisans, not only by providing them with guns, ammunition, and medical supplies but also by offering safe havens in their countries for injured fighters and battered units seeking refuge from royalist offensives.[83] The Yugoslavs in particular were enthusiastically engaged on behalf of the Greeks. In 1946–1947, they supplied the Greek partisans with heavy weapons, artillery pieces, and mortars. In January 1947, they even allowed them to move the headquarters of their armament supply operations to Yugoslavia in order to evade the investigators of a United Nations commission.[84] In addition, they helped equip hospitals, a radio station, and other buildings for the Greek Democratic Army. Once the Yugoslavs had begun relying on Tirana for filtering arms to Greece, the Albanians were also helpful to the Greek partisans, though they worried that their help might prompt Greek royalist attacks. If we are to believe one Greek communist report, the Albanian communists were even more sympathetic to the Greek cause than the Yugoslavs and behaved in a "comradely" fashion.[85]

In any case, Dimitrov, Hoxha, and Tito all felt greater affinity for the revolutionary struggle of their Greek comrades than did the Soviet leaders, whose assessment was based strictly on the calculations of great power realpolitik. Forget your feelings of "moral obligation" concerning the Greeks, Stalin told the Bulgarian Traicho Kostov at the February 10, 1948, meeting; the key issue was "the balance of force."[86] Of course one should not assume that the policies of the Balkan communist leaderships toward the Greeks were not also motivated at least in part by their respective countries' own immediate security concerns. The Albanians were acutely aware of Greek claims to Northern Epirus, while the Yugoslavs and Bulgarians were seriously worried about the fate of Macedonia.[87] Therefore all three leaderships were supportive of the Greek partisans' disruptive actions against royalist adventures in the north. Stalin's viewpoint was different. On various occasions, he stated that the Greek partisans should give up their struggle, which, as he saw it, was doomed.[88] If the Greeks carried on fighting a losing battle, he told the Bulgarians and Yugoslavs, then this only made it more likely that the Americans and British would intervene in the Balkans and force Soviet military action. If, on the other hand, the Greek royalists won, Stalin predicted, the effect on the rest of the Balkans would remain limited.[89]

Both the Bulgarians and the Yugoslavs tried repeatedly to move on to economic and supply questions during the course of the crucial February 10 meeting, but Stalin and Molotov persistently returned to the unacceptability of sidestepping the Soviet Union in foreign policy matters. Whenever Kardelj or Dimitrov readily admitted their "mistakes" and tried to proceed to other questions, Stalin and Molotov insisted that these issues constituted much more than mistakes and indicated serious and deeper problems in both parties.[90]

Stalin made no secret of the fact that he thought Dimitrov, in particular, was behaving like an old fool. Still, as Djilas remarked in his notes of the meeting, the Soviet leader maintained "a friendly tone" even amid all the invectives and name-calling.[91] Mostly likely, Stalin's focus on Dimitrov and the obedient Bulgarians, who could always be relied upon in the end, was a way to warn the more intransigent and difficult Yugoslavs about embarking on a dangerously independent path. That said, Stalin and Molotov also brought up the fact that Tito had not aired his differences with Moscow about the possible consequences of the transfer of the Yugoslav division to Albania. Tito had calculated—no doubt correctly—that the West would only kick up a fuss in the press, nothing more.[92] As a result of these discussions, the Soviets and Yugoslavs signed a special protocol in Moscow on February 11, according to which the Yugoslavs promised to consult the USSR in all significant foreign policy questions.[93]

Before leaving Moscow, Edvard Kardelj told Molotov that Tito wanted to come to meet with Stalin in March or April to straighten out the problems between the two sides but could not be there at the moment "because of the dangers on account of Albania." Kardelj also used the occasion to reiterate Belgrade's main expectations from the Soviets: the delivery of military supplies and a major loan to cover the Yugoslav balance of payments deficit.[94] Meanwhile, back in Belgrade, Tito was upset by his representatives' reports that Stalin had downplayed the problems of both Albania and Greece at the February 10 meeting. In a coded telegram of February 13, 1948, he vented his frustrations to Djilas and Kardelj. The Albanian army, he complained, was in terrible shape.

The Soviet military instructors in Albania were of no help; they should be under the supervision of their superiors in Belgrade, who served within the structure of the Yugoslav People's Army and were viewed as "instructors in our army."[95] Moreover, nothing of value was produced in Albania, and communications between the country's north and south were basically nonexistent. What would happen, Tito asked, if Albania were attacked? "This is very important for us because in case of the success of such an attack our southern Macedonia would fall into a strategically difficult situation. We may have to reexamine our policies—we need to take effective measures to protect our borders. Our hands are tied to do anything about it."[96]

Despite the growing differences, Tito still tended to downplay the problems with Stalin. There was no major divergence in their respective foreign policies, Tito told the Yugoslav politburo on February 19. As far as the disagreement about sending a Yugoslav division to Albania was concerned, "[Our] mistake is that we did not inform [them] in advance; it would have been enough to inform, without asking."[97]

The actual message that Tito was getting from Moscow, though, was that Stalin and the Soviets would not help the Yugoslavs achieve the kind of military power that they sought; Belgrade's ongoing complaints about problems with arms deliveries underlined that fact. "It is not clear that the USSR wants us to be a strong, well-armed country," Tito told his comrades. The Yugoslav people, he concluded, would have to build a powerful military by themselves. He also was nonplussed that the Soviets seemed to interpret the Yugoslavs' well-meaning policies in the Balkans as injurious to the socialist cause. His response was "Let's not send our people for schooling to the USSR." The Yugoslav party should stick to "our line" and call a party Congress.[98]

The Yugoslavs' stubborn defiance of Stalin's wishes reflected their increasing annoyance with Moscow's unwillingness to fulfill their requests for increased military aid and supplies and to sanction their freedom of action in Albania and Greece, which, they felt, belonged to their sphere of influence. The Yugoslav leaders—Tito, Kardelj, and Djilas—met with the leaders of the Greek Communist Party, Nikos Zahariadis and Ioannis Ioannides, in Belgrade on February 21, 1948, and told them about Stalin's position as expressed at the February 10 meeting. Nonetheless, the Yugoslavs granted the Greeks' request for continued aid to the communist partisans.[99]

At an enlarged meeting of the Yugoslav politburo on March 1, Tito reviewed the "dead-end of late" in the relations with Stalin and the Soviets. The worsening of relations with Albania because of Spiru's intrigues during the previous year occupied a central place in his analysis. Once Spiru was out of the way, Tito thought, the problems with Albania would come to an end. But that turned out not to be the case, despite everything the Yugoslavs claimed they had done for the Albanians, especially for their army. Kardelj opined that while the Albanians had to fulfill their agreements with the Soviet Union, they were also obliged to coordinate their outside trade agreements with Yugoslavia. "We have the right to control what the Albanians are doing, what kind of agreements they make," he stated. Moreover, Tito expressed unhappiness with Stalin's advocacy of federation with the Bulgarians. "Now I am not for federation," he declared, while Kardelj stated later, "It is [our] impression that with this federation they [the Soviet Union] want to create stronger influence by the NKVD."[100]

The Yugoslav criticisms of Soviet policy at the March 1 meeting indicated a serious breach of trust. The Yugoslavs chastised the Moscow leadership for ignoring the needs of Yugoslavia and the other "people's democracies" and for pressuring them to conform with Soviet policies. Sreten Žujović—a pro-Soviet member of the Yugoslav politburo— immediately passed on these complaints, as was his wont, to the Soviet ambassador Lavrent'ev in Belgrade, who promptly forwarded them to Moscow. Molotov wrote back to the ambassador on March 7, advising him to thank Žujović for exposing "the sham friends of the Soviet Union in the Yugoslav C.C."[101] Tito must have understood that these negative remarks about the Soviet Union would get back to Stalin, but he did not seem to grasp that the Kremlin leaders could and would not accept complaints about Soviet policies as part of their relations with their younger socialist brothers.

During the late spring of 1948, the tensions between the Soviet Union and the Yugoslavs shifted focus. Sparring about Albania, the South Slav Federation, and Greece gave way to serious disputes about the penetration of Soviet influence in Yugoslavia itself. What had begun in the fall of 1947 as a seemingly innocent set of complaints about Soviet advisors working at cross purposes with Yugoslav ones in Albania now assumed major proportions, as the Soviets played up alleged Yugoslav complaints about the interference of Soviet advisors in internal Yugoslav policy decisions and about the ostensible withholding of information from them. As a protest against these alleged actions, but really to put pressure on the Yugoslav leadership to conform to Moscow's directives, the Soviets withdrew all their civilian and military advisors from Yugoslavia on March 18–19. Tito immediately sent Yugoslav ambassador Popović to Moscow with two letters for the Soviet government, which were delivered to Molotov on March 24. Popović asked the Soviets to reverse their decision. "We don't know," he told Molotov, "what we would do without the Soviet specialists, who are extremely necessary to us." Popović promised that those government members responsible for what he characterized as misunderstandings about the advisors would be "strictly punished" by the Yugoslav party. Molotov, however, was impervious to Popović's pleas—perhaps not least because Tito's letters showed less contrition than surprise at the Soviets' actions. In them, the Yugoslav leader noted that the treatment of the advisors, which he claimed had been perfectly respectful and open, could not be the real reason for Moscow's unhappiness. "We want to know frankly what the story is, what it is in the Soviet [government's] opinion that is disturbing the good relations between our two countries."[102]

The attitude of Moscow toward Belgrade in March 1948 was unremittingly critical of the Yugoslavs and their "anti-Soviet line." On March 18, the Foreign Policy Department of the Soviet Central Committee had presented an investigative report on the "anti-Marxist positions" of the Yugoslavs to its chief, Mikhail Suslov, which concluded that the Yugoslavs "overrate their achievements and allow elements of adventurism to enter into their estimation of their future prospects and foreign policy, laying claim to a leading role in the Balkan and Danubian countries."[103]

By the end of the month, the Soviets started a campaign to enlist Cominform members to support the disciplining of Tito. To this end, they circulated a letter to the Yugoslav leadership from March 27, signed by Stalin and Molotov, which harshly condemned the Yugoslavs' errors.

Interestingly, it focused primarily on issues of revisions of Marxism-Leninism, alleged opportunism, and the pursuit of an anti-Soviet line rather than on Yugoslav ambitions in the Balkans.[104] Tito and the Yugoslavs did not cave in: on April 13, they wrote in their response to Stalin and Molotov, "As much as we love the USSR, the country of socialism, we in no way love our own country any less."[105]

Hoxha's Gambit

The Albanians carefully registered the growing signs of a rift between the Soviets and Yugoslavs in the spring of 1948. In this new situation, Hoxha sought to reposition himself in such a way as to maintain Yugoslav military involvement in the case of the anticipated incursions of the Greek royalists, while simultaneously attracting Soviet economic and political support for his government.[106] His instincts were to remain loyal to the Soviet camp and continue his special relationship with Belgrade, while resisting Tito's pressure to create joint institutions that would, as Xoxe put it, "operate de facto as a federation."[107] Using almost identical words, Hoxha explained to the March 30 session of the politburo that it might make sense to continue with the informal "de facto" federation with the Yugoslavs.[108]

Hoxha played a complex game. On the one side, Tito, who registered the Albanians' reticence and mistrust, threatened in an April 22, 1948, letter to withdraw the Kuprešanin mission and to cut off the subsidies the Albanian army was receiving from the Yugoslav budget. Why help the Albanians, he wrote to Hoxha, when they seemed to distrust Yugoslav intentions and good will? Tito was clearly insulted that his noble efforts to defend Albania and repulse the royalist Greeks were questioned not only by Stalin but by the Albanian upstarts.[109] Meanwhile, Hoxha faced similar pressures from the Soviets, who also threatened to withdraw their military personnel from Albania because of Tirana's unwillingness to take sides in the tug-of-war between Belgrade and Moscow. But Hoxha managed to assuage the Soviets' fears of Albanian subservience to the Yugoslavs, and on April 13 Moscow suspended these threats.[110]

What complicated Hoxha's calculations even more was his justifiable concern that the Yugoslavs were keen to replace him with their long-term client, Koçi Xoxe, who controlled the feared Albanian secret police, the Sigurimi. In all likelihood, Hoxha was already exploring through the Soviet envoy Chuvakhin in Tirana what support he might expect from Moscow if the Yugoslavs pressured him further.[111] While Hoxha tried to keep his distance from the developing Moscow-Belgrade conflict, he also frustrated the Yugoslavs' desires to incorporate Albania by refusing to request formal economic integration.[112] When Stalin and Molotov's March 27 letter denouncing the Yugoslavs was shared with the Albanian leadership, Hoxha knew his hand had been strengthened in his desire to maintain both his political dominance and Albanian independence.[113]

Tito grew increasingly impatient with his erstwhile Albanian clients. At the end of April, he removed Yugoslav military aid and advisors from the country, citing the worsening of relations. Kuprešanin and Zlatić were recalled to Belgrade as well, and trade ties were broken off. In a May 23 letter to Tito, Hoxha picked up the gauntlet, declaring that Albania sided with Stalin against the "very mistaken positions" of the Yugoslav representatives in Tirana: "for the Soviet Union and the praiseworthy Bolshevik Party act for our peoples and our parties, Albanian and Yugoslav, and are our dearest and closest friends who assist us with all their strength and who illuminate our path."[114] Shortly thereafter, Hoxha, together with the Bulgarians, approached the Greek government in Athens to offer a cessation of hostilities along the border.[115]

Once the Soviet-Yugoslav split became public with the expulsion of the Yugoslavs from the Cominform at the end of June 1948, Hoxha lost no time in aligning himself unambiguously with the Soviets, portraying his earlier Yugoslav sympathies as a product of Belgrade's deceptions.[116] He had indeed believed that the Yugoslavs had acted on behalf of Stalin and the Soviets in their earlier actions. When this was patently no longer the case, he quickly abandoned his former sponsors. For him this was also the safest and most politically acceptable way to shed what he saw as Yugoslav overlordship and arrogance. In addition, he wanted to remove the perception in Europe and the United States that Albania was "little more than a Yugoslav republic."[117] Hoxha now came out in defense of the deceased Nako Spiru, whom he characterized in a meeting with Molotov in Warsaw on June 24, 1948, as "a victim of the intrigues of the Yugoslavs."[118] Hoxha admitted in this conversation that he had made a severe mistake by falling under Belgrade's influence. But he blamed that on the machinations of Xoxe, who had been the point man for the Yugoslavs in the Albanian politburo.

Koçi Xoxe no doubt found himself in an extremely difficult position, especially if he wanted to retain his power in the Albanian communist government. Initially he went along with Hoxha's pro-Moscow, anti-Belgrade course. He was even put in charge of purging the "anti-Cominformists" from the Albanian party. But his earlier role in attacking Spiru and purging the party of his comrades who had been close to the Soviets soon caught up with him. Hoxha rehabilitated Mehmet Shehu, the former chief of the general staff, who had also been attacked by Xoxe, and he systematically isolated Xoxe in the politburo.[119] Thus Hoxha sought to evade responsibility for the Yugoslavs' dominance by shifting all blame onto Xoxe.[120] At the Central Committee plenum of the Albanian party in September 1948, Hoxha formally denounced Xoxe, not only for working on behest of the Yugoslavs but for instituting, as minister of interior, a reign of secret police terror against the Albanian party and working class.[121] In this connection, he compared Xoxe to Yugoslav secret police chief Aleksandar Ranković, whom the Soviets accused of being a central figure in the Tito "clique." With Soviet approval, Hoxha also moved to assume greater powers in Albanian affairs at the September plenum. Xoxe was expelled from the Albanian party in November 1948 and, in June 1949 he was tried and executed for his alleged treachery. On the occasion of Stalin's birthday, December 18, 1948, the Albanian party leaders expressed their gratitude to the Soviet dictator for saving them from "the dangers of colonialization by Tito's nationalist-Trotskyist group" and for providing them the aid necessary to realize their state's two-year plan, which would serve "as the basis for the industrialization of our country."[122]

Hoxha proceeded to expunge all Yugoslav influences from Albania, to the point of closing down Yugoslav bookstores, removing the portraits of Tito that hung in many official (and unofficial) buildings, and banning the Yugoslav-Albanian Friendship Society. He stopped scheduled deliveries of coal and oil to Yugoslavia and withdrew the 225 Albanians who were studying at Yugoslav universities and academies as well as other Albanian students who attended Yugoslav schools. Military cooperation came to a complete halt, and by the end of June and beginning of July 1948 almost all of the Yugoslavs had been evacuated from the country. The twenty-two economic agreements between the two countries were abrogated.[123]

As the CIA noted, the cutting off of oil supplies from Albania certainly hurt Belgrade, but the sanctions ". . . would appear to be felt even more acutely by the Albanians, since none of the Yugoslav specialists, who were recalled in July 1948, had up to September 3 yet been replaced by the promised Soviet experts." This meant that work stopped at major projects, like the Shkodër cement and textile works and the Tirana oil refinery, as well as on high-priority fortification projects along the Adriatic coast.[124]

Stalin, who had earlier talked to the Yugoslavs about removing Hoxha from power, not "hastily and crudely—the boot on the throat—but gradually and indirectly," now accepted Hoxha's Albania as a Soviet ally and potential counterweight to the Yugoslavs.[125] His disinterest in the country was only overcome by the desire to put pressure, politically and geographically, on the Yugoslavs. But he was still not ready to invite Hoxha to Moscow. Instead the Albanian leader went to Bucharest along with Ambassador Chuvakhin to meet with Soviet foreign minister Andrei Vyshinskii. Hoxha's primary mission was to get as much in terms of aid and food reserves as possible, since the Yugoslavs had cut off Albanian supplies and sealed its borders. Vyshinskii promised aid and reassured Hoxha that Albania "should never feel isolated" in any way: "That is the instruction of Comrade Stalin."[126]

Stalin finally agreed to meet with Hoxha in Moscow on March 23, 1949. This was their second postwar encounter and the first since the split with Yugoslavia. The meeting was punctuated by the Kremlin dictator's derogatory remarks about Albania's backwardness. Stalin insisted that the Albanians slow down their moves to Sovietize their economy. There was no need for kolkhozes (collective farms), Stalin said; Albania was a primitive and mountainous land. Even in the USSR there were no kolkhozes in the mountains. The Albanians should also learn to incorporate their patriotic bourgeoisie into the political and economic life of the country rather than attacking them. Essentially, Stalin was not ready to treat Albania as a full-blown people's democracy.[127] He agreed to send military advisors for the purposes of establishing order and discipline in Albania's ragtag army, something the Yugoslavs had been unable to accomplish. At the same time, the Soviet politburo approved a project to bring twenty Albanian police officers to the Soviet Union for special training by the Ministry of State Security (MGB) and to send Ministry of the Interior (MVD) instructors to Albania to help organize the work of the Albanian militia.[128] In order to make sure that Tirana became more firmly embedded in the Soviet camp, the Soviet leadership committed to the continued supply of trade goods to Albania, despite the inability of Albania (as earlier with the Yugoslavs) to meet their promises of delivering raw materials and goods in return.[129] In Albania itself, Soviet advisors moved into the positions of Yugoslav ones, while Yugoslav installations were turned over to the Soviets.[130] Finally, Stalin—who had always been skeptical of the Greek partisan effort—now urged the Albanians to get out of the business altogether of helping the Greeks by providing them safe haven, supplies, and weapons. There was nothing to fear from the Greek royalists, he explained, as long as the Albanians behaved in a restrained fashion.

The Soviets, not content with simply issuing advice to the Albanians, also took matters into their own hands. On April 29, 1949, Ambassador Chuvakhin informed Hoxha that the Albanian-Greek border would be shut down on May 1 in accordance with an agreement between Nikos Zahariadis, general secretary of the Greek Communist Party, and the Soviets.[131] For their own reasons, the Yugoslavs soon did the same with their border to Greece, as Belgrade now sought the Western Allies' approval and, most importantly, aid. After the Soviet-Yugoslav split, the Communist Party leaders in Greece and throughout eastern Europe blamed the Yugoslavs and their cooperation with the Americans for the defeat of the Greek partisans.[132]

According to a report from a Greek communist who had been involved with both the Yugoslavs and the Albanians in the transfer of arms to the Greek communists, the Yugoslavs stopped their cooperation completely in October 1948. They would no longer take in wounded fighters, they stated, having no more room for them, and they closed roads that were critical to the Greeks' operations. The Greek communists even claimed that the Yugoslavs had allowed the Greek royalists to operate on Yugoslav territory![133] As a consequence of both Soviet and now Yugoslav and Albanian indifference to the Greek cause, the communist-led revolution was doomed. The Democratic Army was decisively defeated in August 1949, and some eight thousand Greek fighters made their way into Albania to escape further repressions from Athens.[134]

• •

Stalin certainly thought that removing Yugoslavia from the Cominform would enable him to defeat Tito and discipline the Yugoslavs for their insubordination. Khrushchev noted later that Stalin had predicted that "he would wiggle his little finger and Tito would fall."[135] Stalin subsequently tried a number of additional tactics and forms of pressure, even a military buildup and the threat of war on Yugoslavia's borders. Yet the Yugoslav party held firm behind Tito, not least because its leader responded with arrests, internment in fearsome labor camps, as on the deserted Adriatic island Goli Otok, and executions of members of the "Cominformist" (pro-Soviet) opposition. The idea was not just to punish the violators but to break their resistance and restore their loyalty to the Yugoslav party.[136]

When it became clear that Stalin's attempts to bully the Yugoslav party into removing Tito were failing, the Soviet dictator turned to organizing a series of assassination plots. With a white-hot hatred reminiscent of his enmity for Trotsky, Bukharin, Zinoviev, and other old Bolsheviks in the 1930s, Stalin condemned Tito to death and ordered the NKVD to come up with a plan for his elimination.[137] Simultaneously, he prepared the propagandistic ground for this act. Where Tito and his Partisan chieftains had once been the emblem of the glorious struggle of Slavs against the fascist beasts, Stalin now told the Bulgarians that the Yugoslav "clique of scoundrels allow themselves to say that the USSR exploited Yugoslavia. . . . These are dishonorable people, there is nothing Slavic in them."[138] Shortly before being felled by a stroke and dying two days later, March 5, 1953, at his Kuntsevo dacha, Stalin found out that the last of these plots to rub out Tito had failed.[139]

Enver Hoxha, meanwhile, had negotiated a perilous road to the kind of absolute power in Albania that rivaled that of his first mentor, Tito, and his newest, Stalin. (Eventually, he would break with the Soviets in the early 1960s while seeking the protection of another communist dictator, Mao Zedong. In the early 1970s, as a consequence of Mao's decision to pursue rapprochement with the United States, Hoxha broke with China and pursued an autarkic and isolationist stance within the international system.) Already during the war, Hoxha had revealed himself as a violent and dangerous political fighter.[140] As a former lycée student, teacher, and "bourgeois intellectual" who had spent several years at the beginning of the 1930s studying and working in France and Belgium, Hoxha was deemed insufficiently "hard" and revolutionary by the Yugoslavs and, in all likelihood, by the Soviets. Certainly the Yugoslavs preferred his tough-minded, working-class rival Koçi Xoxe, who had a crucial power base in the Ministry of Interior and secret police. Nako Spiru, a specialist on the economy and another rival in the party, had ties to the Soviet embassy and through the envoy Chuvakhin to Moscow. But not unlike Stalin on his path to power in the Soviet Union in the 1920s, Hoxha knew how to hew to the middle of the road, avoiding taking stands that would associate him too closely with either of his rivals, Spiru or Xoxe, and gaining adherents in the party and state bureaucracy by turning his back on the West and supporting Albanian national causes. Like Stalin, he showed considerable patience, but he also understood when it was to his advantage to take sides and claim victory. Despite his readiness to use violence to achieve his aims, notes a 1947 CIA report, Hoxha was "an attractive person" and "he makes friends easily and gives the impression of an accomplished politician."[141]

Hoxha also cleverly evaluated the potential threat of Yugoslav overlordship. He wanted to use the Yugoslavs for the benefit of his power and the Albanian nation; through the Yugoslavs he also harbored hopes of unifying the Albanians in Kosovo with Albania proper. In this sense it is correct to call him an Albanian nationalist. As it became clearer that both causes—that of his own power and that of Albanian national glory—could be seriously diminished by Tito's moves to make Albania the seventh republic of Yugoslavia, Hoxha found ways to drag his heels and delay integration. Here his political struggle with the pro-Yugoslav Xoxe was crucial, since Xoxe was undoubtedly designated by Tito to be the future leader of the Albanian Yugoslav Republic. The Soviet-Yugoslav break brought the perfect opportunity for Hoxha to lead the Albanian party to reject Yugoslavia altogether and join up with Stalin's Soviet Union and eastern bloc. This move also allowed Hoxha to isolate, oust, and eventually put on trial and execute Xoxe and his supporters. With the hard-won support of Moscow, the backflip was complete: Hoxha reigned supreme over a sovereign Albania. This was one of those cases where small states could both resist the influence of major powers and use their rivalries for their own purposes.

Stalin initially viewed the Albanians as an isolated and primitive mountain people of the Balkan peninsula. He encouraged the Yugoslavs to take control and bring Albania into their republic as long as this caused no friction with the West. The Albanians' intense revolutionary commitment and successful resistance against the Germans and Italians during the war did not elevate their status in Moscow in the least. Stalin only got interested in Hoxha and the Albanians when the Yugoslavs became a problem for him in the spring of 1948. Here Hoxha saw his chance to escape the increasingly uncomfortable embrace of Belgrade and pursue his own political interests and what he saw as the national interests of his people in an independent communist Albania under Soviet sponsorship. This met Stalin's needs. So Hoxha's gambit worked; Albania was his.

CHAPTER THREE

THE FINNISH FIGHT FOR INDEPENDENCE

1944–1948

The development of Soviet-Finnish relations at the end of the war and beginning of the peace is critical in understanding the perspectives of Stalin and Moscow on the evolution of Europe as a whole. It would be misguided to consider Finland—and the eventual "Finlandization" of the country—an anomaly that falls outside the norm of the supposedly predetermined cases of western and eastern Europe. In reality, there were no hard-and-fast models for the development of Moscow's relations with specific countries, though, to be sure, wartime allies of Nazi Germany, like Finland, could expect to be treated with particular harshness. Although both Great Britain and the United States had made efforts to get Finland out of the war and guarantee her independence afterward, they understood that, by dint of geography and military entanglements with the Third Reich, the country would fall under the influence of the Soviet Union after the defeat.

There was very little difference in the views of the Big Three about the future of Finland. They agreed during their wartime negotiations that Finland would pay reparations and be subject to an Allied Control Commission (ACC) that the Soviet Union—with the acquiescence of the Americans and British—would dominate. Since the Americans had not been in a state of war with Finland, they did not sign the armistice on September 4, 1944, unlike the British, who had declared war on Finland but not engaged in any military operations. The Americans would play no significant role in Finnish affairs, and the British unambiguously acknowledged Soviet dominance in the country as well.[1] Sweden was the only Western country for whom Finland was very important, and Sweden, neutral during the war, had no say in the determination of the peace.[2]

Moscow's proconsul in Finland was Andrei Aleksandrovich Zhdanov. A senior politburo ideologist who had been in charge of the defense of Leningrad during the war, Zhdanov had not forgotten Finland's crucial military role in helping the Wehrmacht encircle the city. He was also an experienced Finnish "hand," having been deeply involved in the "Winter War" (1939–1940) in his role as head of the Regional Military Council of the Leningrad district, in negotiating with the defiant Finns before the Soviet attack, and in preparing what became a victorious, if catastrophic, military assault. Zhdanov also helped set up a new Finnish "democratic" government, headed by the Finnish communist Otto Kuusinen—the so-called Terijoki government—which was preparing to assume power in a conquered Finland, and participated in the negotiations and signing of the peace treaty of March 12, 1940. Finally, Zhdanov was assigned the task of evaluating the horrendous performance of the Red Army during the war, which was recognized not only by Soviet authorities but, unfortunately for Moscow, by the Nazis as well.[3] To the extent that any Soviet leader could hope to earn Stalin's confidence and trust, Zhdanov seems to have attained that rare, if revocable, status by late 1944 and the end of the war

Zhdanov's main task was to see to it that Finland would never again become the base for an invasion of the Soviet Union. The Soviets did not tire of reminding the Western Allies and the Finns that Finnish forces had taken part in the murderous siege of Leningrad, and that the prewar Soviet-Finnish border, located just thirty-five kilometers from the city, would of necessity be redrawn according to the 1940 treaty following the Winter War.

The Finns thus held a very weak hand at the end of the war. Still, despite reports of a depressed and deeply anxious public given Soviet control of their destiny, Finnish political life underwent a remarkable revival in the months following the signing of the armistice on September 19, 1944.[4] After having lost the Winter War (1939–40) and then the "Continuation War" (1941–1944), both of which cost the country dearly in territory, men, and materiel, the Finns nevertheless bolstered their spirits and those of their political leaders by taking active part in the revivification of parliamentary life and supporting the presidency. Like the peoples of many other European countries, the Finns were sometimes overwhelmed by poverty, devastation (especially in the north of the country), refugees (from Karelia), and reparations payments to the Soviets. Yet they tackled their social and economic problems determined to hold on to their sovereignty despite sometimes severe political differences.

The Finnish communists, after years of operating as an illegal party, emerged from the underground at the end of the war with substantial support in segments of the Finnish working class. They turned their back on their traditional "iron proletarian dictatorship" policies and were one of the first parties in Europe to advocate the formation of a "people's democracy."[5] But splits in the party as a consequence of many communists' support of the Finnish cause in the Winter War weakened the party considerably. Moreover, Finnish communists suffered terribly during Stalin's purges, leaving only a very few alive in the Soviet Union at the time of the war. Many of those, including the party's leader Otto Kuusinen, were badly compromised by their participation in the Terijoki government, which had been constituted by Stalin to take over Finland during the Winter War. The more powerful Social Democratic Party, which had a fervent anti-communist streak that dated back to the civil war in Finland in 1918, dominated the politics on the left.[6] The political landscape at the end of the war was commanded, above all, by the imposing figure of Baron Carl Gustaf Emil Mannerheim, who as field marshal of the Finnish Defence Forces was known since the civil war as a staunch defender of Finnish independence against the Soviet Union.

Soviet Strategic Thinking and Finland

As early as December 1941, Solomon Lozovskii, deputy foreign minister and senior specialist on Scandinavian questions in the Soviet foreign ministry, wrote to Stalin and Molotov about the importance of the Baltic and Black Sea regions for Soviet security. He underlined the fact that "the questions about our land and sea borders need to be thought

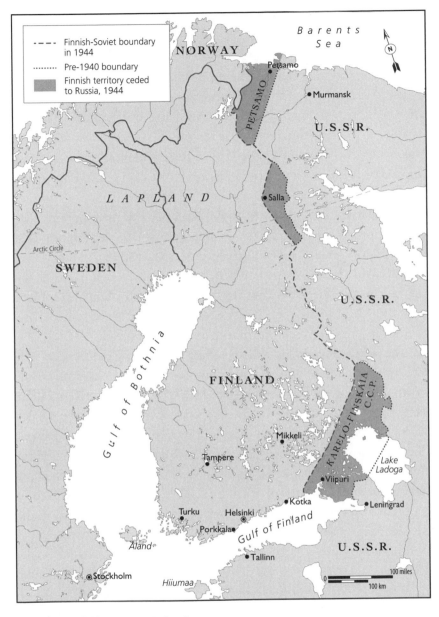

4. Territorial Changes in Finland

through in the context of [our] security and freedom of communications."[7]

Lozovskii articulated what occupied many Soviet military and strategic thinkers during the war, Stalin included: the need for the Soviet Union to extend its European security zone beyond what they considered the narrow and excessively constricted lines of the interwar period. The Soviets' desire to reduce their territorial vulnerability, which the Nazi attack had brutally exposed; to counter potential postwar British imperialism; and to exploit opportunities for expanding their political influence in Europe as a whole all required a much firmer network of secure sea lanes and land bases. In the Black Sea this meant unimpeded egress through the Dardanelles, guaranteed by a Soviet military base in the region. The Bornholm adventure, described in Chapter 1, was part of a plan to keep the Danish Belts and Sound open to the Soviet Baltic fleet and defensible against British domination, and negotiations with the Norwegians about Spitsbergen and Bear Island aimed at securing sea lanes between Murmansk and the North Sea.

The policies toward Finland, including the securing of a base at Porkkala on the Gulf of Finland and the acquisition of Petsamo in the north, which created a common border with Norway, reflected these same larger strategic goals. For the Soviets, control of the eastern Baltic region was also important for preventing resistance groups in Estonia and Latvia from using the sea lanes for moving men and materiel in and out of their forest redoubts, mostly to and from Sweden. Finland, in Maxim Litvinov's optimistic wartime scheme for the future, was to be part of the "security zone" of the Soviet Union, along with Norway and Sweden, while Denmark was to be in the neutral zone.[8] In Ivan Maiskii's notes on the future peace, Finland would cede Petsamo to the Soviet Union and, like Romania, would be tied to the Soviets through a long-term agreement on mutual help, which would include the establishment of Soviet army, air force, and navy bases. The Soviet Union and Finland would also be linked by a series of strategic and economically beneficial railway lines and roads.[9]

The Western Allies consistently supported Soviet territorial demands on Finland, while emphasizing the importance of the reconstitution of Finnish independence, much as they did with Poland at the conferences at Teheran (November–December 1943) and Yalta (February 1945). In December 1941, British foreign secretary Anthony Eden noted in a conversation with Stalin in Moscow that the Finns could not expect better terms for a settlement than those concluding the Winter War in March 1940, meaning the loss of Karelian territory and the Soviet right "to maintain naval and military bases on Finnish territory."[10] Even in their spirited defense of Finnish independence at the conference in Teheran in December 1943, neither Churchill nor Roosevelt challenged Stalin's territorial claims.[11] In his curiously worded reply to Roosevelt's speech, which would have surely unnerved the Finns, the Soviet leader cited a wartime communication from Moscow "to the effect that Russia had no designs on the independence of Finland, and Finland, by its behavior, did not force the Russians to do so."[12]

Since the United States had not declared war on Finland, Washington was more restrained in dealing with Finnish questions during and after the war. Both Roosevelt and Truman were aware of the popularity of the Finns in the West after their dramatic struggle against the Soviets in the "Winter War," which had been played up in the press, and both leaders were lobbied by Finnish-Americans to support Finnish independence, which they did. But beyond this, there was not much they could do. In the Allied Control Commission, the Americans would, according to the State Department, play "a passive role and avoid as much as possible being involved in Finnish politics."[13]

In fact, the United States held no position in the ACC in Finland. Anthony Eden returned to the theme of Finland's dependence on the Soviet Union in August 1944: "Although we shall no doubt hope that Finland will be left some real degree of at least cultural and commercial independence and a parliamentary regime, Russian influence will in any event be predominant in Finland and we shall not be able, nor would it serve any important British interests to concede that influence."[14] Thus, even though the British were a signatory of the armistice, there was no reason to expect that they would do anything to impede the Soviets from running the ACC for Finland. British instructions to their representative in the commission, F. M. Shepherd, were unambiguous in this regard: "It is recognized that during the war Finland falls with the Soviet sphere of military operations, and that the Soviet government must therefore be allowed to play the principal role in enforcing the Armistice. . . . As members of the commission you will be under his [Zhdanov's] control."[15]

Not least because of the long border it shared with the Soviet Union, Finland could expect to receive from Moscow the same kind of close attention to its internal political developments as Poland and Romania, and given Prague's concession to Stalin of the Carpatho-Ukraine, as Czechoslovakia and Hungary. As a neighbor that had fought against the Soviet Union during World War II, Finland was frequently considered by Moscow in tandem with Romania, especially since both countries pulled out of the Axis effort before being overrun by the Soviet armed forces. But for the Soviets Finland did not have the same critical strategic military value as Romania. While the latter would serve as a staging area for further Soviet operations in the Balkans, Finland bordered on neutral Sweden, and with only a few remaining German divisions in the north of the country, which could be handled by the Finnish forces themselves, there was little reason, either military or political, for the Soviets to occupy the country during the war.[16]

The Swedish factor was particularly important. As long as Sweden remained neutral, the Soviets could afford to allow Finland its independence. This logic also included Stockholm's calculations: if the Soviets abrogated Finnish independence, the Swedes might feel compelled to abandon neutrality and join the Western camp.[17] Still, the Soviet Union counted Finland within "her immediate defensive orbit," wrote British intelligence. Her coastal defenses east of Porkkala would be limited, while the gun emplacements on the Gulf of Bothnia that faced Sweden and the West would be strengthened and reorganized.[18]

Finland's domestic political trajectory also remained a matter of intense debate in Moscow during the war. There were those Soviet leaders, especially in the military (Kliment Voroshilov and Boris Shaposhnikov), who advocated the occupation of Finland and the use of Finnish forces to join the attack on Germany. There were others, mostly among the Finnish communists, who suggested the incorporation of Finland into the Soviet Union as the 16th Republic.[19] In a remarkably frank admission to Zhdanov, one of their leaders, Yrjö Leino, declared on May 10, 1945, that their ultimate goal was "the inclusion of Finland in the body of the Soviet Union," while the immediate task was to follow a course like that of Poland, Czechoslovakia, and Yugoslavia. Historically, such ideas were not so far-fetched: the precedent of the absorption of the Grand Duchy of Finland into the Russian empire in 1809 and the relatively harmonious history of Russian-Finnish relations in the imperial period were on everyone's mind, Soviets' and Finns'. Yet in the end Stalin and Molotov determined the outcome with their notion that Finland should and could proceed down the path of a "new democracy," a people's democracy dominated by anti-fascists and democrats with Soviet sympathies, just like the other countries of eastern Europe. Stalin had specifically noted that these new democracies would be implemented in different countries at different stages and with a variety of individual economic and social factors at work. Finland would follow its own distinct path in this direction. The hope in Moscow was that the Finnish Communist Party would emerge from the catastrophic war with greater strength given the fact that the nationalist and conservative forces had incited and prosecuted the war in the first place. That Finland's road would turn out differently than anticipated by the Soviets depended on a number of factors. The most important of these were the acuity and determination of Finnish political leaders, on the one hand, and Zhdanov's and Stalin's political flexibility on the other.

The Armistice

The Finns joined Nazi Germany in its all-out assault on the Soviet Union in Operation Barbarossa, helping to encircle Leningrad in the winter of 1941–1942, starving the city and causing immense suffering and mass death to its inhabitants. When Soviet troops finally succeeded in ending the stalemate on the northeastern front—and the agony of Leningrad—in the early summer of 1944, they did so by breaking through Finnish defense lines on the Karelian Isthmus. Initially, the Soviets had insisted on the unconditional surrender of the Finns, planning to occupy Helsinki and its surroundings. Along with unconditional surrender would have come the imposition of a Soviet military administration, not unlike what was planned for Germany or Austria, including the arrest of Finnish political leaders and of paramilitary civilian bands.[20] But after the fall of Vyborg on June 20, 1944, the Soviets withdrew half of the fifty-five divisions they had concentrated in Finland. These troops were needed for the assault on Berlin, and Stalin did not seem intent on occupying Finland, except for those Karelian territories that Moscow determined would be annexed to the Soviet Union. The Soviets ordered six or seven divisions north to Petsamo to continue the offensive against the Germans in Norway. When this task was completed by September 1944, Moscow was ready to accept a negotiated armistice with the Finns.

What prompted this turn to compromise? It may well be that Stalin and the Soviets still felt the sting of the Finnish fighting spirit they had experienced both during the Winter War of 1939–1940 and during July 1944, even after the fall of Vyborg. The British archives contain a revealing document from October 10, 1945, in which Stalin, in conversation with the leaders of the Finnish Communist Party, compared the Finns favorably to the Belgians. If the Finns had been located where Belgium was, they would have fought the Nazis to the end, claimed Stalin, instead of giving in, like the Belgians. "We like the Finnish people," Stalin stated, "because it is a capable and hard-working and intelligent people. You live the Lord knows where. You have built a country out of a marsh."[21] He might well have reasoned after engaging in two wars with the Finns within the previous five years that this was a people who fought harder and more effectively than their numbers and resources might indicate; it was best not to put too much pressure on them. Given the Soviets' priority to push into central Europe, it would have been completely unacceptable, especially after the Allied invasion of Normandy, to prolong the war in the northeastern Baltic region.[22] At any event, it would have been understandable if the Soviets had had no desire to fight the Finns again.

On their side, the Finns were anxious to strike a deal with the Soviets. Marshal Mannerheim, leader of the Finnish armed forces and first president of the reconstituted Finland after the war, had hoped that the armistice and the Finns' subsequent entrance into the war against Germany would gain his country some leverage with the Allies and enable it to sign a regional defense treaty with the Soviet Union.[23] But while Zhdanov, as head of the ACC, was interested, though with some serious concessions from the Finns, Soviet foreign minister Molotov discouraged any developments of the kind and scolded Zhdanov for overstepping his competence: "Your main task at this stage consists of elucidating Mannerheim's position, and not in scaring him off with radical proposals."[24] Finland would first have to be subjected to the conditions of the armistice, and only afterward to those of a formal peace treaty. At this point, the Soviets were still punctilious about following prearranged Allied procedures for securing peace treaties.

Mannerheim and his prime minister Juho Kusti Paasikivi were both convinced that the Finns had no other choice but to try to convince the Soviets of their good will and their readiness to protect Soviet strategic interests in their own way. Mannerheim detested Bolshevism and mistrusted Soviet intentions; Paasikivi, a former banker, focused on making a virtue out of necessity.[25] Despite their personal and political differences, both were at heart monarchists, yet both were ready nevertheless to devote their energies to rebuilding Finnish parliamentary democracy and shoring up the morale of Finnish society. Both were "Old Finns" who knew the Russian empire well and felt they understood the mentality of the "Russians." (The "Old Finns" were a political grouping of conservative Finnish patriots who believed that the best way to preserve Finnish sovereignty in the Russian empire was to promote Finnish culture and language rights, while accommodating to the demands of the St. Petersburg bureaucracy.[26]) From this background, they saw their task in convincing Moscow that it had nothing to fear from Finland; that the Finns would protect the Soviets' northwestern flank and not allow any enemies to gain foothold in their country.[27]

In October 1944, Mannerheim explained their position to his confederates: "Finland can no longer assume the role of a Western fortress against the East. We must leave all such talk behind. We cannot lend ourselves to any such policies. Our army will never again fight a war against Russia."[28] In the view of Finnish leaders, the vulnerability of Leningrad during the war justified Soviet demands for security guarantees from Helsinki. At the same time, they, and Paasikivi in particular, had the model of the Grand Duchy of Finland on their minds, which had enabled the Finns to live in relative harmony with the Russians, at least until the turn of the century.[29] The so-called "Paasikivi

3.1 Andrei Zhdanov, in military uniform, and Juha Kusti Paasikivi at the signing of the reparations agreement, December 17, 1944. AMANITA OY, LTD.

line"—a Finnish "good neighbor policy"—underlays Finnish foreign policy considerations toward the Soviets even up to today.[30] In order for Finland to survive as an independent state, Moscow had to be convinced, through a delicate combination of Finnish acquiescence to Soviet interests and Finnish political determination, that no foreign power would be able to use Finland to invade the Soviet Union.

With the threat of Soviet occupation constantly in the air, the Finns, fearing the worst but hoping to maintain their independence, accepted the Soviets' terms for the armistice. First of all, they would surrender the territories on the Karelian Isthmus that the Soviets had gained in the war of 1940, as already assumed by the Finnish political leadership. The Soviet Union would also gain control of Petsamo in the north, which gave it both important access to the Arctic Ocean, especially in winter when Murmansk was closed due to ice, and a common border with Norway. (This meant, of course, the elimination of "Finland's window to the Arctic Sea.")[31] Moreover, the nickel mines in the Petsamo region were of intense interest to Moscow. The Soviets also insisted on a long-term lease-holding arrangement on Porkkala (*Porkkalanniemi*), situated directly across the Gulf of Finland from Tallinn in Estonia, for maintaining a military and naval base. British ambassador to Moscow Sir Clark Kerr commented that the Russian "vision of a 'New Gibraltar' is spacious, including as it does the whole of the Peninsula and a cluster of islands south of it."[32] As Molotov told Kerr, the purpose of controlling Porkkala was "to cork up the Gulf of Finland," which at this narrow point measures less than twenty-five nautical miles in width.[33]

Perhaps equally important, a base at Porkkala would put a significant concentration of Soviet military power only twenty-five kilometers west of Helsinki, a threat that made the Finns exceptionally nervous. Located between Vyborg and Porkkala, where the Soviets would station some ten thousand soldiers and sailors, the Finnish capital would be very hard to defend if the Soviets decided to occupy.[34] There was even some talk in Finnish circles of moving the capital from Helsinki.[35] The Porkkala lease was to be for fifty years, which seemed like an eternity at the time. (Hardly anyone would have predicted that the post-Stalin Soviet leadership would make a concession to the Finns by returning Porkkala in 1956.)

The Soviets placed other demands on the Finns as well. If the Finns did not want Soviet troops on their territory, then they would have to agree to disarm and expel all German troops from the north of the country, where the Wehrmacht's 20th Mountain Army, two hundred thousand strong, was still stationed in late 1944. Some sources suggest that the Soviet demand for the Finns to fight the Germans was a way to break Finnish-German ties for the foreseeable future.[36] After several delays and feints, sometimes coordinated with the German army as it retreated toward northern Norway, the Finns faced a Soviet ultimatum to either engage the enemy or be prepared for a Soviet military attack on the Germans in Finland.[37]

So the Finns did the job asked of them, at the cost of some one thousand men killed. Under Mannerheim's command, the Finns fought hard and well to dislodge the Germans from Lapland, which was accomplished in the main by January 1, 1945, and entirely at the end of April 1945. The terrain was difficult and the dark winter hard to deal with.[38] Retreating toward Norway, the Germans also engaged in a typically fearsome scorched-earth policy, destroying buildings and stores of food and blowing up bridges and road junctions to hinder the potential pursuit of Soviet troops.

The combined Soviet demands for the demobilization of the Finnish army and continued Finnish military involvement against the Germans in Lapland, essentially the third war for the Finns within five years, were difficult to reconcile. Demobilization was accomplished but not until the ACC brought considerable pressure to bear on the Finns, who actively attempted to evade the Soviets' restrictions. Units not involved in the Lapland war with the Germans were the first to be demobilized. The Finns also agreed to the Soviets' demand for $300 million in reparations payments (since the sum was calculated in 1938 dollars, the actual worth in postwar dollars came closer to $600 million).[39] The reparations payments, mostly in food products and timber, which Molotov insisted had to commence immediately, were complicated by the need of the Finnish government to deal with nearly a half million refugees, mostly Karelians, from the territories ceded to the Soviet Union. Moreover, the devastation caused by the Lapland war in the north would require a great deal of rebuilding.[40] The Finns had their work cut out for them. But any attempts by the Finns to find relief from the burden placed on their people and economy were rejected outright by Moscow, which was, in Clark Kerr's terms, "stern and unyielding."[41]

Besides demanding that the Finns demobilize their army and disband allegedly fascist organizations, including the important paramilitary Civil Guards, the Soviets insisted that the Finns arrest and try as war criminals the major figures of their wartime government. This proved extremely problematic, especially for General Mannerheim, who, after all, was the leading political figure of wartime Finland associated with the alliance with Berlin and thus could have been arrested and brought to trial himself. Paasikivi, on his part, took issue with Zhdanov's demands for immediate and conclusive judicial processes. As a principled conservative committed to preserving the integrity of Finnish institutions, he repeatedly reminded his Soviet interlocutors about constraints imposed by the Finnish legal code, although without particular success.[42] In any case, whether as a matter of conscience or personal interest, the problem of postwar justice became one of the most contentious issues in the relationship between the Soviets and the Finns.

Zhdanov and the Finns

Zhdanov's appointment as head of the Allied Control Commission in Finland in October 1944 was logical given his recent experiences in Finnish issues. Other commissions—in Hungary, Romania, Austria, or Germany—were headed by Soviet officers with less political standing than Zhdanov, who was an important member of Stalin's inner circle. It seems likely that Stalin understood that Finland would require greater political skills than those countries where Red Army troops were stationed or which the Soviets occupied outright. Some historians believe that Stalin sent Zhdanov to Helsinki in order to get him out of Moscow and away from the center of power, given his growing reputation, resented by the Soviet dictator, for successfully leading the resistance to the Germans as head of the party organization in Leningrad during the blockade.[43] Others believe that the importance and sensitivity of the job was the main reason for this decision.[44] Still others think that Zhdanov's assignment to Finland was an ominous indication that the country would be Sovietized, as had happened to Estonia under Zhdanov's supervision in 1940–1941.[45]

In any case, Zhdanov was not known for his special sympathies for Finland. On the contrary, he had been a strong advocate of going to war in 1939 in the Winter War; had supported the communist-dominated government in the Karelian-Finnish republic, led by Otto Kuusinen, that was to serve as the new center of Finnish communist power during the "Continuation War"; and he unquestionably adopted the Leningraders' resentment of the Finns because of their participation in the Blockade. Later on he even expressed some regret that the Soviets had not occupied Finland. "We made a mistake in not occupying Finland," he told Milovan Djilas in January 1948. "Everything would have been set up if we had." Molotov responded, "Oh (well,) Finland . . . that's a peanut [a small matter]."[46]

Zhdanov came to Helsinki cognizant that shaping Finnish affairs according to Moscow's needs required more flexibility and give-and-take than his earlier missions.[47] He was convinced that the building of a people's democracy in Finland could take place only slowly and carefully, and that he was capable of managing this process because of his knowledge of Finnish affairs, Finnish politicians, and the Finnish national character. The work of the Allied Control Commission in Finland was also different than in other Soviet-dominated countries. For example, there were no provisions for commission (meaning Soviet) censorship over Finnish publications, theater performances, film, or literature.[48] Hence Zhdanov had to use persuasion and veiled threats to get the Finns to show restraint on sensitive issues. There were frequent clashes between Zhdanov and various members of the Finnish government over censorship, trials of alleged Finnish war criminals, irregularities in Finnish demobilization, and the payment of Finnish reparations, among other issues. But, in general, Zhdanov's time in Finland was judged a success by Stalin, since he was made head of the renamed and revamped Department of Foreign Affairs of the Central Committee when he was recalled to Moscow in early 1946. Even before his important new position, Zhdanov spent only a fraction of his time on Finnish affairs. For all practical purposes he was replaced during his frequent and long absences from Helsinki by his deputy Grigorii Savonenkov, who formally became head of the ACC in February 1947 with the signing of the Paris Peace Treaty.

Yet Zhdanov remained closely involved in Finnish affairs at least until the Soviet ratification of the Friendship Treaty in July 1948. (He died of a heart attack in August.) His intentions were consistent, and that was to create in Finland a "new democracy," a people's democracy. Periodically, he noted that there was much left to do to reach that goal.[49] At the first meeting of the Cominform in Poland in September 1947, where

Zhdanov delivered his important "two camps" speech, in which he divided the world into capitalist and socialist antagonists, Zhdanov included Finland "in part" with those former enemy countries that, like Bulgaria, Romania, and Hungary, had joined the "antifascist front" in the struggle "for peace, for democracy, and for freedom and independence" against the British and American "imperialists."[50]

Zhdanov kept the Finnish authorities on edge, making sure they understood that the Soviet Union could, at any time, occupy Finland and install in power the increasingly influential Democratic Union of the Finnish People, which was supported by the Soviets and anchored by the Finnish Communist Party. There was always the specter of the Winter War, when Soviet troops, after crossing the border on November 30, 1939, had established Kuusinen's Provisional People's Republic of Finland (the "Terijoki Republic"), and there was also the continuing threat of the Karelian-Finnish Republic, headed up by Kuusinen in Vyborg, becoming the core of a new communist Finland.[51] In order to get the Finns to comply with the difficult armistice terms, Zhdanov was perfectly happy to have them treat him, as he told F. M. Shepherd, head of the British mission in Helsinki, as if "he had come with a regiment of tanks in one pocket and a squadron of airplanes in the other."[52] When he could, he bullied and cajoled them into fulfilling the Soviets' demands. To the dissident Social Democrats, the so-called "Six," who had spent the war years in prison due to their opposition to the alliance with Hitler and who had separated from the mainstream Finnish Social Democratic Party, Zhdanov said (regarding those who opposed the armistice treaty), "Try to bring it about that the panic which we have created will continue. Keep them in fear. . . ."[53] He insisted that the Finnish government keep strictly to its reparations delivery schedule, which it for the most part did. And he constantly rode Paasikivi on the issue of prosecuting Finnish war criminals.

At the same time, Zhdanov and his staff reiterated their commitment in the Allied Control Commission not to interfere directly in Finnish politics. He stuck strictly to the Kremlin's general principle of not using Soviet military units or police to support his policies in Finland, and he underscored Stalin's advocacy of strong Soviet-Finnish relations. He also seemed to have accepted with a certain appreciation that

Finnish attitudes toward the Soviets had radically improved, given the "many years, I would say decades long, I'm afraid to say thousand year enemy relationship to the Soviet Union."[54] He admitted to having found the Finns more accessible and less "taciturn" than he had anticipated. "When receiving Soviet singers and artists," he claimed, "they expressed their feelings as spontaneously as the Russians."[55] Generally the Soviets in the ACC were pleased with the Finns' warm reception to visiting Russian artists, ensembles and cultural representatives of various sorts.

Zhdanov's attitude toward both Mannerheim and Paasikivi was deeply ambivalent. On the one hand, he exhibited a grudging respect for these grand old men of the Finnish establishment, both of whom had political experience that stretched back to the Grand Duchy of Finland in the Russian empire. The Soviet politician spoke positively of Mannerheim's antique, imperial-tinged Russian and of Paasikivi's long and unwavering commitment to carving out a realm of Finnish independence while making sure that Soviet security interests were fully respected. Paasikivi also impressed Zhdanov and especially Stalin with his superb Russian and knowledge of the people and the country, as well as his ability to deal with Soviet officials over the years. During the imperial period, Paasikivi had been a student of history in Novgorod and had a profound knowledge of and deep interest in the Russian past. His wartime advocacy of a separate peace with the Soviets on Moscow's terms also impressed Stalin and Molotov, who had met him in Moscow and were known to appreciate his knowledge and diplomatic skills.[56]

Despite his respect for the prime minister's (later president's) qualities, Zhdanov would often lose patience with Paasikivi's stolid insistence on Finnish parliamentary and judicial procedures. He also complained to Finnish communists about Paasikivi's duplicity in covering up his reactionary domestic actions with his ostensibly pro-Soviet foreign policy. "This person is conservative to the very marrow of his bones," he told them, disturbed in particular, that Paasikivi would do everything possible to limit the "democratic transformation" of the parliament.[57] Mannerheim, on the other hand, irritated Zhdanov with his recalcitrance about the arrest and trial of Finnish war criminals and his hesitancy to disband the "reactionary," in Zhdanov's words, veterans' organization the Comrades in Arms Association. But Zhdanov was unwilling to go along with the confidential plans of the communists and the Finnish People's Democratic Union (SKDL) that they controlled to bully Mannerheim into resigning. Too great were his concerns about the possible reaction of the other parties (the Agrarians and the Social Democrats), given that Mannerheim, in the words of the communist minister of interior Yrjö Leino stood "a foot and a half taller" than any other political figure in the country.[58] Besides, taking such a route turned out to be unnecessary. The seventy-nine year-old Finnish icon was frequently sick and tired out, as well as subject to "a kind of mental illness."[59] Once Mannerheim was assured by the Soviets that he himself would not be arrested and tried as a war criminal, he resigned the presidency in favor of Paasikivi in March 1946.[60] For all practical purposes, Paasikivi had already assumed the duties of president, given Mannerheim's long absences from the capital for medical treatment. Although himself described as "a quite elderly and somewhat feeble gentleman," Paasikivi's general health was good and he was driven by a deep sense of moral duty to lead Finland through its postwar crisis.[61]

Zhdanov's relationship to the Finnish Communist Party was testy and difficult, though it is worth remembering that tensions between Soviet plenipotentiaries and local communists were common throughout those parts of Europe where the Soviets held some political power, and even in some where they did not. At the time of the armistice, the Finnish Communist Party was small and illegal. Counting no more than two thousand active members, it lacked the kind of forceful internal leadership and organization that characterized some of the other European parties. To be sure, Otto Kuusinen, the "father" of Finnish communism was alive and well in Moscow. Yet as head of the Karelian-Finnish Republic, he had become part of the Soviet political establishment and was not allowed to return to Finland after the war because of his identification with the unpopular Terijoki government.[62] Stalin might also have held him in reserve to install him in the right circumstances as the leader of a full-fledged Finnish people's democracy. Kuusinen's daughter, Hertta Kuusinen, also a communist, did meet regularly with Zhdanov at the Allied Control Commission, along with Ville Pessi, the party secretary, and Yrjö Leino, Kuusinen's husband, who became minister of internal affairs in the Finnish government. Leino, who had been in Soviet military intelligence during the war, reported frequently in confidence to Zhdanov about the proceedings of the Finnish cabinet.[63] He was thus a special asset for the Soviets, but he was also a problem. As a member of the government, he tended to support coalition policies and turn a deaf ear to the efforts of the Communist Party of Finland (CPF) to push the program of people's democracy in Finland. Not unlike a number of Finnish politicians at this time, he also drank to excess and fell into semi-competence as his problem with alcoholism grew more serious. The British noted that Leino "has taken to Wein and Weib in a big way!" He was also known to join British representatives during their hunting forays, which no doubt aroused suspicions about his loyalties.[64]

While Zhdanov told his ACC staff to refrain from getting involved in politics and giving the Finnish communists advice on how to behave, he constantly did so himself. He urged the Finnish comrades, for example, to stifle their unruly "sectarian" left, which opposed parliamentary tactics, and he warned them against extreme programs of land reform, not to mention collectivization, for fear of alienating the Finnish small farmer.[65] He also provided the communists with an election strategy, exhorting them to focus on their ostensible surprise that the same bourgeois politicians who had driven reactionary Finland into war with the Soviet Union were now singing songs of friendship with the Soviets. The communists needed to prepare some real revelations, "bombshells" as he put it, to spring on the public right before the election.[66] At the same time, Zhdanov admitted to the Finnish communists that he was not sure how one should handle Paasikivi's unwillingness to countenance a Soviet-style "democratization" of Finnish law, with "tactics of pressure or tactics of concessions."[67]

Zhdanov wanted much more from the Finnish communists than he was able to get, and he was irritated that they constantly asked advice about matters in which he expected them to take their own initiative. But this also reflected a larger problem that the Soviets had with communist parties abroad (the Austrian Communist Party was a case in point): the Soviets wanted these parties to be strong and robust, and to move resolutely along the lines of the people's democracy outlined by Moscow. At the same time, the masters in Moscow also harshly criticized and punished mistakes by these parties, especially when they appeared to be too radical or revolutionary, thus fostering a kind of infantile dependence of the national communist leaderships on Moscow. The Finnish communists, like the Austrians, would have liked for the Soviet occupation of their country to settle their political problems. (The difference was that the Soviets occupied at least Lower Austria.) Leading Finnish party members, wrote Zhdanov, thought that "it was a mistake for the Soviet tanks not to go all the way to Helsinki" in 1944. The Soviet plenipotentiary responded brusquely: "The Soviet Union rejects the idea of achieving success 'by riding through a foreign country.' Every country must win its own victory by its own forces. Every step (forward) of an independent communist movement is worth more than hundreds of tanks."[68]

Zhdanov felt this particularly acutely in the Finnish case because it was amply clear that neither the British nor especially the Americans had offered any serious help to the centrist or Social Democratic Finnish parties.[69] The Finnish left could do the job of instituting a people's democracy on its own. In this sense, the absence of serious political involvement on the part of the Western powers in Finland can be seen as an important deterrent to a Sovietization campaign in Finland. Zhdanov (and Stalin) had no intention of attracting Western attention to the political development of Finland by overtly and forcibly helping the communists achieve power.

In this spirit, the elections of March 17–18, 1945, were observed to take place in a fair and orderly manner, with a record turnout of 80 percent of the electorate.[70] The CPF, embedded in a national front, the Finnish People's Democratic Union, with several other "progressive" parties, but notably unable to break the unity of the Social Democratic Party, won a fourth of all the seats in the Diet, which was a substantial increase in their representation. By 1947, the Communist Party had grown from a mere two thousand to some forty thousand members. But the CPF still showed no signs of being able to muster a leadership role in society or in politics, despite the support and counsel of Zhdanov and the Allied Control Commission. Nor could they outpoll the powerful Finnish Social Democrats. Rather like the communist parties in France and Italy, though without their numbers, the

Finnish Communist Party in the view of their Soviet advisors was unable to exploit its favorable position in the parliament and society. The communists were not invited to the Cominform meeting in Poland in September 1947. Moscow tended to treat them as second-class allies.

The "Paasikivi Line"

During the fall and winter of 1944–1945, the Finnish military engaged in two operations that reflected its supposition that there would inevitably be another war with the Soviet Union, triggered either by the Soviet occupation of Finland or by a bigger war between Moscow and the West. "Stella Polaris," arranged in secret with Swedish military intelligence, was a well-designed operation to preserve Finnish intelligence materials and communications equipment by shipping them off to Sweden for later use. When the armistice agreement was signed and no occupation appeared to be in the offing, the operation was suspended and the equipment that made it to Sweden sold.[71] The other, related effort consisted in the concealed stockpiling of valuable Finnish weapons for future use. During the demobilization of the Finnish army at the end of the war, some members of the Finnish high command ordered the burying of caches of arms and munitions in preparation for an anticipated war with the Soviet Union. One historian writes,

> Arms were hidden in the archipelago or in forest areas with the help of the foresters, sometimes they were stored in official depositories but uncounted in the bookkeeping, while in one place petrol for the military was stored in the Shell depot, while in northern Savo weapons from demobilized troops to equip two battalions were left under the control of the local civil guard.[72]

As the British representative to Finland, Francis Shepherd, put it, "Were the Russians seeking grounds of justification for more direct intervention they might have found them in the discovery of thirty (some reports say fifty) hidden stores of arms in various parts of the country."[73] A number of high-ranking Finnish officers were implicated in the affair, and the ACC accused the Finnish general staff of being involved. But significantly, the Soviets were content to let the Finnish government take control of the investigation, which was conducted in due course through the communist-led ministry of the interior. The Finnish government handled the scandal with skill, and the Soviets seemed satisfied with the result.[74] The Operations Section of the General Staff was found to be deeply involved and numbers of officers resigned, while others were arrested. Of the roughly ten thousand men and women bound up in this effort altogether, six thousand were interrogated and 2,012 eventually brought to trial.[75]

Zhdanov and the ACC were not always so patient. There were many other cases where they ordered the communist minister of interior Leino to arrest and imprison targeted opponents. The ban on Finnish veterans' associations and a variety of paramilitary groups was carried out by ACC administrative fiat, as usual through Leino. The British report on these moves notes that "once again, the control commission has bypassed the Finnish prime minister." As a member of the commission, Shepherd noted, "I have not (repeat not) been informed about any of the above events by my Soviet colleagues."[76]

Nonetheless, Paasikivi managed to keep the palpable threat of Soviet military intervention off the agenda by skillfully and doggedly sticking to his pro-Soviet foreign policy, while maintaining control of domestic politics. At the same time, Paasikivi understood that there were some domestic issues where he had to make concessions to the Soviets—including their insistence on trying Finnish war criminals, which stuck in his craw (and earlier Mannerheim's) and proved difficult to get past. The question was really less about "war criminals" per se than about "war politicians": those Finnish leaders who had instigated the alliance with Hitler, fought against the Soviet Union, and delayed the signing of the armistice.[77]

The prosecution and trial of those responsible for Finland's war against the Soviet Union, called for in article 13 of the armistice, was a symbolically and emotionally charged demand. Like the return of Soviet displaced persons in the West, it was one of those issues that seemed to touch a central nerve regarding the Soviets' self-image and sense of justice. But it also served as a barometer of Soviet-Finnish relations: Could the Soviets trust the Helsinki government to do what they

3.2 On the occasion of Finnish independence, December 6, 1947, Helsinki photographer Eino Partanen decorated his store window with the installation "Scapegoats," depicting the politicians charged in the ongoing war crimes trial demanded by the Soviets. Partanen was himself indicted with "vandalism" for "endangering the public order" and "defaming the authorities." The charges were eventually dropped. FINNISH HERITAGE AGENCY.

insisted was the right thing, when confronted with resistance from the Finnish middle class and their "bourgeois mentality"?

While Zhdanov talked about executing all Finnish war criminals, Paasikivi stood by the principle that their arrests and trials be conducted strictly according to Finnish legal procedures. To the British representative Shepherd, Paasikivi stated that the creation of a special court and the retroactive passing of special laws—there were no provisions in Finnish law for trying the past leaders—were "contrary to Finnish conceptions of justice."[78] The prime minister also had to face considerable opposition in parliament, the judiciary, and noncommunist political parties to putting on trial former members of a legal Finnish government.[79] He argued directly with Zhdanov that doing so would only stoke anti-Soviet feelings in Finland and make the defendants into heroes and martyrs.[80] Removing the accused from public life, he added, should be enough to satisfy the spirit of article 13 of the armistice.[81]

Zhdanov rightly interpreted these arguments as foot-dragging. He was well aware that trials of wartime generals would have been tremendously unpopular among Paasikivi's supporters in Finland, even if, as Zhdanov suggested, Mannerheim could be excluded from the indictments because he had signed the armistice with the Soviets and, like Marshal Pietro Badoglio in Italy, could be considered to have assuaged his guilt.[82]

Once the Potsdam Agreement of August 1945 had reaffirmed the principle of trying German war criminals and those of its allies, Zhdanov turned up the pressure on Paasikivi. Already several months earlier, the Soviets had encouraged meetings and demonstrations, sponsored by the Finnish left, to call for the setting up people's courts to try war criminals, an idea that was completely alien to Paasikivi's mentality.[83] The Finnish leader understood that he had no choice about proceeding with the indictments, especially given the relative indifference to the issue on the part of the British and Americans. Zhdanov wanted to make clear that the Soviets "did not intend to tolerate further delay." As Zhdanov told the Finnish communists Leino and Kuusinen, "[I]t is important not only to crush the bourgeoisie but we need to know how to compel them to serve us. Therefore in Finland it is very important to have the bourgeoisie itself punish those guilty of the war."[84] Still, Zhdanov was so frustrated by Paasikivi's procedural stalling that he queried Stalin and Molotov whether it might not be preferable for the ACC to become officially involved in the trials, maybe even to take them over. Molotov, worried about accusations of meddling, answered in the negative.[85]

Still, Zhdanov did not give up. In private talks with Paasikivi, he told the prime minister that he had to answer to Moscow about what was happening about the trials in Finland and that he needed to know whether the Finns were reneging on their friendly stance to the Soviets. "I should say to you that they often call me on the telephone and ask: what are you doing there; what's going on there; how come this has happened. There is lot of bewilderment [about the trials]," Zhdanov told Paasikivi, "a lot of bewilderment. . . . So that this crisis does not end in a dead end [for you] and so that it does not destroy our relations, it is necessary to take the appropriate measures." Zhdanov added that he had no right to meddle in internal Finnish affairs, but if Paasikivi did not do something quickly, the situation could get very serious.[86]

At the same time that Zhdanov complained about protests "from Moscow," he also requested from his Kremlin colleagues that critical articles on the Finnish trials appear in the Soviet central press.[87] That way he could increase the pressure on Paasikivi to speed up the process. After the trials had finally begun, Zhdanov was not satisfied either. He took out his frustrations about the Finns on the local communists. He was especially angry that some of the defendants fought the charges by making anti-Soviet statements in court. Not only that, none of the Finnish media criticized the court for allowing them to do so. "Nothing has changed!" Zhdanov ranted.[88]

The Allied Control Commission had drawn up a list of sixty-one people the Finns should arrest for war crimes, mainly in connection with their treatment of Soviet prisoners of war. Forty-five of them were held in a detention camp in Miehikkälä, some for as long as three years, but two-thirds were released without having been indicted. Eight politicians were brought to trial for having instigated the Continuation War in alliance with the Nazis, which started on June 25, 1941, a few days after Operation Barbarossa, and for having delayed the armistice. The Soviets were particularly interested in prosecuting Väinö Tanner, a Social Democrat, who, though only a member of the foreign relations committee of the parliament during the war, bore for Zhdanov particular responsibility for deceiving the Finnish working class into supporting the war.[89] (Since Lenin's times, anti-communist Social Democrats typically aroused even greater ire from the Soviets than stolid conservatives.) Tanner and the others, including the former president, Risto Ryti, and two former prime ministers, Jukka Rangell and Edwin Linkomies, were finally tried and convicted for their crimes. Tanner received a sentence of "only" three and a half years in prison.

The courtroom proceedings attracted little attention from Finnish society and were sparsely attended, except for uniformed Red Army officers and visiting journalists, mostly from the Soviet Union.[90] Zhdanov and the Soviets were incensed by what they thought were inconsequential prison terms for the guilty, and protested Tanner's sentence in particular. As a result, the Paasikivi government was forced to abandon its principles and go against public opinion by pressuring the court to increase the sentences, which it did on February 21, 1946. Tanner, for example, would now serve five and a half years in prison and former president Risto Ryti ten, which was the longest sentence of those indicted.

The Finnish public was unhappy with the trials and sentencing. Throughout the country, photographs were pasted on shop windows showing the convicted politicians with the caption "They Served Finland."[91] Most Finns understood the trials as a clear case of Soviet "victors' justice," especially since the British were not involved at all. Moreover, the Soviets had started the Winter War against Finland in November 1939, they complained, and were not subject to criminal prosecution as a result. But beyond the blow they delivered to Finnish self-esteem, the trials had little concrete impact on the country. The sentences were reduced by the generous parole options built into the Finnish judicial system, and Paasikivi pardoned a number of the convicted after the signing of the Paris Peace Treaty and the withdrawal of the Allied Control Commission in August and September 1947.

The problem of prosecuting alleged war criminals remained the most serious crisis in Soviet-Finnish relations in the immediate postwar period. Paasikivi had an easier time dealing with the issue of the Marshall Plan, not least because he steered a less confrontational course in this regard. He and his government had entered into treaty obligations with Moscow about reparations and mandatory deliveries of goods. While the Marshall Plan was popular in the parliament and society in general, Finland's participation in it would have complicated the already difficult negotiations with the Soviet leadership about the two countries' future relations. Besides, the Soviets made it amply clear that such a decision would be viewed as a "hostile act." As a result, Helsinki rejected the offer of attending the Marshall Plan conference in July 1947 with the official explanation that "Finland has not yet exchanged the treaty ratifications with Moscow and could not now undertake any obligations unless her political stability was more firmly established."[92]

When Zhdanov returned to his post as head of the ACC in early 1947 after a long interlude in Moscow, he seemed pleased with the maturation of Finnish politics during his absence. Even when Leino and Pessi complained about Paasikivi—Pessi called him a "real reactionary"— Zhdanov was more conciliatory. Paasikivi was "the godson of the DSNF [the People's Front] and the ACC," he stated. "We supported him; we helped get Mannerheim out of the way." Now Paasikivi would remain under the influence of the People's Front and the ACC. But Zhdanov also called for the radicalization of the communist tactics urging the Finnish comrades to focus harder on economic issues, including the nationalization of industry and banks, and on agrarian reform, so as to win the masses to their banner. "The communists will be the complete victors in the country and this means that they will transform [Finland] into socialism via a peaceful road without civil war." The time had come, he declared, for the Finnish communists to catch up with the rest of eastern Europe.[93] Yet when Zhdanov met with representatives of the other Finnish parties and the government, he reiterated that the success of Soviet-Finnish relations depended on the good will of both sides and on mutual respect for the views and desires of the other.[94] In the end, Zhdanov's pious wishes for socialism in Finland were subordinate to Stalin's apparent choice to foster good relations with Paasikivi and the Finnish middle class.

The Treaty of Friendship, Cooperation, and Mutual Aid

The initial period of postwar Soviet-Finnish relations from the conclusion of the armistice in September 1944 to the signing of the Friendship Treaty on April 6, 1948, is justifiably called the "dangerous years" in Finnish history.[95] Two skilled and determined political leaders, Andrei Zhdanov (on behalf of Stalin) and Juho Paasikivi, first as prime minister and then as president of Finland, negotiated the relationship between the two countries without forcing either's hand. The British, though closely watching the Finnish negotiations, prudently kept a low profile.[96]

Zhdanov and Paasikivi did not agree about the trajectory of Finnish internal developments: Zhdanov looked to the creation of a people's democracy, not unlike in Romania or Hungary, while Paasikivi sought to protect the future of Finnish parliamentary democracy and the rule of law. Periodically, Paasikivi broached the subject of the return of

Karelia, which annoyed Zhdanov and aroused his doubts about working with the Finnish conservative.[97] Yet both understood that Finland would have to be a "friendly" neighbor of the Soviet Union. Without steadfast Finnish guarantees that the country would not be used to threaten Soviet security, Moscow would force Finland into its alliance system, which was already taking shape in other parts of eastern Europe. The combination of Paasikivi's skillful handling of Moscow's demands and the relative weakness and lack of initiative on the part of the Finnish communists kept the prospects of people's democracy low, although the vision—for the Finns, the specter—remained prominent in the minds of both Zhdanov and Paasikivi.

A military agreement between the Soviets and the Finns had been on the agenda between Zhdanov and Mannerheim since early 1945, originally as a way of deterring German attacks on Finland in response to the Finnish withdrawal from the war. But Molotov argued that according to the norms of the Grand Alliance those talks were inappropriate given the absence of a peace treaty. Once the peace treaty with Finland was signed by the Allies in Paris—it is worth reiterating that the United States was not a signatory—and ratified by Moscow on September 26, 1947, Paasikivi, his prime minister Mauno Pekkala from the leftist SKDL, and the Soviets began exploring the possibilities of a friendship and mutual assistance treaty that would regulate Soviet-Finnish relations and security questions. Paasikivi noted in his diary that he would have preferred not to negotiate a treaty at all, but that the Soviets left him no choice.[98] For him, the main challenge was to formulate an agreement on military questions that would not sign away Finland's sovereignty and would avoid an outright alliance with Moscow.

According to the Paris Peace Treaty, Finland's borders were to be those of January 1, 1941. This confirmed the losses of Finnish territory after the Winter War, much to the disappointment of the Finns, who had hoped for the return of at least some of the parts of Karelia they had ceded to the Soviet Union by the armistice. Yet in Paris the Finns were excluded from the negotiations and even expelled from the visitors' gallery.[99] In addition to the Karelian losses, Finland had to cede the territory of Petsamo to the Soviet Union, as agreed in the armistice. Already in April 1946 the Finns had asked the Soviets for modifications of the agreement on the Porkkala concession, seeking access to the Helsinki–Turku railway that ran through the Soviet leased territory. They also asked to use the Saimaa (*Samuskovo*) Canal that ran to Vyborg. Stalin conceded on both issues, despite some objections from the military, making it clear that he sought to develop positive relations with the Finns. Paasikivi on his side was anxious that Moscow understand that Finland would not serve as a base for enemies of the Soviet Union. In February 1947 he stated that "Finland would fight with all her resources, against any aggressor seeking to strike the Soviet Union across Finnish territory . . . however if her strength would not suffice for this, help would have to be sought from the Soviet Union."[100] Here Paasikivi set out his basic idea about how Soviet-Finnish security relations could and should develop. Finland should have the means and determination to defend its territory against any outside aggressors. But at the same time, if Finland were unable to do so, then she would invite the Soviet Union to join the defense of her territory. In other words, the Finns would be a strictly defensive power. They would not join an alliance to attack any other countries, and they would allow Soviet incursion on their territory only as the result of a formal request from Helsinki to Moscow.

The history of the signing of the Friendship Treaty can be seen as a confirmation of Paasikivi's calculations, despite a great deal of legitimate nervousness on the Finnish side about whether it would hold. Molotov invited Prime Minister Pekkala to Moscow in November 1947 to talk about "some kind of military treaty" to improve security cooperation between the Soviet Union and Finland. On February 22, 1948, Stalin wrote Paasikivi that it would be a good idea to conclude a Finnish-Soviet agreement "which would be similar to the treaties between Hungary and the Soviet Union and Romania and the Soviet Union."[101] This worried Paasikivi to no end, since it would signify the inclusion of Finland in a Soviet-led military bloc, which he firmly opposed, and perhaps even the stationing of Soviet troops on Finnish soil, which might spell the end of the Finnish democratic governmental system. The "Old Finn" wanted to avoid being drawn into the emerging conflict between East and West and had turned down Marshall Plan aid to this end. He had no intention of bringing Finland into a position where its military would be forced to engage an enemy outside of Finland itself. Paasikivi was ready to sign a bilateral treaty with the Soviet Union to protect Leningrad and the Soviet flank from outside aggression. But he was decidedly opposed to joining a larger bloc.[102] "It would be best for us if we did not need to sign a treaty," he wrote, "[but] since the Russians want negotiations, we can't say no."[103]

The final treaty negotiations in Moscow upheld Paasikivi's conception of Soviet-Finnish cooperation. Surprising to many in the Finnish delegation, the treaty resembled Moscow's treaties with France and Czechoslovakia more than it did those with Romania or Hungary. Unique to the Finnish Treaty was the stipulation that it was limited to an attack through Finnish territory, precluding any obligation to fight against a third-party aggression outside of Finland.[104] Apparently, the Finns succeeded in convincing Stalin, Molotov, and the Soviet leadership that they could be relied on to resist Western entreaties to become part of an incipient Western alliance, even though this would have strengthened the country's military and economic potential. From Moscow's point of view, it was best to allow the hullaballoo aroused in the West by the February 1948 communist-led coup in Czechoslovakia to die down before forcing a potential political crisis in Helsinki as a result of the treaty negotiations with the Finns, who still had many friends in the West as a result of their plucky defense during the Winter War. At the same time, Moscow was appreciative of regular Finnish reparations payments and looked forward to increased trade possibilities. Zhdanov praised the exactitude of the Finnish deliveries in a January 1948 Kremlin meeting: "Everything on time, expertly packed and of excellent quality."[105]

The desperate need of the Soviet Union for this kind of a reliable infusion of equipment and goods in the immediate postwar period should not be underestimated as a factor supporting Finnish sovereignty. There was famine in the Soviet Union in the years 1946 to 1948; despite its own shortages, Finland was nearby and a good source of food.

People's democracy might come later; for the moment, the important thing was to make sure that Finland did not fall into the Western camp. NATO negotiations were underway at the same time, and Moscow wanted to keep Finland in its own security orbit.[106] As a result, the critical article in the Treaty of Friendship, Cooperation and Mutual Aid, signed on April 6, 1948, defining Helsinki's security role, conformed to the Finnish position:

> In the event of Finland or the Soviet Union across the territory of Finland, becoming the object of military aggression on the part of Germany or any State allied to the latter, Finland loyal to her duty as an independent State, will fight to repulse the aggression. In doing so, Finland will direct all the forces at her disposal to the defence of the inviolability of her territory on land, on sea and in the air, acting within her boundaries in accordance with her obligations under the present Treaty with the assistance, in case of need, of the Soviet Union or jointly with the latter.
>
> In the cases indicated above, the Soviet Union will render Finland the necessary assistance, in regard to the granting of which the parties will agree between themselves.[107]

In the end, then, Paasikivi got the treaty he wanted. Apparently in the presence of Stalin, Finnish prime minister Kekkonen later called the treaty the "Paasikivi diktat," and Stalin himself supposedly called it "the Finnish diktat."[108] In any case, Finland could concentrate on rebuilding its economy and reviving its society after a disastrous war without having to commit to the newly emerging Soviet bloc. When the Warsaw Pact was formed in May 1955, there was no discussion about the Finns.[109] With the disbanding of the Allied Control Commission in September 1947 and the signing of the Friendship Treaty, the Finns could operate domestically with considerably more freedom than allowed before. There was no more Zhdanov or ACC to worry about.

Yet the Soviets profited from the agreement as well. They gained a buffer zone in the northwest, firm control of the Gulf of Finland, and a common border with Norway. Finland, with heavy-gun emplacements on the Gulf of Bothnia, would resist any incursions from the West. With the addition of Porkkala, the Soviets gained a major military base in Finland that guaranteed that the Finns would not go back on their agreements. The Soviets could not station their troops elsewhere in the country, which no doubt limited their security profile in the northwest and reduced their potential influence on Finnish politics. Soviet assistance could only be proffered "subject to mutual agreement."[110]

Despite the limitations on the Soviets, Paasikivi did not like the treaty. "It has become clear to the Finnish nation and the whole world," he wrote in his diary, April 14, 1948, "that we would rather be without such a treaty if circumstances had allowed it."[111] It tied the Finns' hands when it came to an independent foreign and security policy. But especially with the coming of the Cold War, circumstances did not allow it, and the agreement on mutual defense gave Finland a way to steer clear of the Sovietization, not to mention Stalinization, that other countries in the Soviet East European sphere were forced to endure.

The Finnish Communist Party grew in numbers, but it remained a minor force in Finnish politics. Paasikivi removed Yrjö Leino from his position as minister of interior in the spring of 1948 on charges that he had mistreated Ingrian deportees to the Soviet Union in 1945. But the main problem for the communists at this time were the rumors and denunciations that swirled around the alleged threat of a communist takeover, which many Finns feared would follow upon the Czechoslovak coup of February 1948. It did not help that in a March 24 report on a speech by the CPF member Hertta Kuusinen (daughter of Otto Kuusinen), *Vapaa Sana,* the main newspaper of the Finnish Communist Party and Democratic Front, ran the headline "The Czechoslovak way is our way."[112] The negotiations in Moscow about the Friendship Treaty raised the level of tension in Helsinki in April 1948 to the point where Paasikivi anchored two Finnish gunboats nearby the presidential palace and ordered the Finnish security forces to take precautionary measures.[113] The Finnish military secretly mobilized its forces to protect against a coup attempt, careful not to provoke any kind of Soviet response.[114] But whatever the vain hopes of the CPF, there is no evidence that the Soviets thought a coup would work in their interests in Finland.[115]

Similarly, the Soviets restrained the Finnish communists from engaging in a large-scale strike movement at the end of May 1948 to protest the removal of Leino from his ministry post, which left the government with no communists. Instead of allowing the communists to disrupt the upcoming July 1948 elections, the Soviets tried to influence their outcome by sharply reducing the remaining Finnish reparations obligations (from $147 million to $73.5 million).[116] Although this was a very welcome concession—the Finnish economy remained in the doldrums because of the heavy burden of reparations, 16.1 percent of the budget in 1945 and 14.8 percent in 1948[117]—the Finnish people were determined to keep their independence. The turnout at the polls remained extremely high, with nearly 80 percent of the eligible Finns voting. The SKDL bloc, with the communists as the lead party, suffered a severe defeat, which, together with the loss of eleven parliamentary seats and the exclusion of the communists from the new government formed by the Social Democrat Karl-August Fagerholm, relieved Paasikivi's fears of some kind of a coup.[118] In addition, the president's complete control of the military and his deft handling of Soviet security needs in the Friendship Treaty meant the "Paasikivi Line" in one iteration or another would continue to dominate Soviet-Finnish relations.

• •

For a number of reasons, Finland managed to escape Soviet domination at the end of the war and beginning of the peace. Some of them had to do with Finland's geostrategic position in Stalin's view of Europe. As long as Sweden remained neutral, Finland was not seen as a "front-line" nation that had a high priority in Soviet security calculations, especially given Finnish concessions in Porkkala and the ceding of Petsamo to the Soviets. But it is also true that the Finnish leaders made certain that the Soviets could rely on the fact that Finland, which had a very long and vulnerable border with the Soviet Union, would not fall into the hands of political forces that might invite Western powers to use it as a base against Soviet interests. In fact, given Zhdanov's and Stalin's lack of confidence in the Finnish communists, stolid "Old Finns" like Mannerheim and Paasikivi, who in the postwar period consistently followed a pro-Soviet security policy, were preferable to the unreliable Finnish communists and the "anti-Soviet" Finnish Social Democrats. One historian astutely notes that as a result of Helsinki's policies and relative Western disinterest, which came out of the specifics of the history of Finnish involvement in World War II, "domestic conflicts in Finnish politics were neither 'internationalized' nor were they transformed into a test of prestige and power among the Big Three as elsewhere in eastern Europe."[119]

Juho Kusti Paasikivi made a huge difference to the unpredictable outcome of Soviet-Finnish relations after the 1944 armistice. He managed to follow his conception of Finnish foreign policy, emphasizing careful bargaining and tactical concessions, while maintaining Finnish domestic independence. Despite his often anti-communist domestic policies, he successfully kept the Soviets (and Stalin, in particular) on his side, even if he sometimes clashed with Zhdanov and aroused the latter's suspicions. Paasikivi received the Order of Lenin when he finally retired in 1956, before dying a few months later at the age of eighty-six. Soviet-Finnish relations had their tense moments during his time as prime minister and president, but he managed to define and pursue a course of Finnish foreign policy that continued to be relevant almost to the very end of the Soviet Union.

CHAPTER FOUR

THE ITALIAN ELECTIONS
1948

Italy had been liberated by American and British troops from the south, beginning with the invasion of Sicily in July and the landings at Salerno, Calabria, and Taranto in September 1943. Until the final surrender, on April 29, 1945, of the remnants of those German troops who had occupied the remaining parts of the country soon after the fall of the fascist regime (and the start of the Allied offensive), the Soviets played no role in the Italian campaign whatsoever. The early worries of Italian anti-communists that the Soviet army presence in Austria and the victory of Tito's Yugoslav partisans "would mean Stalinism soon in Lombardy" were allayed by the military victories of the Western Allies in the boot of Italy.[1] The absence of the Soviet army in Italy also meant that, unlike many fraternal continental parties, the Italian Communist Party (PCI) never had to explain away the violent behavior of Red Army soldiers and could instead focus on alleged, sometimes quite real, depredations of the Western forces. At the same time, the interests of the Americans and British in the Italian peninsula became more pronounced over time, as the country, dominating the north-south and east-west axes of the Mediterranean, became increasingly important geostrategically given the bitter civil war that enveloped Greece. From the West's point of view, it was essential that Italy not fall into communist—and therefore Soviet—hands.

The Soviet Union, on the other hand, did not show great interest in participating in the determination of Italy's future for most of the war. For example, in the revealing Ivan Maiskii memorandum of January 1944, the foreign ministry official dealt with the country only in passing: "The USSR need not play an active role here."[2]

Toward the end of the war Moscow surprisingly undertook serious initiatives to inherit Italian colonies in the Mediterranean, but the Americans and especially the British blocked such moves. Still, the growing strength of the Italian communists and the dynamism of the leftist partisan movement led by them during the war and liberation kindled Moscow's hopes that a form of a people's democratic government might win control of the country. The Soviets calculated that this would not only bring about socialist or quasi-socialist reforms in the economy but also keep Western, and especially British, interests at bay. The challenge for Moscow was that the continuing presence of British and American troops in Trieste, a part of the Allied attempt to defuse hostilities between the Yugoslavs and Italians there, meant that whatever Stalin's designs on Italy, they had to be pursued without the threat of armed conflict.

Under these circumstances, Italy provided an early test case for Stalin's continental national liberation strategy. Absent the presence of the Red Army, a national liberation partisan army of leftist and centrist antifascists was to destroy the Nazi forces and emerge from the underground to seize control of the government. Many groups of communist-led partisans in the north of Italy thought quite differently; they planned to capitalize on their leading role in the struggle against Mussolini to lay the bases for establishing communist power, pushing aside the (still formally existing) monarchy and its supporters, many of whom had been involved in the fascist cause. "We will do this as in Russia," they trumpeted.[3]

But Stalin opposed any attempt by the Italian communists to strike for power, especially after the armistice was signed between the Allies and the new government of General Pietro Badoglio on September 8, 1943, for fear that it would provoke a sharp Western reaction. After a meeting with Stalin on March 3–4, 1944, Palmiro Togliatti, the supremely capable and inspirational head of the PCI—and a loyal executive of the Comintern—returned to Italy from his long-term exile in the Soviet Union and pronounced his famous *La svolta di Salerno* (the Salerno turn), which set out the surprising communist policy for years to come. cooperation with the bourgeois government (which meant, at that moment, with the Badoglio government) in the name of promoting

5. Postwar Italy

democracy and defeating fascism and its remnants at home and on the continent.[4]

An entry in the diary of Georgi Dimitrov from March 5, 1944, offers a good picture of the arguments Stalin presented to Togliatti for conciliation rather than striking for power. A division between the left and right among the democratic forces in Italy, Stalin maintained, would help only the British, "who would like to have a weak Italy [that they could control] on the Mediterranean." According to Dimitrov's notes, Stalin added that "for Marxists, *form* never has decisive significance," and that even "a king is no worse than a Mussolini." Therefore, it was a positive step for communists to join the much-maligned Badoglio government and make their compromises with the despised monarchy in order to ensure that a strong and independent Italy emerge from the social and political conflict that threatened to divide the country in two. Communists should be at the forefront of defending the national cause— this was the approach that Stalin advocated all across Europe and that inherently appealed to Togliatti, if not to all or even most of his comrades.[5]

The communist-led Italian partisans, who were itching to seize power and institute an Italian socialist republic, were instructed by their leaders to conceal their weapons in the underground and keep their organizations intact but not to oppose the new government. Stalin essentially told the Italian (and French) communist partisans to keep their powder dry unless they needed to defend themselves against "enemy attack."[6]

As Elena Aga-Rossi and Victor Zaslavsky write, "Togliatti's personal responsibility for preventing the outbreak of outright civil war in Italy should not be underestimated. With great skill the PCI transformed the armed troops of the resistance into a political organization, persuading partisans to hide their arms and abandon violence."[7] Only Togliatti's unchallenged authority to represent Moscow's wishes kept the PCI grassroots organizations in line with a parliamentary strategy of coalition with the Party of Christian Democrats. At the same time, Stalin's preference for communist leaders like Togliatti, who had been trained in Comintern circles and spent the war years in Moscow, over home-grown communists who had fought in the resistance, provided Togliatti with invaluable prestige at home. Togliatti, in short, managed to enjoy the confidence of both Stalin and the PCI rank and file.

Although the stated policy of the PCI was to use its growing power and prestige at the end of the war and beginning of the peace to contribute to the building of democratic institutions in Italy, the option of armed insurrection was never far from the surface. Moscow even eventually helped fund an underground network of former partisan units (sometimes known as the "Gladio Rossa") led by PCI militant Pietro Secchia that was well-trained and ready to provide military force if need be.[8] It was also not beyond Togliatti to allude periodically to the threat of violence in political campaigning in the postwar period as a way to impress his audience with the power of the PCI. In September 1947, for example, he repeatedly brought up the potential use of violence and boasted about having some thirty thousand well-armed partisans "at our disposal."[9] These cross-cutting signals from the PCI were matched by similar mixed signals from the Soviets, who periodically criticized Togliatti for being too docile and too committed to parliamentary methods.[10]

Despite the ongoing desperate economic situation in Italy and the sharpening political tensions between right and left—what orthodox Leninists would consider a "revolutionary situation"—Togliatti, who was in constant contact with Moscow either directly or through the Soviet embassy in Rome, pursued a policy of cooperation with the parties of the left and center. Until May 1947, he even participated in a series of Christian Democratic–dominated coalition governments led by Alcide De Gasperi, who had close links both to the Vatican and to the Americans, who now demonstrated increasingly serious interest in Italian politics. De Gasperi was a social progressive who believed that it was "impossible to think of a sane democracy where . . . the founding elements of Christianity, fraternity and solidarity, do not enter into the system of governance."[11] He was convinced that Italy's fundamental problems were unemployment and rural poverty and that "social solidarity" should become the hallmark of Italian democracy.[12] Where De Gasperi parted ways with Togliatti was his genuine attachment to the Catholic Church and Italy as a Catholic nation. Accordingly, he frequently emphasized his commitment to containing the spread of "atheistic communism." In doing so he was able to keep both the conservative and socially progressive wings of the party acting in concert.[13] Togliatti's insistence in his speeches that "we respect popular religious convictions" did not get far with the thoroughly anti-communist De Gasperi.[14]

Nevertheless, at the outset of the coalition government, De Gasperi successfully enlisted Togliatti's aid to restrain communist protests and attempts by scattered PCI activists to break up rallies and demonstra-

4.1 Christian Democrat leader Alcide De Gasperi speaking at Duomo Square in Milan during the election campaign, April 13, 1945. TOSCANI ARCHIVE / ALINARI ARCHIVES MANAGEMENT, FLORENCE. PHOTOGRAPHER FEDELE TOSCANI.

tions called by the Christian Democrats.[15] Togliatti's ability to contain the impulse to seize power among many PCI veterans of the partisan movement and his unwillingness to unleash the traditional rebelliousness of large segments of what might be called the Italian underclass was essential to De Gasperi's ability to govern.[16] The two postwar Italian leaders worked together for the betterment of the Italian people more than many communists or, for that matter, Christian Democrats, would have liked. Still, there was never a genuine coalition, as CD member Attilio Piccioni observed, but rather "forced cohabitation."[17]

Within the PCI itself, Togliatti tended to downplay the models of the Soviet Union and of the "new democracies" of eastern Europe and to focus on the need to build the political and economic influence of the communists in Italy. In his speeches and writings after returning from the Soviet Union, Togliatti underlined his goal of making the PCI "a big party, a mass party" that would, in addition to representing the working class, of necessity, find a way to work "with the Catholic peasant masses." He added, "The unity of the anti-fascist resistance of liberal and democratic forces should not be broken" but "rather extended and reinforced."[18] His view was that communist strength was too heavily concentrated among factory workers in the northern industrial centers and that the PCI needed to expand its influence among agricultural workers in the south as well as among social groups such as women and youth. Togliatti encouraged his comrades to develop their relationships with allied parties in the government and to perform their functions conscientiously as members of the ruling elite on behalf of the Italian people.[19] With a strong partner in De Gasperi on his right, Togliatti could then concentrate his efforts on marshaling the forces on the left under communist leadership.[20] He was exceptionally proud of having built the PCI into a 2.3 million–member party, which made it the biggest Communist Party in any European country, east or west, and of having deep influence on the nearly seven-million-member United Trade Union Confederation. In an interview with an American journalist, the "short and shrewd" PCI chief stated,

> At present, we don't want communism in Italy. We stand simply for an end to foreign intervention, for the control of industry, and for agrarian reform. We want an advanced democracy to prevent the return of fascism. We want to nationalize chemical production, mining, electricity, the banks, about as much as in Britain.[21]

The emergence of Cold War rivalries between the United States and the Soviet Union mooted Togliatti's ideas of progressively increasing the communist penetration of Italian society and control over the making of government policy. The Americans increased their influence on the Italian government, which alienated both the Kremlin and Togliatti. Stalin and Molotov made it clear to Pietro Quaroni, the first postwar Italian ambassador in Moscow, that they did not believe his protestations that the De Gasperi government sought a middle ground between east and west. "You Italians reserve your words for us and your deeds for the Americans," Molotov said to Quaroni in a December 1945 conversation, adding that Italy should not expect as much interest from Moscow as, for example, Romania for simple geographical reasons.[22]

Moscow's growing frustrations with the De Gasperi government overlapped with those of Togliatti.

At the end of 1946, De Gasperi signaled to the Americans at the Paris Peace Conference that he would be glad to visit the United States. Having received reassurances that his visit would be welcomed and that he would not return empty-handed, De Gasperi accepted an invitation to a world affairs conference in Cleveland sponsored by Henry Luce, editor of *Time* magazine. He was met by outgoing Secretary of State James Byrnes and shepherded around Washington by the energetic Italian ambassador, Antonio Tarchiani. High-level meetings between Italian and American financial and commercial officials produced a significant loan from the Export-Import Bank and assurances of American payments for the stationing of U.S. troops in Italy. According to his daughter, who accompanied him, De Gasperi was thrilled with the traditional ticker-tape parade on Broadway, sponsored by Italian-Americans.[23]

The Italian prime minister returned to Italy on January 17, 1947, determined to expand cooperation with the Americans. This would require considerable convincing of opponents within his own party, where Catholic activists expressed frequent misgivings about Washington's policies. More crucially, it meant the step-by-step undermining of the role of the communists and socialists in the ruling coalition. De Gasperi understood that a pro-American policy could well be compromised by Togliatti and his PCI comrades. The pro-Moscow head of the Italian socialists, Pietro Nenni, wrote about the Christian Democratic prime minister, "The trip to America has changed De Gasperi more than I could have believed. At one point, he said to me, 'I am not the same man.' We shall see what he meant by that."[24]

Already in December before going to the United States, De Gasperi had reshuffled his cabinet by introducing ministers from small moderate left parties, which he calculated would reduce the influence of the PCI and the Italian Socialist Party (PSI) on the Italian workers.[25] De Gasperi had spent the war years working in the library of the Vatican and was a thoroughgoing anti-communist, if progressive, Christian Democrat, as were many similar European Christian Democrats (and founding fathers of the European Union) at the time, most notably Konrad

Adenauer of Germany and Robert Schuman of France. He required little encouragement from the Americans to dispense with the communists in the government. But first he needed the cooperation of Togliatti and the PCI to get the unpopular Peace Treaty signed on February 10, 1947, and article 7 of the constitution, which renewed the Lateran Pact with the Vatican (which Togliatti supported against the wishes of many in his party) approved by the parliament. With these goals achieved, De Gasperi resigned from the government on May 13 in order to form a new one without the PCI and PSI. The accompanying negotiations must have been painful for Togliatti, who seemed willing to compromise on almost any issue in order to continue in the ruling coalition, even in a greatly diminished role. PSI leader Pietro Nenni even got the impression that the PCI leader suffered from an excess of political "cynicism," which others have called "cold realism," not unlike that often attributed to his ostensible mentor Josif Stalin.[26]

Togliatti's preparedness to compromise notwithstanding, De Gasperi understood that in the long run he could not hope to secure American capital for and engagement in Italy while maintaining an alliance with the PCI and PSI. Besides, for the Christian Democrat, this was also a matter of principle. He was convinced that the communists and socialists had never abandoned the goal of "the conquest of power, albeit through elections," and he had no illusions that their victory would mean a different kind of democracy that would be "non-Western" and untenable for the Christian Democrats.[27] He was therefore happy to put behind him the uncomfortable situation of sharing power with parties that, in his view, followed a "dual track" policy of participating in the government while simultaneously remaining opposed to it.[28] Eliminating the PCI and PSI from the coalition also freed De Gasperi's hand for launching a number of financial reforms led by the renowned liberal economist and Bank of Italy director Luigi Einaudi, and, more generally, turning for support to what he called "'the fourth party,' those who have money and economic power."[29]

The announcement of the Marshall Plan in June 1947, which in its broadest outlines De Gasperi had known to be coming, put the Italian communists in an even more difficult situation. Togliatti knew as well as anyone that Italy desperately needed funds to rebuild industry, and therefore he did not initially criticize the overall program. But he had hoped—no doubt naively—that it would be possible to make "selective" use of the Marshall Plan, attracting investment to Italy, while rejecting the debt repayments demanded by Washington.[30] To no avail: neither the Soviets nor, for that matter, the Americans, would countenance partial allegiance.

The Cominform and the Italians

Although the French and Italian communist parties followed scrupulously Moscow's directives regarding their political and economic programs, Stalin was increasingly unhappy with the results of the parliamentary strategies pursued by both parties. He also was concerned about the attractiveness of the Marshall Plan to French and Italian communists, not to mention to the governments of eastern Europe. He was upset that the various European parties did not coordinate their stances on the Marshall Plan with Moscow. The French communists, he said, had unjustified fears that "France would collapse without American credits." It would have been better to leave the coalition governments than to wait to be thrown out.[31] He no doubt thought the same about the Italians. In an era of growing hostility demonstrated by the capitalists, the Italian and French communists should feel in no way constrained about agreements within their respective coalitions, just as Stalin felt little constrained by the agreements with Great Britain and the United States about Europe. As he had noted already in a speech in October 1938 regarding the possibilities of a coming conflict in Europe, "All states adopt masks: if you live among wolves, you must behave like a wolf."[32]

As a result of his growing lack of confidence in the communist parties of western and eastern Europe to represent Moscow's interests, as well as those of their own countries as he saw them, Stalin initiated in September 1947 the founding meeting of the Cominform in Szklarska Poręba, a resort town in western Poland, as a way to deliver a number of important, essentially radicalizing, messages to the assembled party leaderships. Although the initial idea for such a meeting came from Władysław Gomułka, the leader of the Polish party, and was strongly supported by the Yugoslav communists, the real impetus behind the meeting came from Moscow and from Stalin himself.[33] Anticipating that his conciliatory moves in the spring of that year would be subject to severe criticism at the meeting, Togliatti declared that his health would not permit him to go on such a long trip and sent his deputies Luigi Longo and Eugenio Reale in his place. "Should they reproach you for not having been able to seize power or for letting us be ousted from the government," Togliatti instructed them, "tell them that we could not turn Italy into a second Greece."[34]

Led by the Yugoslav delegation, the attacks on the Italian and French parties at the Cominform meeting were indeed sharp and unremitting. The Western communists were accused of harboring parliamentary illusions and of having been unprepared for the counterattacks both had suffered at the hands of the ruling parties. They were charged with having lost their revolutionary spirit and with making illegitimate concessions to the bourgeoisie.[35]

After his return to Rome, Luigi Longo passed on Moscow's message to his comrades at a meeting of the PCI directorate in early October. The PCI "did not have a sufficiently aggressive attitude and did not fight after its exclusion from the government, and did not succeed in mobilizing the masses against it." Moreover, the PCI had failed to take the lead in the struggle against Anglo-American imperialism and instead had allowed Italy to take a neutral stance "towards the two blocs."[36] This issue became particularly important for Moscow when the respected Italian communist Umberto Terracini, president of the Constituent Assembly, was rebuked by the PCI for the "even-handed" suggestion that both the United States and the USSR refrain from intervening in Italian domestic affairs.[37]

The sharp criticism of the Italian (and French) parties at the Cominform encouraged radicals in the PCI like Pietro Secchia to engage in "active resistance," encouraging strikes and violent confrontations with the police by the PCI's increasingly restless armed supporters in the north. Togliatti seemed to go along with this ramped-up radicalism in the fall of 1947, calling for the working people to "go into the piazzas for the defense of democracy and the republic." There were temporary seizures of towns, like that of Perugia in November, and hundreds of bomb-throwing incidents and impromptu strikes. In Bitonto, near Bari, the communists took over the city hall for one night. A temporary strike of transport workers in Rome brought the city to a halt for several hours. Given their brevity, these communist-led actions seem to have been intended to remind the government and society of the PCI's strength but not to prompt civil war.[38] According to the Italians socialist leader Pietro Nenni, the increasingly anti-American tone of Togliatti's public utterances during this period made it almost impossible for him to rejoin the government even if he wanted to; it was clear that De Gasperi also noted this shift in PCI aggressiveness.[39]

In the face of these radical street actions and sharp propaganda attacks, Stalin, in a meeting with the militant Secchia in December 1947, once again urged caution. There should be no uprising, which would inevitably, in his view, arouse the Western powers, especially the Americans, and potentially lead to full-scale military intervention. The Soviet leader repeated his fundamental advice to the West European communists: "We maintain that an insurrection should not be put on the agenda, but one must be ready, in case of an attack by the enemy."[40] When Secchia responded that the PCI's activities were not a matter of an uprising but of conducting "a determined economic and political struggle," Stalin rebuked him with the observation that the result would be the same. "This is not due at this time. You must, however, become stronger, and prepare yourselves well."[41]

In a similar meeting with Maurice Thorez, the leader of the French Communist Party, Stalin also urged preparations for an active defense, as a way to avoid inviting counterrevolution and of repulsing it if it occurred, but not—under any circumstances—to initiate an armed uprising. The main message Stalin tried to impress upon the French leader was that one should not be vulnerable to attack. "It is important to remember," Stalin lectured Thorez, "that the enemy takes no pity on the defenseless, the weak."[42]

Even more so than the meeting with Stalin, Secchia's meetings with Zhdanov in December 1947 proved delicate and difficult for the Italian. Parliamentary elections were coming up in April, and the PCI's hopes were high for a victory at the polls. Given the rising economic dissatisfaction of Italian workers and peasants from ongoing poverty and unemployment, not only did the party see itself rejoining the government, but it counted on winning the election outright and leading a new popular front government of the PCI and PSI. But for this to happen it was important that a majority of the Italian public perceive the communists as pursuing a policy of responsible government and independent national goals—which conflicted, as both Secchia and Zhdanov were aware, with the admonition from the PCI's critics at Szklarska Poręba to raise the level of struggle and communist partisanship. The Hungarian delegate Mihály Farkas had criticized the Italians for "parliamentary cretinism," and the Yugoslav Edvard Kardelj denounced them for "opportunism and parliamentarism." Secchia understood that such criticism did not go over well with Togliatti or with the greatest number of PCI-PSI voters. To navigate the treacherous waters between advancing the PCI's electoral interests and agitating for social revolution could destroy the PCI's chances in April. Given the contradictory signals, Moscow appeared willing to let the PCI leadership deal themselves with the inevitable internal arguments about how to proceed.[43]

The December 1947 meetings with Stalin, Zhdanov, and other members of the Soviet leadership also gave Secchia the opportunity to ask directly for financial aid for the party's propaganda efforts in the election campaign. Secchia mentioned the quite substantial sum of $600,000 as needed for keeping the party's various publication efforts up to speed.[44] Although there is no record of the actual delivery of such funds, the U.S. ambassador James Clement Dunn got the impression that the PCI election campaign was extremely well funded. The communists, he wrote, seemed to have "unlimited" resources for "posters, leaflets, buses, flags, banners, and general paraphernalia" to entice the masses to their cause.[45] In fact, over the next several decades the PCI was probably the best-funded Communist Party outside the Soviet bloc, though help from the Soviet Union usually did not come in cash payments (the dollars the Secchia requested) but in the delivery of raw materials from Yugoslavia (at least until mid-1948) and the other people's democracies that the PCI would then sell for Italian lira.[46]

If Secchia entertained any ideas in December 1947 of using Moscow's support for him to gain control of the Italian party from Togliatti—and some think that was his intention—he was quickly disabused of any such notions. During Secchia's meeting with Stalin, the Soviet leader provided a clear signal that Togliatti remained the Kremlin's favorite to continue to lead the PCI by demonstrating elaborate and solicitous concern about Togliatti's health and about his eating and sleeping habits. Stalin also demonstrated a certain prescience when he pressed Secchia on making sure that the PCI provided sufficient personal security for their leader. The party, he told Secchia, should form its "own security service, a small guard of experienced people. The opponent tries to murder the best party leaders."[47]

In March 1948, in the edgy international atmosphere provoked by the February 1948 communist coup in Czechoslovakia, Togliatti sent a secret message to Stalin stating that the PCI was prepared to stage an uprising. In the same message, though, Togliatti underlined that he personally was against doing so, given the bloodshed that would result and the possibility of unleashing a new world war. Stalin and Molotov agreed. They also let Togliatti know that he should resist Yugoslav pressures to become a more "revolutionary" party. It was increasingly clear that Moscow disagreed politically and ideologically with Belgrade's advice and was deeply annoyed with Tito's cheeky interference with the Italians.[48] Tensions between Stalin and the Yugoslavs grew markedly in the spring of 1948, and Togliatti was pointedly advised not to mediate.

The Elections of April 1948

Notwithstanding the Cominform's criticisms of the Italians' parliamentary tactics, Stalin encouraged Togliatti's efforts to garner support among the Italian middle classes for the Popular Democratic Front, the electoral alliance of the PCI and the PSI, led by the socialist Pietro Nenni. The symbol of the Popular Democratic Front was the Italian national hero Giuseppe Garibaldi, and the PCI's strategy was to appeal to Italian patriotism, the heritage of the Risorgimento, and the unity of Italians in the face of alleged threats to their sovereignty from the Americans.

Despite De Gasperi's high level of popularity in the beginning of 1948—it was never stronger, before or after—Stalin was still confident in the PCI's success. There were, however, some signs of trouble for the Popular Front from the outset. The widely admired anti-communist socialist Giuseppe Saragat led a splinter group, the Italian Workers' Socialist Party, which seceded with a small group of dissidents from the Nenni-led PSI because it had joined the Popular Front.[49] The formation of this group of independent social democrats proved consequential, since it sapped support from the popular front.

The Czechoslovak coup had a powerful effect on the Italian left, in part because of the proximity of the country, in part because the political systems of the two democracies were seen as comparable. In both, the communist parties attracted a substantial minority of the electorate; in both the labor movement was heavily dominated by the communists, and not the social democrats; and in both the Soviet Union enjoyed considerable popularity for its defeat of Nazi Germany. Yet the Italians were in a weaker position to engage in the kinds of country-wide demonstrations and parliamentary machinations that characterized the Czechoslovak coup. Moreover, unlike the Czechoslovak case, the Italian army and police, especially the Carabinieri, the Italian militia, were firmly in the hands of anti-communists. Some PCI and PSI radicals no doubt thought that the Italian communists should follow the lead of their Czechoslovak comrades and instigate a process of striking for power, an alternative suggested in Togliatti's message to Stalin above. But there were also significant segments within the PSI that were disturbed by the coup and concerned about its meaning for Italy's future. PSI leader Riccardo Lombardo noted that when Jan Masaryk fell to his death in a Prague courtyard—either having been pushed or, more likely, committing suicide—"his body plunged into the Piazza del Duomo in Milan, the Piazza Castello in Turin, the Piazza del Popolo in Rome. There are many Socialist workers who can no longer turn their heads."[50]

Interestingly, the effects of the Czechoslovak coup were profoundly ambivalent. U.S. ambassador Dunn, for example, believed that, besides frightening some Italians away from supporting the PCI, it could also "increase the prestige of the local communist party" in the eyes of others and encourage some workers to join "the Communist bandwagon."[51] The PCI's positive official reaction to the coup deepened the differences between the "soft" and "hard" left, exacerbating the already poor relations between the Popular Front of the PCI-PSI and Saragat's Independent Socialists, who were outraged by the Prague events.[52]

Togliatti still had legitimate grounds for optimism in the coming election. In addition to their traditional strong support among Italian factory workers in the north, the communists had made considerable inroads among landless and poor peasants in the south since the previous election in 1946. In Sicily, the Popular Democratic Front demonstrated surprising electoral prowess on April 20, 1947, by winning the plurality of the vote in local elections with some 30 percent versus 21 percent for the Christian Democrats. Ten days later, on May Day, a criminal mafia gang opened fire on an assembly of communist farmers who were celebrating the electoral victory at Portella della Ginestra (in the municipality of Piana degli Albanesi), killing eleven demonstrators and wounding twenty-seven others. The exact political motives behind the "massacre of Portella della Ginestra" remain unclear to this day, but the publicity surrounding it, in which the victims figured as saints and martyrs for the left, gave the communists even greater confidence that they would garner an unprecedented victory in the south during the April 1948 elections.

In addition, there was the powerful Italian labor confederation, the *Confederazione Generale Italiana del Lavoro* (CGIL), led by the PCI veteran Giuseppe Vittorio, which was one of the few united labor unions of its type in Europe and was heavily influenced by the communists. Togliatti had also fashioned an appealing political platform for Italian intellectuals and academics, "half Croce and half Stalin" as he called it. One historian of postwar Europe writes, "The PCI gathered around itself a court of like-minded scholars and writers, who gave to the Party and its politics an aura of respectability, intelligence and even ecumenicalism."[53] Thus with support from intellectuals and peasants, workers, and, increasingly, civil servants, the PCI could claim a nationwide and multiclass basis of support.

The Italian communists were not the only ones who predicted their victory in the upcoming elections. George Kennan was so worried about the PCI coming to power through the ballot box that on March 15 he wrote a panicky memo, suggesting that rather than take the chance of losing the elections to the communists, which would inevitably mean the end of democracy in Italy, the U.S. government should advise the Italian government to outlaw the PCI, provoking a civil war and using American troops to reoccupy parts of Italy. Kennan wrote, "This would admittedly result in much violence and probably a military division of Italy," meaning the north would fall to the armed communists while Rome and the south would be democratic and protected by the Americans. But to him, even this would have been preferable to a "bloodless election victory" by the communists, which would have constituted a disastrous political defeat in Italy and Europe as a whole.[54]

Kennan's worries about Italy were shared by the American government, including its highly engaged ambassador in Italy, James Dunn. The ambassador, however, seemed more concerned about a communist uprising and a subsequent civil war in case of a PCI election defeat than about a possible communist victory at the polls, and he drew up plans for the protection and potential evacuation of American citizens in Italy in the event.[55] The U.S. leadership interpreted the communist coup in Czechoslovakia in February 1948 as confirmation that communist parties could not be trusted to participate in democratic parliamentary politics without taking advantage of them by attempting to seize political power for themselves. The Americans were convinced, as exemplified by a March 1948 intelligence report, that a communist victory in the April elections would set Italy on the same path as the East European countries. With its victory, the PCI

> would demand and receive the ministries of control such as those of the Interior, Justice, Communications, and Defense. There would follow a discreet, but rapid, Communist infiltration of the armed forces, the police, and the national administration. The time required to complete the transition might be a matter of months or of years, but the end would be a fully developed police state under open and exclusive Communist control.[56]

The pattern of "takeover" in eastern Europe left a deep impression on American officials. The Soviets understood this as well. Molotov wrote decades later in the spirit of the first generation of Cold War historians,

"What does the 'Cold War' mean? We were simply on the offensive. They became angry at us, of course, but we had to consolidate what we conquered."[57]

U.S. foreign policy, military, and intelligence leaders mobilized their resources to try to influence the upcoming election. Their efforts were justified by a series of National Security Council documents that emphasized Italy's centrality to American security interests in the Mediterranean. National Security Council (NSC) document 1 / 1 of November 14, 1947, stated unambiguously that "the United States has security interests of primary importance in Italy . . . and the measures to implement our current policies to safeguard these interests should be strengthened without delay."[58] Italy was deemed a key object of American policy, and according to NSC 1 / 2 of February 10, 1948, the United States "should be prepared to make full use of its political, economic, and if necessary, military power" to assure that Italy took a democratic and anti-communist path.[59] The document went on to recommend the deployment of U.S. troops to Sardinia, Sicily, or both if a communist-dominated government were to take over the peninsula.[60] NSC 1 / 3, which was issued on March 8, less than two weeks after the Czechoslovak coup, was even more darkly foreboding in language and tone, suggesting that the potential electoral victory of the PCI would mean that U.S. interests in the Mediterranean were "imminently and gravely threatened."[61] At the same time, the U.S. military, already stretched thin by its commitments in Europe and Asia, was extremely hesitant about using force in Italy and expressed the view that military action was not a serious option.[62]

Motivated by these assessments of the upcoming election as an important test for the fate of postwar Europe, the American government initiated a broad campaign of propaganda and economic measures to support De Gasperi and the Christian Democrats. On De Gasperi's urging, the Americans also aided the other non-communist parties, including liberals, anti-clerical urban elites, and Social Democrats like Saragat's independent socialists as an additional way to erode support for the Popular Democratic Front. American ambassador Dunn likewise urged his superiors in Washington not to focus exclusively on the Christian Democrats, given the "historic Italian distrust of clericalism."[63] If the Americans were overly reliant on the Christian Democrats, there was a danger that anti-clerical liberals, especially, would be drawn to the communists.

Still, the Christian Democrats were the main beneficiaries of U.S. assistance and largesse. The newly created Central Intelligence Agency delivered large sums of money to them for their campaign coffers—according to ex-CIA agent Mark Wyatt, at the astronomical level of $8–10 million a month—helping them match up to the communists' extensive propaganda efforts funded in good part by Moscow.[64] The American embassy served as "election central," with Ambassador Dunn traveling all over the country by train on a whistle-stop tour, distributing American goods and foodstuffs while touting the benefits of American friendship and good will.[65] The fundamental idea was to win votes for the anti-communists. But the Americans also campaigned to convince the Italians that it was in their interests to join the American-backed Organization for European Cooperation, formed on April 16 to plan for the investment and distribution of Marshall Plan funds; and the West European Union, which was being formed at the time of the elections by Great Britain, France, Belgium, the Netherlands, and Luxemburg to coordinate their collective defense programs. (On March 17, 1948, these countries had signed the Brussels Treaty.) The Italians were also enticed by U.S. support for Rome joining the United Nations, and, of course, by the financial aid they would receive through the Marshall Plan. By the end of the election campaign, the message that none of this would be possible if the communists won became increasingly explicit.[66] De Gasperi stated,

> I would not like to see that day when those who attacked the Americans entered into the government. I would not like to see that day because I would fear that the Italian people, waiting on the shore for ships loaded with coal and wheat, would see them turn their bows to other shores.[67]

Hundreds of copies of Greta Garbo's darkly anti-Soviet *Ninotchka* were dubbed in Italian and distributed throughout the boot of Italy for popular viewing. The movie became even more in demand after the Soviet ambassador protested to the Italian government against its showing.[68] The U.S. government also encouraged Italian-American groups to engage in a widespread letter-writing campaign to their relatives in Italy, warning them of the dangers of communism and promoting the cause of liberal democracy. Italian-American letters, packages, and promises of more aid if the elections turned out right were apparently most successful in the south of Italy, which remained buried in endemic poverty and unemployment.[69] The "Sons of Italy," which was heavily involved in the letter-writing campaign, also raised substantial sums for the anti-communist efforts of the Christian Democrats. Gary Cooper, Bing Crosby, Joe DiMaggio, and Frank Sinatra were recruited to the effort to stimulate support for the pro-American cause in Italy. Stepped-up visits of American warships to Italian ports were designed to demonstrate Washington's resolve, as well as ability, to resist Soviet or Yugoslav intimidation.[70] A month before the elections, Washington also carried out a major publicity campaign around handing back twenty-nine merchant marine vessels to the Italians, another gesture to demonstrate the benefits of American friendship.[71]

Perhaps most important, the Americans made a series of barely veiled threats about the curtailment of Marshall Plan aid to Italy if the elections turned out in favor of the communist-socialist coalition.[72] As much as the Italian communists tried to soft-pedal this threat and suggest that the Americans—capitalists to the end—would surely continue the Marshall Plan help in any case since they needed markets to sell their products, already the implicit threat proved very effective. But just to make sure, Ambassador Dunn and the State Department convinced the secretary of state to make a public statement to the effect that American aid would be suspended and all Italian communists denied entry into the United States if a Popular Front government were elected. On March 19, 1948, in a speech widely reported in the Italian press, Secretary of State Marshall stated at the University of California, Berkeley, that in that case, "This Government would have to conclude that Italy had removed itself from the benefits of the European recovery program." The communist newspaper L'Unità noted in its editorial: "Marshall's language clearly shows how the U.S. intends to use aid as an electoral weapon of blackmail against Italian people."[73] The liberal Milan paper Corriere della Sera stated essentially the same in its headline about

Marshall's speech: "Italy will decide with its vote whether it accepts aid plan."[74] The same newspaper noted on the day before the election that "another eight million dollars of Marshall Plan [aid had been] given to Italy."[75]

The American electoral tactics were so successful, and worried Togliatti so much, that he urged Stalin, initially with limited results, to bolster the cause of the left by initiating high-level USSR-Italian trade talks and promising shipments of Soviet grain and coal to Italy in case of a communist election victory.[76] In a meeting with Secchia on December 16, 1947, Zhdanov responded to the PCI requests by saying that one should avoid the impression that the USSR was mixing into Italy's affairs and that Italy was therefore not an independent state. If the Soviets intervened in the politics of a sovereign state like Italy, Zhdanov noted at a second meeting, they would "look like the Americans."[77] Stalin at least feigned confidence that the Italian communists would do well regardless of the outcome of the election: "In Italy and France our position is so strong that we need not fear any election or any change of government. In time of necessity, the majority of the population of the country will be with us, notwithstanding all the contriving in selling themselves out to the American capitalist bourgeoisie."[78] The Soviet leader also backed Togliatti's hard-driving and effective propaganda tack of counterposing Italian nationalism and the interests of the Italian people to the outside interference of the Americans and their West European marionettes.[79]

With that said, the Soviets made some last-minute concessions by concluding new trade and commercial agreements with the government in Rome and withdrawing reparation claims, steps that were noted positively in the Italian press.[80] Perhaps most critically, the Soviets also made several important concessions to the Italians regarding their claims on their former colonies—in contrast to the Americans and British, who insisted that these territories be turned over to UN and British trusteeships until they would be "ready" for independence, as the Italian Peace Treaty demanded. For the Soviets, this was not just election politics. They were convinced that it would be better if the Italians kept their previous colonies than placing them under what would effectively be British and American control.[81] (Molotov's initial efforts to negotiate Soviet control of Tripolitania after the defeat of the Italians at the end of the war were resolutely and successfully opposed by the British and Americans.)

Soviet support on the colonies issue, however, could not completely offset the poor image of the communists in the Italian public that resulted from the Soviets' continuing resolute backing of Yugoslav claims to the city of Trieste, which set off a serious international crisis in May and June of 1945. This issue was especially important in Venice and the Veneto region, where anti-communist propaganda related to it was further fueled by the many stories that circulated about Yugoslav partisan massacres of Italian civilians and mass burials in the *foibas,* the karst crevices that cover Dalmatia and the border regions of Istria and Veneto.[82] In this context, the Soviet rejection, announced just one week before the election day, of a U.S.-British-French proposal to return Trieste to Italy was interpreted by some as "evidence that the Soviet Union had given up hope of a Communist victory in Sunday's election."[83]

A later CIA study, which assessed the American propaganda efforts in Italy at that time as more effective than anywhere else in Europe, emphasized the central importance of the March 20, 1948, declaration on Trieste: "The statement caused a tremendous sensation in Italy, and contributed substantially to the Center victory."[84] Manlio Brosio, Italian ambassador to Moscow from 1947 to 1951, was more skeptical, writing on March 22, 1948, "The Soviets offer us the colonies that the English do not want to give us, the English and Americans propose Trieste to take the initiative away from the Russians. But in the meantime nothing is decided, what will the promises come to after the election?"[85]

The PCI understood that the Americans had made important inroads into the Italian media outlets. American attitudes dominated Italian cinema, radio, and the press, complained Secchia at the second meeting of the Cominform in Belgrade, June 21, 1948. The American-led anti-communist "campaigns of lies" were supported, he maintained, by the Vatican and the Christian Democrats. He recognized as well that the PCI's propaganda failed to communicate the many accomplishments of the Soviet Union and the "new democracies." Secchia urged his Italian comrades to be bolder in juxtaposing Moscow's peace policies to the "danger of the division of Europe" posed by the Marshall Plan and its advocates.[86] In the PCI's postmortem discussions of the April 1948 election catastrophe, the attractiveness of the Marshall Plan was brought up repeatedly. Even communist workers assessed its benefits for their own factories and industries.[87] Personally, Togliatti would probably still have welcomed Marshall Plan aid to improve the conditions in and productivity of Italian factories, yet he had no choice but to follow Moscow's rejectionist line.[88]

Perhaps even more important for the outcome of the competition between the Soviets and the Americans to win support for their respective clients among the Italian population was the intense campaign by the Catholic Church to mobilize the faithful to vote against the communists in the election. Pope Pius XII was convinced that the vast majority of nonpolitical Catholics were anti-communist. The Vatican therefore launched a get-out-the-vote campaign that would use the local churches' lay leaders and priests as voting agents.[89] Having worked in the Vatican library during the war to escape fascist repression, De Gasperi himself had excellent ties with the church. The increasing evidence of the persecution of priests in communist eastern Europe and especially the specter of the Prague coup in February 1948 motivated the Catholic Church and its social organizations to hold electoral campaign meetings and to publish and distribute anti-communist literature. Sunday sermons focused on the potential disaster for Italy if the Popular Democratic Front won. The archbishops of Milan, Turin, and Palermo even threatened to deny communist voters absolution, never mind that it would have been hard to know who these were.[90] In a post-election discussion of what had gone wrong in the election campaign, communist leaders would later complain about the use of "terror and intimidation" by priests and monks against the Popular Front.[91] While such language might sound like an exaggeration, in some parishes the election was framed as a vote "For or against Christ."[92] Holding an election audience with sixteen hundred Roman tram workers, the Pope emphasized that "the doctrine of Christ, the doctrine of truth and faith, is irreconcilable with materialistic maxims, the acceptance of which means to desert the Church and cease to be Catholic."[93] Just as he did with the issue of the Marshall Plan, Togliatti tried in the election campaign to soft-pedal the actual risk of Church sanctions against communist voters.

His comrades also tried to portray themselves and their PCI-PSI front as supportive of Catholic believers, much to the disgust of more militant PCI members.

In any case, the PCI attempts to present themselves as moderates fell short among the electorate. The Church campaign for "Christianity" and against "godless Communism" was met with a groundswell of popular support. Christian pilgrimages wound their way to Rome from various parts of the country to pray for an outcome of the election that would be agreeable to God. One priest stated that "our Lady . . . will not allow the enemies of religion to prevail." Marian visions of a bleeding, weeping, or levitating mother of Christ appeared to both young and old in various parts of Italy, though mostly in the south. Carlo Ginzburg noted that "only after the victorious outcome of the election did this Marian fever gradually die down."[94]

In the end, the communists were much more soundly defeated than anyone anticipated. The Christian Democrats won 48 percent of the vote, an increase from 35.2 percent in 1946, which secured them an absolute majority in the House of Deputies. The PCI-PSI Popular Democrat Front dropped from 40 percent to 31 percent, some of its loss explainable by the creation of the independent anti-communist Social Democratic Party, which won 7 percent of the vote.[95] The antifascist academic Mario Einaudi noted that the communist front (the PCI and the PSI) polled eight million votes, while the Independent Socialists, a pro-government party which represented for the PCI little more than "traitors to the cause of the working class," received some two million.[96]

As the Americans and the Christian Democrats became increasingly confident of victory by early spring, they started to worry about whether the communists would stage an uprising either before the elections, to preempt a loss at the polls, or afterward, to disrupt the Italian political system with the goal of conquering power. "If, as seems probable, the communists fail to secure representation in the new government," predicted an April 9, 1948, CIA report, "they will then launch a new program of strikes and sabotage to wreck the recovery program and discredit the government."[97] That the electoral campaign was characterized by a lot of small-scale violence, mostly incited by the left but also

involving the government and the right—fistfights, attacks on deputies, shootings, beatings, police excesses, sometimes leaving dead and
wounded—fueled concerns that more serious violent uprisings could
be in the offing.[98] Minister of Interior Mario Scelba claimed to have un-
covered a communist "Plan K," dated April 21, 1948, that supposedly
outlined the stages of a Bolshevik-style coup d'état in case of a communist election victory. He deployed carabinieri to strategic points
around the country to make sure that this did not happen. Already the
previous fall Scelba had issued directives to track the movements of "for-
eigners" in Italy, to assemble reliable lists of Soviet citizens in the
country, and to develop police methods of controlling demonstrations
and strikes.[99]

The communists did indeed make preparations for an armed uprising in March 1948, but eventually both Togliatti and Stalin concluded
that such a move could provoke another war.[100] The communists' hard-
worn tactics were consistent with those of the early postwar period:
they made sure they could defend themselves should the government
declare them illegal, but they would not violently seize control of the
government. In secret meetings with the Soviet ambassador, M. A. Kostylev, Togliatti received the same message from Moscow; pay no attention to the Yugoslavs, who were encouraging the PCI to strike for
power, and engage in armed conflict only if attacked. Clearly, the danger
of a military confrontation with the Americans was very much on Moscow's mind.[101]

The De Gasperi government understood the potential threat from
the PCI and prepared itself, with American help, for the eventuality of
an uprising. Italian army and carabinieri units were strategically deployed around the country in anticipation of a civil war.[102] In addition,
the Christian Democrats created their own skeleton paramilitary structure which was supposed to mobilize anti-communist social forces in
the case of civil war, though these units were nowhere as well organized
and numerous as those of the communists.[103] Moreover, there is some
indication that Rome used the specter of a communist insurrection as
a way to increase American resources and commitment.[104] Still, the
threat was real, and the Christian Democrats needed and received
American help to counter it. The delivery of weapons for the Italian

police and militia was especially important, and at the same time a delicate issue prior to the elections because De Gasperi worried that the revelation of the delivery of American arms could be used against him by the communists.[105]

Togliatti reportedly boasted of having thirty thousand well-armed partisans at his command in the so-called *apparato,* and electoral rhetoric by the communists that matters in Italy would soon be settled one way or another, made De Gasperi and his advisors even more nervous.[106] Meanwhile, Cominform activists in Belgrade talked about the "huge implications" of the Italian elections and planned to set up support points and train specialists in sabotage techniques in the case of a civil war in Italy.[107] The atmosphere in Washington was tense, not least because of the February 1948 Czech coup, which had left everyone on edge about the possibility of a dramatic shift in communist fortunes on the European continent.

Though there were advocates of an uprising among the northern partisan groups, Togliatti was firmly opposed and was able to maintain discipline. The PCI Central Committee communiqué about the elections of early May 1948 spoke only of the "religious terror" to which the communists were subjected, "distortions" of their platform propagated by the government, the "anti-Soviet and anti-communist calumnies" resulting from the interference of the imperialists, and the "falsification" of the electoral results.[108] In a party meeting of April 26, after the results were apparent, Togliatti also spoke about problems in the cooperation between the PCI and PSI, where some socialist rank-and-file members, especially in more remote areas of the country, did not go to the polls at all because of poor communications and a lack of cooperation from party headquarters.[109]

The lessons of the April elections were not lost on Togliatti or Stalin. It now seemed highly unlikely that the Italian communists would come to power by legal means, and neither the Soviet nor Italian party leaders were ready to force an armed confrontation that would provoke a civil war, like in Greece, if not a wider conflict that would involve the Americans, British, and Soviets. Instead, both Stalin and the Italian party leadership continued to think defensively. Togliatti sought to strengthen the role of the PCI in local affairs. By penetrating the decentralized and sometimes chaotic Italian local and provincial government institutions, the party, he hoped, would be able to foster its social and political programs. Although remaining loyal to Stalin and the Cominform, Togliatti gradually, if perceptibly, developed his own strategy for preserving the PCI's role in Italian politics and society. He always seemed to keep one eye on the communists' ability to contribute to the development of Italian democracy and to participate in governing it. He also maintained the alliance with the PSI, though the Popular Democratic Front, about which he had never been terribly enthusiastic, was soon formally disbanded. Pietro Nenni, the leader of the PSI, likewise continued to maintain good relations with the PCI, although he was now less willing than he had been during the election campaign to compromise his own socialist principles, especially if he thought that this required holding back criticism of the USSR. Meanwhile, Stalin, according to Italian ambassador Brosio in Moscow, still hoped for an election victory at some point that would put Italy in the anti-imperialist camp and reverse the country's approach to the Marshall Plan.[110]

Still, the disappointing results of the elections affected Stalin's view of the West European communists. The strongest Communist Party in western Europe had proven incapable, even under seemingly fortuitous circumstances—including forging a functional alliance with the socialist party, something the French communists were unable to accomplish—to overcome the stalwart resistance of established social forces like the church, centrist social organizations, and some anti-communist labor unions, especially when these were backed by American money and interests. Not only that, Stalin seemed to have learned that the communist parties would not be able to stop the process of West European economic and political association promoted by the European Recovery Plan. Counter to Moscow's declared interests, Italy, like France, would soon become part of a larger western European community with the strong encouragement of the United States. Italy joined the West European Union in late 1948 and was an original signatory of the NATO alliance treaty in 1949. Stalin's influence over Italian politics would remain minimal and restricted to state-to-state diplomatic relations, apart from the still-vibrant ties between the Italian and Soviet communist parties. Meanwhile, the Soviets would pay more attention to their own "realm," the countries of east central and southeastern Europe, one of which—Yugoslavia—was causing myriad problems for Moscow's ambitions of a hegemonic role in the communist world.

The Assassination Attempt on Togliatti

As Togliatti left the Chamber of Deputies on the morning of July 14, 1948, in the company of his PCI comrade and lover Leonilde Iotti—but by chance not with his usual bodyguard—he was shot three times in the chest with a .38 caliber pistol. The lone assassin was a young neo-fascist student by the name of Domenico Pallante, who carried among his possessions a copy of Hitler's *Mein Kampf* and sundry fascist scribblings of his own.[111] Pallante confessed that he was upset that Togliatti had brought Italy into the Cominform.[112] Reportedly, when questioned by the police, Pallante calmly defended his actions with the accusation that the communist kingpin "was an enemy of the country and has ruined Italy."[113] Meanwhile, Togliatti was rushed to the hospital in an ambulance. Most likely, he did not expect to survive. But although his injuries were severe—one of the bullets had entered his left lung and had to be extracted in a dangerous two-and-a-half-hour operation—they did not prove fatal. Ultimately, Togliatti recovered and returned to political life.

Stalin responded almost immediately to the assassination attempt with a telegram sent to the PCI. Aside from the obligatory mention of distress, his message to his Italian comrades was downright insulting. It read, "The CPSU is grieved that Comrade Togliatti's friends were not able to protect him from the foul underhanded attack."[114] While the PCI wanted to place the responsibility for the assassination attempt squarely on the Italian government, Stalin blamed the Italian communists themselves. Secchia, who took over the party leadership during Togliatti's surgery and hospitalization, could do little else but raise the "problem of vigilance" within the party. At a meeting of the party directorate in August, he called for the formulation of a document that would establish the party's position on the need to mobilize the masses in the defense of the party itself and the country's democratic institutions. Longo added that the party also needed to engage in serious

4.2 The assassination attempt on Palmiro Togliatti outside the Italian parliament, July 25, 1948, as portrayed in the communist illustrated magazine *Illustrazione del Popolo*. NATIONAL LIBRARY, FLORENCE.

self-criticism for not having provided sufficient personnel for Togliatti's protection.[115]

The Italian government took the dangers posed by possible reactions of the PCI and rank-and-file communists to the attempt on Togliatti's life quite seriously. Already in his first public response De Gasperi did what he could to defuse the crisis:

> I hope my colleague the Honorable Togliatti can quickly resume his activities and his fight for the ideas that inspire him by exercising his rights to free debate and [participating in] the parliamentary democracy. The attack, abhorrent in itself, is meant not only against the person of the Honorable Togliatti but in the end targets the democratic system, creating an atmosphere of hatred and resentment, in which the call to force, to violence, to revolt makes impossible every effort to reconstruct a peaceful democracy in Italy. Facing this deplorable attack we reaffirm our faith in the democratic system and in the fair competition of parties for the progress of liberty and social justice.[116]

What the Christian Democratic–led government could not know then was that the communists faced total disarray in their ranks about how to react. The attempt on Togliatti's life brought a number of tensions on the Italian left to a head. For many communist workers in the northern regions, the act marked the ultimate insult to the PCI and its work toward improving the status of Italian labor within the framework of Italian democracy. Many union members immediately took to the streets in protest, occupied their factories, and proclaimed a strike. The labor actions had a spontaneous character, and the episodic violence that accompanied them in some places could be attributed both to the behavior of local worker groups and to the more or less aggressive reactions of the local authorities. Due to the strikes and demonstrations, Milan was paralyzed; Genoa's factories and city districts were seized by militant workers; and many cities in the north of the country came to a standstill. Some of the clashes between workers and police were extremely bloody. Generally, however, the government was well-prepared for a potential uprising, and the civil strife did not presage a seizure of power.

Pietro Secchia, who had been itching for a fight with the authorities, especially since losing the election in April, almost immediately after the assassination attempt proclaimed a general strike on behalf of the party directorate of the PCI. Secchia claimed that the government response to the strikes and demonstrations constituted a systematic attack on the working class, threatening "democracy and liberty" among the Italian people and designed "to provoke [a] civil war."[117] Labor confederation leader and PCI member Giuseppe Di Vittorio, who arrived back from the United States the night of the attempt on Togliatti's life, was unhappy about the fait accompli of the general strike. He believed, as did many of his comrades in the union leadership and in the PSI and PCI, that the unions were not properly prepared for it, and that it might therefore well fail and result only in bloody repression. The Italian army and the carabinieri were known to be loyal to the government and could easily be mobilized to crush the workers. In a tense meeting with De Gasperi on the morning of July 15, Di Vittorio promised to call off the general strike but demanded a guarantee of amnesty from the Italian president Luigi Einaudi for the thousands of strikers who were under arrest and faced potential prosecution. Unlike some members of his government, De Gasperi understood that the general strike was not a communist conspiracy intended to overthrow the government. He agreed to guarantee that individual workers would only be tried for specific crimes.[118]

In meetings of PCI leaders at the Soviet embassy it quickly became apparent that the Kremlin also disapproved of the general strike, fearing that it might provoke a larger conflict.[119] Tensions with the West were high already, given the February Czechoslovak coup, the Soviet walkout from the Allied Control Council for Germany on March 20, and the increasing restrictions on Allied access to Berlin in the spring and early summer of 1948. Problems with the Yugoslavs were coming to a head, and while the prospect of a Soviet intervention to aid the Italian communists was unlikely, to say the least, Moscow worried as much as the Italian government about potential Yugoslav military intervention in Italy in the case of an uprising. Even Secchia thought, as he told the Soviet ambassador Kostylev, that the best possible outcome of an all-out struggle with the government was communist control of the north and middle of Italy, "while the forces of reaction will keep Rome and the territory south of Rome."[120] The American assessment of the balance of forces was very much the same, and neither side relished the scenario. As a consequence, the PCI directorate, which was coordinating its activities with Di Vittorio, called off the strike on July 16, declaring that it had accomplished its goals of demonstrating that the working class could assert its rights against the government.

With scattered exceptions of continuing worker militancy, the situation in Italy returned to normal. Ninety-two thousand people had been arrested, with some seventy thousand of them slated to be brought to trial. Fourteen people, seven of them policemen, had been killed during the disturbances, and 206 were wounded, 120 of them policemen.[121] While Minister of Interior Scelba could finally assure De Gasperi that the situation was under control, the prime minister fretted that the communists could always stage an uprising that would establish a dictatorship. At the same time, De Gasperi was unwilling either to outlaw the PCI, convinced that it had not sought the overthrow of the government, or to create a "second De Gaullism" of the right, which would have meant the erosion of Italian democracy and of the Christian Democratic Party itself.[122]

As he emerged from his hospital bed, Togliatti himself made it clear that the policies of the party would not change. "Calm down," he told his comrades, "don't lose your heads."[123] Togliatti recovered quickly and continued his advocacy of a gradualist strategy in domestic politics. He had to accept one important defeat, when Catholic workers led by Giulio Pastore denounced the general strike, seceded from the communist-dominated labor federation, and formed their own Catholic union in mid-October 1948—the first serious break in the unity of the Italian labor movement. Togliatti's determined efforts to overcome the disappointment of the lost election and the failed general strike were complemented by his attempts within the Cominform to reach an accommodation with the Yugoslav comrades, who had been expelled from the organization by the resolution of June 28, 1948. But his efforts to find points of rapprochement between the Yugoslavs and Moscow, like those of Władysław Gomułka in Poland and Czechoslovak party leader Klement Gottwald, ran afoul of Stalin. Already on July 4, 1948, Stalin had sent Togliatti and Gottwald a note in which he had ordered them not to talk to the Yugoslav "political acrobats" and to let the Cominform resolution condemning Tito and the Yugoslavs speak for itself. As for the invitation to the Yugoslav party congress which Tito had issued to the Italians and a number of European communist leaders shortly before in an obvious attempt to break out of the isolation imposed by Moscow, Stalin instructed them that they should turn it down in any way they wanted.[124] The Soviet leader was determined to deal with Tito and the Yugoslav renegades in his own fashion—including, as access to former Soviet party archives has revealed, a series of planned assassination attempts on Tito.[125]

· ·

Stalin was not particularly happy with Togliatti, yet he could not find a graceful way to remove him from the leadership of the PCI, especially because of the wide popularity and respect the senior Italian communist enjoyed within the Italian party as well as in broad leftist circles of Italian society. At the end of 1950, when Togliatti was in Moscow to recover from an automobile accident, Stalin suggested to the Italian leader that he take over the leadership of the Cominform. But Togliatti would have none of it and did not hide his pique at being asked to step down from the helm of the party he had worked so hard to turn into a mass organization.[126] In a letter to Stalin of January 4, 1951, Togliatti stated his reasons for staying at the leadership of the PCI as follows: First, he did not want to weaken the PCI, for which his own person was of major symbolic importance. Second, he did not want to undermine in any way the "national" character of the PCI by his moving from Italy to Moscow. And third, he wanted to stay where his work would have the greatest effect and that was, he was convinced, in his own country.[127]

Under the impression of the fears of an insurrection that had accompanied the election and the threat of a nation-wide uprising led by the PCI which had become palpable in the wake of the assassination attempt on Togliatti, the American government stepped up its already considerable presence in Italy. Since the country was seen as critical to NATO's position in the Mediterranean, the United States was committed to supporting the Italian government in every way possible to keep the PCI from gaining power and influence in the Italian peninsula.[128] When the Italian municipal elections of 1951 yielded a voter breakdown similar to that of the national elections of April 1948, Washington was distraught that all the economic aid and political advice that had been lavished on Italy in the years since the momentous national election had accomplished so little in changing voting patterns. The United States experienced the same disappointment in the elections to the French Chamber of Deputies in 1951, when the PCF showed consistent support among the electorate. American government officials decided that it was not enough just to support the Italian and French anti-communist parties and military institutions. The deputy director of the CIA, Allen Dulles, went so far as to suggest in September 1951 that the purpose of American and NATO policy should be "to cripple" the communist parties of Italy and France, "to uncover their true intentions, to sow discord in their ranks and promote defection, to deprive them of privilege and respectability, and to drive them underground."[129] On the part of the Americans, this was no longer a matter of competing propaganda claims, but an all-out covert attempt to dislodge the communists from western Europe, as the Soviets had eliminated the noncommunist opposition from eastern Europe in the late 1940s, though without the same level of violence.

The Italian elections of April 1948 represented an important new stage in the development of the U.S. commitment to countering communist influence in western Europe and the coming of the Cold War. The victory of the Christian Democrats gave Washington the confidence that it could combat communist subversion with its own form of clandestine struggle. U.S. policy was now committed to fighting communism in Europe and eliminating potentially crippling internal civil strife in Italy and France, in particular. Meanwhile, both De Gasperi and Togliatti, though from opposite ends of the ideological spectrum, continued their commitment to Italian democracy. Togliatti's goal was to increase the PCI's influence at the local and provincial levels as a way to build electoral strength for new national elections. Stalin wanted more from Italy, counting on the PCI's electoral strength and Moscow's own subversive activities in Italy to advance Soviet interests in Europe. The elections of 1948 and the events surrounding the attempt on Togliatti's life indicated that they still had much to hope for from the country and its Communist Party.

CHAPTER FIVE

THE BERLIN BLOCKADE

1948–1949

The history of the Berlin blockade provides inspiring images of cowboy pilots dropping candy to the wide-eyed eager children of Berlin, of brave Berliners hovering around their cooking stoves for the two nighttime hours a day they had for using electricity, and of the U.S. Commander General Lucius Clay looking every bit as worn and gaunt as the hungry population he sought to feed through the miraculous airlift. There is no question that such a dramatic portrayal of the blockade and airlift ("Operation Vittles," as the pilots dubbed it) captures important aspects of this seminal crisis of the early Cold War.[1]

Yet these popular images can easily obscure the role of the blockade in the development of Soviet policy in Germany. Perhaps more importantly, they can lead us to neglect the significance of the German reaction to Soviet initiatives on the continent. During the blockade, the Western Allies—and the Americans in particular—committed themselves to the maintenance of West Berlin as an outpost in the middle of Soviet-controlled eastern Germany, a commitment that turned Berlin into a flashpoint for Cold War tensions on the European continent for decades to come. On the heels of the lifting of the blockade, on May 23, 1949, the Federal Republic of Germany ("West Germany") was created, and, almost in lockstep thereafter, on October 7, 1949, the German Democratic Republic ("East Germany"). These were not just administrative and legal state entities but two separate societies of survivors of a terrible dictatorship and a ruinous war that had defiled the German people and destroyed their cities, the families, and their livelihoods.

There may be some exaggeration in General Curtis LeMay's description of the Germans' situation when he arrived in Berlin in fall 1947. But it is worth recalling how bleak the future looked for them:

The war had been over for more than two years, but the Germans were still in a state of utter shock. They looked like zombies, like the walking dead. . . . There was an eternal nothingness about the place: nothing happening, no work going on; nothing much to eat at home. People sat and stared. . . . When you passed, their eyes followed you, but blankly, blankly. There was no response, no enlivening humanity in any countenance. The place was bewitched.[2]

The Allied occupation, American, British, and French, not to mention Soviet, did little to improve the Germans' mood. As chief of the Policy Planning Staff in the State Department, George Kennan wrote on February 28, 1948,

They [the Germans] are emerging from the phase of the post-hostilities period in a state of mind which can only be described as sullen, bitter, unregenerate, and pathologically attached to the old chimera of German unity. Our moral and political influence over them has not made headway since the surrender. They have been impressed neither by our precepts nor by our example.[3]

Both LeMay and Kennan were subject to particularly American perspectives of Germans at the time, but their views also capture the desolation and hopelessness that overwhelmed German society in this period.

Bombed-out and hungry, Berlin, the former Nazi capital—in Hitler's mad plans, the future capital of the world—was particularly prone to this mood. The terrible violence involved in the taking of Berlin and its occupation by the Soviets was gradually brought under control. But despite providing some upswing to the economy, especially black-market activities, the Four-Power occupation of the city compounded the moral and spiritual problems that were produced by the Nazi defeat. Along with this came a deep pessimism, reflected in the conviction of two-thirds of Berliners that there would be another war within a generation.[4]

Germans had a "strangely distant relationship to the events of their own epoch," wrote the author Alfred Döblin, who had returned to Berlin after the war. They could only focus on the needs of daily life and lacked perspective on the destruction that they themselves had brought about.[5] Ironically, at least for Germans in the western sectors, the Berlin blockade and the physical suffering it brought to the people of the city provided the kind of jolt they needed to rally their spirits and defend the values of freedom and justice that most observers suggested they had lost.

The currency reform of June 1948, which coincided with the beginning of the blockade and indeed was one of its major causes, worked miracles at invigorating the economic life of the western zones. The blockade turned Germans in the western sectors of Berlin into West Berliners. Responding to the political and existential challenges that the Soviets forced on them, they joined ranks with the Americans and British (less so with the reluctant French) to forge the identity of West Berlin. By embracing the new economic opportunities and allying themselves with the West, the Germans pulled themselves out of the trance described by LeMay. There would be further challenges and other difficult times, but after 1949 there was no question that West German society had learned to respond.

Stalin and Germany

There is still a great deal we do not know about Stalin's intentions and aims when he ordered his troops to interfere with Allied access to Berlin in the spring of 1948 and then to implement a general blockade of the western sectors in the second half of June.[6] From a number of declassified Soviet military documents and post-Soviet interviews with veteran leaders of the occupation, we learn that throughout the time of the blockade Stalin neither placed his forces in the Soviet zone on a war footing nor mobilized additional Red Army troops at home. There were no plans for reinforcing the troops in the Soviet zone, and training and military exercises during the period of the blockade were routine.[7]

Despite the intensified border controls and surveillance that enforcing the blockade required, Stalin did not inveigh on the East Germans to increase their police and paramilitary forces. Contemporary CIA reports also indicated that neither the Soviet military nor East German police were preparing for a major military confrontation.[8] This did not prevent the Pentagon and the Joint Chiefs of Staff from expressing serious worries about the coming of war and the lack of preparedness for dealing with a Soviet attack. Altogether, there is little evidence, at least until an important 1951 meeting in Moscow with his East European allies, that Stalin thought war with the United States might be imminent.[9] Certainly before the first successful Soviet nuclear bomb test, in August 1949, Stalin was cautious in the extreme about confronting the West.

Almost everything about Soviet behavior during the blockade itself indicates that Stalin was using it to further his general aims in Germany and not to provoke a military conflict with the West. The Soviets after all refrained from imposing a total blockade on the city, which would have included interrupting not only all supply and transportation routes but also water, electricity, sewer, and gas networks and would certainly have caused widespread starvation and disease. The Soviet forces did not even try to interfere with air traffic during the airlift nor did they interfere with the Allies' radar system for air traffic control in Berlin. Instead of taking potentially much more radical measures, they thus exerted carefully calibrated pressure on the Allies and German authorities in western Berlin.[10]

At the same time, it is hard to call Stalin's moves in the blockade a "policy," since serious diplomatic approaches were for the most part suspended during the actual crisis; instead, it was, in the words of a Russian historian of the period, "a very crude and one-sided administrative action."[11] The ultimate goal was to prevent the formation of a separate West German state, which the Western Allies had been working toward over the first half of 1948. The minimum goal was to evict the Western Allies from Berlin, which would have allowed the Soviets to consolidate their hold on the eastern zone and provided them with an easy propaganda victory.[12]

During World War II, the leaders of the Grand Alliance had bandied about ideas of carving up Germany into smaller units so as to prevent the Germans from causing another war on the continent. There was consensus that Austria would be decoupled from Germany and that the bulk of German territories in the East, including at least parts of East Prussia, Silesia, and Pomerania, would be given to Poland in compensation for Polish eastern territories claimed by the Soviet Union. In addition, Germany would be subject to de-Nazification, de-cartelization, demilitarization, and forceful democratization measures. As the war came to an end, none of the Allies was willing to initiate further territorial partitions of Germany. None of them wanted to be accused by the Germans of denying their country a minimum of territorial integrity. Stalin, like Roosevelt and Truman, sought to make junior partners out of the Germans, not perpetual enemies. Moreover, all of them worried that a series of small German statelets might ultimately give rise yet again to a fiercely revanchist Germany. Still, Stalin led the Allies in their joint program of dismantling the Third Reich. Austria was separated from Germany, the Polish border was moved westward to include Silesia and parts of Pomerania, and East Prussia was divided between Poland and the Soviet Union.

At the Potsdam Conference in July and August 1945, the Big Three reaffirmed their commitment to the reconstruction of a unified German state, one that would be treated as a single economic entity. Yet in a fateful decision, the Soviets, Americans, and British also agreed that each occupying power (including France, which was given an occupation zone as well) would be free to draw reparations from its own zone, which effectively nullified this principle.[13] At the Yalta Conference in February 1945, the Allies had agreed to extract from Germany reparations in the sum of roughly $20 billion, half of which would go to the Soviet Union. By the end of the war, however, the Western powers, unwilling to further impoverish the citizens of a thoroughly demolished country, quickly abandoned this plan. For the Americans and the British (the French did extract considerable sums from their zone of occupation), this policy change was motivated less by worries about the well-being of the Germans in their zones than by the unwillingness to pay for the minimal upkeep of the German populations in their own zones out of their own budgets. Meanwhile, the Soviets used the agreement at Potsdam to remove German industry and eventually to demand huge quantities of finished goods as reparations from the Soviet zone.

Stalin paid a great deal of attention to what he called the Potsdam principles. Whenever the Soviets accused the West of misdeeds in the Four-Power administration of Germany, they condemned these as violations of the sanctity of Potsdam. Yet the question arises just how interested the Soviets were in the territorial integrity of Germany. Some historians maintain that the Soviet wartime plans for dividing up Germany into small statelets simply morphed into a determination to divide the country between a Soviet occupation zone and the West.[14] By controlling the eastern part of the country, the Soviets could deprive Germany of its ability to challenge Soviet hegemony on the continent and at the same time extract reparations as they saw fit. Moreover, the Soviets could transform the eastern part of Germany along the lines of the "people's democracies" that were being created everywhere in the eastern half of the continent under Moscow's tutelage. This new Germany could conceivably serve as a counterweight to the incipient West German state emerging from the three zones in the West and, in the event of serious economic or social problems, might just surrender its sovereignty to the Soviet-controlled and supported entity of the East.

Although there is scattered evidence for this kind of argument about Stalin's thinking, it seems more likely that the Soviet dictator was—at least for the first two or three years after the end of the war, and even thereafter—averse to the idea of dividing Germany between east and west, especially since the eastern part was both significantly smaller, with roughly one-third the territory of Germany and one-fourth of its population, and less capable of operating independently than the rest of Germany. If the western zones could look at the Ruhr as a potential engine for economic growth and revival, the eastern zone had more economic perspectives, not to mention that the divided Four Power city of Berlin was located in its center. Moreover, as Stalin correctly foresaw, the western sectors of Berlin could be used for espionage and for attempting to destabilize the Soviet presence in eastern Germany and in east central Europe as a whole.

Much preferable from Stalin's point of view would have been a united Germany, one that was weakened politically and economically by the dismantling and removal of industries, the financial burdens of reparations, the elimination of its Nazi and "reactionary" officialdom, and the destruction of it war-making potential. Stalin was not all that interested in the institutionalization of Soviet-style "socialism" in Germany. As elsewhere on the continent, he envisioned forming a progressive "national front" and a potential "new democracy," a planned transition stage between bourgeois democracy and socialism.[15] Even if his political visions for the future of Germany were challenged by the West, the Soviets, given their overwhelming superiority in ground forces in central Europe, would still be able to control the destiny of Germany and ensure its friendly "neutrality." Like Finland, though much more crucial to the fate of Europe as a whole, Germany would thus be denied to the West and controlled through Moscow's military preponderance and ability to intervene whenever necessary.

As the West began to develop its ideas of an independent West Germany in late 1947, in part as a reaction to Soviet political and economic initiatives in the East, in part as a way to deal with the growing economic malaise in western Germany and Western Europe, Stalin began to doubt the potential success of his Germany policy. Serious differences between the East and West had become apparent during the July 1947 meeting of the sixteen prospective participants in the European Recovery Program (Marshall Plan), where representatives of Bizonia (the British and U.S. combined zonal government) presented their claims for economic help. At the time, Molotov had protested: "Under the guise of formulating a plan for the reconstruction of Europe, the initiators of the conference in fact desire to establish a Western bloc with the participation of western Germany."[16]

The abysmal failure of the London Council of Foreign Ministers Meeting in November and December 1947 indicated that these differences could not be bridged. While the Soviets proposed to unify Germany and extract reparations from it, the three Western powers insisted on the integration of the western zones of Germany with each other and their joint participation in the Marshall Plan. Neither could the Soviets convince their former allies to halt the process of creating a distinct German entity in the West, nor were they prepared to compromise with them. Finance and politics worked hand in hand in placing the future of Germany on two disparate tracks.

The diplomatic stalemate prompted the Western Allies to concretize their plans for creating a separate West German administrative unit, not least to supervise the implementation of a much needed currency reform. Beginning in February and March 1948, they met, together with representatives of the three Benelux countries, at the London Conference. By late spring, they had agreed on the creation of a West German state, its inclusion in the Marshall Plan, and its participation in the Western European Union, a collective defense organization that came about as a result of the March 1948 Treaty of Brussels. To Stalin, the London decisions were anathema, since they violated the Potsdam principles of four power decision-making about Germany and of treating Germany as a single economic unit, both of which he had counted on to keep some modicum of control over the evolution of Germany as a whole. "The decisions of the London Conference," Molotov wrote to Stalin, "are directed towards accomplishing the division of Germany."[17] The anger that Western initiatives in Germany elicited among the Soviet leadership was typified in a memorandum from A. Smirnov, head of the third European Section of the Ministry of Foreign Affairs, to Soviet foreign minister Molotov, dated March 12, 1948: "The Western powers seek to turn Germany into their stronghold and to include it in their newly formed military-political bloc directed against the Soviet Union and the new democracies." Smirnov added that simple protests were no longer enough: the Soviets had to "actively interrupt their plans."[18]

Three days earlier, Stalin had already recalled Marshal V. D. Sokolovskii from his post as head of the Soviet military administration in Berlin to Moscow to discuss limiting communications between the western occupied zones of Germany and Berlin. While Stalin did not call a politburo meeting to discuss this issue, the Soviet leader weighed a variety of possible courses of action, including imposing transportation restrictions on Allied access to Berlin, with both military and political leaders during frequent consultations at the Kremlin about possible courses of action.[19]

Since diplomatic efforts had failed to stop the Western Allies from pursuing their plans to form a West German political entity, Stalin was determined to undertake more palpable measures—short of war—to force them back to the bargaining table. As a first step directed against the Allied authorities, in January and February of 1948 the Soviets stopped and delayed trains on their way to Berlin from the west, inspecting freight and personal documents when they had not done so before. These disruptions were annoying but not particularly problematic for the Western Allies, who were expecting some Soviet response to their preparations for creating a Western German state and introducing a separate currency reform.[20] Yet these initial inconveniences were merely the prelude to the most serious confrontation of the immediate postwar period.

The Blockade

By early March 1948, it was clear that Marshal Sokolovskii had orders to increase the pressure on the Allies to back away from their commitment to Berlin. In the eastern zone, the Soviet and East German authorities confiscated literature from the West, although the Four Powers had agreed on the free circulation of printed materials both in the East and West. They harassed German and Allied citizens for little reason and at any opportunity. The practice of kidnapping political opponents and critical journalists from the western sectors to the east seemed to grow more intense and frightening. Acrimonious attacks in both the Allied Control Council and Berlin Kommandantura (the Allied governing body of Berlin) became more pronounced. The Soviets did not try to limit air flights in and out of Berlin, but an April 17, 1948, memorandum from two of Sokolovskii's deputies stated, "[W]e intend to institute [such restrictions] later."[21] Still, it is fair to say that no full-scale blockade of Berlin was yet planned.[22]

"Within the last few weeks," wrote General Clay on March 5, "I have felt a subtle change in Soviet attitude which I cannot define but which now gives me a feeling that it [war] may come with dramatic suddenness."[23] This is just what Stalin wanted Clay to feel, calculating that the overwhelming Soviet preponderance in ground forces in central Europe would convince American military leaders that sticking their necks out because of Berlin was not a good idea. Stalin correctly calculated that there were many in Washington—and particularly in the Department of Defense, Secretary of the Army Kenneth Royal and Army Chief of Staff Omar Bradley among them—who believed that the Germans were not worth a war with the Soviets, and even if they were, that the military was completely unprepared to fight battle-tested Soviet troops in Europe.[24] Soviet intelligence was reporting to Stalin that the Americans were ready to pull out of Berlin.[25] As of February 29, 1949, the Soviets still had some half million men in Germany alone, far outweighing the 160,000 U.S. and 120,000 British troops in the western zones.[26]

The Joint Chiefs of Staff and the Central Intelligence Agency believed that neither the airlift nor Clay's proposals for breaking through the blockade on the ground could solve the Berlin problem. The State Department was also skeptical. Robert Murphy, political advisor for Germany, wrote in March 1948 that Clay was "psychologically" mesmerized by tensions with the Soviets, too anxious to "reorganize" the West German zones, and too ready to advocate the use of force in dealing with the issue of access to Berlin.[27] Still, the Washington foreign policy establishment did not want to be pushed out of Berlin. The influential senator Arthur Vandenberg stated that there was no way to get out of Berlin "under satisfactory circumstances."[28]

James V. Forrestal, secretary of defense, came up with a similar formulation on behalf of the Joint Chiefs of Staff. Committed to making an airlift work while preparing for the eventuality of war, he noted that "some justification might be found for withdrawal of our occupation forces from Berlin without undue loss of prestige."[29] The CIA was one of the most pessimistic Washington agencies about the Berlin crisis, predicting that "any of the courses predicated on the Western Powers' remaining in Berlin is likely in the long run to prove ineffective. The Western position in the city would increasingly deteriorate and ultimate Western withdrawal would probably become necessary."[30]

On March 20, 1948, Marshal V. D. Sokolovskii, commander of the Soviet forces and head of the Soviet military government in Germany, staged a Soviet walkout from the Allied Control Council and, as its chairman at that point, effectively ended its functioning. Meanwhile, the harassment of Allied trains to and from Berlin intensified. The Soviets ordered not only that passenger trains be stopped, travel documents checked, and baggage subjected to inspection but also that each freight train receive formal permission to pass through the Soviet zone. This violated a series of informal and makeshift agreements about guaranteed Allied access to Berlin that had been in place for almost three years (apparently, there was nothing binding on paper).[31] But Clay agreed to provide documentation on the personnel and freight that was transported through the corridors. "However," he wrote to the Pentagon in March, "the right of free entry into Berlin over the established corridors was a condition on precedent to our entry into Berlin and to our evacuation of Saxony and Thuringia, and we do not intend to give up this right of free entry. I regard this as a serious matter because it is my intent to instruct our guards to open fire if Soviet soldiers attempt to enter our trains."[32]

Clay tested the Soviets by sending in military transport trains to Berlin, ordering the personnel to refuse inspection. But these were shunted off to side rails and forced to return to their zone. Clay was still convinced that the Soviets were bluffing and suggested that an armed military convoy be sent to Berlin through the zone, with orders to shoot if Soviet guards tried to stop the convoy. Yet U.S. Army chief of staff General Omar Bradley was so alarmed by Clay's plan (which became known as the "shoot our way into Berlin" policy) that he wrote, "Had I had enough hair on my head to react, this cable would probably have stood it on end."[33]

Meanwhile, Clay had already been flying supplies in and out of Berlin as a way to get around some of the restrictions on the ground. When two further trains were shunted off on side rails on April 1, he suspended rail traffic altogether. Unwilling to obey the Soviets' orders, he decided to "lay on" an airlift instead, which, he stated in a cable to Bradley "will meet our needs for some days."[34] General Albert Wedemeyer, director of combat operations and strategy for the general staff of the U.S. Army at that time, later took credit for the idea of the airlift, which he had employed during World War II in China.[35] This was the beginning of the "Little" airlift, sometimes also called the "Baby" airlift, whose purpose was to provide the Western forces with sufficient supplies and food to support their mission in Berlin.[36]

Just as Stalin would ratchet up the pressure on the Allies and, starting in June, on the Germans in Berlin, Clay increased the capabilities of the airlift as a way to supply his troops and the city. Seeing the situation in Berlin in the context of the communist takeover in Prague in February 1948, the bleak outlook at the time for Finnish independence, and the critical upcoming Italian elections (on April 18), he felt that he was in the middle of a battle for freedom in Europe. Clay also rejected out of hand the Pentagon's suggestion that he fly American family members out of Berlin; he wanted to show no signs of weakness and no hints that the Americans might abandon the city. "[The] German people—would be frightened elsewhere," he wrote, "but in Berlin [they] might become hysterical and rush to communism for safety."[37] He made sure that his interlocutors in Washington recognized Berlin's importance as an outpost of freedom and a "symbol of the American intent."[38] Anticipating what was to come, he told Bradley on April 11,

> I do not believe that we should plan on leaving Berlin short of a Soviet ultimatum to drive us out by force if we do not leave. At that time we must resolve the question as to our reply to such an ultimatum. The exception which could force us out would be the Soviet stoppage of all food supplies to [the] German population in western sectors. I doubt that [the] Soviets will make such a move because it would alienate the Germans almost completely, unless they were prepared to supply food for more [than] two million people.[39]

On June 7, 1948, the London Conference issued a final communique that called for elections to a constituent assembly in the West and the creation of the Basic Law, which would serve as the constitutional backbone of the new federal entity. For many West German politicians and public intellectuals, this new state still was a provisional one, given the temporary, they hoped, absence of the eastern zone and Berlin. The Soviets, predictably, were outraged. They saw these moves, quite correctly, as a departure from the 1945 Four Power agreements about the future of Germany. The Western Allies responded, somewhat disingenuously, that the German states of the Soviet zone could join the new federal entity if they wished. Soviet propaganda dismissed the Western fiat and excoriated the Western powers for violating the Potsdam Agreement and undermining the unity of Germany with their actions. Many

German political leaders agreed and were concerned that moving forward on the London Conference measures would mean the permanent division of their country. German politicians also generally opposed the proposed internationalization of the Ruhr and limitations on their foreign and defense policies.[40]

Stalin tried to use the appeal of a "unity" platform to mobilize the Germans against the Allied "splitters." In a late March 1946 conversation with Wilhelm Pieck and Otto Grotewohl, the leaders of the Socialist Unity Party, the SED (created through the forcible merger of the German Communist Party and the Social Democratic Party in the Soviet zone in April 1946), Stalin had made it clear that they should not, on their part, form a separate government in the east but rather develop some "surrogate or better embryonic" institutions of an all-German character. Even more importantly, they should work out a constitution for all of Germany that would appeal to both the West and the East, neither too democratic nor too restrictive. "This would be very good. It would form the psychological basis," Stalin stated, "for the realization of a united Germany." Don't just talk unity, Stalin admonished the East German leaders, take concrete steps toward accomplishing it. "The British and the Americans are trying to buy the Germans by putting them in a privileged position. Against this there is only one means—prepare the minds of the people for unity."[41]

The successful currency reform in the western zones, which was formally announced on June 18 and introduced on June 20, soon demonstrated to the Germans the advantages of integration into the West.[42] Political change was accelerated by monetary reform. Negotiations between the currency experts of the Four Powers on June 22 broke down, as it became clear that the Soviet side would only accept the Soviet zone currency for Berlin, in effect seizing control of the finances of the city. The chief of the financial administration of the Soviet military government, Pavel Maletin, threatened his Western counterparts, "We warn you as well as the German population of Berlin that we will impose economic and administrative sanctions that will force the transition to a single currency in the Soviet zone of occupation."[43]

Without consulting Washington, Clay went ahead and initiated the introduction of the new Western currency in the western sectors of

Berlin on June 23. Colonel Frank Howley, commandant of the American sector, ordered the Berlin municipal government to ignore the Soviet order to use exclusively the new Soviet-sponsored currency.[44] The British agreed with the Americans; both hornswoggled the reluctant French into going along.[45] But the Western commitment to reforming the currency in their sectors was less forceful than in western Germany. No sooner than the financial institutions in the western sectors of Berlin started adjusting bank accounts to the new German mark, the American military government announced that the Western powers were ready to reverse the decision for introducing the German mark.[46]

With no agreement on the currency question from the Western powers, Stalin finally imposed a full-scale blockade of the western sectors of Berlin, closing down all land, railway, and canal traffic in and out of the city. This took place on the night of June 23, under the pretext that "technical problems" prevented normal passenger and freight service on the Berlin to Helmstedt rail line. Quickly, similar technical reasons were given for closing down road and canal access to the city. Delivery of electricity to the city was also drastically cut back. Meanwhile, Sokolovskii implemented the long-planned currency reform in the Soviet zone of occupation, with plans to spread it to all of Berlin on June 24. In short, both the East and the West planned a currency reform in their zones that they sought to implement in Berlin. The situation, George Kennan wrote in his memoirs, "was dark and full of danger."[47]

In a note to the U.S. government of July 14, the Soviets claimed that they had no choice but to cut off Berlin from the western zones in order to protect the economy of the eastern zone. But they also tried to convince the Western powers that it would be best for the Berliners to share one currency with eastern Germany. The introduction of a Western currency in the western zones of the city was unacceptable when all of the surrounding territory would have a different currency. The note added that "if necessary, the Soviet government has nothing against supplying from its own means 'Greater Berlin' with sufficient provisions."[48]

Some historians of the blockade have appropriately pointed out that West Berlin was by no means completely cut off economically from the surrounding Soviet zone.[49] Despite intensified border controls, black-market entrepreneurs managed to bring goods and foodstuffs into the city from the nearby farms. Gradually, the Soviets were able to suppress much of the black-market activities, but still, goods found their way into the western zones thanks to a variety of subterfuges thought out by inventive Berliners and abetted by corrupt or indifferent (even sometimes sympathetic) East German police. The Soviets also continued to supply restricted materials on contract to factories in the western sectors, and they offered to supply milk to western zone infants in exchange for manufactured goods.[50] In addition, the Soviets offered rations to western sector inhabitants, for which, however, the Berliners in the west had to register in the east. Besides, after some initial interference with air traffic in April, the Soviets did not take any actions to obstruct the airlift.

The West, on its part, immediately imposed a counter-blockade on the Soviet zone, which created, in the words of one SED leader, "serious problems" for Soviet zone industries and undermined the Two-Year Plan, which communist leader Walter Ulbricht would announce with great hoopla in January 1949.[51] Its effects eventually reached the other countries of the newly formed Soviet bloc. Already in June 1948, in response to the closing down of land access to the western sectors of Berlin, General Clay had stopped the delivery of coal and steel from the Ruhr to the Soviet zone. At the same time, Clay continued to encourage inter-sector trade in Berlin. Thus some give-and-take continued even at the height of the blockade during the winter of 1948–1949.

Stalin had no intention whatsoever of starving out the Berlin population with the blockade measures. Few things could have done greater harm to Soviet aims on the continent than Movietone newsreels of hungry, pathetic women and children in Berlin showing in theaters in Rome, Paris, Munich, and London. The blockade was developed in the spring of 1948 as an instrument of Soviet German policy, to be tightened or loosened depending on the circumstances, with offers of food and coal from the east used to entice the West Berliners to join the campaign for a united Germany and abandon the Western Allies' moves to institutionalize a separate West German government and currency. Stalin put pressure not just on the Allies but even more emphatically on the Germans.

Much like his later March 1952 note, in which he offered to withdraw Soviet forces from Germany in return for German neutrality, Stalin used the blockade as a political and propagandistic ploy. In June 1948, he staged the crisis in Berlin as a last-ditch effort to prevent the formation of a German government in the West, just as in 1952 he sought to prevent the West German government from joining NATO. Meanwhile, his minimum goal in 1948 was to prevent the adoption of the new West German currency in West Berlin and to absorb Berlin as a whole into the Soviet zone of occupation, in effect expelling the Western powers. If he had to make do with a weak German statelet in the east, then at least it would have all of Berlin as its capital. Frustrated by the SED's continuous lack of popular support in Berlin and in much of the Soviet-occupied zone of Germany, the East German Communist leader, Wilhelm Pieck, told Stalin during a March 26, 1948, meeting that his party would be glad "if the [Western] Allies were removed from Berlin." Stalin replied, "Let's do it, with our common efforts, let's try, and maybe we'll be successful."[52] A gamble on Stalin's part, no doubt, but one that he and the Soviet leadership had thought through as a way to minimize their losses and perhaps even make some gains on the German question.

There was great optimism among Soviet officials in Berlin that these new limits on transportation would, in Political Advisor Vladimir Semenov's words of June 11, be "a further blow" to the prestige of the Western Allies in Berlin. Reportedly, Sokolovskii's staff were ecstatic about the move. In a telegram to Moscow at the same time, Semenov enthusiastically talked about "smoking" the Allies out of Berlin.[53]

General Clay responded to the June escalation of the Soviet blockade measures by suggesting again to his superiors that the United States call Stalin's bluff by sending an armed convoy through the Soviet zone to Berlin. Rebuffed again, he argued, supported by Murphy, to the National Security Council on June 20 that the airlift could supply Berlin if he could get 160 C-54s, which had a freight capacity of ten tons each, four times as much as the C-47s he was using to supply the city. The air force agreed, and Clay began his preparations to keep West Berlin alive by air.[54] Later in the summer of 1948, Clay also made preparations for a possible Soviet attack, which he thought possible (though highly un-

5.1 Berlin children watch a C-54 airlift plane approach the Tempelhof runway.
GERMAN PICTORIAL COLLECTION, ENVELOPE MN, HOOVER INSTITUTION ARCHIVES.

likely) if the West continued its policy of forming a West German government. Troops and supplies would be assembled on the western bank of the Rhine to prepare for the eventuality of war.[55] Strategic bombers capable of carrying nuclear weapons had been sent to England to counter a potential Soviet attack by bombing Soviet bases. Still, the strong assumption of the American military was that the Soviets, with their overwhelming preponderance of infantry and armored units, could easily take the western zones of Berlin and sweep across Germany.

Despite some skepticism in the Pentagon that Berlin could be supplied by air, President Truman backed Clay's requests for more cargo airplanes. Unlike a number of senior officials in the White House and State Department, Truman clearly sensed the critical symbolic importance of the city to American efforts to stimulate the economic and political development of Europe. Thus the president backed Clay in his determination to hold the line in Berlin, despite Soviet pressure, French wavering, and some skeptical officials in Washington. Truman "read" the Berlin crisis just as Stalin did: as a confrontation of will and prestige in Europe.[56] If Stalin hoped to gain an important victory over the Western powers by driving them out of Berlin, Truman was determined to avoid that loss at all costs short of war.

The Allied Control Council ceased to function in March 1948 as a consequence of the increasingly bitter relations between the Soviet and Western occupation authorities. The Kommandantura, which brought the heads of the Four Powers together for the purposes of administering the city, likewise became the site of mutual accusations and acrimonious exchanges, especially between the Soviet commandant, General A. G. Kotikov, and Colonel Frank Howley, commander of the American sector in Berlin. "To me," Howley wrote, "Kotikov's attacks seemed all part of the new campaign by the Russians to kill the Kommandantura, blame the West for its demise, and then try to drive us out of the city." Unlike the land access routes to Berlin, the three air corridors to the city were agreed upon in writing by the Four Powers in the Allied Control Council on November 30, 1945, and updated by a convention of October 22, 1946.[57]

The confrontation came to a head on July 1, 1948, when Howley stomped out of the meeting, allowing Kotikov to declare an end to the Kommandantura as well.[58] Given the crescendo of hostility between the Soviets and the West over the resolution of the German question, the Four Power machinery that had been set up at the end of the war to deal with Germany and Berlin had proven incapable of resolving serious disputes between the two sides. Even the formerly amiable relations between Generals Clay and Sokolovskii, which had been characterized by much good-natured banter, joking, and entertaining with plenty of food and drink, came to a sudden halt. With the closing of the Allied Control Council and the Kommandantura, the Four Powers ceased to adjudicate their disputes and regulate the actions of their respective German clientele in an institutional format. Now the Allied powers and the German politicians lined up in two firmly opposed camps, fighting with salvoes of mutual press and propaganda attacks for the hearts and minds of the Berlin population.

During the summer of 1948, the Four Powers held episodic meetings to try to deal with the difficult currency issue, and the technical questions related to the blockade (or, as the Soviets called them, "disturbances in the transportation networks"). But there were no signs that the Soviets were ready to alter their stance. At the same time, there were still indications that neither side had entirely ruled out the possibility of a negotiated settlement at the highest level. On the Soviet side, Stalin and Molotov still hoped to extract concessions from the West on the calling of the constituent assembly and the introduction of the new West German currency in Berlin. On the former issue, the Western Allies—the French hedged their bets on some issues—were unwilling to compromise. The constituent assembly was scheduled to meet in mid-September 1949, and nothing, at this point, was going to stop the formation of a West German government short of military confrontation. As George Kennan noted, the work on creating the West German state "assumed an irrevocable character" as the months went by, "and the idea of suspending or jeopardizing it for the sake of a wider international agreement became less and less acceptable."[59] Moreover, the Americans completely rejected the incessant Soviet claim that they had forfeited their rights in Berlin as a consequence of supporting the formation of a German government in the West.[60] Instead, the Western Allies hoped that some concessions on the currency issue in Berlin might bring the blockade to an end and return an acceptable modicum of Four-Power control to the city.

At the beginning of August 1948, Walter Bedell Smith, American ambassador to the Soviet Union, led a delegation of the ambassadors of Great Britain, France, and the United States to meet with Stalin and Molotov in Moscow with the goal of finding a compromise on Berlin.[61] Usually in meetings like this, Stalin played the good cop and Molotov the bad cop, though Smith noted that Molotov was almost excessively gracious: "Stalin and Molotov were undoubtedly anxious for a settlement. Doubt if I have ever seen Molotov so cordial and if we did not know [the] real Soviet objectives in Germany [we] would have been completely deceived by their attitude as both [were] literally dripping with sweet reasonableness and desire not to embarrass."[62]

Stalin, too, was good-natured, affable, and approachable. The Soviet ruler indicated that there were serious grounds to believe that an agreement could be reached, despite the unwillingness of the Western Allies to slow down, much less reverse, the process of the formation of a German government. He did not mind, he said, if the West wanted to integrate their three zones of occupation, and even considered it "progress."[63] The issue was the planned German government. "The Soviet zone also formed a unity but they [the East Germans] had not the right of creating a government there."[64] (Stalin could have added that he had repeatedly rejected initiatives to do so by SED leaders Walter Ulbricht and Wilhelm Pieck.[65]) Stop the London Conference process and withdraw the B-Mark (as the West German currency, marked "B" for Berlin, was called in the western sectors of Berlin), "then there would be no difficulties," he stated.[66] In addition, Stalin brought up the issue that the West was taking "large quantities of equipment" out of the city—but like the so-called "technical issues" associated with the blockade, this was something of a red herring.[67]

The Western ambassadors did express the willingness to delay the implementation of the London decisions until a new meeting of the Council of Foreign Ministers reviewed, at Stalin's request, contentious issues regarding reparations, demilitarization, and the conclusion of a German peace treaty. The real hard nut of the negotiations that prevented a resolution of the crisis came down to the question of which currency would be used in Berlin and who would control its emission. But even here, the two sides reached an apparent consensus at an August 24 meeting of Smith, Stalin, and Molotov. There was no need to extend the use of the new (West) German mark into Berlin. In exchange for the lifting of the blockade, which was to coincide with the lifting of the counter-blockade, the parties also agreed that the new Soviet zone currency would be introduced in all of Berlin and the "B-mark" withdrawn, with the understanding that a "financial commission comprised of representatives of the four [Allied] commanders" would control the issuing and distribution of that currency through an emissions bank.[68]

In short, Berlin would be reconstituted as a Four Power city within the Soviet zone of occupation, using a single currency from an emissions bank that the Western Allies would be able to control along with the Soviets. In the absence of a Western agreement to postpone the implementation of the London agreement, the Soviets refused to sign a communiqué. Instead the ambassadors sent instructions to their respective commanders in Germany to resolve the currency technicalities with the help of a committee of experts.[69] Ambassador Smith explained that the agreement required the commanders "within a week, to find practical ways of doing two things at the same time: lifting the blockade and introducing [the] Soviet currency in Berlin under effective four-power supervision."[70]

Neither Moscow nor Washington had much faith in the outcome of the negotiations. In a telephone communication between General Sokolovskii and his political advisor Vladimir Semenov in Berlin and Molotov in Moscow on August 30, the former pair complained about making concessions to the West, suggesting that the Western powers were only interested in an agreement because the Berliners would quickly tire of their difficult position with the coming of fall.[71] Molotov sent a telegram back to Sokolovskii on August 31, instructing him to "take under consideration the fact that the western representatives above all will try to expand the competencies of the Finance Commission. This should not be allowed."[72]

Ambassadors Smith and Roberts thought that the deal reached in Moscow might work and urged their respective governments to agree. General Clay was justifiably more suspicious; he wanted to be absolutely sure that the West had a constituent role in resolving all currency issues in Berlin. On consultation with Clay, Secretary of State George C. Marshall insisted that U.S. acceptance of a Soviet currency for Berlin was contingent upon a satisfactory agreement regulating the emission and availability of the currency under "some form of quadripartite control."[73]

Despite Stalin's assurances in Moscow, there was little confidence in the West that the Soviet side intended to grant the Allies any significant role in the printing or distribution of the Soviet currency in Berlin.

These misgivings were confirmed in the Four-Power negotiations between the respective commanders on August 31 and September 7. From Molotov's instructions cited above we know that Sokolovskii was not acting on his own when he insisted in these talks that the Soviets would control Berlin's currency. He supported this position with the already familiar assertion that the Western Allies had forfeited their rights to be in Berlin when they had abandoned the Potsdam principles on the unity of Germany and Four-Power control by taking steps toward creating a West German state.[74] The commandants' talks were "getting nowhere," reported Robert Murphy, and were quickly abandoned.[75] Consequently, the "war of words" between East and West intensified in late September and October 1948, with both sides blaming the other for the breakdown of the talks. Even more important in the failure of these negotiations, no doubt, was Stalin's and Molotov's conviction that the coming winter would push the West Berliners to the limit of their endurance and force them to join up with the rest of the Soviet zone in a campaign for German unity. In order to be fed and warm, Stalin no doubt calculated, the Berliners themselves would take the kinds of actions that would delegitimize the Allied presence in Berlin and foster the integration of West Berlin into the rest of the city and the Soviet zone.

The Berliners

Finding provisions grew increasingly difficult for the two million plus population of the western sectors of Berlin in the late summer and fall of 1948 as the Soviets reinforced their previously haphazard control over the borders between the western sectors and the surrounding Brandenburg countryside.[76] They also severely cut back deliveries of food, fuel (both coal and firewood), and electricity to the western sectors. Normal inter-zonal thoroughfares were blocked off by barriers manned by Soviet soldiers and East German police, and automobile traffic back and forth between the western zones of occupation and Berlin was severely limited. The post was delayed and post office rules were changed; parcel deliveries were held up for weeks.[77] Passengers were inspected on stations of the numerous U-Bahn and S-Bahn lines that ran through the eastern and the western sectors.[78] Some commuters, noted one contemporary letter writer, "have their bags taken, purses searched and money (westmarks) seized; one Berliner from the east who wanted to give his mother in West Berlin a potted plant had it taken by the police."[79] Soviet zone residents were given new identity cards as a way of cutting back the traffic between the western sectors of Berlin and the rest of the Soviet zone. Although some deliveries continued, residents of the western sectors most definitely felt the severity of shortages in the late fall. Soviet kidnappings continued to rattle the population, raising levels of tension, and, according to the memoirist Ruth Andreas-Friedrich, contributed to a growing suicide rate, which jumped from one and a half to seven per day. "Kidnapping across the border. Police raids. People being dragged into the other sector. People protest. Shots are fired, stones are hurled. People are arrested. People are wounded. Who is the enemy?"[80] Many Berliners would have fled to the West if they could have. Being "caught" in the city only added to the trauma experienced by the population.[81]

After some initial glitches, including the accidental collision over Berlin of a Soviet YAK fighter and a British passenger plane on April 5, 1948, the airlift itself worked extremely well. Berliners themselves rushed to help where they could. In just three months in 1948, German workers, many of them women, took on the task of building in three shifts, twenty-four hours a day, a third airport (Tegel) in the French sector. General Curtis LeMay, generally skeptical of the Germans' commitment to the West, wrote extremely positively about the work of the German teams: "[I]t would astonish the life out of you to see how quickly those Germans got the sacks out of the airplane; and how soon they helped to get the airplane loaded again."[82]

The Western powers quickly began to feel the propaganda benefits among the Berliners for their efforts to keep the population fed and warm. After Sokolovskii introduced the new Soviet-backed "German mark" in the eastern zone and all of Berlin, the Western Allies forbade its use in their sectors and introduced the B-mark currency, which was specific to the western sectors of Berlin, but was tagged to the German mark in the West, which also began to show up in the West Berlin economy. The value of the B-mark quickly exceeded that of the Soviet

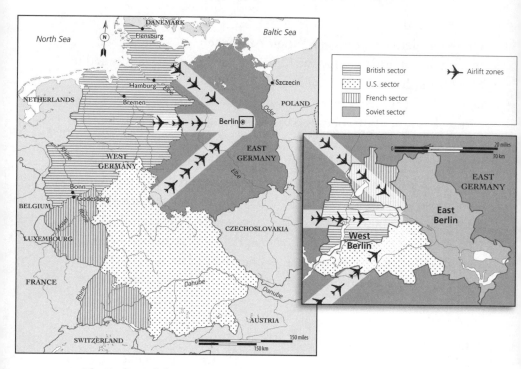

6. The Berlin Airlift

zone currency (roughly at one to three, eventually between one to four and one to five). The Soviets understood that what they denounced as the "Clay-mark" tilted the balance between the economies in the eastern and the western sectors of the city. Those who worked for the western zonal governments and Western-oriented firms, some still located in the eastern sector, found themselves in a privileged position, whereas the opposite was true for those, including West Berliners, who worked in the East, where they were paid in the Soviet currency.[83] Moreover, the best goods from the Soviet zone were smuggled over to the western sectors of Berlin in order to earn B-marks.[84]

As the months went by, the issues involved in the Berlin blockade became obvious to both sides. The Soviets kept telling anyone who would listen that the blockade would be lifted if the proclamation of a West German state were put aside and the introduction of the Western B-mark in Berlin was reversed. Although the Western Allies continued to offer concessions on the currency issue according to what had been negotiated in Moscow, Stalin played his hand to the hilt. He was certain that the Western powers would cave in once they realized that they could not supply the West Berliners with sufficient food and fuel through the airlift to survive the winter. Not even the calling of the constitutional assembly for the new West German state on September 1, 1948, shook his confidence in the plan. While the SED waged a fierce propaganda campaign against the counter-blockade, in their own Russian language newspapers, the Soviets denied that there was a blockade at all, only rarely referring to it as "the so-called blockade," and dismissed the "air bridge" as an "air bluff." According to their propaganda, more was being taken out of Berlin, especially "finished products and other valuable materials," than was being brought in.[85] If Western planes dropped candy and toys for the children of Berlin, then they did so only in order to draw a curtain over the history of the vicious Western bombing campaign against Berlin's children.[86]

As it turned out, Stalin completely miscalculated the effects of the blockade on the population in the western sectors. Since there was already widespread griping and scattered cases of civil disorder, he expected that growing shortages and unemployment would intensify the dissatisfaction of the locals with the Western Allies. Some scholars have speculated that the lack of experience of the Soviets with airlifts made them more skeptical than otherwise of the Allies' potential success.[87] With food and coal supplies assured to their compatriots in the eastern sector, the Berliners in the western sectors would surely put pressure on the Allies to concede, even demanding to join the East. As early as July 20, 1948, *Tägliche Rundschau,* the German-language Soviet newspaper in the East, announced in a full-sided, front-page article, "The Soviet Union will assume the provisions of the people of all of Berlin."[88] Sokolovskii was willing to offer the West Berliners cooking oil, potatoes, and other goods at the same ration norms as were available in the East.[89]

This promise, periodically renewed by the Soviets, required that citizens of western Berlin register in the eastern sector in order to receive the appropriate ration cards. The SED made every effort in their propaganda and organizational activities to entice the West Berliners to enlist in this program. "Mothers! No one needs to be hungry or freeze. Buy in the East" was one of the slogans used.[90] Thousands of West Berliners followed the calls to use Soviet sector ration cards—according to official Soviet statistics 21,802 in August 1948, and a maximum of 99,246 in January of 1949.[91] Yet out of a population of some two million, these were remarkably few enlistees. Many West Berliners were suspicious of the Soviets' motives and feared the consequences of signing up.[92] Many of those who did register in the eastern sector withdrew once it became clear that the airlift could supply enough foodstuffs for survival. The Soviets tried to explain this lukewarm response to their enticement in part by emphasizing the West Berliners' fear of "repressions by the Western powers" and manipulation by "the SPD's furious propaganda campaign." But they also saw that the population in the western sectors was receiving products at a fairly stable rate from the airlift.[93]

The propaganda officials of the Soviet military administration in Germany understood that the airlift itself produced significant propaganda gains for the Western powers. Lt. Col. V. A. Zdorov noted with some frustration that myriad problems experienced by the Berliners at the time were all blamed on "our security measures" (i.e., the blockade): the speculation, the shortages, the closed factories, the unemployment, the lack of heating supplies; these were all seen as "the result of the Russian policy of blockading the city." Zdorov added that the Soviet measures in Berlin led to the "strengthening of the West's position" not just in the western sectors but in the Soviet sector as well. (Sokolovskii wrote in the margins of the report at this point, "Absolutely!")[94] On September 20, 1948, General A. G. Russkikh, deputy commander of the Soviet Occupation Administration for Political Questions, reported to Mikhail Suslov in the Central Committee and General Sergei Shatilov of the Red Army political administration in Moscow:

> The very fact of the daily flights over the city at low altitudes of several hundred heavy transport planes creates a great psychological effect on the German population. [This leads to] the strengthening of the anti-Soviet mood of the western sectors of Berlin.[95]

Russkikh recommended more intense efforts of the SED to demonstrate the nefarious effects of the counter-blockade. But in a report three months later to his superiors in Moscow, the propaganda chief noted that these measures had not yet borne fruit.[96] Especially the results of the December 5, 1948, elections to the city council in the western sectors of Berlin, he wrote, showed that the Anglo-Americans and the "reactionary" SPD had "succeeded in gathering behind them the majority of the population of the western sectors and sharpening the anti-Soviet, anti-SED mood."[97] There was a stunning turnout of some 86 percent of the population. The SPD was the clear winner, with 64.5 percent of the vote (an increase from 50.8 percent in 1946).[98] General Russkikh complained: the population remains "indifferent or even hostile" to us. Then, in a typically contorted Soviet formulation, he noted, "The masses have not succeeded to a sufficient degree in being convinced of the soundness and correctness of [our] position." This attitude makes one think of Berthold Brecht's ironic poem, "The Solution," about the June 17, 1953, uprising in East Germany, which asked, "Would it not be easier / In that case for the government / To dissolve the people / And elect another."

Stalin and the Soviet authorities in Berlin had decided not to allow the eastern sector of Berlin to take part in the local Berlin elections, scheduled for December 1948.[99] Pieck admitted to the Soviets that his party would have been trounced in open elections.[100] Groups of SED agitators even attempted to keep the population of the western sectors from voting in the December election, but to no avail. Instead, the best the Soviets and SED could do was to hope that the difficulties of the winter would erode the confidence of the western sectors in their political parties. But fortunately for the Western suppliers of the city—and for the Western parties vying for power in the elections—the winter of 1948–1949 was relatively mild, especially in comparison to the previous winter and, in particular, to the fierce winter of 1946–1947, one of the coldest in modern German history, when many thousands had died of the cold.

As was their wont, the Soviets combined the carrot (of increased food supplies for the population) with the stick of bullying the local German authorities. In the latter respect, their first move after imposing the blockade was to seize control of the city police force by firing the police chief and replacing him with Paul Markgraf, a well-known communist supporter. This prompted the Western Allies to set up their own German police force for the western zones under Johannes Stumm.[101] The next target was the city administration, the Magistrat. At its seat located at the provisional city hall on Parochialstrasse in the eastern part of the city, Soviet- and SED-inspired crowds held demonstrations against the elected, anti-communist Magistrat leadership, which included the Social Democrats Louise Schroeder as mayor and Ernst Reuter (who had been elected to this post, but was not allowed to assume it because of Soviet opposition), as well as Ferdinand Friedensburg, a Christian Democrat who served as acting mayor. Ultimately, the conflict got so nasty and threatening that the democratic leadership reconstituted their government in the western part of the city, eventually in the Schöneberg city hall in the U.S. sector. If the Soviets' intentions were to force the West German authorities to capitulate to eastern institutions, then their tactics were a failure; if the intention was to cement the division of the city, then one could count their actions a success.[102]

In the political arena, the Soviets' ability to further their cause during the blockade were limited as well. The leaders of the Socialist United Party (SED) realized that despite three years of intense communist propaganda and organizing in Berlin at large they had relatively little leverage over the western sectors of the city. Not only was the party weakly developed in the West, in some parts of the city, General Russkikh reported to his superiors, it was completely paralyzed. As a consequence, neither the SED nor the democratic Magistrat with communist participation could exert "any noteworthy influence" on the views of the western sector population.[103]

As Hermann Matern, a SED leader, told General Kotikov, chief of the East Berlin Soviet administration, "in the Berlin trade union movement, there is a strong tendency to oppose the [SED led-] campaign under the slogan: 'Berlin—a part of the Soviet zone.'" The Independent Union Opposition (UGO), in which the anti-communist SPD held sway, had split off from the Free German Trade Union Federation (FDGB), which had been founded and developed largely under SED auspices since 1945. There were even serious problems with the SED control of the FDGB in the East. As for the SPD in the West, Matern stated, exemplifying the uncompromising stance of many East German communists, "we deal with the leadership of the Berlin SPD on the principle that we cannot have any common efforts with this center of Anglo-American spying."[104] Matern blamed the Western powers for the blockade and attributed the pro-Western and anti-Soviet stance of the population in the western sectors to a "smear campaign without equal."[105] In a greeting to the Women's Congress in the east, Matern called the anti-communist "defamations" of the Social Democrats "worse than those conducted by the Nazis."[106] Otto Grotewohl, an important SED leader, the future first prime minister of the GDR, and a former SPD member, stated that the SED constantly underestimated the strength of the "chauvinist, warlike, anti-Soviet" denunciations from the West and that these made their way even into the SED party ranks.[107]

Due in part to the splendid leadership of Berlin's elected mayor Ernst Reuter, leader of the West Berlin SPD, who had returned to Germany in November 1946 from exile in Turkey, the inhabitants of the western sectors rallied behind the Allied cause. In many ways, this was unexpected, given the hardscrabble existence and anti-occupation attitude of Berlin's population. Convinced that his battered people were fully capable of regeneration, Reuter went about his work "with honest enthusiasm and an unbroken optimism that perhaps only a returned exile could muster," writes his biographer. His skills as a brilliant, charismatic orator and an indefatigable administrator proved invaluable when he had to lead the city's efforts to deal with the overwhelming burdens of the occupation and then the blockade. This he did "with the mixture of sobriety, expertise, closeness to the people, and appeals to collective solidarity that was typical for him."[108] His speeches and writing were inspiring paeans to the need for freedom and the importance of the West Berliners' struggle for their right to sovereignty. Typical was an interview with *Nordwestdeutscher Rundfunk* (NWDR, Northwest German Radio) on August 12, 1948, in which he spoke about the confidence of the Berliners in the Magistrat and City Assembly in the West who "will do everything that is humanly possible, also to survive these times, because we have to survive them, because only when they are surmounted will we be free at last. And that is finally and at long last the goal of our struggle at the moment."[109]

Before launching the airlift, General Clay had a serious conversation with Reuter and asked whether the Berliners would support the action, given the cold and hunger that they would still have to endure, even with Allied support. In what Clay would later consider the most dramatic moment of the blockade's history, Reuter assured him that the Berliners would stand up to the Soviets and take the hardships of the blockade without complaint.[110] Clay knew that the airlift could not succeed if the Germans succumbed to the Soviet's entreaties and bullying. Reuter (and the other democratic leaders of the city) made sure that this would not happen. "You worry about the airlift," Clay reported Reuter telling him, "let me worry about the Berliners."[111]

In fact, Reuter was concerned, as were many Berlin politicians, that Allied support of a West German state might weaken the West's willingness to defend a free West Berlin in the face of overwhelming Soviet pressure.[112] But as he let Clay and others know, he was also determined that the Germans in the western sector resist Soviet encroachments with or without Western help. In fact, the more pressure the Soviets applied, the readier the Berliners seemed to fight back with volunteer work, defense of their freedoms, and enthusiasm for the Western Allies. At an emotional rally at the Brandenburg Gate on September 9, 1948, as many as three hundred thousand people protested against the violence committed against the Magistrat in the East. Reuter called out to the world to look at the city of Berlin and see how its people were ready to defend freedom and liberty. Not just in Germany but internationally his speech was one of the most dramatic—and effective—of the early Cold War period.

Today is the day when it's not diplomats and generals who do the talking or negotiating. Today is the day when the people of Berlin lift their voices. Today, this people of Berlin call the entire world. . . .

You people of the world, you people in America, in England, in France, in Italy! Look at this city and realize that you must not, that you cannot surrender this city and this people. There is only one possibility for all of us: to stand together until this struggle is won, until this struggle is finally sealed at last through the victory over the enemies, through the victory over the power of darkness.

5.2 "Cruel, brutal, aggressive powers will not beat us to our knees": Ernst Reuter addresses a rally in front of the Reichstag, September 9, 1948. GERMAN PICTORIAL COLLECTION, ENVELOPE MN, HOOVER INSTITUTION ARCHIVES.

The people of Berlin has spoken. We have done our duty, and we will continue to do our duty. People of the world! You, too, do your duty and help us in the period that stands before us, not only with the drone of your airplanes, not only with transport capabilities that you have brought here, but with the steadfast and unbreakable commitment to the common ideals which alone can secure our future, and yours as well. People of the world, look at Berlin! And people of Berlin, be certain of this, this struggle we will, this struggle we shall win![113]

While Clay and his supporters worked the corridors of power in Washington, trying to convince the waverers in the administration that Berlin was strategically crucial to the American position in Europe, and with Reuter using his formidable rhetorical and political skills to commit the people of the western sectors of Berlin to resist

Soviet offers of food and succor in the blockaded city, a critical alliance was forged between the leader of the American occupation, who was known to have little truck with Germans as a consequence of the war, and a German Social Democrat (and a communist in the Soviet Union in the early 1920s), who was skeptical of American-style democracy but committed to efficient, freely elected, and effective municipal institutions.[114] Clay's success depended on Reuter and the Germans; Reuter's on Clay and the Americans. In this relationship, Reuter was anything but a puppet of the Americans who merely fulfilled their wishes. He answered such taunts, which emanated from some West German circles, communist and others, himself: "The situation is the reverse, the Americans are the voice of Berlin, because we did not carry out American policy but we caused the Americans to carry out Berlin policy and not to leave Berlin to its fate."[115] Among Germans in the western sectors, meanwhile, expressions of support for the Western Allies only increased as the situation grew more critical. Although a large majority of Berliners in the western sectors—82 percent—worried about the imminence of war in July 1948, almost all—98 percent—stated that the Western powers did the right thing by staying in Berlin.[116]

The commanders of the occupying forces on both sides, meanwhile, were not keen on letting the situation escalate even further. Clay was unhappy about the fact that the British had allowed the huge Reuter-led demonstration at the Reichstag. After the event itself, matters had turned ugly when several hundred Germans converged on the Soviet war memorial near the Brandenburg Gate, throwing stones at Soviet soldiers and East German policemen and spilling across into Pariser Platz in the Soviet zone. When youths managed to tear down the Soviet flag from the Brandenburg Gate and began to rip it up and burn parts of it, several guards from the war memorial rushed over and fired shots into the crowd.[117] Reports vary about how many were killed, but Colonel Howley noted that four demonstrators were buried in the east the following week.[118] Five alleged perpetrators whom the Soviets had seized were promptly tried and convicted to twenty-five years each in prison. General Russkikh, worried about the propaganda consequences, was critical of these "harsh and undifferentiated" sentences.[119]

Clay felt that he could not publicly condemn the German demonstration, which he thoroughly disliked, without undermining the German will to resist the Soviets. At the same time, he suggested instead that he and General Robertson, commander of the British occupation forces, talk secretly to the German leaders to make sure they would thenceforth prevent such demonstrations, which, he feared, could otherwise become routine and eventually turn into violence against the occupation regime as a whole.[120] Clay also worried that the Soviets, if faced with an openly hostile population in West Berlin, might simply decide to take the city by force, which, as everyone agreed, would not have been at all difficult.[121]

The End of the Blockade

Following the failure of the August 1948 Moscow talks to produce a compromise and the subsequent collapse of the commanders' negotiations about the Berlin currency, efforts to lift the blockade and resolve the disputes about Berlin shifted at the end of September 1948 to the United Nations, with the encouragement of Argentinian foreign minister Juan Atilio Bramuglia, who was at that time president of the Security Council. Though Molotov was no fan of the Security Council and would have preferred that the Council of Foreign Ministers take up the Berlin question, he sought to convince Stalin that continuing talks were necessary. The negative publicity following the breakup of the Berlin Magistrat on November 30, he argued, "might leave the impression that we did not want any kind of agreement on the Berlin question," which would have been undesirable.[122] Stalin concurred and agreed to the formation of a UN committee to study the currency situation in Berlin. Its discussions resulted in a compromise solution not unlike the one concluded in Moscow, but with fewer Western controls over the emission bank. Washington's opposition ultimately killed the effort in March 1949. But even earlier, Stalin tried playing good cop once more when answering questions from American journalist Kingsbury Smith on January 27, 1949. This time, he did not bring up the daunting issue of the currency reform at all, suggesting instead that the limitations on transportation to Berlin could be lifted if the counter-blockade was brought to an end.[123]

The UN efforts overlapped with secret talks between Yakov Malik, Soviet ambassador to the UN, and the American deputy chief of mission to the UN and Ambassador-at-Large Philip Jessup. The progress of the talks between Jessup and Malik gave both sides the hope that the situation could be resolved short of war.[124] Stalin, initially through Molotov, supported Malik's efforts to find a compromise with the Americans; Dean Acheson, American secretary of state, similarly supervised Jessup's negotiating stance. At about the same time, significant personnel changes on the Soviet side signaled that Stalin intended to take more active steps in resolving the crisis. In early March, Molotov was replaced as foreign minister by his previous deputy Andrei Vyshinskii.[125] On March 29 Marshal Sokolovskii was replaced as commander of the Soviet zone by General of the Army Vasilii Chuikov. Jessup had asked Malik on February 16 whether Stalin's omission of the demand for a single currency in Berlin in his interview in late January had been intentional.[126] On March 12, Vyshinskii wrote to Malik, "Meet with Jessup and tell him that you have received . . . an explanation from Moscow regarding the Berlin question that interests him. . . . You have the opportunity to inform him that according to the explanation from Moscow it was not an accident that Stalin's answer to correspondent Smith did not contain the mention of a single currency for Berlin."[127]

By the early spring of 1949, it was clear to Stalin that the blockade had not accomplished its goals. With Allied airplanes landing every five to seven minutes at three airports in the western sectors, the city was reasonably well supplied and the Berliners in the western sectors were hardly suffering from a shortage of the essentials. Roughly the same tonnage of supplies was delivered to Berlin by air as had been delivered before the airlift by other transportation means. It seemed that the Western Allies could continue with the airlift indefinitely, which was precisely the impression they wanted to convey to Stalin. On March 20, the Western Allies declared that the German mark would become the only legal currency in the western sectors. A historian of the currency issue exaggerates only slightly when he writes that "this date marks a turning point in the history of postwar Berlin."[128] In reality, there still remained great unease among some officials in Washington about concentrating so much of U.S. military air transportation capacity in and around Berlin and about perpetuating an operation that could trigger an armed conflict at any moment.[129] On March 10, 1949, Murphy wrote to Clay from Washington that there was no doubt "a certain amount of fatigue regarding the Berlin situation"; many officials wanted out of Berlin, and there were even the "backsliders" who were ready to make concessions on the formation of a West German government.[130]

Meanwhile, the counter-blockade was taking its toll on the productivity of the Soviets' own factories in the eastern zone. In short, both the Americans and the Soviets were weary of the conflict. In the Malik-Jessup talks of March 21, the two sides agreed to put the currency issue on the back burner and to take measures to lift both the blockade and the counter-blockade. Each of the Four Powers issued a communiqué on May 5, agreeing on the conditions to bring the blockade to an end. Stalin gave orders to lift the blockade on the same day; on May 10 the politburo formalized the resolution. One day earlier General Chuikov issued Order no. 56, which rescinded all measures related to the blockade and was published in *Tägliche Rundschau*.[131] Clay was determined to keep the airlift going in the case that the Soviets reimposed restrictions on the traffic to Berlin. Supplies for Berlin were to be warehoused in western Germany in anticipation of a new blockade.[132] Both the U.S. Joint Chiefs of Staff and the British Foreign Office insisted on maintaining the men and materiel necessary to quickly bring the airlift back into action.[133]

All in all, 2.35 million tons of goods were delivered to Berlin throughout the airlift. 405 American and 170 British planes were involved—575 altogether, nineteen of which crashed during the period.[134] Most of the 101 fatalities (forty British and thirty-one Americans) were caused by accidents on the ground.[135] Although the Allies did continue the airlift until late September, their fears did not materialize. Stalin shifted his tack on the German problem, launching a highly visible propaganda campaign for peace in the vain hope of keeping Germany out of the Western camp. On May 23, 1949, a new Council of Foreign Ministers meeting, agreed to in the Malik-Jessup talks, took place in Paris to revisit the disputed issues of the status of Germany and the currency situation in Berlin, yet in the end to no avail. There were some concessions on interzonal trade, which was important to both sides.[136]

But the Soviets looked to return to the status quo ante, including the Potsdam principles, while the Americans and British would have none of it. U.S. secretary of state Dean Acheson greeted the Soviet proposals to conclude a German peace treaty with derision. For him, they were "as full of propaganda as a dog is of fleas; in fact it is all fleas and no dog."[137]

Both Berlin and Germany were divided even more than before the crisis had started. Now there was a mobilized population of western Berlin with a sense of Western identity and the élan of a society that had won a battle for its sovereignty after just having lost such a terrible war. As a CIA report at the time put it (note the agency's unceasing skepticism regarding the Germans), "On the Soviet side, the blockade has increased the anti-Soviet sentiment of Germans and temporarily, at least, strengthened their attachment to the Western camp."[138]

• •

Despite his instinctual understanding of the realpolitik inherent in the successful management of foreign affairs, Stalin often misread public opinion on the continent, and especially its fragile relationship with "democracy" and the Western community. Instead of turning their back on the Western Allies, the West Berliners—urged on by their charismatic leader Ernst Reuter—rallied to the side of the Allies despite the serious economic and political pressures on their city. This was critical for turning the airlift not only into a military and logistical success but into a symbol of defiance against the Soviet Union and Stalin. Before the events themselves, it would have been impossible to predict the outcome, as Berliners spent most of their efforts in the daily struggle for economic survival. Postwar escapism was still rampant and the citizens' commitment to politics tenuous. The growing division of the city and the gradual isolation of the western sectors from the eastern sector compounded the indifference many in the western sectors felt toward politics. Paradoxically, the blockade forged the demonstration of political will among the Berliners in the western sectors for the first time since the war. As Frank Howley noted, the Soviets ceased to be an ally of the West; instead the Germans had taken their place.[139]

As a consequence of the blockade, the Western Allies themselves had moved closer together; by the end, even the French, who sometimes shared Soviet policy prescriptions for the Germans and Germany, stood solidly with their British and American allies. As the Paris CFM talks in June 1949 confirmed, they, too, were determined that the Americans stay on the continent to serve European security needs.[140] Differences over Germany paled in comparison. Stalin's ideological disposition had led him to believe that the capitalist West, especially Great Britain and the United States, would come to blows over their rivalries in Europe and around the world. The excellent cooperation between Washington and London during the Berlin crisis proved him wrong.[141] Instead of dividing the West, the blockade contributed to the building of the Atlantic Alliance.[142]

The failure of the blockade left Stalin with no alternative but to accept the fact that a new "Bonn Republic" would soon be born under the protection of the Western powers. In response, he intensified his efforts within Germany along two contradictory lines. First, in a mid-December 1948 meeting in Moscow, he encouraged Pieck, Ulbricht, and Grotewohl to pursue an "opportunistic" policy of advancing the formation of a "provisional German government" in the Soviet zone. This government would not be considered a people's democracy, nor would it institute a dictatorship of the proletariat or join the Cominform.[143] There was, however, talk of building such state-like institutions as a standing military and a State Security Service. In mid-1948, the SED declared itself "a party of a new type," a thoroughly Marxist-Leninist entity to lead the "new democracy" that was being formed in the eastern zone.[144]

The second line of Stalin's efforts was to keep hopes alive to unite all of Germany in the German People's Congress, which had been created in 1947 in the Soviet zone to develop the communist-dominated anti-fascist front into an all-German organization. At the Peoples' Congress second meeting in Berlin in March 1948, the People's German Council (*Deutscher Volksrat*) was proposed to pursue all-German elections and draw up a constitution for all of Germany. The idea of the People's Council was to appeal to German national feeling and to use the issue of German unity to disrupt the Western Allies' plans to form a separate West German state. At the beginning of May 1949, Stalin urged the People's Council to insist on a unified state at the Foreign

Ministers' Conference to take place in Paris later in the month. To no avail. The Western Allies and the West Germans would not halt their plans, and the Soviet Union rejected the invitation at the Paris Conference to join their zone to the new West German entity, which was founded on May 23. The successful founding of the West German state meant that the German National Council simply became the vehicle by which the new German Democratic Republic was created on October 7, 1949, and the division of Germany completed.[145]

The Berlin blockade turned the western sectors of the city into West Berlin, and the vast majority of their population into friends and defenders of the West. As Reuter correctly put it in a parting word of thanks to General Clay, "The common experience of these months has made us more closely tied to your people, and your people more closely tied to us."[146] It also hardened the opposition of the West to Soviet entreaties for negotiations about Germany and elevated suspicions in the West of Soviet intentions to the point where the United States found itself leading an effort to develop military resistance to counter them. The CIA correctly pointed out that the Soviet "hard" policy in Berlin "has been driving the Western Germans more firmly into the Western camp" and that the prospects of communists gaining serious strength in western Germany were highly reduced.[147] On January 14, 1949, the American State Department made public its plans for a North Atlantic Treaty Organization (NATO) with a combined command that would be comprised of the United States and Canada, as well as the members of the West European (Brussels) Union, plus Portugal, Denmark, Norway, and Iceland. "Russia's toughness and truculence in the Berlin matter," Truman wrote, "had led many Europeans to realize the need for closer military assistance ties among the western nations, and this led to discussions which eventually resulted in the establishment of NATO. Berlin had been a lesson to us all."[148]

West Berlin remained a constant irritant for the East Germans and the Soviets. It served as a major center for American spying in Berlin and the eastern bloc. The Soviets seemed as concerned about the perpetuation of that outpost for espionage as the CIA had been about losing it.[149] More importantly, West Berlin's very existence in the middle of the Soviet zone, and later the German Democratic Republic, served as an example of a functioning West German democratic society and economy that undermined the negative propaganda about western Germany that was incessantly disseminated in the East. The blockade and its outcome also meant that until the fall of the Berlin Wall in October 1989, there would be further Berlin crises that would threaten the stability of the international system.

CHAPTER SIX

GOMUŁKA VERSUS STALIN

1944–1949

At first glance, Poland may well seem like an open-and-shut case to demonstrate Stalin's brutal domination of what should have been a sovereign European country after World War II. The Nazi-Soviet Pact of August 23, 1939, opened the door to a series of fierce attacks on Poland and the Polish people. In a speech to the Supreme Soviet of the USSR on October 31, Soviet foreign minister Molotov exulted, "One swift blow at Poland, first by the German army and followed by the Red Army, and nothing was left of this ugly offspring of the Versailles Treaty."[1] After the Nazi invasion of the Soviet Union on June 22, 1941, Stalin demanded at the Allied conferences at Tehran, Yalta, and Potsdam that Poland be "friendly" and "democratic" according to the Soviet definition of those terms, which meant that the rulers in Moscow would determine the character of Poland's postwar government as well as its political leadership. In wartime meetings with potential partners in the postwar Polish government Stalin was frequently conciliatory.[2] But in his own mind he was clear that the new Poland would serve Soviet aims and that no Polish government would compromise the security of the USSR's western borders, which German armies— whom he expected to be ready to attack again in twenty years—had been able to cross in World Wars I and II. A high-level report from the British Joint Intelligence Service stated what all the Allies understood: ". . . a major Russian strategic interest [is] to ensure that Poland can never again become a base for hostile activities and operations."[3]

In addition to his old-fashioned "realist" view that the Soviets needed to control Poland's geostrategic position on the continent, Stalin quite simply mistrusted and disliked the Poles. From the time of the Polish-Soviet War in 1919–1921 through his anti-Polish "actions" and terror campaign of the 1930s, for Stalin the Polish nation was defined by what he considered the devious, effete Polish noblemen, the ubiquitous Polish "Pans," and the ultramontane, conservative, and anti-Soviet stance of the Polish Catholic Church. The Polish military and intelligence services, he frequently complained in the 1930s, sought to undermine the Soviet Union by recruiting agents, fashioning a variety of underground conspiratorial organizations, and supporting Ukrainian separatism.[4]

In order to eliminate what he saw as the nefarious Polish threat, and thus to strengthen the Soviet state, Stalin insisted to the Allies that Poland's borders be substantially redrawn. What had been interwar eastern Poland—in Soviet terms western Belorussia, western Ukraine, and parts of Lithuania, lands that included the major cities of Wilno (Vilnius) and Lwów (Lviv)—would become part of the Soviet Union. Stalin's territorial claims were based on the 1919 Curzon Line, drawn in preliminary fashion after World War I to divide Poland from the Soviet Union roughly along the Bug River. Stalin cut a deal with Churchill (and eventually Roosevelt) that Poland would be compensated with German territory that bordered in the west on the Oder and Neisse Rivers and included the major cities of Breslau and Stettin, along with Silesia and parts of East Prussia. By shifting Polish territory westward in this fashion—which implied the forced deportation of Germans from Poland and Poles from the Soviet Union—Stalin increased the Poles' dependency on the Soviet Union and thus put additional pressure on them to conform to his policies.[5] Who, after all, would defend the integrity of their newly carved national territory from a likely revanchist Germany if not the mighty Soviet Union?

Stalin also ensured that Poland would conform to his wishes through his proven methods of violence and intimidation. This had begun already in the period of the Nazi-Soviet Pact, when close to four hundred thousand Poles were deported from Soviet-occupied eastern Poland to central Asia and many others were killed, including the twenty-two thousand Polish officers and administrators who were interned and then executed in the Katyń forest and elsewhere in NKVD camps in April and May 1940. After the Nazi invasion of the Soviet Union in June 1941

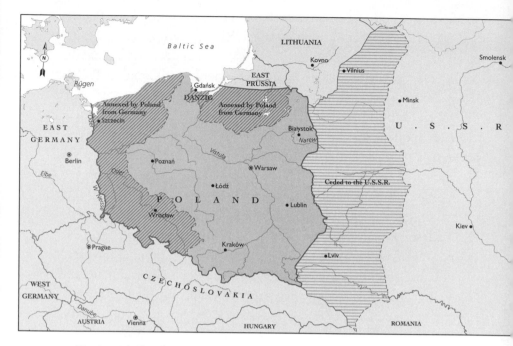

7. Territorial Changes in Poland

and a brief period of amnesty for those Poles deported to the Soviet Union, Stalin abrogated relations with the London government-in-exile in April 1943 in response to the questions it raised about the Polish officers who had disappeared at Katyń and its insistent claim on the eastern Polish territory demanded by the Soviets. Despite these Soviet actions and the murderous German occupation policies, the Polish government-in-exile and its underground organizations carried on a well-organized and extensive resistance movement dedicated to the struggle for Polish liberation. In August 1944, the London government and the powerful Polish underground Home Army, the Armia Krajowa (AK), instigated the Warsaw Uprising, which, it was hoped, would both throw off the Nazi yoke in Warsaw and prove the value of the Polish democratic movement to the Allies.[6]

The Germans eventually crushed the uprising, physically demolished most of Warsaw, and deported most of the surviving citizens of the city to concentration camps. The Soviets, whose armies had reached Praga on the other side of the Vistula in early August, stood idly by, offering the uprising no help and letting it fail, despite some last-minute attacks by units of the Soviet-supported Polish First Army commanded by General Zygmunt Berling.[7] In the end, there were some twenty-two thousand military casualties on the Polish side and seventeen thousand on the German side—and 150,000 to 200,000 Polish civilians who had died from German massacres, artillery bombardments, fires, and collapsing buildings.[8]

The violence continued in the wake of the Soviet advance. As Red Army soldiers marched into Polish territory in early summer 1944, finally seized Warsaw on January 17, and crossed the Oder in mid-April 1945, they were accompanied by NKVD, SMERSH (military counterintelligence), and other Soviet security units. NKVD General Ivan Serov was put in charge of Soviet repressive policies behind the lines of the Red Army; his formal title, "NKVD advisor to the Ministry of Public Security in Poland," belied his unlimited powers to chase down, imprison, torture, and ultimately eliminate enemies of the new order that was being imposed on Poland. His directives from Stalin and Beria were clear: eliminate the danger from the Home Army, which had fought the Nazis from the underground. Stalin and Serov shared a deep antipathy for these resistance fighters, who, on their part, were in their majority fervently anti-Soviet. In his memoir notes, Serov blustered, "These liars! These blackguards! We fight and they wait until they can seize power in Warsaw."[9]

Aside from the regular military authorities, Serov proceeded to divide Poland into districts, each of which was overseen by NKVD units whose job it was to destroy the opponents of the Soviet Union. He himself led the effort to infiltrate AK units, arrest those members who refused to leave the underground and turn over their weapons, and torture and brutalize those captured, ferreting out information about other resistance members and their units. According to Soviet figures, by the end of the war, some twenty-five thousand Poles, mostly AK fighters, were in NKVD camps; thousands more had been killed in a series of coordinated "actions" or in outright battles between the Soviet police units and the AK.[10]

While Polish units were engaged in this desperate struggle with the Soviets, the London government, in a last-ditch effort to influence the

development of postwar politics, tried to set up a provisional government in the underground led by its vice prime minister, Jan Stanisław
Jankowski, and the commander of the AK forces, General Leopold Okulicki. Serov enticed them into "negotiations," which ended in the arrest of sixteen underground Polish leaders and their abduction by airplane to Moscow.[11] Once there, they were placed before a military
tribunal, convicted of engaging in anti-Soviet disruptions in the rear
of the Red Army, and sentenced to various prison terms. While most
received relatively short terms, three never returned from Russia,
including Okulicki, who was summarily "liquidated," to use Serov's
words, while in the central NKVD prison and headquarters, the
Lubianka.[12]

The Polish Communists and Gomułka

This dismal picture of the chances for any real Polish sovereignty after
the war is made only bleaker by the history of Polish communism
in the 1930s and 1940s. Accused of various forms of deviation, including
the most dangerous, Trotskyism, the Polish Communist Party (KPP)
was abolished by Stalin in 1938 and many of its leaders were executed
or disappeared into the camps of the Gulag. Some Polish communists,
the later party leaders Bolesław Bierut and Władysław Gomułka (comrade "Wiesław") among them, survived the purges because they were
in Polish prison at the time. Others, like Jakub Berman and Hilary Minc,
spent the war years in Moscow, where they worked with small groups
of Polish communists. One result of the murderous purges of the KPP
was to make most of the survivors all the more subservient to Stalin
and willing to do anything to earn his confidence. Those who stayed in
Moscow during the war dutifully performed the assignments they received from the Comintern and, after its dissolution in June 1943, by the
International Committee of the Central Committee, both of which
were led by the famous Bulgarian communist activist Georgi Dimitrov,
who enjoyed direct relations with Stalin. It was these Polish communist leaders in Soviet exile who formed the "Central Bureau of Communists in Poland." With Berman as its "informal director," the group
eventually took control of Polish administrative and internal security

functions after the war and ensured that Moscow's injunctions would be followed to a tee.[13]

The group of Polish communists who remained in Poland during the war formed the core of the Polish Workers' Party (the PPR), so named because Stalin, no doubt correctly, deemed that the name "communist" would alienate too many Poles. Nevertheless, the PPR was the legitimate "in-country" heir of the KPP, and some of its members continued to operate under the prewar communists' maxim that following Moscow's orders was the only road to success in Poland, where communism had such a terrible reputation. Some even believed that the only way to achieve their aims was for Poland to join the Soviet Union as the sixteenth republic.[14] Others thought that a small revolutionary cadre, on the model of the Bolsheviks, should seize power in a violent revolution, establish a dictatorship of the proletariat, and proceed to transform Poland's social and economic life by force. But there were also communists and PPR members, Władysław Gomułka most prominent among them, who thought differently. They believed that the problem with the KPP had been its excessive reliance on the orders of the Comintern and its lack of understanding of the special character of the Polish people.

For a good part of the war, Gomułka and the PPR were cut off from any potential channels of communication with Moscow. During this time, they were absorbed with the everyday struggle of supporting their small army of anti-Nazi fighters, the Armia Ludowa (People's Army, AL), issuing printed proclamations, dealing with Gestapo infiltrators and assaults, and combating the sometimes hostile actions of the AK and the right-wing underground. Even after December 1941, when the Soviets sent the Comintern-trained Polish communists Marceli Nowotko, Paweł Finder, and Małgorzata Fornalska into Nazi-occupied Poland to impose discipline on the PPR, communications with Moscow remained poor, and the problems of sheer survival lessened the pressure of ideological conformity.[15] Nowotko was likely assassinated by a party comrade under mysterious circumstances in November 1942, and Finder and Fornalska were seized by the Gestapo in November 1943 and later shot. With the Comintern emissaries gone, the codes for communications with Moscow also disappeared. This left Gomułka without

direct guidance from Moscow and ready and able to shape PPR policies in his own way. Dimitrov and the Kremlin leaders found out about
Gomułka's election as First Secretary of the PPR only in February 1944—
and were none too pleased. Especially Dimitrov distrusted those Polish
communists he did not personally know.[16]

Gomułka's views from the beginning of his involvement with the
PPR seem to have diverged from those of the more Moscow-oriented
Polish communists, in part because he had little to do with Stalin or
Dimitrov during the war. He sought ways to make the PPR program
and communism more palatable to the Polish masses, and to workers
in particular. Gomułka was an autodidact and prolific reader (Stalin derogatorily called him a "scholastic"[17]). He had risen through the ranks
of the Polish trade union movement in the 1920s and 1930s and actively
nurtured ties with Polish laborers in factories and workshops in Nazi-
occupied Poland.[18] He was also deeply influenced by the Comintern's
popular front thinking of the mid- and late 1930s, and he was less prone
than the PPR leaders Bolesław Bierut and Franciszek Jóźwiak to seek
Moscow's advice on every action and thought. Despite the fact that the
Soviets were valued allies, Gomułka wrote in his memoirs, he believed
that the Poles understood their own conditions better than the comrades in Moscow.[19] This related in particular to such Soviet programs
as collectivization, which Gomułka accepted on ideological grounds—
he was, after all, a Marxist-Leninist—but rejected nonetheless as alien
to the Polish character.[20] Gomułka had also personally witnessed the
economic and moral effects of the horrible famine that had resulted
from the collectivization drive during his visit to the Soviet Union in
1934–1935, and he worried about similar consequences if collectivization
came to Poland.[21] Moreover, he was more open to unconventional political alliances than most of his comrades. As part of his attempt to
spread the influence of the PPR in Polish society, Gomułka even sought
to establish contacts with AK units. But the AK both loathed and feared
the Polish communists, and Gomułka learned that there was little
chance of working with them as partners in the future government.

Some of Gomułka's more Moscow-oriented comrades, Bolesław
Bierut among them, frowned on his initiatives to broaden the PPR's
contacts in the underground. Bierut held considerable influence as head

of the KRN (Krajowa Rada Narodowa, National State Council), the PPR-founded national liberation movement, which was meant to serve as the basis of the future government of Poland. On June 10, 1944, Bierut sent a report to Dimitrov in which he denounced Gomułka and his closest PPR comrades for their "zig-zag" politics, "from sectarianism to extreme opportunism," and "lack of principles."[22] Gomułka reached out too far to other underground groups, Bierut complained, and needed to be disciplined. Meanwhile, Gomułka himself tried to convince the Soviets to turn over arms to the AL (People's Army), suggesting that a more active struggle by the communists against the Nazis would win the KRN support among the Polish people. But he was faced with considerable mistrust from Moscow, something, he wrote later, that he found unjust and that "disturbed me a lot."[23]

In fact, at this point the Soviets were more interested in building the reputation of the newly formed Lublin government (PKWN, the Polish Committee of National Liberation), which they had established in liberated Polish territory in July 1944, than in talks with the recalcitrant AK or even building up the communist dominated AL. Earlier, they had supported the Union of Polish Patriots (ZPP), a group of Moscow-oriented communists, tied to Dimitrov, as the core of a future Polish leadership. Given the problems of the PPR and the lack of Soviet support, Gomułka's comrades in the underground insisted that he go to Moscow and meet with Stalin and Dimitrov. He did so in the second week of August 1944, but to little avail. His meeting with Stalin was brief and unremarkable. The one with Dimitrov hardly went better; predisposed to dislike the Central Committee official because of his dismissiveness of the PPR, Gomułka took umbrage at what he perceived as Dimitrov's "tone of superiority."[24] Yet the trip, which remained without tangible results, was only the first of nearly monthly pilgrimages to Moscow that Gomułka would undertake over the next several years, usually together with fellow PPR leaders, to meet with Stalin and the Soviet leadership.[25]

During one of these meetings with Stalin in March 1945, with Poland cleared of the Nazis and the Lublin provisional government, now with Gomułka's participation, having moved to Warsaw, the PPR first secretary decided to raise a difficult issue.[26] Gomułka was upset that

Okulicki, Jankowski, and fourteen other representatives of the underground organization had just been arrested by "General Ivanov" (Serov), especially without any previous notice to the PPR.[27] This was not a matter of their guilt or innocence, Gomułka argued, but of the sovereignty of the Polish Provisional Government. In general, he stated, the way Serov conducted NKVD operations in Poland had alienated Polish society and made it more difficult for the PPR to spread its influence. Serov, Gomułka added, "did more political harm to us than the entire activities of the Council of National Unity [the underground Polish government group] that was arrested."[28]

These arrests would only encourage the AK to go further underground in opposition to the Polish Provisional Government and do even more damage. What Gomułka did not say, but Stalin surely knew, was that he and Serov did not get along at all. They constantly clashed about the extent of the danger of the AK and about Gomułka's persistent desire to negotiate with the less violent groups within the scattered units of the underground army. Stalin was unhappy with both Gomułka's tone and his words. "You are talking like you were the head of a great power, but you are the leader of a weak party in a weak country, which we liberated. They shot at our people, and we will hold them accountable to us." "But they shoot at our people even more," Gomułka parried. It might even be the case, he continued, that the Polish government would punish them more severely than the Soviets would. Stalin conceded that Serov, while being "a good Chekist," showed "little subtlety" and promised to find him a new assignment.[29] Six weeks later, Serov was indeed transferred to Germany, which Gomułka interpreted as "a great success for us."[30]

Gomułka raised a second important issue during this meeting: his efforts to find common ground with Wincenty Witos's Polish Peasant Party, the Stronnictwo Ludowe (SL). For Gomułka, this was another attempt to broaden the PPR's influence in society and to create a "people's democracy."[31] Stalin agreed with this approach and noted that the main bugaboo of the SL, collectivization, was essentially off the table for Poland. There was no need for it; in the Soviet Union it had taken years to accomplish and reflected different historical circumstances. As Gomułka understood Stalin's remarks, Poland did not need to even think about collectivization for another fifteen or twenty years. Poland would also need alliances with France and Great Britain, and would need to maintain friendly relations with the United States, Stalin explained; the Soviet Union would not be Poland's only ally.[32] In the end, Gomułka was pleased with the "pragmatism" that, he thought, the Soviet leader had demonstrated at every stage of their discussions.[33]

Stalin's articulated views about the future of Polish communism as Soviet troops cleared Poland of the Nazis and the war came to an end closely concurred with those of Gomułka and his closest comrades, Zenon Kliszko and Marian Spychalski among them. Stalin provided an outline for a new kind of democracy and a parliamentary government that would reflect the needs of the Polish people as a whole. There would be no reason for a "dictatorship of the proletariat," as he repeatedly told the Polish communists. To a delegation of them, he explained in May 1946, "In Poland there is no dictatorship of the proletariat, and there is no need for it . . . the capitalists and large landowners have been overthrown in Poland with the help of the Red Army. This is why there is no basis for a dictatorship of the proletariat."[34] The bloodshed of the Russian Revolution was unnecessary in Poland; Moscow had already assured those social and political changes that were needed for forming a "new democracy," sometimes called people's democracy, a transitional form of government on the way to socialism, not a bourgeois, capitalist-dominated parliamentary state but one controlled by progressive, democratic, and anti-fascist forces. But neither Gomulka nor Stalin had a pluralist country in mind, one that would be controlled by non-communist forces. The "Polish road to socialism" would be one dominated by the PPR.[35]

Gomułka and the Soviets

The new Polish Government of National Unity, which was formed under Soviet auspices in Lublin on January 1, 1945, and moved to Warsaw soon thereafter, was based on the previous, communist-dominated Lublin government. As a concession to the Western Allies, in June 1945 Stanisław Mikołajczyk, the former premier of the London government-in-exile, was included as minister of agriculture and second deputy prime minister. But neither Stalin nor the Polish communists, including Gomułka, who was first deputy prime minister, were going to allow Mikołajczyk and his political supporters from the newly established Polish Peasant Party (called *Polskie Stronnictwo Ludowe*, or PSL, to distinguish it from the now communist-dominated SL) to seize the initiative from the Democratic Front controlled by the PPR. After a series of arrests of anti-communist politicians and manipulated elections, including the cruical falsified "referendum" of October 1947, the widely admired Mikołajczyk fled the country in the same month.[36] Despite considerable pressure on him, Mikołajczyk had done his best under life-threatening circumstances. As early as February 1946, the American ambassador had reported to the State Department that "Mikołajczyk's life is in danger," and in January 1947 he had warned again that Mikołajczyk could be tried for treason and executed, given shrill public statements by Bierut and Gomułka.[37]

Along with the other PPR leaders, Bolesław Bierut, the new president of Poland, Finance Minister Hilary Minc, and Jakub Berman, the head of public security, Gomułka became an important member of the new government leadership. He continued as first secretary of the PPR but assumed government duties as first deputy prime minister and, against Stalin's advice, as minister of the Recovered Territories *(Ziemie Odzyskane)*. In the latter position, Gomułka oversaw the flight and sometimes brutal removal of some six million Germans from the lands in the west and south of the new Poland.[38] In his orders to party officials, he stated, "We must expel all the Germans because countries are built on national lines and not on multinational ones."[39] At the same time, he oversaw the resettlement of millions of Poles both from the Soviet Union and, more haphazardly, from central Poland, to these same areas.

In this function, he crossed swords with the Soviets once again. The Recovered Territories were justifiably described as Poland's "Wild West," and for the first years after the war, Gomułka was busy trying to bring order to chaos. Both Red Army occupation units and Soviet reparations teams tied to economic ministries in Moscow wreaked havoc on the ground. Soviet army commanders in the Recovered Territories seized formerly German agricultural stores, housing, and even some workshops and factories to support their troops, often paying little

6.1 Polish president Bolesław Bierut speaks at a National Youth Rally, July 21–22, 1946. Vice Premier and First Secretary of the Polish Workers' Party Władysław Gomułka is on the right. POLISH PRESS AGENCY.

or no attention to the needs of the incoming Polish administration. And while the Poles also had legitimate claims to reparations from the Germans, the economic ministries in Moscow had independent authorization from the Soviet government to seize German factories and materials and send them back to the Soviet Union. Gomułka did what he could to stem the flow of these assets and to impose some limits on the plundering Red Army units, yet his complaints found little resonance in his own government and among the more Moscow-oriented PPR leadership, let alone in Moscow itself.[40]

The behavior of Soviet troops on Polish territory, and especially in the Recovered Territories, also drove Gomułka to distraction. In a memorandum to the Soviet politburo from September 11, 1945, a copy of which with Gomułka's handwritten edits can be found in the Polish archives, the Polish leadership complained about the frequent cases of murder and robbery committed by drunken groups of "soldiers-marauders," who plagued the roads and railways with their depredations. "The rape of women is a constant phenomenon," stated the memorandum. Combined with other immoral and illegal behavior, this played into the hands of "anti-Soviet agitation" and damaged the popularity of the PPR as well. "There is nothing easier [for our opponents] than to create among the masses the impression that the PPR is also responsible for all the marauding of the soldiers of the Red Army in Poland. . . ."[41] When Gomułka confronted Stalin about this problem at one of their meetings in the summer of 1945, the Soviet leader admitted that during the war the Red Army had learned to plunder. But just as he did when dealing with other East European communist leaders with similar complaints, Stalin downplayed his soldiers' illicit behavior, responding to Gomułka with the story that in Berlin two hundred thousand watches had been stolen and that demobilization would soon bring the issue to an end anyway.[42]

Negative Soviet actions in Poland, whether it was the confiscation of food for the occupation troops, the dismantling and removal of industrial plants in the Recovered Territories, the seizure of already scarce housing, or the drunken and criminal depredations of Soviet troops, indeed caused serious problems for the PPR and the Polish communists. The populace perceived the PPR as Moscow's party. Its members could not complain publicly about Soviet behavior and show solidarity with the population because that would have alienated the Soviet partners and, in some cases, fellow Polish communists. Among the PPR leaders, Gomułka stood out by trying everything he could to deal with these problems. He even went so far as to give orders to shoot Red Army soldiers in the Recovered Territories who removed assets from the region without official approval.[43]

Of still greater significance, especially in the long term, was that Gomułka also developed the ideology of what became known as the "Polish road to socialism," though he himself rarely used the phrase.[44] Many of Gomułka's ideas were already set out during the war. At least initially, they dovetailed neatly with Stalin's efforts to convince the Poles and the West that he had no intention of taking over Poland. There seemed to be full agreement between Gomułka and Stalin that there would be no "dictatorship of the proletariat," no collectivization, and no "socialization" of large industries, only some limited nationalization. The Peasant Party (SL) and the Polish Socialist Party (PPS) would be allowed to operate within the Democratic Front of parties, led by the PPR. There would be normal contacts with both the East and the West, though Soviet influence would predominate. As Stalin told Gomułka in a 1945 meeting, the PPR should, above all, "maintain its ties with the Polish people" and also "continue its relations with the British and the Americans," since "otherwise the Polish people would not understand it."[45]

Despite Gomułka's episodic complaints about Moscow's heavy hand in Poland, the policies of the Polish road to socialism took hold in the immediate postwar period. There was general agreement between the PPR leadership and Moscow, though, that any developments that might lead to an anti-Soviet government would not be tolerated. Moreover, the Polish communist-dominated Security Service (*Urząd Bezpieczeństwa*, or UB) worked closely with NKVD units in eliminating underground opposition and anti-Soviet activities, which were defined very broadly. Yet, as everywhere in Europe immediately after the war, Moscow enjoined the communists to drop their revolutionary rhetoric and seek broad coalitions with left and bourgeois parties to stimulate the formation of anti-fascist "people's democracies."

Gomułka's efforts to increase the PPR's popularity frequently led him to clash with more orthodox Polish communists. At the February and May–June 1945 Central Committee plenums, for example, he inveighed against "sectarians" among party members who did not share "the spirit of the Polish people" and were not open to the "honorable people" in the "pro-London" camp, who were ready to join the struggle for a new Poland. He also criticized the security forces of the UB for pursuing their own radical ends as if they were "a second government." They were prone, he charged, to working in tandem with NKVD and Red Army units, which gave the appearance of the dependence of the new Poland on the Soviet Union and of the PPR on the Soviet party. "The masses should consider us a Polish party," Gomułka stated. "Let [our opponents] attack us as Polish communists, but not as 'agents' [of Moscow]."[46] No doubt Gomułka felt empowered to give voice to his opinions by the success of his policies; Polish politics and government were indeed controlled by the PPR and undergirded by Stalin's apparent approval and direct Soviet support.

6.2 Poles visit the Kremlin, March 5, 1947. From left to right: unknown; Józef Cyrankiewicz; Joseph Stalin, Władysław Gomułka, Hilary Minc, Viacheslav Molotov. EAST NEWS (POLAND).

Gomułka and the Cominform

During his vacation and health cure in the Soviet Union in June 1947, Gomułka met with Stalin in Moscow and discussed with the Soviet dictator the development of the people's democracies in Europe. It was on this occasion that Stalin first broached the idea of holding a meeting of European Communist Party leaders in Poland for an "exchange of experiences" and for founding a journal to explore the theoretical and practical implications of this new, transitional form of government.[47] When Jakub Berman met with Stalin and several other Soviet leaders on August 20, 1947, possible places in Poland for such a meeting of representatives of the communist parties were discussed. As he had told Gomułka, Stalin described the proposed get-together to Berman as a "private, informational consultation." When Berman inquired whether the meeting was to pass a resolution, Molotov answered only that there would be a communiqué that would adumbrate the creation of "a newspaper, which would be a common organ of the parties."[48] Later Gomułka claimed that he had been "hoodwinked" by Stalin into hosting what became the first meeting of the Cominform (Communist Information Bureau) in September 1947, whose agenda, set by Moscow, went much beyond Gomułka's expectations of general discussions and a new socialist publication.[49]

It may well be, as Gomułka later indicated, that Stalin had had right from the beginning far more radical aims in mind for the Cominform meeting than he had initially disclosed to Gomułka. But it is also true that tensions between the Soviet Union and its former Western Allies increased over this same period, and that Stalin's attitudes hardened over the summer of 1947, after the U.S. secretary of state General George C. Marshall announced the Recovery Plan for Europe (the so-called Marshall Plan) at the Harvard commencement in June 1947.[50] Initially, there were signs that the Soviets might participate in the Paris meeting where Marshall Plan aid would be discussed. But Stalin and Molotov quickly concluded that the Americans would not agree to Moscow's conditions for loans, and in turn not very subtly instructed the Poles and the Czechoslovaks, who were desperate to receive Marshall Plan credits, to denounce the plan as an American plot to exploit their economies.

At the meeting of the Cominform, held in the Silesian resort of Szklarska Poręba on September 22–23, 1947, Stalin's representative, Andrei Zhdanov, turned the proceedings into an effort to establish firmer control over the East European parties' approaches to their political tasks and to force the French and Italian parties to radicalize their tactics for achieving power within their respective countries.[51] While the attacks on the Western parties, spearheaded by the militant Yugoslavs, violated Gomułka's understanding of individual roads to socialism, the Polish communist leader also worried that Zhdanov's "two-camp" speech, which raised the temperature of the ideological struggle between East and West, would cause his own party problems at home, given the still powerful attraction of the Western Allies. He later wrote that he tried to convince his Polish comrades and others at the meeting to resist the radicalizing tenor of the discussions but was rebuffed in no uncertain terms.[52] When he turned to Minc for support, for example, the Moscow-true PPR leader declined, saying, "I'm not so stupid."[53]

Yet even after the meeting dispersed, Gomułka continued to work to limit the damage he felt that the notion of the Cominform as a potential new Comintern would cause the PPR's image in Poland by calling into question the sovereignty of the European communist parties.

He also rebuffed the suggestion that the Cominform headquarters should be located in Poland.[54] Gomułka's long-time confederate, Marian Spychalski, stated in an interrogation protocol in December 1950 that Gomułka had invited him to his home to talk about the Cominform meeting after his return to Warsaw from Szklarska Poręba. Reportedly, the "furious" Gomułka told him that he understood better than the other comrades "the nationalist character of Polish society, which is very sensitive to the issue of sovereignty vis-à-vis the Soviet Union. . . ." Polish reactionaries would denounce Polish communists' participation in the Cominform as a blow to Poland's independence; using this argument, Gomułka told Spychalski, he would convince the politburo that the Cominform headquarters should be located somewhere else.[55]

In contrast to Gomułka, the other members of the PPR leadership, Bierut, Berman, Minc, and Zambrowski, understood that Zhdanov's position at Szklarska Poręba reflected Stalin's demands for ideological conformity to the Soviet model across the East European parties. The Yugoslavs, led by wartime leader Josip Broz Tito, initially cheered this new, more radical line. But they quickly found out that it also entailed the subordination of their own brand of Stalinist socialism to Moscow's desires and control, something they were unwilling to do.[56] When Soviet ambassador Viktor Lebedev showed Gomułka the March 27, 1948, letter in which the Soviet leadership denounced the Yugoslavs and insisted that Gomułka present it to the PPR politburo, Gomułka apparently assented, although not without calling the Soviet action "premature" and stating his unhappiness about the pernicious influence of the Yugoslav affair on the rest of the East European communist parties.[57] After Gomułka had shared the letter as well as his own critical comments with the politburo, Minc warned him that "he should proceed very carefully." When asked years later why he had seemed so ready to take on both Stalin and his fellow PPR leaders, Gomułka answered that he had wanted to take no responsibility for the new "line" and that he had been ready to resign his positions if he failed to convince his comrades of the correctness of his position.[58]

By June 1948, the conflict between Stalin and Tito had escalated to the point that the Yugoslavs were expelled from the Cominform meeting, which took place in Bucharest. To no avail, Gomułka had appealed to the Central Committee of the Yugoslav party to take part in the meeting. "Non-attendance at the conference," he wrote, would "inevitably lead" to "breaking away from the world revolutionary movement, with all the consequences entailed."[59] But even after the meeting, Gomułka was still reluctant to criticize the Yugoslavs; he understood that their expulsion meant that his own brand of socialism, which deviated from the Soviet model even more significantly than the Yugoslav version, was seriously endangered. He even offered to mediate between Moscow and Belgrade, but Tito rejected his offer, and his proposed visit to Belgrade never took place.[60]

Meanwhile, Gomułka's stance on the Yugoslav issue was drawing increasing criticism from his more Moscow-friendly comrades in the party leadership.[61] Eventually the tensions around his position in the PPR exploded into a series of events that led to his being purged from the party, removal from the government, and eventual imprisonment and interrogation. It seemed, then, that Gomułka's fears about the ramifications of the Yugoslav case had been justified. At the same time, the story of his downfall was also entangled with another major issue: his attitude toward the Jews.

Gomułka, the Jews, and His Fight with Stalin

From the very beginning of the Polish Communist Party (KPP) in the 1890s, when Rosa Luxemburg and Leo Jogiches, among others, organized the Social Democratic Party of the Kingdom of Poland and Lithuania (SDKPiL), Jews had played a disproportionately central leadership role in it. When Stalin destroyed the KPP in summer 1938, it included a very large number of Poles of Jewish background.[62] In its successor organizations, the Union of Polish Patriots, formed in the Soviet Union in 1941, and in the PPR, though less so in the underground, Jews also played a prominent role. This high Jewish participation was not only well known but also, significantly, almost always exaggerated both by the party's adherents and opponents. Soviet lists of leading Polish party members from the time of the war onward identified everyone by their nationality—Pole or Jew (or sometimes Polish Jew). Stalin was very aware of the perceived problem of a large Jewish presence in the Polish (as well as Romanian, Hungarian, and Czech) communist leaderships.

The destruction of the European Jews—the Shoah—only seemed to exacerbate the Jewish "problem," as Stalin and the Soviets saw it. Already in 1946, officials in Moscow expressed serious concern that there were too many Soviet Jews in the occupation administration in Germany, and that this might offend the Germans.[63] The assertion of Jewish national identity among Soviet Jewish activists and veterans after the war and Holocaust alienated Stalin and increased his suspicions of their motivations.[64] Moreover, there were tensions between the Moscow-based Jewish Antifascist Committee and the Soviet government about identifying the special losses suffered by the Jews during the "Great Patriotic War." This conflict eventually resulted in the banning of the organization, the NKVD's brutal murder in January 1948 of its leader, the famous Yiddish actor Solomon Mikhoels, and the arrests of many of its members. These domestic events were accompanied by a shift in the Soviet stance toward Jews in the international arena. Until early 1948, the Soviets had been crucial supporters of the UN-sponsored creation of a Jewish state, mainly in order to bring to an end the British mandate in Palestine, and with it British influence in the Middle East more generally. Yet after the founding of the state of Israel in May 1948, Soviet backing quickly turned into antagonism, which further radicalized into official anti-Zionism, "anti-cosmopolitanism," and anti-Semitism in 1949 and 1950.

Soviet attitudes toward leading Jewish members in the PPR, which was merged with the Polish Socialist Party (PPS) in December 1948 to form the Polish United Workers' Party, or PZPR, similarly soured in this period. In March 1948, the Soviet ambassador in Warsaw, Viktor Lebedev, wrote to Soviet foreign minister Molotov that there were two wings of the Polish party, the nationalist "Gomułka group" and the so-called "Minc group" (after Hilary Minc), which constituted in his view a virtual Jewish lobby. Lebedev's central point was that despite being valuable party members, Minc and other Jews were vulnerable to intimidation and attacks from the right because of their Jewish backgrounds. Polish chauvinists in the PPR could "very easily" vilify

Minc as a representative of Poland's "eternal enemy," the Jews, or even as a "Jewish beast." There was a "fierce hatred of Jews in Poland," Lebedev wrote, and the anti-Semitic attitudes of the Polish Socialist Party and of the Vatican made matters only worse. At the same time, stated the ambassador, the more Minc tried to combat Polish anti-Semitism in the PPR, the more the Poles viewed him as a Jewish leader.[65]

Lebedev and the Soviets faced a difficult question in formulating their policy toward this growing split in the Polish party. On the one hand, they were worried about the overrepresentation of Jews in the leadership: Berman, Minc, and Zambrowski, most notably. On the other, they were suspicious of what they considered Gomułka's nationalist proclivities, which had become especially unacceptable at the Cominform meeting and after. Stalin's moves to create homogeneity among and control over his East European "allies" during the winter of 1947–1948 meant that Gomułka's open advocacy of the distinctiveness of the Polish road to socialism had to be suppressed. The expulsion of Yugoslavia from the Cominform in June 1948 for alleged Trotskyism, nationalism, and anti-Sovietism was very much a public affair and widely reported in the international press. The attack against Gomułka was less open, though already in April 1948 the Foreign Department of the Soviet Central Committee had prepared a document entitled "On the Anti-Marxist Ideological Tendencies in the Leadership of the PPR," which listed Gomułka's alleged sins, most prominently his "rightist-nationalist deviation."[66]

Gomułka himself soon added to them with a provocative speech at the June 3, 1948, plenum of the PPR Central Committee in which he stated publicly that in the history of Polish socialism the PPS had represented the wishes of the Polish working-class movement better than the SDKPiL and the KPP, both of which—no one could miss the connection in that speech—were closely associated with "the Jews" and their supposed indifference to legitimate Polish patriotic causes. It is also significant that Gomułka's speech was timed to coincide with the intense campaign to join the PPS with the PPR, which culminated in the unification congress in December 1948. The PPS was growing in popularity, and many of its leaders considered the PPR, in the words of Józef Cyrankiewicz, "Russian agents."[67] The time had come, in Gomułka's view, to force a merger. In the face of the increasing "internationalist" dogmatism of both the majority of the PPR's leadership and the Soviets, Gomułka sought to lay out a more thoroughly "Polish" line for the new united party by "harnessing" the patriotic traditions of the PPS and its followers to the Marxism-Leninism of the PPR.[68]

Gomułka's pro-Moscow comrades in the PPR leadership were incensed by his June 3 speech and especially by his depiction of the history of Polish socialism. They accused him of making a "grave concession to the cause of the nationalist-bourgeois and reformist traditions represented by the PPS" and demanded that he engage in a round of self-criticism.[69] At the second Cominform meeting in Bucharest where the Yugoslavs were expelled (June 19–23, 1948), Berman, representing the Polish communists, denounced the "serious danger of right-wing opportunist, nationalist character." Without mentioning Gomułka by name, he called for a cleansing of the united party of all such "elements."[70]

At the August–September plenum of the party's Central Committee, Berman made himself clearer: while making many references to "Wiesław's" services to the party, he took Gomułka to task for his "stiffening" to the Soviet Union, his "mistrust" of Moscow, and his unwillingness to participate in the "Bolshevization of our party."[71] Mieczysław Moczar, Gomułka's later partner in the expelling of thousands of Jews from Poland in 1968, dwelled on the fact that the Soviet Union "is our fatherland" and "the good fortune of our people."[72] Meanwhile, Ambassador Lebedev had already reported to Moscow that Gomułka exhibited "sharply anti-Soviet outbursts on different issues" and pursued a "'shameful' line in relation to propaganda about getting closer to the Soviet Union."[73]

Gomułka engaged in a battle he could not win. But he was obdurate and committed to his views. Pressure from Lebedev and the Polish party leadership to engage in self-criticism only seemed to strengthen his resolve to defend his vision of a distinct Polish road to socialism. Though ostensibly performing the ritual act of admitting his "mistakes" at the Central Committee plenums, he carefully avoided core issues and remarked periodically that "he wasn't sure that he wasn't right."[74] At one point in his frustrated attempts to get Gomułka to admit his sins, Bierut tried to convince him to go to Moscow to see Stalin. But Gomułka replied, "[W]hy should I go? I am now [nothing but a] corpse."[75] Already in July 1948, Gomułka had withdrawn from active participation in Central Committee meetings, claiming health problems; he speculated that his political life might well be finished.[76]

Differences between Gomułka and the Soviets that dated from the period of the war came to the surface again.[77] He was repeatedly attacked for his alleged lack of vigilance as PPR leader in the underground; questions were raised about his responsibility for the killing of Marceli Nowotko and Paweł Finder and about his contacts with the anticommunist AK resistance. These and other wartime issues were to emerge again and again during his interrogations in 1951. Bierut, who was advised by the Soviets and appropriately called by one historian "a stool pigeon of the most obvious ilk," led the campaign of removing Gomułka from his posts.[78]

On August 16 Bierut flew to Moscow for a meeting with Stalin and Molotov. There he accused Gomułka of "serious rightist-nationalist tendencies," which, he asserted, had revealed themselves already in the spring of 1944. Bierut asked Soviet Central Committee official Mikhail Suslov for a copy of the letter he had written to Dimitrov in June 1944. In it, he had denounced Gomułka's leadership of the wartime PPR as "dictatorial" and "insufficiently collective" and characterized Gomułka as following no consistent political line but "zigzagging from sectarianism to extreme opportunism and back again." Especially pertinent for the growing case that was being assembled against Gomułka in 1948 and 1949 was Bierut's criticism in the same letter that Gomułka had been in contact with "reactionary groups who supported the London government."[79]

At the August–September 1948 plenum of the Central Committee, Gomułka was accused of holding to "a system of rightist and nationalistic views for a period of nearly five years." Bierut denounced him for Titoism and Rajkism, while Minc insinuated that he was responsible for the deaths of Nowotko and Finder. The plenum's final resolution stated that "increased national solidarity with the CPSU" was the only way to assure Poland's sovereignty and independence, which marked a clear repudiation of Gomułka's course.[80] The Soviets demanded that this kind of language be included when they approved the draft resolution on "Comrade Wiesław."[81] Gomułka himself was ousted as general secretary of the PPR at the plenum and replaced by Bierut. In January 1949, he also lost his position as minister for the Recovered Territories (in fact, the entire ministry was shut down). In November 1949, Gomułka was expelled from the Central Committee of the newly formed PZPR, together with his close confederates Marian Spychalski and Zenon Kliszko.[82]

In most circumstances in communist-controlled Eastern Europe, Stalin would have given the party leadership the go-ahead to imprison, interrogate, put on trial, and likely even execute Gomułka for the "nationalist" and "rightist" deviations of which he was accused. There is little doubt the other Polish communist leaders would have complied. They were rock-solid Stalin enthusiasts who followed the Soviet dictator's orders unquestioningly, even seeking to anticipate them.[83] But in this instance, the Soviets faced several problems. First of all, Gomułka was well known in Polish society for having resisted the German occupiers in the underground and for having overseen, as minister of the Recovered Territories, the expulsion of the German populations from the lands that had now become Poland—which was enthusiastically greeted by the vast majority of Poles. He had given well-attended speeches all over the country and was lauded for his modest lifestyle and lack of pretensions.[84]

Compared to the other communist leaders, Gomułka enjoyed at least a modicum of popularity in the country. He was also known in government and party circles for his opposition to the return of the several hundred thousand Polish Jews who had managed to escape or were deported from occupied Poland to the Soviet Union during the war, as well as for his advocacy—along with many other PPR leaders—of their immediate emigration once they had returned.[85] Gomułka was an outspoken proponent of a mono-ethnic Poland—Germans, Ukrainians, and Jews should all leave—a vision that was popular both within the party and among the general population. Moreover, except for Boleslaw Bierut, a man of notably modest abilities, Gomułka was the only non-Jew remotely capable of exerting leadership in the Polish communist movement. From Moscow's point of view, the Jews Berman, Minc, and Zambrowski could not be allowed to run the Polish party themselves.[86]

No doubt with these considerations in mind, Stalin tried to woo Gomułka back to party work at the end of 1948. The Moscow leadership did not like Gomułka at all. (Andrei Vyshinskii once said that he was no better than Władysław Sikorski, the Polish general and leader of the Polish government-in-exile until his tragic death on July 4, 1943, in a mysterious airplane crash.) But they felt they needed him to complete the upcoming unity Congress of the PPR with the PPS.[87] Therefore, Stalin summoned Gomułka to a personal meeting at his Kuntsevo dacha on December 9, 1948. Gomułka understood that he was in an extremely difficult position and expected nothing good from the meeting, but he had no choice but to go.[88] At the meeting, attended at times by NKVD chief Lavrentii Beria and perhaps Molotov, Stalin asked him to stand for elections to the newly formed politburo of the Polish United Workers Party (PZPR). Gomułka replied that there was no way he could work with Bierut, Minc, and Berman. Beria showed his annoyance: "How can you turn down something Stalin proposes to you," he barked, but Stalin promptly chided Beria, "You prosecutor," and asked him to leave the meeting.[89] When Gomułka departed Stalin's dacha, he had agreed to consider joining the Central Committee of the new party.

Yet only five days later, on December 14, Gomułka wrote to Stalin and rejected the idea of assuming any significant role in the PZPR. In this startling letter, he placed much of the blame for the woes of the Polish party and his own fate directly on "the Jews." Claiming that most rank-and-file party members knew that he had done everything he could to limit the influx of Jews into elevated positions in the party and the security services, he wrote that the sheer number of visible Jews encumbered party work "among the intelligentsia, also in the countryside, but, most importantly, among the working class." Part of the responsibility for the overrepresentation of Jews in the leading party and state organizations Gomułka took on himself, having been the leader of the party. But primarily, he asserted, his Jewish comrades were to blame. They ignored his admonitions to limit the number of Jews they recruited and did what they wanted in the realm of cadre policy. Not only had they thwarted his attempts to deal with the problem of too many Jews at various junctures of party history since the war, but they had even threatened to "end" his party activities if he persisted. One of the major reasons he did not want to go back to the politburo, Gomułka wrote Stalin, was the problem of the Jewish leadership; they would again employ all their devious methods to defeat him on this important issue.[90]

Gomułka pointedly explained to Stalin in the letter that the problem with the Jews in the party was not just their numbers and the popular perception of their ubiquity. Years of observation, he wrote, had convinced him that at least a very large number of Jewish comrades "do not feel tied to our Polish people" and did not have particularly warm feelings for the Polish working class. Gomułka did not accuse the Jews of "cosmopolitanism," a denunciation that was only just beginning to become widely used in Soviet official discourse, but rather of "national nihilism." Everyone understood this issue, he claimed, but no one had the courage to talk about it openly. Especially now that he was under attack for supposed "nationalism," it would have been hard for non-Jewish Polish party members to criticize Jewish comrades for recruiting so many of their own in the leadership. "I believe it is necessary not only to curtail the further percentage growth of Jews in the party and state apparatus," Gomułka asserted, "but also gradually to decrease this percentage, especially in the ranks of the apparatus."[91]

Gomułka's rhetoric about Jewish difference and the Jews' inability to conform to the norms of Polish nationhood echoed a powerful theme in the history of Polish nationalism both in and outside the socialist movement. Though his wife, Zofia Gomułka (Szoken), came from an Orthodox Jewish family (and was a devoted communist), and his son, Ryszard Strzelecki-Gomułka, was forced to hide from the Nazis during the war, Gomułka was nevertheless unrelenting in criticizing his Jewish comrades. Was Gomułka an anti-Semite? Perhaps. As one Polish expert writes, "It's hard not to recognize Gomułka's views as a form of capitulation to anti-Semitism or even as anti-Semitic themselves."[92] Another notes that except for the immediate postwar period and in 1968, Gomułka actually seemed to get along well with his Jewish comrades and shared important decisions with them.[93] But there is no question at the time that he saw the Jews as a liability for Poland as a whole, as well as for the Polish party.

Gomułka put Stalin and the PZPR leadership in a difficult position. Stalin's goal in insisting that he rejoin the party leadership had no doubt been to balance its heavily Jewish contingent, of which the Soviet leader himself had grown increasingly suspicious. Now Gomułka sought to link his return to a leading position with a purge, or at least demotion, of his rivals of Jewish descent—Berman, Minc, and Zambrowski. From the Soviet point of view, however, this would isolate Bierut and permit Gomułka to reshape the party according to the "Polish" agenda he sought to pursue. Essentially, Gomułka pitted his own patriotism and close ties with the Polish working people against the alleged "national nihilism" of his party rivals. As Stalin and the Soviet leadership raised the flag of the struggle against "cosmopolitanism," barely concealing its anti-Semitic essence, the other leaders of the Polish party were forced to walk a precarious tightrope between denouncing cosmopolitanism in the spirit of the international class struggle and countering Gomułka's brand of Polish patriotism and exclusive nationalism. For Berman, Zambrowski, Minc, and others, these acrobatics required considerable skill, strong nerves, and patience.[94]

For his part, Stalin was not at all pleased with the response he received from Gomułka. In a note to Bierut of December 16, 1948, he and Molotov suggested that Gomułka was hiding something and that his activities should be carefully monitored.[95] Gomułka had miscalculated; giving in to the Polish leader's "road to socialism" would be far more dangerous in Stalin's view than dealing with Jews—well-proven and extremely loyal ones at that—in the Polish party leadership.

Gomułka's comrades warned him of Stalin's displeasure and urged him to conform to party norms. "Do you know what you are risking?" Hilary Minc asked him. He answered, "I know."[96] Nevertheless Gomułka kept up his attack on the Jews in his address to the unity congress of the PPR and PPS (December 15–21, 1948). "We internationalists have fought and will fight not only with nationalism [a concession to his critics] but also with cosmopolitanism [now this term had entered his political lexicon as well] and national nihilism. We hold in contempt those who do not respect our people, [who] do not value its greatness and its capabilities, those who diminish our contributions to international culture over its thousand-year history."[97]

The Soviet ambassador Lebedev watched the infighting in the Polish party leadership with a jaundiced eye. His reports back to Vyshinskii and Molotov in Moscow, which were often passed on to Stalin as well, were foundational for Soviet policy.[98] Lebedev was pleased that Bierut and his comrades had beaten back the "right wing nationalist" tendencies represented, in his view, by Gomułka, Spychalski, and others in their camp. But he continued to express his dissatisfaction that in the leadership group, only Bierut was of Polish nationality. Lebedev admired Bierut and thought of him as an able and competent leader. He was therefore all the more annoyed that, after the removal of Gomułka, the Jewish party leaders acted as if they had saved Bierut's position and seemed even more full of themselves than before. In a letter to Soviet foreign minister Vyshinskii from July 10, 1949, he complained that the Jews would not let any other non-Jews into the party leadership.[99] He pointed in particular to the case of Władysław Wolski (A. Piwowarczyk), a Polish party member (and NKVD informant), whom Lebedev sought to promote within the Polish state hierarchy.[100] Berman and Zambrowski, claimed Lebedev, were suspicious of Wolski's close ties with the Soviets and therefore kept him away from Bierut. Even worse, in the ambassador's view, they justified his isolation from the party leadership with the fact that he was often seen at the Soviet embassy.[101]

Lebedev also expressed annoyance that the Jewish politburo member Jakub Berman was not just an important leader of the Polish party but also responsible for the Polish security services. It was Berman's fault, Lebedev alleged, that the "notorious" Jewish organization "Joint" (Joint Distribution Service) of the American Jewish Congress continued to operate in Poland until 1950, even though Moscow had advised that its offices be liquidated as outposts for spies and saboteurs.[102] Furthermore, Lebedev leveled the charge that "the apparatus of the Ministry of Public Security, beginning with the deputy minister and including all the heads of departments, are not led by a single Pole." He added, "All are Jews. It is only Jews who work in the department of intelligence." From the viewpoint of those who were not opposed to the worldwide influence of the Jews, namely the Jewish communists, the investigation of foreign agents in Poland was therefore "in welcome hands"; materials about such agents were "cooked" even before they reached

Bierut. To make matters worse, Lebedev continued, the Jew Roman Zambrowski was in charge of the Central Committee's administrative apparatus. Like Jakub Berman (whose brother, Adolf, was a famous Zionist activist), Zambrowski constantly made concessions to Zionist Jews who wanted to emigrate to Israel, as well as to Zionist delegations from Palestine, who were seeking recruits in Poland, Lebedev asserted.[103]

Given his undisguised anti-Semitic views, Lebedev's conclusions were not surprising. The Jewish leaders suffered in his eyes from "Jewish nationalism" and should, their services to the party notwithstanding, be cleared out of the party and state hierarchy.[104] Berman's Ministry of Public Security required special attention. Lebedev suggested that a Polish confidant of Bierut replace Berman and deal with the problem of cadres. Although he did not mention him explicitly in this context, Lebedev clearly had Wolski in mind, whom he considered a good Pole and loyal friend of Moscow. The problem with this scheming was that, these qualities aside, Wolski had nowhere near Berman's political savvy, not to mention connections with Stalin and Molotov. (In an interview in the early 1980s with the Polish journalist Teresa Torańska, Berman described how he had danced with Molotov during an evening at Stalin's dacha: "Molotov led; I wouldn't have known how," while Berman whispered party business in his ear.[105]) Meanwhile, Wolski's own attempts to draw the new Polish defense minister, Soviet-born Konstantin Rokossovskii, into his careerist anti-Jewish machinations also remained fruitless.[106]

In the end, Lebedev's Wolski gambit did not work out as he had hoped. The embassy-sponsored upstart was expelled from the Polish party on May 13, 1950. Several days later Stalin put an end to the affair when he wrote to Bierut that he had Wolski checked out with "the appropriate authorities" (that is, the secret police), the conclusion being that "Wolski did not deserve political trust."[107] Apparently, Wolski had criticized the "Jewish" party leadership publicly, something even Gomułka had avoided doing. Most likely, he had misjudged both Lebedev's power and Stalin's unwillingness to sacrifice the leaders of the Polish party just because of their Jewishness—something that Gomułka had had to learn as well.[108]

Bierut ended up charging Wolski with following in Gomułka's footsteps: "Wolski accused the leadership of the party of not believing in the strength of the working class. This serious accusation . . . is completely unfounded. For the TsK [Central Committee] of the party, this is not new. Gomułka also tried to undermine the authority of the leadership of the party. Wolski is proceeding along the same lines [analogichno]."[109] Within a year of Wolski's fall and subsequent relegation to an obscure position in the provinces, the Soviet ambassador Lebedev was removed from Warsaw and called back to Moscow.[110] Bierut had successfully defended his Jewish comrades by discrediting Wolski's attack as a case of Gomułka-style Polish right-wing nationalism. Now he could not only expect support and loyalty from them, but also, precisely because they were Jews, he did not have to fear that they would be rivals for his top position in the party.[111]

Trials and Internment

Anti-Semitism would continue to figure prominently in the political struggle within the Polish leadership. The case of Marian Spychalski, one of Gomułka's closest allies, is instructive in this regard. Spychalski and Gomułka had worked together in the underground and shared a common understanding of the need for a Polish road to socialism. Consequently, both were accused of "rightist nationalist deviations." Since the PZPR leadership was not ready to put Gomułka on trial in 1948–49, they ordered security officials to open a case against Spychalski first. As deputy minister of defense, Spychalski was charged with complicity in a "military conspiracy" to turn the Polish military into a haven for anticommunist attitudes. Ironically, simultaneously to being removed from the party Central Committee for his "nationalist" leanings, he was also denounced as being of Jewish background—falsely, as it turned out. Gomułka understood very well that what became the "Trial of the Generals," which implicated Spychalski, also constituted an important stage in bringing him, Gomułka, "before a tribunal at a later date."[112] Some of Spychalski's accusers even suggested that Gomułka had been doing Spychalski's bidding rather than vice versa. In the fall of 1949, the leading politburo members personally subjected Spychalski to intense "conversations;" later on he was imprisoned, tortured, and interrogated by the secret police. Gomułka was left pretty much alone during this period. He continued to work in the insurance administration and recuperated from some health problems, while being constantly watched by the secret police.[113]

Spychalski's interrogators forced him daily to write long, detailed descriptions of his party activities going back to the war, no doubt with the intention of using him as the central witness in a wide-ranging investigation of Gomułka's ties with the Home Army and the London government during that period. Among the accusations against Spychalski was that he had carried out a nationalist program, the "so-called special path to the building of socialism in Poland," as head of the Polish People's Army during and after the war. Moreover, Marshal Rokossovskii, the new Polish minister of defense, complained that Spychalski had withheld funds and materials from the army, and one Soviet military-judicial advisor accused him of packing the military justice system "with reactionary elements from the ranks of prewar jurists, primarily Jews, and of getting rid of Soviet officer-jurists under various pretenses."[114] In fact, both Gomułka and Spychalski had inveighed on Moscow to remove the hundreds of leading Soviet officers in the Polish army in order to build its legitimacy as a Polish institution among the population.

As his close associates were arrested and interrogated, and bits and pieces of the case that was being built against him appeared in the party press, Gomułka fervently defended himself. In multiple letters he wrote to Bierut and Berman, he insisted on his and his comrades' innocence.[115] He should have known that this would be of no help in the least. After having him followed closely for months, the party leadership had Gomułka arrested on August 2, 1951. Stalin, who was immediately informed by telephone of Gomułka's arrest, apparently expressed his doubts about the wisdom of doing so.[116] Col. Józef Światło of the Xth Section of the Ministry of Public Security—and later a renowned defector to the United States—supervised Gomułka's arrest, which was a meticulously planned operation. Gomułka was transferred to a special compound in Miedzeszyn, in the southeast of Warsaw, where he lived in spartan circumstances and complete isolation, separated from his wife, who was also interned in the same compound, and allowed no communication with the outside world or with her. He was not sub-jected to torture and was able to read widely in the classics of world literature in Polish translation. Yet for all practical purposes, Gomułka was imprisoned.[117] In a letter to the Central Committee of June 1952, Gomułka complained that he had no idea why he was being held in isolation, with no access to newspapers, and noted that his health was deteriorating and that he needed medical care, in particular for his leg.[118]

Gomułka also had to endure endless interrogations. Again and again, he was forced to recapitulate one and the same story, told from only slightly different angles depending on the questions, but always in im-possibly dense and boring detail. The central issues were his wartime work in underground Warsaw, his relations with Nowotko and Finder and their deaths, his contacts with the Home Army and the represen-tatives of the London government, and his ties to Włodzimierz Lecho-wicz, who, despite his questionable interwar background, had worked with Spychalski in the AL and joined Gomułka in the Ministry of Re-covered Territories after the war.[119]

Gomułka stubbornly held to his version of events, was absolutely consistent in his presentation of the facts, and the interrogators made little progress in extracting any compromising information from him. He emphatically rejected some of the evidence presented to him as "lies of SPYCHALSKI," with whose "enemy activities" he claimed to have "had nothing in common."[120] When confronted with Spychalski's tes-timony that Gomułka had urged the Polonization of the army and its officers corps, including the acceptance of prewar officers as a way to reduce the numbers of Soviets officers, especially those who could not speak Polish, Gomułka accepted full responsibility, noting not only that the idea of this policy was to take the wind out the reactionaries' claims about Polish dependence on Moscow, but that he shared all of this with the PPR politburo at the time.[121] What he wisely did not mention was that Stalin had told him in a meeting of November 14, 1945: "You should Polonize the army all the way through. You can let go of the Red Army generals and officers whenever you want, as soon as possible."[122]

Gomułka's arrest and interrogation were supervised by Józef Światło, who may or may not have been working for Western intelligence services at the time. During a visit to East Berlin in December 1953, Światło defected to the West, turning over vast troves of information to the CIA during his depositions and broadcasting back to Poland about the excesses of the Security Police's repressive policies.[123] Gomułka was never brought to trial; Lebedev's observation to Stalin was that the Ministry of Public Security had made a "fiasco" of the investigation.[124] Stalin died in March 1953, though Gomułka remained under house arrest until the end of 1954, when Bierut, who continued to conduct business along Stalinist lines, decided he could keep him imprisoned no longer. It is important to remember that not only had Gomułka been interned for three and a half years but that several hundred other party members shared his fate, generally under much more trying circumstances. Moreover, the Stalinist system of terror introduced into Poland by Bierut and his comrades took a huge toll on the population as a whole. In 1952, some fifty thousand political prisoners were held throughout Poland. Between 1949 and 1954, at least fifteen thousand people died as a result of judicial actions, meaning execution or perishing while in prison. Some sixty thousand peasants faced interrogations, prosecutions, and internment in labor camps as a result of having allegedly withheld grain from the state during Bierut's fruitless attempt to collectivize Polish agriculture.[125]

● ●

How was it that Gomułka survived the coordinated attacks of Stalin and his Polish allies, when similar cases against László Rajk in Hungary and Rudolf Slánský in Czechoslovakia ended in show trials and executions? It did seem, as an American embassy official commented in July 1948, that by his actions and statements Gomułka had "probably signed his own death warrant."[126] We also know that Bierut sent Światło and other Polish agents to Hungary to explore evidence from the Rajk case in Hungary and the Slánský case in Czechoslovakia to use against Gomułka, Spychalski, and others.[127] Moreover, there was great pressure on officials in the Polish Ministry of Public Security from their Soviet and East European comrades to construct a case against Gomułka. Clearly the preparations were in motion; Światło, among others, attested to that.[128]

Gomułka himself wavered in his views on this question, sometimes arguing that he was safe: "I am convinced that they will not subject me to any kind of trial. They know me well. A trial would mean that I would say what they want, and I would not do that."[129] But at other times, and especially when hearing about the executions in Hungary, he worried that although he continued to live in palatable conditions and was not physically mistreated, Bierut might still do him in.[130] Berman attributed Gomułka's survival to the fact that the Polish leadership itself resisted Stalin's injunctions to prosecute him. Berman stated, somewhat disingenuously, "We . . . refused to allow Gomułka to be put on trial. We rejected all the charges against him. In this sense we were an exception, because we were the only ones who didn't allow leading figures to be wrested out of the party leadership."[131] But Gomułka rejected any notion that he was saved because of "scruples" on the part of the party leadership.[132] Rather, he thought that if he were put on trial, Berman would soon follow and Bierut could not accept that, for security chief Berman might reveal compromising material about Bierut.[133]

An equally plausible way of thinking about Gomułka's survival is that he was not Jewish while his accusers, for the most part, were. Slánský in Czechoslovakia, in contrast, was of Jewish background, as were almost all of Rajk's close associates and co-defendants in Hungary, though not Rajk himself. They were therefore susceptible to the accusation of being "cosmopolitans" and agents of Zionism. In Gomułka's case, this was an impossible accusation, given his consistent fight against the Jewish presence in the party and in Poland in general since the war. The "deviation" he represented was more akin to "Titoism," which, by the early 1950s had faded in salience to the Kremlin in comparison to the perceived threats of Zionism and American imperialism.[134] At the time of the gathering storm of the "Doctors' Plot" in the Soviet Union in 1952, how would it have looked for a party led by the trusted "Moscow Jews" Berman, Minc, and Zambrowski, not to mention the many prominent Jews in the Ministry for Public Security, including Gomułka's chief warder, Józef Światło, to put on trial and execute the unabashedly anti-Jewish defender of Polish "home communism," Gomułka?

Even after Stalin's death in March 1953, the Soviet leadership, most of whom had been in Stalin's closest circle, did not forget the Jewish question as it related to the Polish party or, for that matter, to the Soviet system. True, they dropped immediately the charges of Zionism and anti-Soviet activities against the Kremlin Doctors, almost all of Jewish origin, whom Stalin had had arrested before his death. But the anti-Semitism of the Soviet elite did not fade so quickly. On December 23, 1953, Nikita Khrushchev, Viacheslav Molotov, Georgii Malenkov, and Nikolai Bulganin met with Bierut in Moscow and ordered that Berman be removed as minister of public security, though they allowed him to retain his position in the politburo and the Council of Ministers. Similarly, Minc was to be relieved of his position as head of Polish State Planning, while retaining his membership in the politburo and Council of Ministers. In some sense, the new Soviet leadership even adopted the program and prejudices of Gomułka, insisting that the Polish party "deal seriously with the promotion of leading cadres from the ranks of advanced and loyal party comrades of Polish nationality."[135]

Ultimately, Gomułka can be seen as having won his struggle with Stalin, over what he saw as the related issues of the Jews in the Polish party and the distinct Polish road to socialism. When Gomułka was again selected as first secretary of the PZPR in 1956, Khrushchev and the Soviet leadership were not initially ready to accept this and tried to bully the Poles into forming a more Soviet-oriented government. But Gomułka managed to convince Moscow that Poland would remain a loyal member of the Soviet bloc under his leadership, while pursuing a socialist agenda according to specific needs of the Polish nation—something Stalin would not have allowed. When Gomułka did return to power in 1956, riding the wave of popular protest in the "Polish October," he began a process of weeding out Polish Jews from the upper ranks of the party. Anti-Jewish riots and scattered violence accompanied the upheavals of that fateful year.[136] Then, in the aftermath of the 1967 war in the Middle East, Gomułka bared his teeth when he learned that many PZPR comrades of Jewish origin sympathized with the Israelis, undermining the pro-Arab and anti-Zionist propaganda being cranked out by the Soviet bloc.[137] Gomułka's long and consistent effort to purge the Jews from the party was completed in 1968, when he conspired with anti-Semitic allies in the PZPR and in the Polish veterans' association to expel some fifteen thousand Jews from party and state positions, which led to the forced emigration of some eleven to twelve thousand Jews from Poland.[138]

Poland had been the lynchpin of the victorious Grand Alliance; sharp differences over its fate disrupted the postwar settlement and helped bring on the Cold War. Yet even in Poland, where the stakes were so high for Stalin and the Soviet Union, Gomułka managed to lead a political struggle within the Communist Party for the integrity of the Polish road to socialism, even after the program no longer conformed to Moscow's interests. The boundaries of the struggle were limited—Gomułka was, after all, a dedicated communist, just like his more notable rebel comrade Josef Broz Tito. Like Tito, he thought he was doing the right thing for the victory of socialism and the interests of the Soviet Union in his country. But the outcome of his resistance to Stalin's injunctions was inevitable. There would be no Finnish or Austrian solutions for Poland. Stalin would not compromise.

CHAPTER SEVEN

AUSTRIAN TANGLES

1944–1949

The story of Austria's pursuit of independence and sovereignty after the war was a complicated one from the beginning. In the Moscow Declaration on Austria, published November 1, 1943, the Great Powers established that Austria was a victim of Nazi aggression and deserved to be returned to a state of independence as it was prior to 1938. They also noted that Austria bore responsibility for its participation on the side of Germany in the war, but this clause received little notice in Austria itself.[1] In any case, none of the Allies expressed the intention to occupy Austria longer than would be necessary to ensure the final defeat of the Third Reich, get the Austrians back on their feet economically, eliminate Nazism as a social and political force, and create a new democratic Austrian government. The Soviet leadership gave no indication that this was not also its position. During the preparations for the occupation, Stalin stated unambiguously to Dimitrov, "We want Austria restored to its status quo as of 1938."[2]

Similar statements by Molotov and his deputies in the foreign ministry corroborated Maxim Litvinov's conception that Austria would belong to a group of independent and non-aligned countries in the middle of Europe. It was important to the Soviets that there be no return to the Habsburg monarchy, as a few prominent Austrians had suggested, and no Danubian federation, as broached by Churchill, which Moscow worried would be dominated by the Vatican or the British.[3] When the Red Army captured Vienna on April 13, 1945, its proclamation "To the Austrian People" reiterated the slogan that Austria fell "as the first victim of German aggression" and that the Red Army would liberate the Austrians from "German-Prussian domination."[4] Yet, in a paradox that would endure for a full decade until the state treaty guaranteeing Austrian independence was finally signed in 1955, the Allied armies occupied and administered a country they had officially liberated from Nazi overlordship as if it were a defeated nation. The mantra of the Austrian liberation from Nazi overlordship was, wrote American political officer, Martin Herz, "a psychologically reasonable and effective fiction."[5]

As in many of the other cases across Europe examined in this book, the Soviets pursued their goals in Austria on a number of levels. In their basic conception, Austria would in time become a "people's democracy" and evolve toward socialism, like the other countries of Europe. To facilitate this development, they encouraged Austrian communists in Moscow to set up initiative groups whose task it would be to create a bloc of democratic parties so as to form a "new"—if nominal—"democracy" in the country. Political officers of the Soviet element of the Allied Commission worked tirelessly with Austrian communists to find ways to radicalize Austria's politics and society in a more "progressive" direction, to no avail. The country remained obdurately anticommunist, despite direct Soviet control of two and a half of Austria's provinces—Lower Austria, Burgenland, and the Mühlviertel—and a quarter of Vienna's districts. Soviet influence was guaranteed, as well, by its membership in the Allied Commission, whose resolutions needed unanimous Four-Power concurrence. The Soviet occupation of Austria also conveniently—and, as we shall see, consequentially—justified the presence of Soviet troops in Romania and Hungary, where desired political transformations were hurried along by the threat and reality of the use of force. The formal Soviet argument was that their troops in Romania and Hungary provided the necessary logistical and communications infrastructure for the Red Army in Austria. At least until the peace treaties were signed with Romania and Hungary, Stalin would be extremely hesitant to remove his troops from Austria.

Unlike Germany, Austria had its own government and administration and fought for and gained a good measure of autonomy under the occupation. Yet unlike Romania, Finland, and Hungary, Austria also had a functioning Allied Commission that was genuinely quadripartite. This prevented the kind of Sovietization that took place elsewhere in Central and Eastern Europe. Moreover, while the eventual "hard" partition of the country into east and west, like Germany, was always a possibility, the combination of the lesser strategic importance of the country, the difficulty of imagining the economic survival of the eastern portion alone, and Soviet anxieties about forcing a potential military confrontation with the West over Austria, made this scenario unlikely. Still, despite the Austrians' fervent efforts and the distinct advantage of having their own government, they were unable to relieve themselves of the burdensome occupation until May 15, 1955, when a state treaty mandating the removal of Allied forces was finally signed. That it took so long to sign such a treaty—not a peace treaty but a state treaty, meaning a treaty with a formally nonbelligerent nation—was yet another anomaly of the Austrian postwar situation.

Karl Renner

The Soviet liberation and occupation of Austria commenced on March 29, 1945, as Marshal Fedor Tolbukhin's Third Ukrainian Front crossed the borders of Austria at Klostermarienberg in Burgenland. Two weeks later, Vienna fell after futile but fierce attempts to defend the city. Although most Austrians were greatly relieved that the war was over and they could focus on getting on with their lives, finding food, and locating their loved ones, they greeted the Soviet occupiers with a combination of resentment and fear.[6] Some of the anxiety dissipated when it became evident that the rumors about a Bolshevik revolution and mass executions in Vienna proved baseless. The Soviets also provided the Austrians with much-needed food supplies and set up effective soup kitchens.[7]

Neverthless, it soon became clear to everyone, including the Soviet authorities in Vienna and in Moscow, that the presence of Red Army troops in Austria undermined rather than furthered the formation of positive Austrian-Soviet relations and made the Austrian Communist Party even more unpopular than it already was. The Austrians were outraged by the violence, plunder, and rape committed by Soviet troops, not just in the taking of Vienna, where, as Martin Herz wrote, Soviet soldiers were "allowed to run hog wild," but in the context of occupation itself.[8] The Soviets themselves understood that the conduct of their

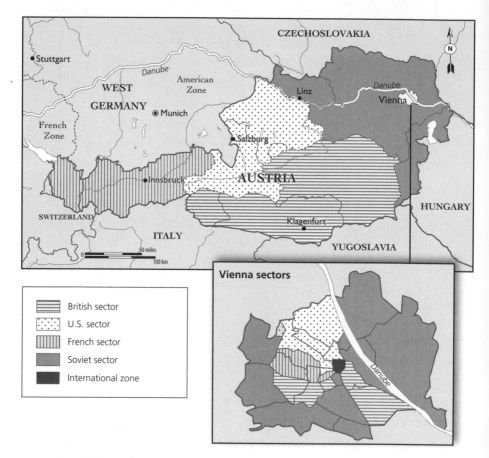

8. The Division of Austria

men diminished the attraction of communism in Austria. Scores of internal Soviet reports, running into the late 1940s, referred to "cases of rape, murder, and plunder. Therefore the population, which has suffered, cannot have a good view of us, even more since every case of violence becomes known literally to thousands."[9] But this was not all: as the Austrian communist Franz Honner complained, "hatred of the Soviet Union" was also fueled by the random arrests of Austrians in the streets of Vienna and elsewhere.[10]

Initial Soviet concerns about the joining of Austria to Germany (a "new Anschluss") or about an Austrian-centered and British-dominated Danubian federation also quickly dissipated. Early on, it was apparent that neither the Germans nor, especially, the Austrians were interested in joining together, and increasing communist control of Hungary, Yugoslavia, and Romania—and after February 1948, Czechoslovakia—soon robbed hypothetical prospects of a Western-sponsored Danubian federation of any basis. Besides, the European Advisory Committee foresaw the Four-Power occupation of Austria already in March 1945. In July, the commission delineated four zones of occupation, with Vienna being divided into four sectors, plus an international district in the inner city. The Potsdam Agreement of July–August 1945 cleared the way for the resolution of Soviet economic claims to "German assets" in Austria, and when the Western powers, who had first marched into Austria in May, assumed formal control of their occupation zones in late August, cooperation between the Four Powers seemed assured.[11] Even the symbolism of the "Four in a Jeep" patrols of the international First District—the inner city—of Vienna, augured well, at least symbolically, for a cooperative, successful, and short occupation of Austria.[12] This was apparently what the Soviets expected at the time. In fact, when Marshal Ivan Konev took over control of the Soviet troops in Austria from Tolbukhin on July 9, 1945, he expressed the hope that the Potsdam Conference would spin off an Allied Commission in Vienna that would produce a final settlement of the Austrian question.[13]

Already, on April 1, in the small town of Gloggnitz, the Red Army political authorities met with the seventy-five-year-old Karl Renner, former head of the interwar Austrian Social-Democratic Party, the first president of the Austrian Republic (1918), the president of the Austrian peace delegation at St. Germain (1919), and the last president of the Austrian Parliament (1933), who had offered his services to run the new Austrian provisional government desired by the Soviets.[14] There are some assertions in the historical literature that Stalin himself sought out Renner to be the first head of the Austrian administration, but the evidence is not convincing.[15] In any case, Renner told the Soviets,

I am old, but am ready with advice and actions to participate in the construction of a democratic regime. Today, communists and social democrats have the same goal—the destruction of fascism.

7.1 "Four in a Jeep," September 25, 1945, an international patrol in Vienna. AUSTRIAN NATIONAL LIBRARY.

As the last president of the parliament I could call a parliament in the time of war as a provisional government of Austria. I would exclude Nazis from the parliament.

With this I could conclude my functions and retire.[16]

When hearing from Tolbukhin about Renner, Stalin was reported to have been pleasantly surprised, "What," he shouted, "the old traitor is still alive? He is exactly the man that we need!"[17] In its return note from April 4, 1945, the general staff—Stalin and A. Antonov—expressed its confidence in Renner and expressed its support for his efforts to build a "democratic regime in AUSTRIA."[18] In their view, Renner was exactly the right politician to set up a broad anti-fascist coalition government that would include a tripartite partnership of socialists (postwar successors to the interwar social democrats), communists, and representatives of the "bourgeois" Austrian People's Party (ÖVP), the heirs of the

Christian Social Party. This was what Renner promptly set out to do under the direct sponsorship of the Red Army. He argued for a strong and highly structured administration in the Soviet zone, so that the other zones, which lagged behind, would have to follow suit, an idea that the Soviets encouraged.[19] The Soviets were less enthused that Renner took as his point of departure the democratic constitution of Austria of 1920, which he felt would serve the needs of the new republic until such time as reforms could be introduced.[20]

Renner was anxious from the first to demonstrate his loyalty to Stalin, the Soviets, and even to socialism. "The future of the country," Renner wrote to Stalin, "belongs to socialism. This is indisputable and requires no special emphasis."[21] He may not always have hit the right keys when professing his fealty, for instance when bragging in a letter to Stalin that he had known and admired Trotsky.[22] More important, however, was his readiness to work constructively with the Soviets as well as the communists, to whom he was willing to grant what they considered an appropriate share in the newly constructed Austrian administration. For the Soviets, this was reason enough to delay an earlier plan of having the Austrian communists organize an initiative group for founding a new communist-fostered bloc of parties.[23]

At seventy-five, Renner's energy, focus, and ability to rally numbers of anti-fascist Austrians to the new administration was astonishing. "The Austrians were very active," remembered a former Soviet occupation diplomat, "and if there had not been the hesitations of many of our organizations, things would have developed in a better fashion."[24] Renner knew how to stretch the limits of the possible with his Soviet interlocuters, sometimes making decisions and informing the Soviets later (for example, about the laws regarding government officials, the *Beamtengesetz*), sometimes strategically offering to resign.[25]

Local communists, in contrast, were less satisfied with Renner, whom they saw as a sworn enemy. When they first learned of his mandate to construct the first government, they sent an emissary to Moscow to try to convince Stalin, to no avail, of Renner's political foibles.[26] Soviet officials in Vienna also tended to dismiss the communists' frequent and noisy complaints about Renner. Colonel-General Zheltov noted that "for the Red Army, the main thing is that the country not be left without administration. . . . He [Zheltov] rejects defending one or the other of the parties."[27] If the communists reacted against what they saw as Renner's authoritarian politics (both Ernst Fischer and Johann Koplenig denounced his "Presidential Dictatorship"), the Soviets praised his effectiveness.[28]

Whether in their endorsement of the provisional government or in the Allied Control Council during the fall of 1945, the Soviet authorities consistently supported recognizing the Renner regime. In doing so, they portrayed themselves as the true advocates of Austrian independence versus the retrograde Western powers. They also moved more quickly than the Western powers in taking up diplomatic relations with the provisional government, hoping to steal the march on the West in the eyes of the Austrian population and to bolster support for the Austrian communists in the forthcoming elections.[29] On April 27, 1945, the provisional government assumed its offices in the Vienna Rathaus with twenty-nine members: eleven socialists, nine Christian socials (People's Party), seven communists, and two independents.[30]

The Western Allies were at first extremely hesitant about Renner and his Austrian Socialist Party (SPÖ). Fearing that he was too much of a leftist and would be too compliant with Soviet wishes, they initially refused to recognize the provisional government and protested to the Soviets in the newly constructed Allied Commission against the spread of its competence throughout Austria. (At this point, Renner's provisional government ruled only in the territory held by the Third Ukrainian Front—Vienna, Burgenland, and most of Lower Austria.) Renner himself noted that the Western Allies, and especially the British, treated him "like a leper."[31] But by the end of September 1945, the Western Allies found that Renner had sufficient backbone to stand up to the Soviets and thus were ready to recognize the competence of his government throughout Austria. At the same time, Renner proved strikingly adept at keeping the trust of the Soviets. He allowed the communists of the KPÖ to join his administration in a trilateral arrangement with the Socialist Party and the People's Party, while following his own "Austrian" national path of reconstructing an Austrian parliamentary democracy. Though earlier a proponent of Anschluss, which he claimed was "falsified and distorted" by Hitler—he never really recanted his

7.2 Austrian state chancellor Karl Renner is greeted by Soviet officers as he walks to the parliament, April 29, 1945. Renner with the beard, City Commander, Lieutenant General Aleksei V. Blagodatov in the center. AUSTRIAN NATIONAL LIBRARY.

stance—Renner successfully portrayed himself as a thoroughgoing Austrian patriot.[32] The Soviets were pleased with Renner's initial moves to work closely with the communists, and especially that he paid at least lip service to the desirability of a unity party. Yet Renner was careful not to compromise the organizational integrity of the much more powerful SPÖ. Moreover, he demonstrated an uncanny ability to resist Soviet blandishments and communist efforts to move quickly to a united Socialist-Communist party, as happened in East Germany and elsewhere in east central Europe. Not without an edge of irony, Soviet political advisor Koptelov wrote that Renner's ideas and judgments "were permeated with extreme optimism, whereby everything will be good; everything will be taken care of; everything will work itself out, and Austria will be filled with a new life and break forever with the Nazis."[33]

An important component of Renner's socialist program was to nationalize—what he called "socialize"—Austria's major industries, especially those seized by the Germans. This was not a matter of "party doctrine," he noted, but a measure that would serve "economic necessities."[34] But he had no chance to implement his plans since the Soviets, empowered by the Potsdam Conference in July–August 1945, seized German assets, including the important Zistersdorf oil fields and refineries. "If the others [the Allies] say no, so our intentions [to nationalize] will fall apart," Renner stated in August 1945.[35] Later Austrian representations about the desirability of nationalization fell on deaf ears in Moscow. "There is no need to return to the subject, it has already been decided," Vyshinskii told Karl Gruber.[36] The Austrian government would not get control of the core of their country's industrial capacities. But the Soviets hoped to appease Renner and the Austrian population by formally recognizing his government on October 24, 1945, before the other Allies.

That the Austrians themselves approved of Renner's path to overcoming these problems was demonstrated strikingly by the November 25, 1945, parliamentary election. From the Soviet and KPÖ point of view, its results constituted an unexpected and catastrophic defeat. Contrary to Austrian and Soviet expectations that the communists would receive in the neighborhood of 20 to 25 percent of the vote (15 percent according to the most "conservative" predictions), the communists received a mere 5.4 percent of the vote, which gave them only four seats in the new Austrian parliament. All remaining seats were divided between the Socialist Party, which received 44.6 percent, and the ÖVP, which, most surprisingly for many, had received 49.8 percent of the vote. The successful ÖVP showing reflected a broader European interest in Christian Democratic political platforms after the war. The KPÖ's defeat was all the more spectacular given the extraordinarily high participation rate. With 94 percent of all registered voters casting their ballots, the 120,000 member–strong Communist Party had attracted no more than 174,000 votes. These numbers left not the shadow of a doubt: the Austrian communists had demonstrated, as one party analyst wrote, "very weak influence" in Austrian society.[37] At least one explanation for this seemed evident: according to the commander of the American forces, General Mark Clark, the election outcome had a lot to do with the "Russians running around killing, looting, stealing, raping."[38] Communist leader Friedl Fürnberg complained that "a Russian psychosis" had spread in the Austrian population.[39]

Although important to the communist defeat, the fear and dislike of the Soviet occupiers was not the only story. The fall of 1945 was a particularly difficult time for the Austrians; refugees and displaced persons converged on the country from many directions but particularly from the Czech lands, raising the specter of disease and epidemics, while the hunger was as bad, if not worse, than anywhere else in Europe.[40] Both the socialists, under Renner, and the People's Party, led by Leopold Figl, proved to be adept campaigners and ardent defenders of interwar Austrian traditions, while providing hopeful visions of a better future to a hungry, bombed-out, and fearful people. Figl's background as a loyal supporter of the Austro-fascist Engelbert Dollfuss was something of an embarrassment, though, like Renner, Figl remained unapologetic about his political past. Indeed, he presented himself as an ardent Austrian patriot, which appealed to broad sections of nationalist-inclined Austrian voters, including the wives and mothers of Austrian POWs and missing, not to mention former Nazi sympathizers. At the same time, Figl could legitimately seize a moral high ground, since he had spent almost six years interned in Nazi prisons and concentration camps.[41] For Austrian farmers, villagers, and most middle-class voters, Figl and the People's Party represented the only acceptable political option.[42]

Whatever plans or expectations Stalin and the Soviets might have had up to this point for the occupation of Austria, the elections made crystal-clear that they could not count on support from the Austrian population or even the vast majority of the working class for their presence. As one senior Soviet military political official put it, "There is no question that the victory of the People's Party in the elections and in the formation of the new government have strengthened the political position of the reaction and of the Anglo-Americans in Austria."[43] As a consequence, the Soviets would from now on seek to tighten their control over the Austrian government through the Soviet element, irrespective of earlier promises of abandoning the need for the Allied Council.[44]

In the face of Soviet disappointment over the elections and growing suspicions of Renner and Figl, the Austrian politicians deftly handled the issue of how to deal with the defeated and humiliated communists. In behind-the-scenes negotiations that were carefully followed by all the Allies, Figl became the chancellor of the new government, as dictated by the election results, while Renner assumed the mostly ceremonial post of Austrian president. As a crucial concession to the Soviets, the communists were able to keep one ministry, that of electricity and energy, under the leadership of Karl Altmann, while the crucial Ministry of the Interior, held by the communists in the provisional government, fell to the socialists.[45]

Between December 1945, when the new government was formed, and June 1946, when it was recognized by the Four Power occupation as having control over its own domestic laws, except for those pertaining to occupation rights and foreign affairs, the attitude of the Western powers toward Renner and the Austrian government changed markedly. By mid-1946, the British and the Americans were much more supportive of extending Austrian government sovereignty than the Soviets, who were frustrated and annoyed by the Austrian government's growing power, independence, and seeming attentiveness to Western interests.[46] On April 12, 1946, the Austrian parliament adopted the 1920 constitution, as amended in 1929, which the Soviets interpreted as "a clear affirmation of the reactionary politics of the Austrian government," while Renner's speeches in this period were characterized as "open attacks on Soviet democracy and the Austrian communists."[47] Despite having been instrumental in setting it up, the Soviets found that they were uncomfortable with Austria's new government, which though still limited in its ability to govern on its own, nevertheless took increasing control of the economic and political life of the country.

The Soviets and the Austrian Communists

The election results reflected not only the popularity of the SPÖ and FPÖ messages with the Austrian people but also the problematic character of the KPÖ leadership. The main figures were Johann Koplenig and Friedl Fürnberg. Koplenig was the party's chairman and also served as vice chancellor in Renner's provisional government, while Fürnberg was the general secretary of the KPÖ's Central Committee. Fürnberg seemed to have enjoyed greater confidence among the Soviets than Koplenig, who, in Martin Herz's words, was a "wild-eyed fanatic of limited intellectual capacities."[48] Both were veteran communists who had spent the war years in Moscow fully involved in the whirl of émigré communist activities led by Georgi Dimitrov. In a memorandum to Stalin of April 3, 1945, Dimitrov suggested that they, as well as fourteen other Austrian communists and "prisoner-of-war antifascists," be sent from Moscow and Yugoslavia to join the Third Ukrainian Front as it moved into Austria.[49] The communists hoped the Soviets would place them at the head of a newly formed bloc of parties and were not at all pleased that Stalin had opted so quickly for the recognition of the Renner government. They never quite got used to the unwillingness of the Soviets to place them clearly ahead of the People's Party and the Socialist Party in their political calculations, and they tended to blame their unpopularity on the missteps of the Soviet occupiers and on the need to explain these to disgruntled Austrians.[50] Still, they were believers, and, like the vast majority of European communists, remained completely devoted to Stalin and Moscow's wishes.[51] In this sense, the burden of having to defend themselves constantly against the epithet "party of the occupation," as the party's later chief ideologist, Franz Marek, put it, was for Austrian communists as much a matter of fate as of choice.[52]

The Soviets and the KPÖ leaders themselves understood how unpopular they were among the Austrian people. The Austrian communists tried concentrating their efforts on the Austrian workers but found that they could not break the socialists' stranglehold on the unions. They also almost completely wrote off the Austrian countryside as a bastion of the People's Party.[53] In both cases, they were quick to blame their predicament on the disinformation spread by the Western Allies and leading Austrian parties. Still even the most pessimistic communist observers did not expect the catastrophic election results of November 1945.

The Soviet element agreed that the superior propaganda efforts of their Western counterparts bolstered the continuing hold of anti-Soviet attitudes on the Austrian population. At the same time, the Soviets blamed both their own and the Austrian communists' propaganda organs for their failure to "provide the necessary counters to the anti-Soviet denunciations [of the West]" and to target the social organizations of youth, labor, women, etc., which were firmly under the influence of the "bourgeois" parties.[54] The propaganda section of the

Soviet element responded to such criticisms by promising to devote more resources and attention to the press, media, and film in order to win over the Austrian population, especially its more "progressive" segments. There was a great deal of talk about the importance of appealing to Moscow to bring more musicians, academics, and exhibitions to Vienna to demonstrate the inherent superiority of Soviet life to the Austrians. At the same time, rigid campaigns of de-Nazification were dropped from the Soviet agenda.[55]

Western propaganda was far from the only problem, as the leaders of the Soviet element knew perfectly well. The announcement of the Marshall Plan in June 1947, the agreement between the United States and the Austrian government regarding imports into Austria at the same time, and the noticeable growth of American investment and aid during the months to follow put the Soviets in an unenviable position. Neither able nor willing to make any comparable economic commitments, they knew no better option than to criticize the United States for infringing on Four Power control agreements and "distorting" the economy of Austria with these highly popular policies.[56]

The Austrian communists pinned their hopes of gaining greater support among the working class in the four hundred and fifty or so industries in Soviet-occupied Lower Austria that were designated as "former German assets" and therefore remanded to Soviet control by the Potsdam agreement. In accordance with Order no. 17 of June 1946, the Soviet element had taken over these factories and plants, which included the important Austrian oil industry, and subjected them to the newly formed Administration of Soviet Properties in Austria (USIA).[57] With the overall management of the USIA controlled by Soviet officials, the Austrian communists figured they could influence the economic and social policies of these enterprises. This, they calculated, would give them leverage over the USIA's workers and increase their own standing in the country.

Yet the KPÖ leadership and the Soviet directors of the USIA industries frequently did not get along. As Fürnberg complained to a visiting Soviet Central Committee representative, the Soviet bosses of the Danube Steamboat Shipping Company and of the Zittersdorf oil industry, who reported directly to ministry officials in Moscow, tended to ignore the suggestions of the KPÖ leaders and even fired communist workers.[58] When Colonel General Zheltov, head of the Military Council of the Central Group of Forces and the chief political officer of the Soviet element, was informed about this, he merely noted that Fürnberg and Koplenig were constantly whining about one thing or another. The Austrian communists suffered from "tendencies to *diktatorstvo* [dictatorial tendencies]," he stated; they exhibited a desire to run everything and sometimes needed to be restrained.[59]

In general, the Soviets did not think terribly highly of their Austrian "comrades." The Austrians' repeated requests to visit Moscow were turned down by the Central Committee, at least in part because it would have made the KPÖ "look like agents of Moscow to the Austrians."[60] On the one hand, the Soviets worried about excessive leftism in the party, in Soviet parlance "sectarianism" or, more seriously, "Trotskyism"; on the other they criticized "elements" of the party for nationalism, kowtowing to "Social-Democratism," and deeming themselves superior to their Soviet instructors.[61] In any case, there is no evidence that the one scenario that might have helped the KPÖ attain some political power in Austria, the division of the country between East and West, with power in the east handed over to the KPÖ by the Soviets, was seriously considered by Soviet leaders either in Vienna or in Moscow at this time or even later.[62]

Despite their reserved attitude toward the Austrian communists, the Soviets still needed and wanted the KPÖ's feedback on a variety of important matters, from the laws passed by the Austrian government that needed the imprimatur of the Soviets in the Allied Council to drafts of a potential state treaty. In almost every case, the Austrians' views were more "radical" than the Soviets', but this did not mean that they were not given serious consideration and sometimes validated by the Soviet "superiors."[63] Whenever they had the chance, the Austrian communists tried to undermine the process of achieving a state treaty. They understood that without Soviet forces to support them, they would have next to no influence on Austrian society. In a comment on an early draft of the state treaty circulated by James Brynes, the American secretary of state, Koplenig and Fürnberg railed that "the acceptance of this or a similar treaty would mean the handing over of Austria to the anglo-american bloc. . . . Foreign fascists and the Austrian reaction would become the rulers of Austria."[64] The Soviets paid attention, and sometimes even repeated the Austrians' language in their communications with each other.

The Soviets understood that the Austrian population resented their presence in the country. Part of this antipathy clearly derived from the unforgotten "excesses" committed by Soviet troops as they marched into Austria on March 29, 1945, and conquered Vienna in the middle of April. Austrian communists, officers of the Soviet element, and other Soviet observers noted how much the reputation of the Soviet Union was dragged down by these repeated incidences, even after the war was long concluded. The communist Franz Marek noted that rape was the first thing that the party central talked to him about when he returned to Vienna in August 1945.[65]

Although Soviet commentators all insist that the Austrians exaggerated the numbers and violence of incidents and that Soviet soldiers were often blamed for actions committed by civilians in Soviet uniform or decommissioned Soviet soldiers who had not yet returned home, the repeated references to the detrimental behavior of the troops underscore the importance of this violence to the political failures of the communists. Similarly, Soviet and Austrian documents emphasize the Austrians' resentment about Soviet seizure and sometimes removal of Austrian industrial establishments. At one meeting of workers where the removal of an entire Viennese factory was decried, there were shouts in the hall: "'That's thievery!' 'The dogs!' Even after the war they continue to plunder!' and so on."[66]

According to the Potsdam agreement, the Soviets had the right to requisition property that had been German owned before the war. But the Soviets' desperate need for materials and equipment for rebuilding made the legal definition of what was "German-owned property" very broad indeed. Moreover, the insistent Soviet demands for Austrian rail cars and locomotives crippled attempts to rebuild the local transportation system. At the same time, the Red Army seized much of what it needed to provision its troops and supply its installations—in contrast to the other occupying forces. Set against the relief efforts of UNRRA after the war and the first stages of the Marshall Plan in the winter of 1947, the Soviet demands on the Austrian economy seemed deleterious in the extreme.[67]

On top of the continuing violence of Red Army soldiers against the population and the seizure of important industries, the Soviets did not endear themselves to the Austrian population by refusing to budge on the question of the repatriation of Austrian prisoners-of-war who were still in the Soviet Union. The Austrian communists were anxious to take the lead on this issue so as to be seen as the party that was able to bring home the POWs. The KPÖ asked to send Ernst Fischer officially and Johann Koplenig secretly to Moscow in 1947 to deal with this issue in the context of the negotiations about the state treaty. The Soviet apparat was not interested.[68] Austrian POWs were treated much like German POWs and were in the hands of the NKVD, which was unwilling to reveal their existence, not to mention their location or allow correspondence. Immediately after the war, most Austrians did not know whether their relatives in Soviet POW camps were dead or alive.

Meanwhile, the increasing incidence of arrests and kidnappings for alleged espionage or anti-Soviet activities left Austrian public figures, journalists, and bureaucrats—those groups who seemed to be most at risk—skittish and worried. Even among the broader public, Soviet actions aroused intense opposition.[69] In one of the most spectacular cases, the Soviet seizure of Anton Marek in June 1948, a senior police official in the Austrian Ministry of Interior, the press and radio were filled with questions about his disappearance. Colonel General Zheltov responded to government and Allied inquiries that Marek had been arrested on "charges of organizing espionage against the Soviet occupation troops and that other officials of the Ministry of the Interior were involved in these actions."[70] For Marek, the publicity had no effect: he was brought to the Soviet Union and sentenced to twenty-five years in prison. (He was released only after the signing of the state treaty in 1955.)[71]

Especially with the heating up of the Cold War at the end of 1947 and beginning of 1948, the Soviet Central Committee also scrutinized its own political establishment in Austria. Already in June 1946, A. A. Kuznetsov had questioned the competence of the military-political leadership in Austria at a Central Committee meeting. "I've worked with them," he stated, "and there is nothing to hope for from them."[72] In face of the continuing loss of Soviet status among the Austrian population, Colonel General Zheltov was heavily criticized and eventually removed from his position in Austria for failing to lead a successful propaganda effort against the West. At the same time, the propaganda section of the Soviet element was sharply attacked for its contacts with "Zionist" organizations in Austria; as also happened with other representative bodies of the Soviet Union abroad during the early years of Stalin's "anti-cosmopolitan" campaign, its Jewish members were singled out and accused of self-indulgence and a lack of vigilance.[73]

Yet as the Soviet leadership in Austria spoke increasingly about tightening up their ideological line, working harder to mobilize social organizations, and providing more support for the KPÖ, they also periodically mentioned that this was necessary because they would soon leave Austria. Hearing both the Austrian political leadership and the Soviets speaking about the withdrawal of all Allied troops from Austria gave the Austrian communists the sense that they could soon be left in the lurch, which in turn undermined their morale.[74]

Soviet support of the communists took two forms: secret and quite substantial financial contributions and unremitting efforts to improve and control their ideological education.[75] By mid-1949, the Soviets wanted the communists to be more explicitly open to the development of an Austrian people's democracy, and criticized them for being too reticent about the Soviet Union's important role in "fostering peace and security" in Europe.[76]

The Soviets also supported the formation of new parties and blocs of parties as a way to split the Socialist Party and weaken the People's Party. Despite these efforts, the elections of October 9, 1949, did nothing to strengthen the communists' marginal position in Austrian parliamentary politics. Their electoral alliance with the leftist socialists stagnated at only 5.1 percent of the votes, unable to benefit from the losses of close to 6 percent, which both the socialists and the Austrian People's Party endured. Instead, these votes went to a newly established political party: the national liberal Federation of Independents (*Verband der Unabhängigen*), whose advocacy to end de-Nazification ensured it the support of former NSDAP members and sympathizers.

The Soviets saw these results as an even more significant failure than those of 1945. "The reactionary camp in Austria has strengthened its position," and: "The government of Austria acts as the agent of Anglo-

American imperialism" were typical of the comments they made internally.[77] In this situation, they turned to ever more Stalinist tactics. On the one hand, the Austrian Communist Party was to be thoroughly "Bolshevized" and purged of those who continued to harbor "Social Democratic illusions of the past;" on the other, the KPÖ needed to stand on an uncompromising platform of establishing a people's democracy in Austria and to demonstrate to the Austrians the advantages of becoming like their neighbors, Czechoslovakia and Hungary. The Soviets seemed to have resigned themselves to the fact that their capacities to influence the course of Austrian politics were severely limited for the time being. The end of the communist participation in the coalition government (the KPÖ had withdrawn from it in late 1947) had provoked no particular reaction from their side, and when the communists looked to gain support from the strike movement that gathered force in the fall of 1950, the Soviets provided minimal support. In fact, they complained later about the loss of workdays in their factories.[78]

Trouble with the Allies

Meanwhile, the Four Powers were still far from any final agreement on how to end their joint occupation of Austria and deliver on their promises to restore the country's independence and sovereignty. Indeed, when examining the protracted history of the negotiations that began in January 1947 and ended only with the state treaty in 1955, the observer is struck by the salience of contingency and happenstance, of bad luck, and sometimes of bad faith on the part of the negotiating powers. Knowing their goals to be at odds with each other, both the Western Allies and the Soviets tried to appear neither too anxious to reach an agreement nor as obdurate as to make it impossible. Such stances, however, led them to send out signals that were often ambiguous, which decreased the chances of arriving at an agreement that would have been acceptable to everyone (including the Austrians).[79]

The larger political context did not help, either. Although of lesser significance in the poker game of influence and control that shaped up between the Soviet Union and the United States and its allies on the European continent, Austria was nevertheless a card that counted and that could be played alongside the German, the Hungarian, or the Polish one. Moreover, developments in other parts of the region—Yugoslavia, east central Europe, Germany—disrupted the settling of internal Austrian issues that would normally have appeared resolvable. Finally, there was the real and difficult issue of security guarantees for the time after the Four Powers would have pulled out. What if the Soviets would put renewed pressure on Austria or even—the nightmare of the American Defense Department—would march back in from the neighboring territories of their allies? On the Soviet side, there were mirroring fears that the Americans would seek to make a "bridgehead" out of Austria for the Western Alliance and use it to its advantage in the "war of nerves" in Europe.[80]

Stalin had no firm plans for Austria that became apparent over the course of nearly a decade of negotiations. But the West was only somewhat more consistent about its strategy, and its negotiating stance suffered from differences between the United States, Great Britain, and France. Unlike the Russians, who were "loath to relinquish their hold on this country," the British generally shared the Americans' desire "to withdraw their armed forces from Austria as quickly as possible," while the French element, "usually adopts a position in between the two extremes"—this, at least, is how John Erhardt, the American minister in Austria, saw it.[81]

Even the Austrians hesitated at certain moments in their program for obtaining a state treaty; sometimes, the price that the Soviets exacted, both financially and politically, seemed too high. One needs to be clear about it: the Soviets were unquestionably the more intransigent and difficult negotiating power. But the insertion of additional problems and issues, most of them unrelated to Austrian developments and therefore out of the control of Austrian politicians, contributed to making the efforts of the Austrians to free themselves from external controls exceedingly difficult.

From the very beginning of the occupation, Karl Renner sought ways to encourage the Allies to leave. His initial position was simple and reflected that of many Austrian politicians; Austria "carried absolutely no responsibility" for the war and, in any case, had been "punished enough" during those years.[82] Now the Austrians wanted to rule themselves, and they wanted to be members of the United Nations organization, which was just being created. Having had little success in convincing the Allies to satisfy these maximalist demands, Renner soon toned down his rhetoric. In September, he declared that the Austrians would take on all the burdens that the Four Powers put on them, "no matter how hard and how little earned they also may be."[83] At the same time, he continued his attempts to persuade the Allies to lower them. To Stalin, he wrote: we "have the hope that soon we will be alone in our land" and that the burden of the occupation itself "can soon be reduced." There was no need for the mass of troops on Austrian soil. It was like having "four elephants on a small Austrian boat."[84]

Meanwhile, Karl Gruber of the ÖVP, the foreign minister of the Second Austrian Republic, and previously Renner's deputy in charge of Foreign Affairs in the provisional government, consistently pushed the Allied governments to sign a state treaty that would lift the occupation and restore Austrian sovereignty. Gruber worked especially closely with British prime minister Ernest Bevin to organize Allied initiatives to unburden Austria of its occupation forces, which placed serious financial, political, trade, and, above all, perhaps, psychological burdens on the country. Bevin proved to be a consistent supporter of the Austrian cause. But whatever Renner, Gruber, or any other Austrian politician could do, the power to decide remained exclusively in the hands of the Four Powers.

The Allied Control Agreement of June 28, 1946, which expanded the authority of the government in Vienna throughout Austrian territory and formally recognized the Austrian government formed after the elections in the previous December, led some Austrian leaders to hope that a state treaty would follow in quick succession.[85] The first realistic opportunity for this came in late 1946 and early 1947, with the preparations for the Council of Foreign Ministers meetings where the peace treaties with Hungary, Romania, Bulgaria, Italy, and Finland were to be finalized. These countries had all been allies of the Third Reich at one point or another during the war and were categorized, unlike Austria, as defeated nations. But the Austrian negotiations got tied up especially with the Hungarian and Romanian treaty considerations. The crucial issue was the stationing of Soviet troops in both of these countries, which the Soviets considered important for both strategic reasons, to secure the western glacis of east central Europe, and domestic ones, to make sure that the transitions in those countries to "new democracies" (and to people's democracies), would go smoothly. Since the Soviets' prima facie legal justification for the presence of their troops in Hungary and Romania was the necessity to provide logistical back-up for their occupation forces in Austria, both the Soviets and the Western powers understood that an Austrian peace treaty and the removal of Soviet forces from Austria would call into question the continued presence of Soviet troops in Hungary and Romania as well, which, in turn, would not only significantly weaken the Soviet military posture in central Europe but also jeopardize the Sovietization of these countries. There were other issues that emerged in the negotiations that ensued at the Paris Peace Conference, among them questions about the large number of displaced persons in Austria, many of whom were identified by the Soviets as "fascists," and the allegedly slow pace of Austrian de-Nazification and demilitarization. But whereas these and many similar issues that would emerge in the negotiations over time were negotiable, the placement of Soviet troops was not.

In general, the documents make it apparent that there was no flexibility in the Soviet position in this period. It would be "premature," noted the Soviet foreign ministry instructions for the upcoming April 1946 Council of Foreign Ministers (CFM) meeting, to turn over "supreme power" to the Austrians. If the Austrian question was placed on the agenda, it should be scuttled by blaming the Austrians for insufficient progress on de-Nazification and demilitarization.[86] At the following Paris CFM meeting in June–July, this line was followed to the letter. As soon as the Austrian question was brought up, the Soviets demanded that Austria fulfill the conditions of "de-Nazification" and "democraticization" before any discussions of independence could begin. An analysis of the Soviet diplomatic documents, including the dense interchange between Allied ministries of foreign affairs during that spring and early summer of 1946, indicates that the Soviets had no interest in reaching an agreement about Austria at this point. One example was Molotov's exchange with Stalin, days before the beginning of the CFM meeting, about the need to sign a new control agreement about Austria independently from the negotiations regarding a state treaty. Signing such an agreement, Molotov suggested, would increase the powers of the Austrian government and limit the role of the Allied Council, which would provide the Soviets with "additional arguments to turn down the consideration of [U.S. secretary of state James] Byrnes's proposed treaty on Austria at the Council of Ministers meeting in Paris on June 15."[87] Stalin's undated notation on Molotov's communication was typically laconic, but unambiguous: "I agree."

The peace treaties with Hungary and Romania were signed at the Paris CFM meeting on February 10, 1947. They encoded the right for the Soviets to maintain troops in these countries until the Austrian State Treaty was signed and Allied troops were removed from the country. As negotiations on the state treaty cranked up again at the same time in London, two new contentious issues emerged. The first was Yugoslav claims for Austrian territory in Carinthia.[88] The Soviets, who backed them in a general way, urged Belgrade to deal with the Austrians on this issue themselves. They were annoyed, however, when the Yugoslavs engaged in separate talks with the British, offering concessions of which the Soviets were initially, at least, unaware.[89] The second, more serious problem revolved around article 35 of the proposed treaty, which dealt with Soviet claims to "German assets" in eastern Austria, the most crucial of which was the valuable oil industry located in the Soviet zone. Bevin wrote that the negotiations were deadlocked on the German assets question; an "impasse" had been reached, and "the breaking point had not yet come."[90]

In October 1947, the French Deputy High Commissioner, General Paul Cherriere, proposed a plan for the Austrians to compensate the Soviets for the German assets with a one-time payment of $100 million, in addition to 50 percent rights to the oil output and a third of the exploration rights. The Soviets countered with a higher number, $200 million, and the demand for sole ownership of the Danube Steamboat Shipping Company (*Donaudampfschiffahrtsgesellschaft*), both of which the Western Allies rejected. But the Cherriere plan at least provided a basis for negotiations, since the Allies and the Austrians accepted the principle that the Soviets had legitimate claims for compensation.

The Moscow CFM Conference in March and April 1947 brought no agreement about Austria, either. At about the same time, the announcements of the Truman Doctrine (in March 1947) and the Marshall Plan (in June 1947) rankled the Soviets and worsened relations between them and the Western Allies. The Soviets, it appeared, were fed up with their situation in Austria. The Austrian government was "an obedient marionette of the U.S. government," and the communists were hopelessly passive. From November 1947, they were not represented in the government, had only four seats in the parliament, and had been outmaneuvered by the Social Democrats and the People's Party even in the Soviet zone.[91] Yet the Soviets seemed unable to find a way to extricate themselves from a bad situation. In their view, the Americans had shackled the Austrian economic system to the West. The Allied Council had ceased to produce any meaningful agreements. Neither side, though, wanted to give up the negotiations altogether, since both felt they needed to gain support among the Austrian population and be able to blame the other side for the hold-up in granting Austrian independence. The British, who had been working closely with the Austrians to achieve an agreement, seemed genuinely perplexed. Wrote Bevin in December 1947: "The Austrian question should have been settled long ago. What has been holding it up? Why is a liberated country still occupied by four Allied armies?"[92]

The Czechoslovak coup of February 25, 1948, had a profound impact on the Austrians, giving them, in the words of U.S. high commissioner General Geoffrey Keyes, "a first class attack of jitters."[93] When the Czechoslovak noncommunist ministers resigned from the coalition government in February 1948 to protest the communist control of the police, the communists mobilized their labor unions to take to the streets and directed the police to undermine the democratically elected government led by Eduard Beneš. By May 1948, the government was completely under the control of the communists and in June, Czechoslovak communist leader Klement Gottwald replaced Beneš as president. The Austrians were petrified that something similar could happen to them, all the more so since neighboring Hungary was also succumbing to a communist takeover, which was formally completed in August 1949. Far from everyone understood that the Austrian communists were in no position to pull off a comparable coup without the direct intervention of Soviet troops, which, in turn, could have provoked a war with the West, something Moscow would hardly have risked at the time, and especially over Austria.[94] Moreover, Austrian politicians as well as the Western Allies overestimated the insurrectionary capabilities of the so-called "Werkschutz," armed groups of Austrian workers, usually communists or left socialists, from the USIA industries.[95]

Along with the apparent strength of the Communist Party of Italy, the Czechoslovak coup therefore "dampened the eagerness of both major [Austrian] parties for a withdrawal of the [Western] occupation troops as a first step toward actual independence."[96] More importantly, the coup also had a marked effect on the Americans, who began to view the possibility of pulling out of Austria as a mistake given apparently insatiable Soviet territorial ambitions. While the State Department, led first by George Marshall and then by Dean Acheson, continued to support negotiations toward a state treaty, the Joint Chiefs of Staff grew increasingly nervous about American (and Western Allied) withdrawal without the creation of an Austrian army that could defend the country against Soviet military action.[97] The Department of the Army's Intelligence Division suggested the possible scenario of a "Soviet-inspired revolutionary attempt" in Austria as soon as the Four Powers withdrew.[98] Despite the Soviets' readiness to make some concessions in connection with Yugoslav territorial and reparations demands and to allow the formation of an Austrian army armed by the Western powers after the conclusion of a treaty, the negotiations on an Austrian treaty were again broken off in May 1948, this time because of Western concerns. The Western powers used the Yugoslav territorial demands as the justification.[99]

A series of new developments converged in early 1949 to constitute what many historians consider the best opportunity to conclude a state treaty prior to 1955.[100] In the fall of 1948, Austrian foreign minister Gruber inquired once more of the Four Powers about resuming the negotiations. From the Soviets, he received encouraging signs that the crucial issue of German assets could be resolved through mutual concessions.[101] Along with the Austrian representative in Moscow, Norbert Bischoff, Gruber made the rounds of the Soviet foreign ministry, indicating a willingness to make a variety of economic concessions, though holding the line on territorial ones. This latter point was now less problematic as Moscow had stopped supporting Yugoslav demands since the expulsion of Tito and the Yugoslav party from the Cominform in June 1948 and the concomitant souring of Soviet-Yugoslav relations. (Although the Soviets still expressed some concerns for ethnic rights of the Carinthian Slovenes out of a vague Slavophilism, they suggested only a few minor border corrections in that connection.) Bischoff argued to Soviet foreign minister Vyshinskii that the Americans were exploiting the slowness of the state treaty process to deepen their influence in Austria, especially among the conservative rural population. Best to conclude a treaty right away, he argued, before Soviet-Austrian relations were irreparably damaged.[102] Similarly, Gruber warned that Austrian chauvinism was on the rise because of a lack of a treaty. Further delay would only increase the dangers from the right.[103] Chancellor Figl was also pushing hard for an agreement, although he insisted that the "independent economic existence of Austria" and the complete sovereignty of the country not be imperiled in the coming negotiations.[104] On the difficult issues involved in article 35 on the German assets, Molotov wrote to Stalin that there were good reasons to think that the differences about compensation "will be eliminated . . . in the course of future negotiations." There was no concern, he added, about Austria joining together with Germany again or having further quarrels about the Yugoslav-related issues.[105]

At the CFM meetings in Paris in May and June 1949, both sides seemed ready to make the necessary concessions to conclude a treaty. The figure of $150 million was agreed to for the German assets, and the Soviets backed off of the need for any territorial concessions from Austria for the Yugoslavs. Secretary of State Dean Acheson reported back to Washington that most of the disputed issues had been resolved and that "the British and French delegations, as well as Austrian Foreign Minister Gruber, are doubtful whether [any] outstanding issues prevent agreement on a treaty."[106]

On June 20, with the broad outlines of a deal sketched out by the ministers, the treaty was remanded to their deputies, whose job it was to hammer out the details by September 1. Gruber pushed especially hard on British foreign secretary Bevin to complete a state treaty right away; Austria was prepared to take on whatever financial burdens necessary to free the country from the Allied occupation, he declared.[107]

But the Austrian foreign minister was constantly up and down about the prospects of an agreement; writes one historian, Gruber was "hectic, nervous, moody, and volatile" throughout this entire period.[108]

The Americans also seemed ready to sign the treaty: one State Department official in the Division of Austrian affairs wrote that the failure of an agreement at that point would be "completely demoralizing for the Austrians" and would have serious adverse effects on the "Austrian national character we had hopes of building up."[109] Moreover, it appeared that the Soviets were open to a solution as well: American deputy for the CFM on Austria, Samuel Reber, reported that the Soviet deputy, Georgii Zarubin, "seems most anxious to conclude negotiations early in August and said that once Article 35 [on the German assets] had been settled he saw no further obstacles to [a] speedy conclusion of [the] treaty draft."[110] The American negotiators were convinced that the agreement reached in Paris was a "huge victory," which would bring about "an independent and self-sufficient Austria."[111]

Such assessments turned out to be premature. The deputies failed to finalize the agreement and adjourned their negotiations until a September 22 meeting in New York. Most importantly, the Soviets dug in their heels on the issue of future oil concessions. They demanded not only the best fields, but a larger percentage of their output (sixty instead of forty) than the Austrians would receive.[112] The Americans hardened their own stance on this issue, in part because of continuing Department of Defense lobbying against the signing of a treaty from a European security point of view. The British were more positive. From a private meeting with Foreign Minister Vyshinskii on September 30, 1949, Ernest Bevin walked away with the impression that Stalin and the Soviets genuinely wanted an agreement, and kept pushing in Washington for concessions that would make this possible.[113] Bevin wrote to Acheson, "I have come to the conclusion that the Russians want a treaty. I can't identify the exact reason for this, but it is clear to me that Stalin has ordered that reasonable attempts should be made to create this opportunity."[114]

With Gruber constantly in his ear, Bevin urged the Americans that "this is a psychological moment for the conclusion of a treaty which we cannot afford to miss." To do so now, would mean postponing an agreement "indefinitely."[115] But the renewed talks of the deputies in

New York foundered on the issue of what should be considered German assets, which the Soviets now defined in such a broad way that the Western representatives stepped away from concluding a treaty. Bevin worried privately that the negotiations would be imperiled by the successful Soviet test of an atom bomb, announced by President Truman on September 23. This "and the general feeling regarding Russia . . . make a settlement very doubtful."[116]

A renewed impetus for an agreement came from the American side, when, on October 26, President Harry S. Truman finally stepped into the debate on Austria between the Defense Department and the State Department and sided with the latter in favor.[117] The relevant National Security Council report states, "The President has determined that it should be United States policy to agree at an early date to a draft Austrian treaty on the best terms attainable. If the recent schedule prevails and agreement is obtained, the Austrian treaty may be concluded by the Deputies within the next few weeks and presented to the four governments for final acceptance."[118] In the following days, Washington offered a number of important concessions to the Soviets on article 35, which dealt with German assets. Essentially, the United States caved in on all disputed issues, including the percentage ownership of the proceeds of the oil fields and the number of businesses to be considered German assets (though some problems with Western-owned businesses would be brought up later). A deal was ready to be signed.[119]

Yet the Defense Department still dragged its feet. Omar Bradley, chairman of the Joint Chiefs, reiterated his fears that "the withdrawal of occupation forces may create a military vacuum in that country [Austria] with which the communists, following their usual practice, may be able to seize power and dominate Austria." This in turn "could shake the very foundations of our national security and that of other noncommunist nations throughout the world."[120] He worried, as did many in Washington, that the Soviets could move their troops back into Austria if they decided for their own reasons that the conditions of the treaty were not being observed.[121] Bradley was not convinced by Gruber's insistence that the Austrians could forge a new army capable of resisting the Soviets in the three months between signing the treaty and the withdrawal of Allied forces, though he was aware that "secret and extremely discrete" talks (and preparations) had been going on between the Western powers and "certain Austrian ministers" regarding the building of an Austrian defense force.[122] Meanwhile Acheson expressed doubts about Gruber's reliability, suggesting that he was too willing to sign a treaty simply because it would gain him "popular support."[123]

Not only the Americans were hesitant. Despite the fact that the Soviet Foreign Ministry recognized that no more concessions could be wrested from the Austrians or the Western powers, Stalin and his advisors were inherently mistrustful of the West's intentions.[124] The Americans and British seemed suspiciously anxious to sign the state treaty. Were they trying to push the Soviets further away from the Yugoslav borders in order to assert increasing influence there? Or were they, as Deputy Foreign Minister Andrei Gromyko warned in an October 22, 1949 memorandum to Stalin, not just trying to remove Soviet troops from Austria, "but also from Hungary and Romania on whose territory the Soviet Union . . . has the right to maintain troops necessary for the maintenance of communication lines with the Soviet Zone of Austria?" Gromyko urged taking a more careful look at the Soviet negotiating posture.[125]

Two days later, on October 24, 1949, the politburo, clearly with Stalin's imprimatur, issued a directive to Foreign Minister Vyshinskii which stated "we are not interested in a quick conclusion of the Austrian Treaty. Therefore make use of the existing contradictions and do not conclude the preparation of the treaty at the New York meeting of the deputies."[126] Just as the Americans were ready to go ahead with the treaty, the Soviets decided, after much internal wrangling, that they would step back from signing, thus effectively destroying the possibility of a state treaty until after Stalin's death. It seems Stalin and his lieutenants had simply lost the will to negotiate a treaty that would free Austria from the occupation. In retrospect, the summer and fall 1949 opening on the difficult issues of the state treaty looks very much like a "missed opportunity" in the history of postwar Austria. Between December 1949 and the middle of February 1950, the Austrian government did everything it could not to let that chance go down the drain. Norbert Bischoff, its political representative in Moscow, sent five separate formal notes to the Soviet government and approached his Ministry of Foreign Affairs contacts to restart the negotiations, but to no avail.[127] The Soviets kept bringing up side issues like Trieste or the supposed debts for feeding the Austrians in the summer of 1945 (the *Erbsenschulden*—literally: "green pea debts") to deflect attention from their unwillingness to leave Austria at this point.

Soviet Perspectives on Austria

Khrushchev claimed in his memoirs that Stalin's desire to support Yugoslav demands associated with Trieste was critical to the Austrian negotiations.[128] After the Soviet-Yugoslav split became public in June 1948 and Tito proved more resistant to Soviet pressure than Stalin had anticipated, there was no longer any obligation or interest to back Yugoslav claims. Khrushchev reports: "I remember Stalin saying, 'We didn't sign any peace treaty [with Austria]. Why did we have to refuse to sign? That was a mistake, all because of Trieste. Now that issue doesn't even exist anymore.'"[129]

The documents of the Soviet element of the Allied Control Commission in Austria during 1948 and 1949 contain repeated references to the imminent withdrawal of all Allied occupation forces in Austria. The question for the Soviet officials in Vienna was not whether the withdrawal would occur, but what would happen when it did. Washington's hesitations in 1948 and 1949 did not help matters. American military leaders made very strong arguments about the importance of maintaining the connections between American troops in West Germany and in Italy, while insuring that the Soviet Union would not seize all of Austria. Once Truman decisively intervened on behalf of a state treaty, the Americans put their negotiating house in order, and returned to the Soviets with a firm proposal in hand in November 1949. But the Soviets were no longer willing to come to the table.[130]

Khrushchev's portrait of Stalin returning to the issue of signing the state treaty is backed up by internal Soviet documents that show Stalin's interest in getting out of Austria even before problems with the Yugoslavs were beyond remedy. When Andrei Zhdanov berated the visiting Austrian communist leaders Johann Koplenig and Friedl Fürnberg in February 1948 in Moscow for being satisfied with the occupation of their country and for looking to the division of Austria between

East and West to solve their problems, he undoubtedly represented not only the Central Committee's position, but also Stalin's personal views: "The TsK [Central Committee] of the KPÖ builds its tactics on the proposition that Soviet troops should stay for an extended period on Austrian territory. The TsK of the CPSU(b) does not agree." The Austrian communists should not be depressed by the "perspective of the liquidation of the occupation regime." Instead, they should seize the moment for defending the full national sovereignty of Austria, which was "the wish of true Austrian democrats and patriots." The presence of Soviet occupation troops in Austria was a "necessary evil" but an "evil" nonetheless that needed to be removed for Austria to develop in a democratic fashion. Zhdanov concluded by advising the KPÖ chiefs to seize the issues of independence, sovereignty, and the removal of occupation troops from the right and center of the political spectrum and staunchly to defend the Austrian national cause. "We believe in your strength," stated Zhdanov disingenuously. "You don't. That's the main difference between us."[131]

We still have no clear understanding of why Stalin allowed the Austrian situation to stagnate after the initiatives of 1948–1949 came to naught. There was every reason to pull out. The number of occupation troops in the western and eastern parts of Austria had dwindled to nominal numbers, and the Austrian government almost completely controlled the country's domestic policies. By this point, the Hungarian government was firmly under Soviet control and there was little need for more than symbolic detachments of Soviet troops to be stationed there. Meanwhile Red Army soldiers in Austria continued to embarrass the Soviet political authorities with periodic sprees of violence and lawlessness, as well as desertion. Soviet intelligence kidnappings on the streets of Vienna heightened tensions between East and West and made the Soviets even more unpopular in the eyes of the Austrian population. The kidnappings, on average three or four a month in 1948, were "just hitting that happy medium," wrote Martin Herz, "which, without completely demoralizing the Austrians, results in maximum abhorrence of the Soviets and their political system."[132] The Austrian public was especially outraged by the November 5, 1948, kidnapping of Margarethe Ottilinger, an official in the Austrian Marshall Plan administration, and her sentencing by the Soviets to twenty-five years hard labor.[133]

That the Austrian population remained obdurately anti-Soviet and anti-communist frustrated Soviet leaders in the zone and in Moscow. One pessimistic report from the propaganda section of the Soviet element on their work in 1949 summed up their predicament. Across the board, the Austrians were convinced that the Marshall Plan was helping them get back on their feet, while efforts to propagandize the accomplishments of the people's democracies fell on deaf ears. Western consumer products had become all the rage, while Soviet encouragement of the role of social organizations only seemed to help the socialists. Meanwhile, in the cultural sphere the Soviet authorities censored hundreds of films and productions. Of the thirty-five Austrian ones, "not a single one was progressive."[134]

The KPÖ remained weak and divided; the party was a constant source of worry and target of criticism from Soviet bosses. Moscow repeatedly berated the leaders of the political and propaganda apparatus of the Soviet element for their passivity, for their inability to make any headway in the Austrian countryside, and for their poor relations with the communists, among other sins. To be sure, among Austrians there were those on both sides, pro-Soviet communists and pro-Western democrats, who saw it in their interests to prolong the occupation. But the Austrian government and the vast majority of the Austrian people longed for an end to the Four-Power presence. The escalation of Cold War tensions in the summer and fall of 1948 may well have played the decisive role in scuppering the hopeful state treaty negotiations. The Berlin blockade made Four Power relations in Vienna even more difficult. The Western powers worried seriously about a blockade of Vienna, especially because they did not have a readily available airstrip to fly in supplies for their zones. When it appeared that the Western fears were misplaced, the outbreak of hostilities in Korea in July 1950 gave military leaders in East and West every reason to think they needed to prepare for war in Europe. Negotiations for a state treaty, then, quickly faded into the background.

Once the Soviets had seized and began to exploit the Zistersdorf oil reserves in the eastern part of the country and removed those industries they deemed useful for rebuilding their own economy back home, there were few economic reasons left to remain in Austria, especially in light of the additional $150 million compensation for the relatively unproductive and uncompetitive industries under USIA direction that the Austrians agreed to pay in 1949. The Austrians' readiness to make a sacrifice on this issue had grown over time as it became increasingly difficult for these industries to sell their products, acquire raw materials, and pay their workers. While continued Soviet interests in Zistersdorf oil and in the Danube Steamboat Shipping Company complicated the negotiations, these issues themselves did not, in the end, stand in the way of signing the state treaty.[135]

Stalin's famous note of March 20, 1952, offering to withdraw Soviet troops from Germany in exchange for the withdrawal of Western troops and the declaration of German neutrality, revived the Austrians' waning hopes for action on the state treaty.[136] Most historians now agree that this Soviet initiative was little more than a propagandistic effort to prevent the Federal Republic of Germany from rearming and joining the planned European Defense Community (EDC).[137]

In any case, few Western diplomats—the exception was George Kennan—were willing to negotiate on this basis. Leading Austrian politicians were paying close attention nonetheless. To be sure, that Austrian communists began to talk about the benefits of Austrian neutrality just at this time gave rise to serious reservations about the extent to which a neutral Austria might be dominated by the Soviet bloc. At the same time, Austrian leaders were startled by the lack of Western response to Stalin's initiatives and increasingly worried that their country would be divided into two, like Germany, for a very long time. Fortunately for them—and for everyone else in the world—Stalin died on March 5, 1953. The Korean War came to an end; and a new leadership in Moscow sought serious negotiations about the German and Austrian questions as a way to relieve tensions in Europe and provide a basis for "peaceful coexistence."

As a consequence of the changing international situation, there was reason to hope that the Berlin Foreign Ministers Conference of February 1954 would come to an agreement on the German Peace Treaty and set out the conditions for the Austrian state treaty. Although none of the participating parties, including the Austrians, were ready to give up potential advantages in the negotiations, the key issues had been resolved. The Soviets would be compensated, as determined already in 1948, for the USIA industries; previous agreements on the continued delivery of Zittersdorf oil and for Soviet interests in the Danube Steamboat Shipping Company were also easily revived. The Austrians were ready to declare their neutrality with an international guarantee "on the model of Swiss neutrality," an idea that had been "in the air" since 1946 and on which all parties were in agreement. Renner had not only talked about neutrality, but also practiced it in some form in previous years, despite what General Keyes rightly noted were "the sympathies and ties with the objectives of the Western nations."[138] Both the Americans and Austrian public opinion were comforted by the fact that the United States had already invested money in and provided arms for the rebuilding of the Austrian army, which, as was hoped, could at least slow down a potential Soviet invasion of the country.[139] The British and the French had already withdrawn all but purely symbolic forces from their zones of occupation.

Yet Austrian hopes were dashed one more time. At Berlin, negotiations foundered on Soviet attempts to link the Austrian treaty with keeping Germany out of the European Defense Community (EDC).[140] The background, as few could know at that time, was internal wrangling in the Kremlin between Khrushchev and his supporters, on the one hand, and Molotov and his supporters, on the other. While the former group was genuinely interested in settling the Austrian question, the latter continued to worry about Western intentions in Austria, especially given the prospect of a rearmed and potentially aggressive West Germany. Standing his ground, Molotov ultimately took a position in Berlin and after that demanded either the continuing occupation of Austria, even if the state treaty were signed, or the right for each individual signatory to march back into the country at their own discretion. Since neither the Austrians nor the West wanted any part of these potential solutions, talks were again broken off. Once more, genuine worries emerged in Austria that the country would remain divided between East and West. Some politicians in the western part of the country even began preparations for what they thought was an impending partition of their country comparable to that of Germany.

We are now reasonably certain that it was Khrushchev's victory in his power struggle against Molotov that led to those Soviet initiatives in spring 1955 that eventually settled the Austrian question. In April, the Soviets invited the Austrians to Moscow to conclude an agreement, and on Sunday, May 15, 1955, the state treaty was finally signed in Vienna.[141] Although Molotov was not formally removed from power until 1957, when his participation in the so-called Anti-Party Group was formally condemned in the Presidium of the party, by January and February of 1955 Khrushchev had managed to align a strong Presidium majority against Molotov's Austrian policy. Essentially, the leadership ordered the Soviet foreign minister to sign the state treaty and agree to the withdrawal of all occupation forces from Austria within three months of that date. This was made much easier by West Germany's joining of NATO in May 1955, which had already been predecided with the signing of the Paris Agreement in October 1954. Now the Soviets could argue that it was to their strategic benefit to construct a neutral belt of Austria and Switzerland that would separate NATO troops stationed in West Germany and in Italy. In fact, Khrushchev's simultaneous and successful efforts to overcome Molotov's objections to a rapprochement with Yugoslavia meant that Soviet strategic interests in central Europe would be protected. Moreover, the Warsaw Pact was signed on May 14, 1955, which made it possible for the Soviets to withdraw from Austria without being vulnerable to Western demands that they withdraw their troops from Romania and Hungary, always a sensitive trip-wire for the signing of a state treaty.[142] The newly elected chancellor of Austria, Julius Raab from the ÖVP, gave Moscow his government's assurances that Austria would strictly observe the terms of the country's neutrality and managed to convince skeptics in Washington that this formula would work.[143] The condition of neutrality would not be included in the treaty itself, but rather voted on by the Austrian parliament.

The Austrians kept their word. As agreed to by all parties, the Austrian State Treaty, signed on May 15, 1955, contained no provisions on neutrality. But the Austrian parliament passed a resolution on the principles of neutrality on June 7, and on October 26, when the last of the occupying troops had left their country, the Austrian government passed a constitutional law that established the permanent neutrality of

Austria. Austrian neutrality was recognized by the Four Powers and Austria was admitted to the United Nations. Ten years of occupation ended; a new era of Austrian independence was inaugurated.

• •

Stalin's policies in Austria demonstrated an unusual lack of decisiveness and purpose on the part of the Soviet dictator. But surely Austria was not his highest priority, which meant that Austria policy floundered between the foreign ministry, the military, and the economic ministries that were seeking to extract resources from the country. Unlike in eastern Germany, Moscow neither engaged in a program of Sovietization in its occupied zone nor empowered the Communist Party to undertake social and economic reforms in its zone. Instead, it worked with the Austrian government to achieve its goals, something that was impossible in Germany. Still, as many Austrian politicians understood, the elusive state treaty was subject to the shifting priorities of the Kremlin as it faced the uncertain but steadily growing challenges of the Cold War.

To be sure, there were economic benefits to be gleaned from the Austrians, oil and manufactured products among them. There were reasons to stay that related to the stationing of troops in Hungary and Romania. Austrian problems intersected with and were complicated by the question of the German peace treaty and the problem of Yugoslav territorial claims. But the consistently poor electoral following of the Austrian Communist Party and the abiding resentment of the Austrian population to the presence of Soviet soldiers on their territory gave Moscow every reason to sign a favorable treaty and depart from the country with some kind of attainable guarantee that Austria would not become a Western outpost. That this did not happen sooner was the product in part of the waffling and indecision of the Soviet negotiators but also of the increasing mutual suspicions between the Americans and Soviets. Chance, contingency, and circumstance also played their roles in the foiled diplomatic negotiations. The signing of the state treaty in 1955 was a great day in the history of postwar Austria, but one that could have happened much sooner and saved the Austrian people a lot of grief.

CONCLUSION

The seven case studies explored in this book prompt a number of general observations about Stalin's impact on the fate of Europe, about European politics in the postwar period, and about the coming of the Cold War. Of course, each case represents a different set of domestic circumstances in relation to the Soviet Union and the coming Cold War. This diversity makes it difficult to generalize and draw broad conclusions. But there are still commonalities that can be identified.

In every case, political leaders in Europe sought to protect and, in some cases, strengthen their country's sovereignty, meaning the right of their nations to govern themselves. They had been largely deprived of this right during the war and had been subject either to German occupation, the rule of collaborators, or combinations of both. Many of the political leaders who emerged after the war had been in prison, exile, or hiding before liberation. In the case of the communists, many had been in Moscow. The severe challenges of physical reconstruction and the reconstitution of their societies made their political tasks all the harder. It was not at all a given that they or their political parties could resist either the internal threats of revolution on the left or right or the external threats posed by the power, the prestige, and sometimes the military presence of the Soviet Union. In fact, given the strength of many communist parties immediately after the war and the chaos of the European economies, it was something of a miracle that democratic, pluralist politics could develop at all. One needs to view the postwar period from the perspective of 1944 and 1945 to absorb the sense of insecurity and foreboding that pervaded the political leadership on the continent. Added to this were growing worries in some quarters, and hopes in others, that the Soviet Union and the West might go to war. Yet, amazingly, traditional political systems did revive and the old parties, if sometimes under different names, defended the reconstitution of the rule of law and parliamentary government.

In Denmark (Bornholm), Finland, Austria, and western Germany (West Berlin), the conservative Christian Democrats, and anti-communist Social Democrats, revived parliamentary democracies and led their countries to resist Soviet blandishments. The Christian Democrats faced the uncertain present and future by developing a strong social orientation to their programs. The Social Democrats, especially those who were outside the direct control of the Soviet military and political authorities, successfully resisted efforts by the communists to submerge them in unity parties or to split their parties. Statesmen like Ernst Reuter in Berlin, Juho Kusti Paasikivi in Finland, Karl Renner and Leopold Figl in Austria, and Alcide De Gasperi in Italy were engaged in a political struggle with Soviet and / or communist domination that defined the national character of their countries for decades to come. Even in those countries with ruling communist parties, Poland and Albania, the struggle for sovereignty went on within the communist movement. In Poland, Władysław Gomułka pursued a "Polish road to socialism," which eventually clashed, like Josip Broz Tito's Yugoslav communist ambitions, with Stalin's demands for subordination and conformity. In Albania, Enver Hoxha used the conflict between Tito and the Yugoslavs and Stalin to protect his weak and undeveloped nation's ability to govern its own affairs from the Yugoslavs, though under his own ruthless and violent dictatorship. Even a Western communist leader, like Palmiro Togliatti, was involved in a complicated balancing act of advancing Italy's national interests against what he saw as the United States' imperialist goals and Moscow's demands for upholding the Cominform line. But Togliatti should also be seen as pursuing Italian sovereignty and building Italian democracy, despite his unquestionable loyalty to Moscow.

Stalin had no firm views in 1944–1945 about how relations with the countries of Europe should develop. As the reader has seen, he looked to the establishment of "new democracies" or "people's democracies," which he saw as an attractive intermediate stage between bourgeois democracy and socialism, as the best way to model the new political systems emerging from the war. There would be no dictatorship of the proletariat, no collectivization, and no socialization of property. The Soviets were not interested in red flags flying over city halls or in insurrectionary workers' demonstrations in the streets. Stalin thought this would also mollify the West; he was rue to antagonize his former wartime Allies and was fearful of a military confrontation of any sort. Moscow dealt with each European country differently, depending on the geostrategic importance of its territories and the strength of its communist parties. Stalin also had a strong sense of "national character" that sometimes influenced his dealings with the European countries: Finns were hardy and stubborn; Germans were brave, unsubtle, "Teutonic"; Poles were subversive and flighty; Albanians were backward and primitive.

From a geostrategic point of view, Poland, Finland, and Germany were crucial to Stalin's calculations. Finland had a long common border with the Soviet Union and had been its opponent in two recent major wars (the Winter War and the Continuation War); Poland, had been a traditional enemy of the Soviet Union (and pathway for invading German armies), and was the object of Soviet territorial ambitions; and Germany, the strongest European country outside the Soviet Union, had invaded the lands of the Soviet Union during World War I and World War II, and had demonstrated traditional hostility to Russian ambitions on the continent. In each case, Stalin's policies produced different results. The Finns were not occupied by the Soviet Union and were able to win their domestic sovereignty by diplomatically ceding their ability to make military and foreign policy that might counter Soviet interests. The Poles lost their independence in the Stalinist period, and Gomułka's attempts to maintain a modicum of Polish sovereignty within the communist movement came to naught within Stalin's lifetime. The outcome of the Berlin crisis of 1948–1949 indicated that Germany would have two distinct states. The struggle for sovereignty in Germany meant the creation of West German and East German political entities, with the former capital divided between a West Berlin and East Berlin.

In those countries where Stalin had less direct interest—Denmark, Albania, Austria, and Italy—compromises were easier to reach. The occupation of Bornholm lasted less than a year, and the Soviets withdrew with minimal assurances of Danish neutrality and promises for trade and good relations. There was no Sovietization on Bornholm and few lasting effects of the Red Army presence. Stalin left the fate of Albania to the Yugoslavs until the rising tensions between Belgrade and Moscow in the spring of 1948 erupted into a full-scale split. To the end of his life, Stalin seemed both uninterested in Albania and unsure how to deal with its remoteness and backwardness. Despite being very close to an agreement over a state treaty with Austria several times, and most notably in 1949, the Austrian problem was only resolved once the dictator died. Stalin was intrigued with the possibility of Soviet gains in Italy (and France) and displayed periodic flashes of hope that the communist parties there might come to power through electoral victories. But he was consistently opposed to suggestions from militants within those parties that they should strike for power in a workers' uprising. From the beginning, Stalin had little interest in fomenting revolutions in Europe.

Numerous issues in Europe and Asia were successfully resolved at Yalta, Potsdam, and even afterward. (Historians tend to concentrate on those that were not.) The Soviet Union needed resources to rebuild from the horrendous destruction of its peoples, resources, and industries. As a result, Stalin wanted good relations with the United States and Britain, and he was ready to deal and did. His withdrawal from Bornholm can be seen in this light, as can, for example, his almost incomprehensible unwillingness to help the Greek partisans or support an insurrection in Italy, when in both cases success for communist-backed actions might well have been in the cards.

The coming of the Cold War unquestionably influenced the fate of Europe in the immediate postwar years, but it was not as dominant a factor as many historians suggest. In 1945 and 1946, there was plenty of room for compromise among the great powers. By 1947, with the American president's pronouncement before Congress of the Truman Doctrine (March 1947), Secretary of State Marshall's announcement at the Harvard University commencement in June 1947 of his plan to reconstruct the European economies, and the Zhdanov's "two-camps speech" and critique of the West European communist parties at the first Cominform meeting in September 1947, the chances of compromise between the East and West began to narrow. It took some months for the impact of these and similar policy prescriptions to harden into divisive actions on both sides.

The Americans, it is well worth remembering, had almost nothing to do with the postwar fate of Finland or Bornholm. In both cases, the British were involved, though in neither were they willing to confront the Soviets or interfere with the policies of the Danes or Finns. Given the brutal Soviet takeover of Poland after the war, symbolically marked by the flight of Stanisław Mikołajczyk from the country in October 1947, the United States and Britain had soon abandoned the country as hopelessly inaccessible behind the "Iron Curtain." The same was true of Albania, though feeble efforts were made in the beginning of the 1950s to overthrow Hoxha. While there were periodic episodes of conflict in Cold War Vienna, the Allied Control Commission functioned remarkably well, and the joint interests of the Four Powers made the evacuation of their respective military contingents a source of constant speculation. Only the Berlin blockade in 1948–1949 carried the seeds of more serious conflict. But here, too, the Four Powers compromised, finding a practical solution for Berlin that lasted in the main until the building of the Berlin Wall in 1961 and then until the collapse of the German Democratic Republic in 1989 and the fall of the Soviet Union in 1991.

The years 1948 and 1949 were a crucial watershed in the history of the Cold War and the division of Europe. Many of the salient events discussed at relative length in this book happened during that short period: the defeat of the communists in the Italian elections of April 1948; the beginning of the Berlin blockade in June 1948; the Albanian switch from the Yugoslav to the Soviet alliance during the Soviet-Yugoslav split of the spring and early summer of 1948; the Finnish-Soviet treaty of April 1948; the removal of Władysław Gomułka as secretary-general of the Polish Workers' Party in September 1948; the lifting of the Berlin blockade in May 1949; and the failure of the Austrian State Treaty negotiations during the summer and fall of 1949. That Denmark joined NATO as an original member in May 1949 in some ways concluded the Bornholm affair, though Soviet withdrawal in April 1946 had ended the occupation.

This book has shown that these events and those that led up to them cannot be understood only in the context of the Cold War between the Soviet Union and the United States. This was, above all, European history, in the sense that the intentions of European political leaders and the results of European elections were of vital importance in determining the outcome of crises and conflicts within European societies regarding their future. The agency of Europeans mattered and mattered a lot. The political inclinations of postwar leaders and the bitter experience of the Nazi domination of Europe influenced their choices and guided their actions when faced with pressure and enticements from the Soviets and Americans alike. To be sure, Soviet pressure was sometimes overwhelming and deprived some Europeans of complete sovereignty in their choices of political futures. But the struggle was real, and there was little that was inevitable about the division of the continent in the immediate postwar period.

In short, the events of 1948 and 1949 inaugurated the Cold War in the form the world knew it until 1989–1991, when communist states, including the Soviet Union, fell one after another until there were none left in Europe and few in the world as a whole. Before 1948–1949, the fate of the continent could have taken different directions, but that was not to be. Instead, as the war came to an end the rivalry between the Soviet Union and the United States over the European settlement drove the former Allies further and further apart. Despite bleak economic and social circumstances, what seemed like open-ended political possibilities with the collapse of the Third Reich and the liberation of the continent narrowed considerably as the former Allies sought to take advantage of their military positions on the continent. After the formal division of Germany and the formation of NATO in 1949, there was no turning back. The opportunities were minimal for an understanding between the United States and the Soviet Union regarding a German peace treaty, which would have signaled the formal end of World War II.

Events in Asia—the victory of the Chinese Communist revolution and the creation of the People's Republic in 1949, and the Korean War (from June 1950 until July 1953)—solidified the division of the world into rival camps, the kind that Andrei Zhdanov had stated already existed at the Cominform meeting of September 1947 and Churchill had anticipated in his Fulton, Missouri, speech of March 5, 1946. Even after Stalin's death in March 1953, during the period of "peaceful coexistence," the Cold War contained the seeds of a new world war, which might well have involved nuclear weapons, between the ideological and political rivals in the East and West.

No observer can fail to notice the hangovers of the hostility between the United States and the Soviet Union in the post–Cold War period. Old habits die hard in both political entities; some institutional cultures in both Washington and Moscow remain intact and easy reflexes of traditional enmity appeal to political actors and mass audiences alike. But one should make no mistake that the ideological and geostrategic determinants of the Cold War are not the same as those driving Russian-American enmity during the era of Vladimir Putin. Marxism-Leninist theory—and what it meant for the division of Europe and the political hostilities between Europeans, left and right—is all but a dead letter in the spectrum of ideologies today. Instead, the new divisions engendered by the emergence of populist political ideologies are much different in form and content and much more susceptible to change.

Germany is united, economically powerful, and, at least for the time being, a stalwart member of NATO and the European Union. A major aspect of its raison d'être is the peaceful and unified development of the European continent, in comity with the interests of Russia. Italy retains some of the "leftism" of its influential communist past but has become, at least until recently, an active and important part of the European Union and NATO. Albania and the former Yugoslav republics of Slovenia, Croatia, and Montenegro are in NATO, as are Poland and other countries of the former Soviet bloc. Finland and Austria, though both still "neutral" in their own ways, are aligned with NATO, and have joined the European Union. One can undoubtedly read their past vulnerabilities vis-à-vis the Soviet Union and their struggle for sovereignty in their present foreign policies. At least during the 1990s, the discussion about the potential joining of the Russian Federation with the European Union and NATO was serious. One need not exclude that possibility at some point in the future, despite the difficult state of relations between Russia and the West today. But Europe has its woes as well, as the threat of anti-immigrant right-wing parties and the development of anti–European Union sentiment threatens the continent's stability and prosperity.

The rise of populism and the disruptive public and clandestine Russian policies in Europe require the kind of political leadership and mature social and political engagement of voters that the Europeans experienced in the immediate postwar period. The dominance of fascism and dictatorship in the interwar period and the horrors of World War II made the attraction of parliamentary democracy and peace all the greater. The danger of Soviet transgressions aroused the determination of Europeans to shape their own futures politically. Then, as now, sovereignty was a crucial objective. The Russian Federation will try to limit the Europeans in this connection at its own peril. Despite a generally conciliatory stance toward Moscow, the Europeans have held strong to the regime of sanctions introduced to warn the Russians away from steps, like the annexation of Crimea, meddling in eastern Ukraine, and attacking its former citizens in Britain, that threaten European sovereignty. The downsides of the European Union—excessive bureaucracy, expensive institutions, and sometimes imperious behavior toward member states—can distort the desire for sovereignty into anti-liberal politics. The EU has to find a way to meet its original European calling of peaceful and harmonious cooperation in economics, trade, finance, and labor without impinging on the rights of its member states to determine their own futures.

In many of the countries of Europe, memory politics play an important role in the way the populations think about the immediate postwar period and the present. There are segments of society in former communist eastern Europe that are nostalgic for the idealism and sense of purpose of those early years of rebuilding their countries' infrastructures and their families' lives. But much more often, the postwar years are painted in the darkest terms possible, as a time of violence and communist excess, of the crushing of freedom and of the valiant but hopeless struggle for independence. Contemporary Polish memory politics, for example, buries the postwar excesses of anti-Semitism, including the scattered pogroms of the postwar period—or Gomułka's campaign against the Jews—in a government-supported campaign to revive the reputation of the so-called "Cursed Soldiers," members of the underground army who switched from resisting the Nazis at war's end to fighting the communists. In western Europe, too, the postwar era is in part romantically recalled as a time of overcoming economic hardship and rebuilding destroyed cities and shattered lives. For a very long time, discussion of wartime collaboration, fascist crimes, and collusion with the Holocaust was—and still is to some extent—submerged on the continent in the rhetoric of resistance, liberation, and restoration. Memories of the postwar years are frequently shaped by the stories of social conflict in the black-and-white tones of the film noir of the late 1940s and 1950s and of the Italian neorealism school, which explored the lives of the poor and indigent. On the left of the political spectrum and among the Italian intelligentsia as a whole, Togliatti and the PCI are remembered with considerable admiration, while the enormous contributions of De Gasperi to social peace and prosperity in Italy tend to be minimized. Like De Gasperi, the founding fathers of postwar West Germany (Konrad Adenauer and Kurt Schumacher) and Austria (Karl Renner and Leopold Figl,) receive little of the admiration and sense of gratitude that they deserve. Paasikivi is an exception to the rule; the Finns understand in myriad ways the crucial role he (and Mannerheim) played in the development of Finnish sovereignty today. In Denmark, criticism from the right still attends the memory of the Danish government's handling of the Bornholm crisis and the potential Soviet threat from that period. At the same time, Gustav Rasmussen, Danish foreign minister from November 1945 to October 1950, has been excoriated for setting Denmark on a "neutralist" path.

Forgetting is as much a part of memory politics of the postwar years as remembering. Both the Austrians and the Germans, for example, tend to minimize and historically compartmentalize the period of the Soviet occupation. Both the Germans and the Poles tend to think of the early postwar period as one of Soviet domination, forgetting that there were large numbers of German and Polish communists who contributed to the Stalinization of the East German and Polish states. For many decades, Germans and Austrians did not want to talk publicly about the problem of rape and other depredations by Soviet soldiers at the end of the war and the beginning of the peace. That changed, especially after the fall of the Soviet Union. Still, both the Germans and Austrians tend to follow conciliatory policies toward Moscow in part because of justified guilt regarding the war. The Austrians and Finns, both of whom tottered on the brink of absorption into Moscow's orbit, remember that their countries' sovereignty depended on the relative restraint of the Soviets after the war. They, too, do everything they can not to antagonize the Russian Federation today. What might be considered pro-Russian Italian policies derive in good measure from the decades of Italian communist dedication to the Soviet cause in Europe, even if relatively critical and open-minded in the period of Euro-Communism in the 1970s and 1980s. Many younger Albanians accuse the contemporary Albanian government of distorting the legacy of Enver Hoxha and the extreme violence that attended his regime. The strong emphasis on the discourse of Albanian nationalism today overwhelms the history of Yugoslav, Soviet, and eventually Chinese involvement in the country's development.

Russian historical memory is divided on the legacy of Stalin. But most Russians admire his role as the leader of the country during the Second World War—the Great Patriotic War—and during the early Cold War, which attracts much less attention. Russian historians and journalists will argue about the Soviet role in Europe after the war, with a minority sharply critical of Stalin's policies and practices that led directly to the communist seizure of power in the countries of eastern Europe. The majority, however, hew a middle path between the traditional and much more benevolent Soviet interpretation of the "liberating mission" of the Soviet troops and the "brotherly aid" of the Soviet Communist Party to its East European comrades, and the more realistic stance of Stalin's critics. They argue that the communist elites of the European countries themselves determined the fate of the success of the revolution in each, not the Soviets, and even sometimes that American intervention prevented the success of the revolution in western Europe. Violence and purges in eastern Europe, therefore, were the product of local communist excesses but not of Stalin and the Soviet leadership.

In virtually all the countries of Europe, World War II continues to occupy a dominant role in the development of memory politics. This is no doubt even more the case today than in decades past. The memory of the immediate postwar period is also important. Yet Europeans would do well to pay more attention to the struggles of that period as a way to understand the character of their politics and societies. They have a great deal to be proud of in the reconstruction of their countries, the rebuilding of their cities, the prosperity of their economies, the strength of their social welfare systems, and the flourishing of their cultures. The European Union, born as the Coal and Steel Community in 1950, is a product of postwar yearnings for peace, cooperation, and economic development. The spread of the EU to eastern Europe after the collapse of communism was intended to demonstrate that the strivings of the postwar period could be shared throughout Europe. Europeans won their struggle for sovereignty. Now they need to learn how to balance the interests of their own countries with the benefits of acting as a single unit. That is not a simple task, but it is one that they have the talent and determination to resolve.

Abbreviations

AVPRF	Archives of the Foreign Policy of the Russian Federation
CREST	CIA Records Search Tool
FIG	Archives of the Gramsci Institute
FRUS	Foreign Relations of the United States
HIA	Hoover Institution Archives
	Allied Commission for Austria
	German Territory under Allied Occupation (GTUAO)
	Jakub Berman
	Bolesław Bierut
	Władysław Gomułka
	Ryszard Gontarz
	Daniel Lerner
	Jay Lovestone
	Stanisław Mikołajczyk
	Robert Daniel Murphy
	Finn Å. Nielsen
	Eugenio Reale
	Ernst Reuter
	Albert C. Wedemeyer
NACP	National Archives at College Park, MD (RG Record Group)
NSA	National Security Archives
ÖS	Austrian State Archives
RGASPI	Russian State Archives of Social and Political History

	Fond 17	Central Committee of Russian / Soviet Party
	Fond 77	Andrei Zhdanov
	Fond 82	Viacheslav Molotov
	Fond 558	I. V. Stalin
SAPMO-BArch	The Archives of the Parties and Mass Organizations of the GDR in the Bundesarchiv	
	NY	Nachlässe und Erinnerungen (Papers and Memoirs)
TNA	The National Archives of the United Kingdom	
	CAB	Cabinet Office Files
	FO	Foreign Office
	JIC	Joint Intelligence Committee
	WO	War Office

NOTES

1. INTRODUCTION

A. J. P. Taylor, "The European Revolution," Broadcast from BBC London, *The Listener*, November 22, 1945, HIA, Lerner Collection, box 38, folder 8.

1. Keith Lowe, *Savage Continent: Europe in the Aftermath of World War II* (London: Penguin, 2013), 28.

2. William I. Hitchcock, *The Bitter Road to Freedom: A New History of the Liberation of Europe* (New York: Free Press, 2008), 270–272.

3. Jan T. Gross, *Fear: Anti-Semitism in Poland after Auschwitz: An Essay in Historical Interpretation* (Princeton, NJ: Princeton University Press, 2006), 30–80.

4. Norman M. Naimark, *Fires of Hatred: Ethnic Cleansing in 20th Century Europe* (Cambridge, MA: Harvard University Press, 2001), 108–139.

5. See, for example, Benjamin Frommer, *National Cleansing: Retribution against Nazi Collaborators in Postwar Czechoslovakia* (New York: Cambridge University Press, 2005), 243–253.

6. Norman M. Naimark, "The Persistence of 'the Postwar': Germany and Poland," in *Histories of the Aftermath: The Legacies of the Second World War In Europe*, ed. Frank Biess and Robert G. Moeller (New York: Berghahn Books, 2010), 13–29; István Deák, "The Crime of the Century," *New York Review of Books*, Sept. 26, 2002; also in István Deák, *Essays on Hitler's Europe* (Lincoln: University of Nebraska Press, 2001).

7. Marcin Zaremba, *Wielka trwoga: Polska 1944–1947: Ludowa reakcja na kryzys* (Kraków-Warsaw: Znak, 2012). See Giovanni de Luna, *La Repubblica inquieta: L'Italia della Costituzione, 1946–1948* (Milan: Feltrenelli, 2017), 19–32.

8. Atina Grossmann, *Jews, Germans and Allies: Encounters in Occupied Germany* (Princeton, NJ: Princeton University Press, 2007), 187–235.

9. Zaremba, *Wielka trwoga*, 15.

10. Frank Biess, "Feelings in the Aftermath: Toward a History of Post-war Emotions," in *Histories of the Aftermath*, 37–38.

11. Konrad Jarausch, *Out of the Ashes: A New History of Europe in the 20th Century* (Princeton, NJ: Princeton University Press, 2015), 403.

12. Ian Kershaw, *To Hell and Back: Europe 1914–1949* (New York: Penguin, 2015), 471.

13. Norman M. Naimark, *The Russians in Germany: The History of the Soviet Zone of Occupation, 1945–1949* (Cambridge, MA: Harvard University Press, 1995), 69–140.

14. Mark Mazower, *Dark Continent: Europe's Twentieth Century* (London: Alfred A. Knopf, 1998), 294–295; Jeffrey M. Diefendorf, *In the Wake of the War: The*

Reconstruction of German Cities after World War II (New York: Oxford University Press, 1993).

15. Jan Gross, "War as Revolution," in *The Establishment of Communist Regimes in Eastern Europe, 1944–1949,* ed. Norman Naimark and Leonid Gibianskii (Boulder, CO: Westview, 1997), 21–23.

16. See Tony Judt's epilogue to *The Politics of Retribution in Europe: World War II and its Aftermath,* ed. István Deák, Jan Tomasz Gross, and Tony Judt (Princeton, NJ: Princeton University Press, 2000), 293–325.

17. Tony Judt, *Postwar: A History of Europe since 1945* (New York: Penguin, 2005), 3, 10.

18. István Deák, *Europe on Trial: The Story of Collaboration, Resistance and Retribution During World War II* (Boulder, CO: Westview Press, 2015), 217.

19. Nina Tumarkin, *The Living and the Dead: The Rise and Fall of the Cult of World War II in Russia* (New York: Basic Books, 1994), 95–125. For an assessment of the numbers, see Boris Sokolov, *Poteri Sovetskogo Soiuza i Germanii vo Vtoroi Mirovoi Voine* (Moscow: Airo-XX, 2011), 24–26.

20. Melvyn P. Leffler, *For the Soul of Mankind: The United States, the Soviet Union, and the Cold War* (New York: Hill and Wang, 2007), 44–45; Michael Neiberg, *Potsdam: The End of World War II and the Remaking of Europe* (New York: Basic Books, 2015), 243–244; David Holloway, *Stalin and the Bomb: The Soviet Union and Atomic Energy* (New Haven, CT: Yale, 1996), 117–118.

21. Holloway, *Stalin and the Bomb,* 129–130.

22. Holloway, *Stalin and the Bomb,* 131–133.

23. Jonathan Haslam, *Russia's Cold War: From the October Revolution to the Fall of the Wall* (New Haven, CT: Yale University Press, 2011), 62.

24. See Marc Trachtenberg, "The United States and Eastern Europe in 1945: A Reassessment," *Journal of Cold War Studies* 10, no. 4 (Fall 2008): 94–132.

25. John Lewis Gaddis, *We Now Know: Rethinking Cold War History* (New York: Oxford University Press, 1997), 19. See also his "The Emerging Post-Revisionist Thesis on the Origins of the Cold War," *Diplomatic History* 7 (Summer 1983): 171–190. For a useful rejoinder, see Melvyn Leffler, "The Cold War: What Do 'We Now Know?'" *The American Historical Review* 104, no. 2 (Apr. 1999): 501–524.

26. See Mark Kramer, "Stalin, Soviet Policy, and the Establishment of a Soviet Bloc in Eastern Europe," in *Stalin and Europe: Imitation and Domination 1928–1953,* ed. Timothy Snyder and Ray Brandon (New York: Oxford University Press, 2014), 270–272.

27. Jonathan Haslam, "Russian Archival Revelations and Our Understanding of the Cold War," *Diplomatic History* 21 (1997): 219. Geoffrey Roberts, *Molotov: Stalin's Cold Warrior* (Dulles, VA: Potomac Books, 2002), 2–4.

28. Norman M. Naimark, "Cold War Studies and New Archival Materials on Stalin," *The Russian Review* 61 (Jan. 2002): 11–14. This is also the conclusion of the most up-to-date biographies of Stalin: Robert Service, *Stalin: A Biography* (Cambridge, MA: Harvard University, 2005); Oleg V. Khlevniuk, *Stalin: New Biography of a Dictator* (New Haven, CT: Yale University Press, 2017); and Stephen Kotkin, *Stalin*, vol. 2, *Waiting for Hitler* (New York: Penguin, 2017).

29. *Khrushchev Remembers: The Last Testament*, trans. and ed. Strobe Talbott (Boston: Little, Brown, 1974), 357.

30. *Sto sorok besed s Molotovym: Iz dnevnika F. Chueva* (Moscow: Terra, 1991), 99.

31. RGASPI, fond (f.) 558, opis' (op.) 11, delo (d.) 99, listy (ll.) 80–95. See the articles by V. O. Pechatnov in *Istochnik*, no. 2 (1999): 70–85; and *Istochnik*, no. 3 (1999): 92–104, that deal with this incident. See also Naimark, "Cold War Studies," 7–11, which covers several aspects of the relationship between Stalin and Molotov at this time.

32. For a recent discussion of Stalin's papers, see Kotkin, *Stalin*, 2:xvi.

33. "Zapiska [. . .] po voprosam budushchego mira i poslevoennogo ustroistva," Jan. 10, 1944, in *Sovetskii faktor v vostochnoi evrope 1944–1953*, vol. 1, *1944–1948*, ed. T. V. Volokitina et al. (Moscow: ROSSPEN, 1999), 23–48.

34. See Litvinov to Molotov and Vyshinskii, Jan. 11, 1945, in *SSSR i Germanskii Vopros 1941–1949*, vol. 1, *22 iiunia 1941g.—8 maia 1945g.*, ed. G. P. Kynin and I. Laufer (Moscow: Mezhdunar. Otnosheniia, 1996), 595–596.

35. I have explored some of these problems in several essays: "Revolution and Counterrevolution in Eastern Europe," in *The Crisis of Socialism in Europe*, ed. Christiane Lemke and Gary Marks (Durham, NC: Duke University Press, 1992), 61–84; "The Soviets, the German Left, and Problems of 'Sectarianism' in the Eastern Zone, 1945–1949," in *Between Reform and Revolution: German Socialism and Communism from 1840 to 1990*, ed. David E. Barclay and Eric D. Weitz (New York: Berghahn, 1998), 421–443; and "The Soviets and the Christian Democrats: The Challenge of a 'Bourgeois' Party in Eastern Germany, 1945–1949," in *The Soviet Union and Europe in Cold War*, ed. Francesca Gori and Silvio Pons (London: Macmillan, 1996), 37–47.

36. Notes of a conversation between Stalin and Hebrang, Jan. 9, 1945, in *Vostochnaia Evropa v dokumentakh rossiiskikh arkhivov, 1944–1953*, vol. 1, *1944–1948*, ed. T. V. Volokitina et al. (Moscow-Novosibiirsk: Sibirskii khronograf, 1997), 132–133. My emphasis.

37. See Alfred J. Rieber, *Stalin and the Struggle for Supremacy in Eurasia* (Cambridge: Cambridge University Press, 2015), 3–8. Rieber argues that Stalin's origins in the borderlands of the Caucasus increased these sensitivities.

38. Sergey Radchenko, "Did Hiroshima Save Japan from Soviet Occupation?," *Foreign Policy*, Aug. 5, 2015; see also Tsuyoshi Hasegawa, *Racing the Enemy: Stalin,*

Truman, and the Surrender of Japan (Cambridge, MA: Harvard University Press, 2005), 268–269, 272–274.

39. "Record of Conversation of Comrade I. V. Stalin with . . . Comrade Thorez," November 19, 1944, trans. Vladislav Zubok, *Wilson Center Digital Archive,* International History Declassified, 5.

40. "Record of Conversation of Comrade I. V. Stalin with . . . Comrade Thorez," November 18, 1947, trans. Vladislav Zubok, *Wilson Center Digital Archives,* International History Declassified, 2–3.

41. See Naimark, *The Russians in Germany,* 9–11, 351–352. Norman Naimark, "Stalin and the Austria Question," in *Austrian Foreign Policy in Historical Context,* Contemporary Austrian Studies, vol. 14, ed. Günter Bischof, Anton Pelinka, and Michael Gehler (New Brunswick, NJ: Transaction Publishers, 2006), 353–361.

42. Vojtech Mastny, "NATO in the Beholder's Eye: Soviet Perspectives and Policies, 1949–1956," *Cold War International History Project Working Papers* 35 (2002): 3–5.

43. *The Diary of Georgi Dimitrov,* ed. Ivo Banac (New Haven, CT: Yale University Press, 2003), 413–414.

44. Stalin and British Labor Leaders, July 8, 1946, RGASPI, f. 558, op. 11, d. 286.

45. *The Diary of Georgi Dimitrov,* 413–414.

46. Peter Kenez, *Hungary from the Nazis to the Soviets: The Establishment of the Communist Regime in Hungary 1944–1948* (Cambridge: Cambridge University Press, 2006), 27–29.

47. T. V. Volokitina et.al., *Moskva i vostochnaia Evropa: Stanovlenie politicheskikh regimov sovetskogo tipa, 1949–1953: Ocherki istorii* (Moscow: ROSSPEN, 2002), 35–36. See also Stalin's discussion with the American priest and Polish-American activist Stanislaus Orlemanski (Apr. 28, 1944) in *Vostochnaia Evropa,* 1:36–42.

48. *Vostochnaia Evropa,* 1:457–458. I. I. Orlik, "Vostochnaia Evropa v dokumentakh rossiiskikh arkhivov, 1944–1945 gg.," *Novaia i noveishaia istoriia,* no. 5 (1999): 192.

49. See Norman M. Naimark, "People's Democracy," in *A Dictionary of 20th Century Communism,* ed. Silvio Pons and Robert Service (Princeton, NJ: Princeton University Press, 2010), 609–610.

50. Gibianskii, "Forsirovanie," 144.

51. Cited in Dietrich Staritz, "Die SED, Stalin und die Gründung der DDR," *Aus Politik und Zeitgeschichte: Beilage zur Wochenzeitung Das Parlament* B5 / 91 (Jan. 25, 1991): 7n20. Wilhelm Pieck's cryptic notes from the meeting state, "The struggle too open . . . careful politics necessary (Comparison Teutons). . . ." Stalin and the SED leadership, Dec.. 14, 1948, *Wilhelm Pieck—Aufzeichnungen zur Deutschlandpolitik 1945–1953,* ed. Rolf Badstübner and Wilfried Loth (Berlin: Akademie Verlag, 1991), 259.

52. See Wolfgang Leonhard, *Child of the Revolution*, trans. C. M. Woodhouse (Chicago: Henry Regnery Co., 1958), 303.

53. See Charles Gati, *Hungary and the Soviet Bloc* (Durham, NC: Duke University Press, 1986), 76–77.

54. Anna Mazurkiewicz, *Uchodźcy polityczni z Europy Środkowo-Wschodniej w amerykańskiej polityce zimnowojennej* (Warsaw-Gdańsk: Instytut Pamięci Narodowej, 2016), 148–150.

55. Andrew Roberts, *Churchill: Walking with Destiny* (New York: Viking, 2018), 895.

56. See Edith Sheffer, *Burned Bridge: How East and West Germans Made the Iron Curtain* (New York: Oxford, 2011), 34–49. For a different view, see Anne Applebaum, *Iron Curtain: The Crushing of Eastern Europe, 1944–1956* (New York: Doubleday, 2012), 193–198.

57. *Text of a Speech Delivered by J. V. Stalin at an Election Rally in Stalin Electoral Area, Moscow, February 9, 1946* (Washington, DC: Information Bulletin Embassy USSR, 1946), 4.

58. Marc Trachtenberg, *A Constructed Peace: The Making of the European Settlement, 1945–1963* (Princeton, NJ: Princeton University Press, 1999), 29–36.

59. These kinds of questions are particularly important to German and Austrian historians of the early Cold War. See, among others, the work of Gerhard Wettig, Hannes Adomeit, Rolf Steininger, Wolfgang Mueller, and Jochen Laufer.

60. Books by Melvyn P. Leffler stand out in this context: *A Preponderance of Power: National Security, the Truman Administration, and the Cold War* (Stanford, CA: Stanford University Press, 1992), and *For the Soul of Mankind: The United States, the Soviet Union, and the Cold War* (New York: Hill and Wang, 2007).

61. See Federico Romero, "Cold War Historiography at the Crossroads," *Cold War History* 14, no. 4 (2014): 685–703. See also the *Journal of Cold War Studies*, edited by Mark Kramer.

62. See, for example, Wolfgang Mueller, *Die sowjetische Besatzung in Österreich 1945–1955 und ihre politische Mission* (Vienna, Köln: Böhlau Verlag, 2005); Alfred Rieber, *Zhdanov in Finland* (Pittsburgh, PA: Carl Beck Papers, 1995); Elena Agarossi and Victor Zaslavsky, *Stalin and Togliatti: Italy and the Origins of the Cold War* (Washington, DC: Woodrow Wilson Center Press, 2011).

63. There are a number of useful exceptions. See, among others, Gerhard Wettig, *Stalin and the Cold War in Europe: The Emergence and Development of East-West Conflict, 1939–1953* (Lanham, MD: Rowman and Littlefield, 2008); and Vladislav Zubok and Constantine Pleshakov, *Inside the Kremlin's Cold War: From Stalin to Khrushchev* (Cambridge, MA: Harvard University Press, 2006).

64. *Soveshchaniia Kominforma 1947, 1948, 1949: Dokumenty i materialy* (Moscow: ROSSPEN, 1998), 297–303. The English translation of the Cominform

documents is available in *The Cominform: Minutes of the Three Conferences 1947 / 1948 / 1949,* ed. Giuliano Procacci (Milan: Feltrenelli, 1994.) For Zhdanov's speech, see 216–251.

65. Cited in Bruce Lockhardt, *My Europe* (London: Putnam, 1952), 125.

66. Radomír Luža, "Czechoslovakia between Democracy and Communism," *The Cold War in Europe: Era of a Divided Continent,* ed. Charles S. Maier (Princeton, NJ: Markus Wiener Publishers, 1996), 97–100.

1. THE BORNHOLM INTERLUDE

1. Milovan Djilas, *Conversations with Stalin,* trans. Michael B. Petrovich (New York: Harcourt Brace Jovanovich, 1962), 114.

2. See L. Ia. Gibianskii, "Problemy vostochnoi Evropy i nachalo formirovaniia sovetskogo bloka," in *Kholodnaia voina 1945–1963 gg.: istoricheskaia retrospektiva,* ed. N. I. Egorova and A. O. Chubar'ian (Moscow: Inst. Vseobshchei Istorii RAN 2003), 124–125.

3. Scholars will argue differently on this question. See Jonathan Søborg Agger and Trine Engholm Michelsen, "How Strong Was the 'Weakest Link': Danish Security Policy Reconsidered," in *War Plans and Alliances in the Cold War: Threat perceptions in the East and West,* ed. Vojtech Mastny, Sven G. Holtsmark, and Andreas Wenger (London: Routledge, 2006), 240–266.

4. See Clemens Meier, "Making Memories: The Politics of Remembrance in Postwar Norway and Denmark," Ph.D. dissertation, European University Institute, 2007, 125–127.

5. István Deák, *Europe on Trial: The Story of Collaboration, Resistance, and Retribution During World War II* (Boulder, CO: Westview, 2015), 132–133.

6. Bent Jensen, "Soviet Remote Control; the Island of Bornholm as a Relay Station in Soviet-Danish Relations," in *Mechanisms of Power in the Soviet Union,* ed. N. E. Rosenfeldt, B. Jensen, and E. Kulavig (New York: St. Martin's Press, 2000), 193.

7. S. G. Holtsmark, "The Limits to Soviet Influence: Soviet Diplomats and the Pursuit of Strategic Interests in Norway and Denmark, 1944–47," in *The Soviet Union and Europe in the Cold War, 1943–1953,* ed. Francesca Gori and Silvio Pons (New York: St. Martin's Press, 1998), 106–112.

8. Memorandum (to Admiral Leahy) by the Assistant to the President's Naval Aide (Elsey), July 1, 1946, FRUS, The Conference of Berlin (The Potsdam Conference), vol. 1, Washington, DC, U.S. Government Printing Office, 322.

9. Natalia I. Yegorova, "Stalin's Conception of Maritime Power: Revelations from the Russian Archives," *Journal of Strategic Studies* 28, no. 2, 159.

10. Yegorova, "Stalin's Conception of Maritime Power," 163–164.

11. Aide-Memoire, The British Secretary of State for Foreign Affairs (Bevin) to the Secretary of State, Jan. 14, 1946. FRUS, 1945, vol. 5:389.

12. TNA, JIC (46) 1(o) Supplementary T. of R., Tab 1, Jan.–Apr. 1946, "Russia's Strategic Interests and Intentions," 19.

13. Bent Jensen, *Den lange befrielse: Bornholm besat og befriet, 1945–1946* (Odense: Udgivelsesår, 1996). I use here the Russian translation, B. Ensen, *Dolgoe osvobozhdenie ostrova Bornkhol'm 1945–1946*, trans. Boris and Liudmila Vail' (Moscow: RGGU, 2001), 51–52. Running through Jensen's study like a red thread is his highly critical stance toward the Danish government for its handling of the Bornholm "affair." For him, the Danish leaders were too "timid," "passive," and "frightened" in their dealings with the Soviets. I disagree with his analysis. Nevertheless, this is a richly researched and extraordinarily detailed book about the Soviet occupation and Danish compliance. It would have been more difficult to write this chapter without his essential contribution to the scholarship.

14. "Maiskii to Molotov (11 January 1944), Zapiska po voprosam budushchego mira i poslevoennogo ustroistva," AVPRF, f. 6, op. 6, papka 14, d. 145, l. 17.

15. Ensen, *Dolgoe osvobozhenie*, 22.

16. See the discussion in Ensen, *Dolgoe osvobozhdenie*, 22–23.

17. Ensen, *Dolgoe osvobozhdenie*, 23–40.

18. M. Litvinov, "K voprosu o blokakh i sferakh vliiania (January 11, 1945)," and M. Litvinov, "Ob obrashchenii s Germaniei," in *SSSR i germanskii vopros 1941–1949*, ed. G. P. Kynin and I. Laufer (Moscow: "Mezhdunarodnye otnosheniia," 1996), vol. 1, 595–598.

19. Ensen, *Dolgoe osvobozhdenie*, 55.

20. Ensen, *Dolgoe osvobozhdenie*, 48.

21. Ensen, *Dolgoe osvobozhdenie*, 166.

22. Ensen, *Dolgoe osvobozhdenie*, 45–55.

23. Ensen, *Dolgoe osvobozhdenie*, 62.

24. Orme Sargent, Foreign Office, to General Ismay, War Office, May 4, 1945. In *Bornholm mellem Øst og Vest: En udenrigspolitisk dokumentation krig*, ed. Jacob Hornemann (Bornholm: Bornholms Tidende, 2006), 87. I thank Prof. Hornemann for giving me a copy of his essential book of documents and for his advice.

25. C. H. M. Waldeck, Admiralty (minutes), May 8, 1945, 23–24, in *Bornholm mellem*, 103.

26. Poul Grooss, *The Naval War in the Baltic, 1939–1945* (Barnsworth: Seaforth Publishing, 2017), 327.

27. Danish foreign minister Christmas Møller's summary of conversation with British charge d'affaires, Rodney Gallop, May 21, 1945.; see also telegram

May 21, 1945 from charge d'affaires, Rodney Gallop, May 21, 1945, Copenhagen, to Foreign Office. In *Bornholm mellem*, 169.

28. See articles by Børge Outze, *Information*, May 5, 1970, *Bornholm mellem*, 408, and P. C. Florian-Larsen in *Politiker*, Dec. 8, 1953, *Bornholm mellem*, 407.

29. Arne Sørensen in *B. T. Iørdag*, Sept. 10, 1946, in *Bornholm mellem*, 405.

30. C. H. M. Waldeck, Admiralty, minutes (A. Haigh), May 8, 1945, *Bornholm mellem*, 103. Planning Office of the 21st Army Group, Plan Directives for Denmark, May 4, 1945, in *Bornholm mellem*, 83. In this latter document it is clear that SHAEF had the intention of liberating all of Denmark, including Bornholm, but the plans were unspecific.

31. Orme Sargent (Foreign Office) to Winston Churchill, May 9, 1945, *Bornholm mellem*, 109.

32. Interview with General Dewing, May 5, 1965, *Berlingska Tidenda*, May 6, 1945, in *Bornholm mellem*, 400–401. In comments on Dewing's interview, former governor von Stemann expressed considerable doubts about the veracity of Dewing's memory given the thorough reports he had forwarded to both the Danish resistance and the Danish foreign ministry.

33. Arne Sørensen in *B. T. Iørdag*, Sept. 10, 1966, *Bornholm mellem*, 405.

34. *Parliamentary Debates* (Hansard), fifth series, vol. 411, sixth vol. of Session 1944–45, House of Commons Official Report (London 1945), 191.

35. "Desant posle Pobedy," Kniga Pamiati Kaliningradskoi oblasti, 1, http://formulyar-polka.narod.ru/t21-desant45BF.htm.

36. General of the Army, S. M. Shtemenko, who was responsible for supply issues, stated that both the Germans and locals faced starvation, which was no doubt true, but he added that the Soviet general staff decided to seize the island in a humanitarian gesture to save the locals from this fate. S. M. Shtemenko, *General'nyi shtab v gody voiny*, kn. 2 (Moscow: Voennoe izd., 1981), 404. Sovinformburo sources stated that there were 12,000 German soldiers on the island, http://eng.9May.ru/eng__inform/m9004260.

37. Poul Grooss states that "the British could easily have flown to Bornholm and received the German surrender." Grooss, *The Naval War in the Baltic*, 330.

38. K. K. Rokossovski, *Soldatskii dolg* (Moscow: Voennoe izd., 1985), 359.

39. I. F. Orlenko, "Krylatye torpedonostsy: Arkhiv 51-go Minno-torpednogo aviapolka," http:www.bellab.ru/51/Book2/Book2012.html. See also A. V. Kuz'min, *V pribrezhnykh vodakh* (Moscow: Voennoe izd., 1967).

40. Rokossovkii, *Soldatskii dolg*, 359.

41. Ensen, *Dolgoe osvobozhdenie*, 101, 127.

42. Ensen, *Dolgoe osvobozhdenie*, 125.

43. Stemann to Danish Foreign Ministry, May 14, 1945, *Bornholm mellem*, 135.

44. Orlenko, "Krylatye torpedonostsy," 1.

45. A. Basov, "Desant na ostrov Bornkhol'm," *Voenno-istoricheskii zhurnal* 8, no. 5 (1966): 34.

46. Boris Vail', "Ob odnom zabytom epizode voiny na Baltike: Datskii istorik o sovetskii okkupatsii Bornkhol'ma," *Zvezda*, no. 8 (1999), reprinted in Ensen, *Dolgoe osvobozhdenie*, 353. For a similar account of the occupation of Bornholm, see Grooss, *The Naval War in the Baltic*, 328–331.

47. Ensen, *Dolgoe osvobozhdenie*, 106. One can pretty much dismiss Rokossovskii's standard mantra: "The residents of Bornholm enthusiastically welcomed their liberators." Rokossovskii, *Soldatskii dolg*, 360.

48. Boris Grigor'ev, "Skandinaviia s chernogo khoda, zapiski razvedchika: ot ser'eznogo do kur'eznogo," erLib.com (2006–2010), 7.

49. Ensen, *Dolgoe osvobozhdenie*, 73. Vail', "Ob odnom zabytom epizode," 350.

50. M. Litvinov, "K voprosu o Baltiiskikh Prolivakh i Kil'skom Kanale, (December 18, 1945)" AVPRF, f. 06, op. 7, papka 17, d. 175, l. 164.

51. See the March 1946 discussions between the British and the United States about the Belts and Sound in FRUS, 1946, vol. 5, 393–397.

52. The Chargé in the Soviet Union (Kennan) to the Secretary of State, February 22, 1946, FRUS, 1946, vol. 6, 699, 702.

53. "11 Maia 1945: Ot Sovetskogo Informbiuro," Nasha pobeda, http://9may.ru/inform/m4261.

54. Governor Stemann to Foreign Ministry, May 23, 1945, *Bornholm mellem*, 175.

55. Report of Bornholm Office of Intelligence to General Commando (Resistance), Office of Intelligence, May 14, 1945, *Bornholm mellem*, 133–134.

56. Grooss, *The Naval War in the Baltic*, 337.

57. One Danish source writes that "Governor von Stemann got along exceptionally well with Colonel Strebkov, who was an esteemed officer of the older school." Bent Jensen, *Bjørnen og haren: Sovjetunionen og Danmark, 1945–1965* (Odense: Odense Universitetsforlag, 1999), 102.

58. Ensen, *Dolgoe osvobozhdenie*, 132.

59. Telegram from General Dewing to General Eisenhower, SHAEF, May 15, 1947, *Bornholm mellem*, 139.

60. It was frequently noted that the Bornholmers would have easily voted to join Sweden rather than stay in Denmark at this time. The resentment of the Danish government was extremely high.

61. Stemann to Foreign Ministry, May 14, 1945, *Bornholm mellem*, 135.

62. FRUS, 1945, vol. 5, 579–580.

63. Notes of Director Nils Svenningsen on the telephone. Conversation with Stemann, May 15, 1945, *Bornholm mellem*, 137.

64. Ensen, *Dolgoe osvobozhdenie*, 146.

65. See Ensen's discussion of Danish politics in *Dolgoe osvobozhdenie*, 148–155.

66. Report of Bornholm Office of Intelligence May 14, 1945, *Bornholm mellem*, 134.

67. Ensen, *Dolgoe osvobozhdenie*, 155.

68. Press attaché Helge Wamberg on meeting with Mikhail Kosov, May 17, 1945, *Bornholm mellem*, 148, fn 197, which states that the Foreign Ministry asked that all newspapers have stories about Bornholm approved by them before publication.

69. See *Århus Stiftstidende*, May 8–June 2, 1945, and *Inllands-Posten*, May 2, 5, 7, 17, 18, and 25, 1945, in HIA, Finn A. Nielsen Collection, box 1.

70. Ensen, *Dolgoe osvobozhdenie*, 238.

71. Ensen, *Dolgoe osvobozhdenie*, 238.

72. Press attaché Helge Wamberg on meeting with Mikhail Kosov, May 17, 1945, *Bornholm mellem*, 148.

73. Meeting of ministers with Stemann, May 18, 1945. *Bornholm mellem*, 236.

74. Telegram from Swedish envoy to Moscow (Söderblom), May 17, 1945, *Bornholm mellem*, 148.

75. Memorandum of Conversation, by the Chief of the Division of Northern European Affairs (Cumming) with Danish Minister Henrik de Kauffmann, Oct. 22, 1945, FRUS, vol. 4, 579–580.

76. Memorandum of Conversation, by the Chief of the Division of Northern European Affairs (Cumming), Washington DC, Oct. 26, 1945. FRUS, 1945, vol. 4, 580–581.

77. "Sovetskii desant na datskom ostrove Bornkhol'm (Dokladnaia zapiska star-shevo leitenanta F. G. Khromushinoi), June 1945 g.," *Istoricheskii arkhiv: nauchno-publikatorskii zhurnal*, no. 3 (1996): 128–129.

78. Bo Lidegaard, *A Short History of Denmark in the 20th Century* (Copenhagen: Gyldendal, 2009), 199.

79. See telegram December 21, 1945 from the Foreign Office to Ambassador Randall, *Bornholm mellem*, 287.

80. Bo Lidegaard, *Short History of Denmark*, 199–200.

81. Land og Folk, May 26, 1945. *Bornholm mellem*, 280.

82. Stemann to the Ministry of Foreign Affairs, June 26, 1945, *Bornholm mellem*, 208–209. Stemann to Foreign Ministry, August 27, 1945, *Bornholm mellem*, 235–236.

83. Stemann to Foreign Minister, Dec. 5, 1945, *Bornholm mellem*, 278. Vail', "Od odnom zabytom episode," 350.

84. Report of Major Streeter's visit to Bornholm (U.S. Army and Chief of Public Relations, SHAEF, in Denmark), who accompanied Ambassador Døssing. Reported by Ambassador Randall, Copenhagen, to Prime Minister Churchill, June 25, 1945, *Bornholm melem*, 206. Grigor'ev, "Skandinaviia," 6–7.

85. Press attaché Helge Wamberg on meeting with Mikhail Kosov, May 17, 1945, *Bornholm mellem* 148.

86. Stemann to Foreign Ministry, July 19, 1945, *Bornholm melem*, 223.

87. Soviet Ministry of Foreign Affairs Note, June 27, 1945, from T. Zhdanova to Section Head M. S. Vetrov, *Bornholm mellem*, 210.

88. See Hornemann note, *Bornholm mellem*, 218. Also see Ensen, *Dolgoe osvobozhdenie*, 208–212.

89. Ambassador Døssing to Foreign Minister, Gustav Rasmussen, Jan. 7, 1946. Notes of conversation with Dekanozov, Jan. 5, 1946. *Bornholm mellem*, 306.

90. Lidegaard, *Short History of Denmark*, 200.

91. Summary of meeting of the British Chiefs of Staff Committee, May 11, 1945. *Bornholm mellem*, 125.

92. G. Lundestad, *America, Scandinavia, and the Cold War, 1945–1949* (New York: Columbia University Press, 1980), 46.

93. Mastny, "Stalin as Warlord," 6. See also Vojtech Mastny, *The Cold War and Soviet Insecurity: The Stalin Years* (New York: Oxford, 1996), 19.

94. In discussions with the Norwegians (July 5, 1945), Molotov put forward "an outright claim" to Bear Island and insisted that Spitsbergen be ruled by a joint Russo-Norwegian condominium to protect Russian communication lines. FRUS, 1945, vol. 5, 91.

95. TNA, JIC (46) 85 (0). Final. Feb. 14, 1947. Chief of Staffs Committee, "Russia's Strategic Interests and Intentions in Europe," 31.

96. A report from the British ambassador in Copenhagen describes Danish diplomacy as sometimes irritating, but also as "shrewd" and "clever," as befits a small country faced by overwhelming power. Ambassador Randall, Copenhagen, to R. M. A. Hankey, Foreign Office, Apr. 15, 1946. *Bornholm mellem*, 393.

97. Ensen, *Dolgoe osvobozhdenie*, 13.

98. Jensen, "Soviet Remote Control," 198.

99. TNA, CAB 81 134, Chiefs of Staff, Joint Intelligence sub-committee, "Attitude of Certain Powers in the Event of a Future War," Aug. 15, 1946, 2. Here the British write: "Fear of Russia amongst the Danes is so great that it is considered most unlikely that the Danes would enter into any military alliance with the Anglo-American powers, at least during the early stage of the conflict."

100. Denmark: Evacuation of Bornholm, Mar. 15, 1946, 25, CREST, https://www.cia.gov/library/readingroom The American evaluation differs from the British, which states, in a report covering Jan.-April 1946, that "they [the Russians] have erected no permanent installations" on Bornholm. TNA, JIC (46) 1 (0), Supplementary T. of R., Tab 1, Jan.–Apr. 1946, "Russia's Strategic Interests and Intentions," 18.

101. V. M. Molotov Diary. Summary of V. M. Molotov's conversation with Danish ambassador Døssing, March 5, 1946. *Bornholm mellem*, 337.

102. "The Chargé in Denmark (Ackerson) to the Secretary of State, March 20, 1946," FRUS, 1946, vol. 5, Denmark, 393.

103. Ensen, *Dolgoe osvobozhdenie*, 321.

104. *Bornholm Tidende*, Apr. 5, 1946, *Bornholm mellem*, 391.

105. As a consequence of growing Cold War tensions, the Danes finally agreed in 1951 to the building of U.S. bases on Greenland.

106. Holtsmark, "The Limits to Soviet Influence," 120. See Melvyn P. Leffler, "The Cold War: What Do 'We Now Know?,'" *The American Historical Review* 104, no. 2 (April 1999): 514–515.

107. Agger and Michelsen, "How Strong Was the 'Weakest Link'?," 248.

108. Mikkel Runge Olesen, "To Balance or Not to Balance: How Denmark Almost Stayed out of NATO 1948–1949," *Journal of Cold War Studies* 20, no. 2 (Spring 2018): 63–98.

109. Agger and Michelson, "How Strong Was the 'Weakest Link'?," 249–250.

110. See Ensen, *Dolgoe osvobozhdenie*, 291, on these talks.

111. "Zapis' Besedy tov. I. V. Stalina s Min. In. Del Danii Rasmussen i Glavoi Torg. Deleg. Danii Printsem Akselem (6 June 1946)," RGASPI, f. 558, op. 11, d. 305, ll. 1–9.

112. Aleksei Chichkin, Aleksandr Rublev, "Ekho voiny: Bornkhol'm i Khiiumaa," *Nochnoi dozor*, June 2, 2008, http:www.dozor.ee/?p=newsView&iNews=1649. The numbers include soldiers who died in various capacities during the bombardment, the capture of German soldiers, the transportation of the Germans, and in the occupation, since there were no shots fired in the actual taking of the island.

113. See the discussion in Vail', "Ob odnom zabytom episode," 352–353.

114. Agger and Michelson, "How Strong Was the 'Weakest Link'?," 250.

2. THE ALBANIAN BACKFLIP

1. Although the Yugoslav party had not formally authorized the mission of Popović and Mugoša, the influence of these two figures was profound, even to the point of participating in the selection of CPA Central Committee members. General CIA Records CREST, "Socialism and Communism in Albania," *Quatreme Internationale* 6 (1948): 10–11. CIA-RDP8000809A000600 250862-7.

2. On Apr. 1, 1944, Tito wrote to Dimitrov, "We have ties with Greek and Albanian comrades. These ties are still rather weak, but [they] are improving, and we help as much as possible with advice and materials, especially with the Albanian comrades. . . . [In Macedonia] a delegate of our TsK and a member

of our General Staff . . . coordinate operations of the Albanian, Greek, Yugoslav, and now also Bulgarian partisans." RGASPI, f. 17, op. 128, d. 6, l. 2.

3. See Greta Delcheva, "Vneshniaia Politika Albanii 1944–1948, *"Études Balkaniques* (Sophia), no. 4 (1984): 20. The Albanian resistance leadership hoped during the war that this might lead to the formation of a greater Albania. See R. Craig Nation, "A Balkan Union? Southeastern Europe in Soviet Security Policy, 1944–8," in *The Soviet Union and Europe in the Cold War 1943–53*, ed. Francesca Gori and Silvio Pons (New York: St. Martin's, 1996), 127.

4. Enver Hoxha, *The Titoites: Historical Notes* (Tirana: "8 Nëntori" Publishing House, 1982), 14.

5. Aleksandar Životić, "Albaniia i iugoslavskoe videnie Balkanskoi federatsii posle Vtoroi mirovoi voiny," in *Balkany v evropeiskikh politicheskikh proektakh xix–xxi vv* (Moscow: Institut slavianovedeniia RAN, 2014), 333. The Albanians came to power, wrote one British observer, "by the enthusiasm of youth." Cited in Elidor Mëhilli, *Albania and the Socialist World from Stalin to Mao* (Ithaca, NY: Cornell University Press, 2017), 32.

6. Discussions between I. V. Stalin and E. Hoxha, Mar. 23, 1949, in *Sovetskii faktor v vostochnoi Evrope 1944–1953*, vol. 2, ed. T. V. Volokitina et al. (Moscow: ROSSPEN, 1999), 70.

7. *The Artful Albanian: Memoirs of Enver Hoxha*, ed. by Jon Halliday (London: Chatto & Windus, 1986), 96.

8. Litvinov to Molotov, "Al'banskaia Problema," Feb. 8, 1945, AVPRF, f. 06, op. 7, papka, 17, d. 173, ll. 110–111. The Americans were also convinced that the British were thinking about the partition of Albania, with "the southern part [being] added to Greece." "Summary of Findings and Recommendations with Respect to the Recognition of 'The Democratic Government of Albania,'" Aug. 15, 1945, FRUS, 1945, vol. 6, 50.

9. "Verbal Note," Italian embassy in Moscow to Ministry of Foreign Affairs," Jan. 21, 1946 (Russian translation), AVPRF, f. 98, op. 29, papka 33, d. 3, ll. 28–29. Here the Italians asked the Soviets to intervene with the Albanians, who had decided not to allow the mission to come. Leonid Gibianskii suggests that complicated Soviet interests in Italy were determined in part by Moscow's hope to use Italy (and the Italian communists) to counter British and American influence in the Mediterranean. See Leonid Gibianskii, "The Trieste Issue and the Soviet Union in the 1940s," *Vojna in mir na Primorskem: Od kapitulacije Italije leta 1943 do Londonskega memoranduma leta 1954*, ed. Jože Pirjevec et. al. (Koper: Založba Annales, 2005), 365.

10. Hoxha, *Titoites*, 503.

11. L. Ia. Gibianskii, "U nachala konflikta: Balkanskii uzel," part 1, *Rabochii klass i sovremennyi mir*, no. 2 (Mar.–Apr. 1990): 172–173.

12. Hoxha wrote to UNRRA that "the Nazi occupiers had burned and ravaged entire regions" "pitilessly killing cattle" and "destroying the economy of our country." See TNA, WO 204 / 9515. Reports from Bari and Albania, Mar. and Apr. 1945. Translation (from French) of Col. Gen Hoxha's message to UNRRA, Mar. 11, 1945. See also TNA, WO 204 / 9514. Jan. 12, 1945 report of a meeting with Hoxha and Col. D. B. W. Warner about the severe deprivation in the country.

13. Životić, "Albaniia," 334. Gale Group, U.S. Office of Intelligence Research, Department of State, Apr. 15, 1948. "East European Political Treaties," U.S. Declassified Documents Online. Tinyurl.galegroup.com / tmyurl / 4KNnPX.

14. Leonid Ia. Gibianskii, "The Soviet-Yugoslav conflict and the Soviet Bloc," in *The Soviet Union and Europe in the Cold War, 1943–53,* ed. Francesca Gori and Silvio Pons (New York: St. Martin's Press, 1996), 226.

15. Greta Delcheva, "Vneshniaia politika Albanii 1944–1948," *Études Balkaniques* 4, no. 20 (1984):18.

16. Gibianskii, "The Soviet-Yugoslav Conflict," 226.

17. D. S. Chuvakhin Diary, Hoxha's Visit to Belgrade, July 3, 1946, *Vostochnaia Evropa v dokumentakh rossiiskikh arkhivov,* vol. 1, ed. T. V. Volokitina et al. (Moscow: ROSSPEN, 1999), 472.

18. Elidor Mëhilli, *From Stalin to Mao: Albania and the Socialist World* (Ithaca, NY: Cornell University Press, 2017), 41.

19. Paskal Milo, "Albania in East-West Relations 1944–1945," Academy of Sciences Conference paper, Moscow, Mar. 29–31, 1994, 10.

20. The Representative in Albania (Jacobs) to the Secretary of State, Feb. 4, 1946, *FRUS,* 1946, vol. 6, 5–6.

21. The Representative in Albania (Jacobs) to the Secretary of State, Feb. 28, 1946, FRUS, 1946, vol. 6, Albania, 14. Generally, however, the Americans overestimated the Soviet influence vis-à-vis that of the Yugoslavs.

22. Hoyt S. Vandenberg (CIA) to the President, Jan. 16, 1947. U.S. Declassified Documents Online. Gale Group. tinyurl.galegroup.com / tinyurl / 4KHR03. See also TNA, CAB, 81 / 130. Chiefs of Staff: J.I. Subcommittee Memorandum, July–Sept. 1945, "Situation in Yugoslavia." Here the British correctly assess that the Yugoslavs would not want to risk a "collision" with the Anglo-Saxon powers and instead incorporate Albania by peaceful means.

23. Hoxha, *Titoites,* 15.

24. D. S. Chuvakhin Diary. Hoxha's visit to Belgrade, July 3, 1946, *Vostochnaia Evropa,* vol. 1, 475.

25. Delcheva, "Vneshniaia politika Albanii 1944–1948," 22.

26. Suslov to Zhdanov, June 13, 1946, "O polozhenii v rukovodstve komm. partii Albanii," RGASPI, f. 17, op. 128, d. 96, ll. 17–18.

27. Report of American representative Jacobs to Secretary of State, Jan. 29, 1946. FRUS, 1946, vol. 6, 2.

28. Nijaz Dizdarević, *Albanski Dnevnik* (Zagreb: Globus, 1988), 20–21, 201. Thanks to Leonid Gibianskii for alerting me to this important source.

29. Gibianskii, "U nachala konflikta," 175–176.

30. In a Washington, DC, meeting between British Foreign Minister Bevin and Secretary of State Dean Acheson, a State Department official noted: "it would be right to seize any opportunity of bringing down the Hoxha regime." TNA, CRA 28 / 3 / 49, Alb 49 / 8. The biographers of the American diplomat, Llewellyn Thompson, write similarly that Bevin sought American commitment "to bring down Hoxha" and wondered if there might be some "kings around that could be put in" to replace him. Eventually, in 1950 and again in 1952, British and American intelligence infiltrated Albanian émigrés into the country to organize uprisings against Hoxha that failed miserably. Jenny Thompson and Sherry Thompson, *The Kremlinologist: Llewellyn E. Thompson: America's Man in Cold War Moscow* (Baltimore, MD: Johns Hopkins Press, 2018), 71.

31. L. Ia. Gibianskii, "Proekty federatsii na Balkanakh v gody Vtoroi mirovoi voiny i v nachale kholodnoi voiny," in *Balkany v evropeiskikh politicheskikh proektakh XIX–XX vv.,* ed. R. P. Grishin (Moscow: Institut Slavianovedeniia RAN, 2014), 302. Halliday, ed., *Artful Albanian,* 92.

32. FRUS, 1945, vol. 4, 51.

33. Delcheva, "Vneshniaia politika Albanii," 22–23n47.

34. Molotov's Diary, Sept. 16, 1946, AVPRF, f. 06, op. 8, papka 2, ll. 9–13.

35. Notes of Conversation with Enver Hoxha, Sept. 21, 1946, Diary of D. S. Chuvakhin, RGASPI, f. 17, op. 128, d. 96, ll. 89–91.

36. Gibianskii, "The Soviet-Yugoslav Conflict," 226.

37. The transcript is cited in Gibianskii, "U nachala konflikta," 176.

38. Molotov Diary, July 15, 1947. Talks with Enver Hoxha, AVPRF, f. 06, op. 9, papka 2, d. 11, ll. 70–79.

39. Gibianskii, "The Soviet-Yugoslav Conflict," 226. Hoxha, *Titoites,* 348.

40. In one such meeting with the Albanian envoy, M. Prifti, Molotov indicated that the Albanians were on the same path as the peoples of the Soviet Union, who had also been deprived of the ability to develop their own culture before the Revolution. From Molotov's Diary, Apr. 26, 1947, AVPRF, f. 06, op. 8, papka 21, d. 1, l. 34.

41. Gibianskii, "U nachala konflikta," 176.

42. Gibianskii, "U nachala konflikta," 175–176.

43. Halliday, ed., *Artful Albanian,* 102.

44. See discussions between Gagarinov and Spiru, Nov. 19, 1947, in *Vostochnaia Evropa,* vol. 1, 737, fn. 3, where the editors state, based on a foreign

ministry document, that Spiru shot himself in front of his coworkers on Nov. 21.

45. Halliday, ed., *Artful Albanian*, 104. Gagarinov and Spiru, Nov. 19, 1947, in *Vostochnaia Evropa*, vol. 1, 735–737.

46. Blendi Fevziu, *Enver Hoxha: The Iron Fist of Albania*, ed. and intro. Robert Elsie, trans. Majlinda Nishku (London: I. B. Tauris, 2016), 138.

47. Gagarinov and Spiru, Nov. 19, 1947, in *Vostochnaia Evropa*, vol. 1, 736.

48. Daniel Isaac Perez, "Between Tito and Stalin: Enver Hoxha, Albanian communists, and the assertion of Albanian national sovereignty, 1941–1948," Ph.D. Dissertation, Stanford University 2017, 220.

49. Discussions between Hoxha and Molotov, June 24, 1948, in *Vostochnaia Evropa*, vol. 1, 905.

50. Gibianskii, "U nachala konflikta," 177–179. Gibianskii has done an effective job of reconstructing the exchanges during the Popović mission from the Serbian archives.

51. Ibid.

52. R. Craig Nation thinks that the Yugoslavs were anxious to proceed with the incorporation of Albania into their federation because they worried about the Soviet interest in Albania. Nation, "A Balkan Union?," 134.

53. Daniel Perez, "Albanian-Yugoslav Relations, 1945–1949," unpublished manuscript, 2010, 17–18.

54. T. Volokitina et al., *Moskva i vostochnaia Evropa: Stanovlenie politicheskikh rezhimov sovetskogo tipa (1949–1953). Ocherk istorii* (Moscow: ROSSPEN, 2008), 502.

55. Elidor Mëhilli, *From Stalin to Mao: Albania and the Socialist World* (Ithaca, NY: Cornell University Press, 2017), 38.

56. See Delcheva, "Vneshniaia politika Albanii," 22.

57. See Pukhlov and Manchkha on the KPA, May 15, 1948, *Vostochnaia Evropa*, vol. 1, 871.

58. Halliday, ed., *Artful Albanian*, 106.

59. Fevziu, *Enver Hoxha*, 139.

60. Leonid Gibianskii, "The Soviet-Yugoslav Split and the Cominform," in *The Establishment of Communist Regimes in Eastern Europe, 1944–1949*, ed. Norman Naimark and Leonid Gibianskii (Boulder, CO: Westview, 1997), 295.

61. Ivo Banac, *With Stalin against Tito: Cominformist Splits in Yugoslav Communism* (Ithaca, NY: Cornell University Press, 1988), 40.

62. Djilas, *Conversations with Stalin*, 143.

63. Djilas, *Conversations with Stalin*, 146.

64. Leonid Gibianskii has reproduced and analyzed these documents in "U nachala konflikta," 180–181.

65. Perez, "Between Stalin and Tito: Albanian Communists and the Yugoslav-Cominform Split," Dec. 1947–June 1948," Workshop Paper, Stanford University, Apr. 2010, 6.

66. Životić, "Albaniia," 344.

67. Gibianskii, "The Soviet-Yugoslav Conflict and the Cominform," 296. *Zapisnici sa sednica politbiroa Centralnog komiteta KPJ (1945–1948)*, ed. Branko Petranović (Belgrade: Arhiv Jugoslavije, 1995), 234.

68. Životić, "Albaniia," 347.

69. The account of the Feb. 10 meeting is taken from the *Cold War International History Project Bulletin*, no. 10 (1998): 128–134. This includes the original translation of the report of Milovan Djilas from the Yugoslav archives, as well as substantial citations from the Bulgarian and Soviet versions of the same meeting. A translation of the Bulgarian account is available in *The Diary of Georgi Dimitrov*, ed. Ivo Banac (New Haven, CT: Yale University Press, 2003) Feb. 10, 1948, 436–444. The fullest documentation of the Feb. 10 meeting is in L. Ia. Gibianskii with V. K. Volkov, ed., "Na poroge pervogo raskola v 'sotsialisticheskom lagere': Peregovory rukovodiashchikh deiatelei SSSR, Bolgarii i Iugoslavii. 1948 g." *Istoricheskii arkhiv*, no. 4 (1997): 92–123. In the following discussion, where I quote some of these documents, I reproduce the original underlining that is preserved in the published versions, but not the brackets in the published version, which indicate where words are abbreviated in the original.

70. Hoxha, *Titoites*, 445; Halliday, ed., *Artful Albanian*, 107. Here Hoxha claimed that this was the first time he had contacted Stalin to get his backing in a confrontation with Yugoslavia. He was especially unsettled by Kuprešanin's announcement of taking over the military effort on the Greek border. The Soviets learned about Tito's move from their Ambassador Lavrent'ev in Belgrade. See also Perez, "Between Stalin and Tito," 20.

71. "Na poroge pervogo raskola," 99.

72. "Na poroge pervogo raskola," 105. Djilas notes.

73. "Na poroge pervogo raskola," 93.

74. Gibianskii, "U nachala konflikta," 180–182.

75. Gibianskii, "U nachala konflikta," 183.

76. *Dimitrov Diary*, Feb. 10, 1948, 440.

77. Notes of Vasil Kolarov on Soviet-Bulgarian-Yugoslav meeting with Stalin, Feb. 10, 1948. "Na poroge pervogo raskola," 96. Emphasis in the original.

78. Notes of Vasil Kolarov on Soviet-Bulgarian-Yugoslav meeting with Stalin, Feb. 10, 1948. "Na poroge pervogo raskola," 97.

79. Notes of Vasil Kolarov on Soviet-Bulgarian-Yugoslav meeting with Stalin, Feb. 10, 1948. "Na poroge pervogo raskola," 98. Emphasis in the original.

80. Notes of Vasil Kolarov on Soviet-Bulgarian-Yugoslav meeting with Stalin, Feb. 10, 1948. "Na poroge pervogo raskola," 100.

81. Kolarov notes, "Na poroge pervogo raskola," 100.

82. Gibianskii, "U nachala konflikta," 184.

83. TNA, JIC (46) 104(0). Annex: Foreign Assistance to the Greek Communists," Dec. 4, 1946, 3–4.

84. See Basiles Kontes and Spyridon Sfetas, *Empylios polemos: engrapha apo ta Giounkoslavika kai Voulgarika archeia* (Thessalonike: Parateretes, 2000), 62–65.

85. Russian translation of a handwritten report by Greek communist "Ilia," Oct. 1948, in RGASPI, f. 17, op. 128, d. 479, ll. 7–8. Since this was written after the Tito-Stalin split, one might doubt the author's judgment.

86. *Dimitrov Diary,* Feb. 10, 1948, 442. Kolarov notes, "Na poroge pervogo raskola," 101.

87. Early on, the Greek communists in the national front had supported Athens' claim to Northern Epirus, though they assured Hoxha that this was only a tactical maneuver.

88. *Dimitrov Diary,* Feb. 10, 1948, 441.

89. Djilas notes, "Na poroge pervogo raskola," 106.

90. Djilas notes, "Na poroge pervogo raskola," 107.

91. Djilas notes, "Na poroge pervogo raskola," 109.

92. Djilas notes, "Na poroge pervogo raskola," 103.

93. Životić, "Albaniia," 349. "Na poroge pervogo raskola," 109.

94. Molotov's diary, Reception for Kardelj, Feb. 11, 1948, AVPRF, f. 06, op. 10, papka 1, d. 2, l. 41.

95. Tito to Djilas and Kardelj, Feb. 13, 1948 in "Na poroge pervogo raskola," 113.

96. Tito to Djilas and Kardelj, Feb. 13, 1948 in "Na poroge pervogo raskola," 113.

97. Minutes of politburo, Feb. 19, 1948, in *Zapisnici sa sednica politbiroa,* 234. Djilas notes.

98. Minutes of politburo, Feb. 19, 1948, in *Zapisnici sa sednica politbiroa,* 234–235. Djilas notes.

99. Gibianskii, "The Soviet-Yugoslav Split and the Cominform," 298.

100. *Zapisnici sa sednica politbiroa,* 236–241.

101. Gibianskii, "The Soviet-Yugoslav Split and the Cominform," 299. At the Central Committee plenum of the Yugoslav party, Apr. 12–13, 1948, Žujović attacked the leadership for its anti-Soviet stance but found no supporters. He was expelled from the Central Committee and the party and arrested on May 7.

102. Molotov's diary, Mar. 24, 1948, Reception of Yugoslav Ambassador Popovich, AVPRF, f. 06, op. 10, papka 1, d. 3, ll. 98–103.

103. Gibianskii, "The Soviet-Yugoslav Split and the Cominform," 300.
104. Gibianskii, "The Soviet-Yugoslav Split and the Cominform," 300–301.
105. Letter of Tito and Kardelj to Stalin and Molotov, Apr. 13, 1948, "Sekretnaia sovetsko-iugoslavskaia perepiska 1948 goda," *Voprosy istorii*, no. 4 (1992): 158.
106. Perez, "Between Tito and Stalin," 38–40.
107. Cited in Daniel Perez, "Albanian-Yugoslav Relations, 1945–1958," manuscript, 33.
108. Perez, "Between Tito and Stalin," 44.
109. Cited in Životić, "Albaniia," 350, 353.
110. Perez, "Between Tito and Stalin," 50–52.
111. Životić writes that Hoxha was "constantly" talking to Chuvakhin about Yugoslav "ideas, mistakes, and demands." Životić, "Albaniia," 348.
112. Hoxha, *Titoites*, 480.
113. Hoxha, *Titoites*, 492–495.
114. Cited in Perez, "Albanian-Yugoslav Relations," 35. According to Perez, the original document (though not the published version) was also signed by Xoxe. Perez, "Between Tito and Stalin," 288.
115. The Secretary of State to the Embassy in Greece, June 9, 1948, FRUS, 1948, vol. 4, The Greek Frontier Question, 249.
116. The Chargé in Yugoslavia (Reams) to Secretary of State, July 7, 1948, *FRUS, 1948*, vol. 4, 1090. Životić, "Albaniia," 356.
117. CIA Research Reports, The Soviet Union, 1946–1976, Reel 1, Central Intelligence Agency, Memorandum for the President, June 30, 1948, 1. This perception was also widespread among European communists. Later critics of the Yugoslavs blamed them for having a colonialist attitude toward the Albanians. Group of Spanish Communists on the Political Situation in Yugoslavia, RGASPI, f. 17, op. 128, d. 494, l. 29.
118. Molotov's diary, discussion with Hoxha, June 24, 1948, *Vostochnaia Evropa*, vol. 1, 905.
119. Mëhilli, *From Stalin to Mao*, 44.
120. CREST, General CIA Records, CIA Information Report, "Consequence of Albania's Rift with Yugoslavia," May 16, 1949.
121. Mëhilli, *From Stalin to Mao*, 45–46.
122. Mehmet Shehu on the occasion of the 69th Birthday of Stalin, RGASPI, f. 17, op. 128, d. 656.
123. Životić, "Albaniia," 356–358.
124. CREST, General CIA Records, "Information Report Albania / Yugoslavia," Nov. 5, 1948.
125. Quote in "Report of Milovan Djilas about Soviet-Bulgarian-Yugoslav meeting, Feb. 10, 1948," *Cold War International History Project Bulletin*, no. 10 (1997), 131.

126. Halliday, ed., *The Artful Albanian: The Memoirs of Enver Hoxha,* 122.

127. Discussion between Stalin and E. Hoxha, *Sovetskii faktor,* vol. 2, 70.

128. "Ob okazanii pomoshchi albanskomu pravitel'stvu v organizatsii raboty organov Ministerstva vnutrennikh del Albanii," RGASPI, f. 17, op. 162, d. 40, l. 146.

129. RGASPI, f. 17, op. 162, d. 40, l. 216.

130. Shifrovka Malenkov to Stalin, Sept. 16, 1948, RGASPI, f. 558, op. 11, d. 112. l. 3.

131. Chuvakhin's Diary. Meeting with Hoxha, Apr. 25, 1949, in *Vostochnaia Evropa,* vol. 2, 83. According to the agreement, only individual members of the Greek Central Committee and heavily wounded fighters of the "Democratic Army" would be allowed to cross the border. Everyone else would be arrested by the Albanians. There continued, however, to be serious problems between the Albanian and Greek parties over the tactics of the Greek partisans. The Albanians repeatedly appealed to Moscow for help in this connection. See Hoxha and Chuvakhin, Aug. 2, 1949, and Hoxha to Stalin, Nov. 16, 1949, in *Sovetskii faktor,* vol. 2, 151, 210. The Americans spotted an opening with Albania in early May 1948, as the Albanians expressed to them their "desire to end tensions on the Greek-Albanian border." Secretary of State to the Embassy in Greece, FRUS, 1948, vol. 4, 249.

132. "'Liudiam svoistvenno oshibat'sia': Iz vospominanii M. Rakosi" *Istoricheskii arkhiv,* no. 3 (1997): 126.

133. Nikos Zahariadis, "Tito Clique's Stab in the Back to People's Democratic Greece," *For a Lasting Peace, for a People's Democracy,* Aug. 1, 1949, 6. Given the desire of the Greek communists to please Stalin, one should read with a grain of salt these Greek accusations against the Yugoslavs after the split.

134. Stavros Dagios, *E diethnes diastase tes rexes E. Hohxa—J. B Tito kai e lexe toy Ellenikoy Emphyloioy Polemoy (1945–1949)* (Thessalonike: Parateretes, 2004), 247.

135. *Memoirs of Nikita Khrushchev,* vol. 2, *1945–1964,* ed. Sergei Khrushchev, trans. George Shriver and Stephen Shenfield (University Park: Pennsylvania State Press, 2008), 158–159.

136. Banac, *With Stalin against Tito,* 247. For a comprehensive history of Goli Otok, see Martin Previšič, *Povijest Golog otoka* (Zagreb: Fraktura, 2019).

137. See Mark Kramer, "Stalin, the Split with Yugoslavia, and Soviet-East European Efforts to Reassert Control, 1948–1953," *Stalin and Europe: Imitation and Domination 1928–1953,* ed. Timothy Snyder and Ray Brandon (New York: Oxford University Press, 2014), 298.

138. Stalin's discussion with Chervenkov, Damianov, and Iugov, *Vostochnaia Evropa,* vol. 2, 201. On the Slavic struggle against German fascism, see RGASPI, f. 82, op. 2, d. 1011, l. 1.

139. See *Cold War International History Project Bulletin,* no. 10 (Mar. 1998): 1.

140. See Fevziu, *Enver Hoxha*, 50–54. Fevziu paints a portrait of Hoxha as an extremely devious and violent politician who systematically eliminated all of his major opponents. On Hoxha's brutality, see also Arshi Pipa, *Albanian Stalinism: Ideo-Political Aspects* (Boulder, CO: East European Monographs, 1990), 10.

141. Central Intelligence Group, "Albanian Political Situation," Aug. 18, 1947, 3, https://www.cia.gov/library/readingroom.

3. THE FINNISH FIGHT FOR INDEPENDENCE

1. Kimmo Rentola, "Great Britain and the Soviet Threat in Finland, 1944–1951," *Scandinavian Journal of History* 37, no. 2 (May 2012): 172–174.

2. Mikko Majander, "Post-Cold War Historiography of Finland," in *The Cold War and the Nordic Countries: Historiography at a Crossroads*, ed. Thorsten B. Olesen (Odense: University of Southern Denmark Press, 2004), 60.

3. Kees Boterbloem, *The Life and Times of Andrei Zhdanov, 1896–1948* (Montreal: McGill-Queen's University Press, 2004), 200–205.

4. Fred Singleton, *A Short History of Finland* (Cambridge: Cambridge University Press, 1989), 137.

5. James H. Billington, "Finland," in *Communism and Revolution: The Strategic Uses of Political Violence*, ed. Cyril E. Black and Thomas P. Thornton (Princeton, NJ: Princeton University Press, 1964), 128–130. See also John H. Hodgson, *Communism in Finland: A History and Interpretation* (Princeton, NJ: Princeton University Press, 1967), 225–231.

6. Kimmo Rentola, "Generations of Finnish Communists," in *Twentieth Century Communism*, vol. 4 (2012), 148. Tuomas Tepora, "Changing Perceptions of 1918: World War II and the Postwar Rise of the Left," in *Finnish Civil War 1918: History, Memory, Legacy*, ed. Tuomas Tepora and Aapo Roselius (Leiden: Brill, 2014), 382.

7. S. Diullen, "Gde prokhodit granitsa? Mesto Finliandii v zone bezopasnosti SSSR, 1944–1956 gg.," M. M. Narinskii, ed., *SSSR, Frantsiia i ob'edinenie Evropy, 1945–1957: Sbornik nauchnykh statei* (Moscow: MGIMO, 2008), 123. See also *Istochnik*, no. 4 (1995), 114–115.

8. Litvinov to Molotov and Vyshinskii, Jan. 11, 1945, in *SSSR i germanskii vopros 1941–1949*, vol. 1, *22 iiunia 1941g.–8 maia 1945g.*, ed. G. P. Kynin and I. Laufer (Moscow: Mezhdunar. Otnosheniia, 1996), 595–596.

9. Zapiska I. Maiskogo, "O zhelatel'nykh osnovakh budushchevo mira," Jan. 11, 1944, *Istochnik* 4, no 17 (1995):125–126.

10. Cited in Jukka Nevakivi, "The Soviet Union and Finland after the War, 1944–53," *The Soviet Union and Europe in the Cold War, 1943–53*, ed. Francesca Gori and Silvio Pons (London: Macmillan, 1996), 90.

11. Tripartite Luncheon Meeting, Dec. 1, 1943, in FRUS: The Conferences at Cairo and Tehran, 1943, vol. 3, *The Tehran Conference* (Washington, DC: U.S.

Government Printing Office, 1961), 590–592. Roosevelt and especially Churchill tried to ameliorate Stalin's demands for reparations from the Finns.

12. Tripartite Luncheon Meeting, *The Tehran Conference*, 590.

13. Washington DC to Foreign Office, Oct. 1, 1944, cited in "Directive for British Section of Allied Control Commission in Finland, 115B," in TNA, WO/06/433.

14. Cited in Tuomo Polvinen, *Between East and West: Finland in International Politics*, ed. and trans. D. G. Kirby and Peter Henning (Helsinki: Werner Söderström Osakeyhtiö, 1986), 283.

15. "Directive for British Section of Allied Control Commission." TNA, WO/06/433.

16. See Diullen, "Gde prokhodit granitsa?," 125–127, on the Swedish factor in Soviet thinking about Finland.

17. Juka Nevakivi, "A Decisive Armistice 1944–1947: Why Was Finland Not Sovietized," *Scandinavian Journal of History* 19, no. 2 (1994): 95.

18. TNA, JIC (46) 85 (0) Chiefs of Staff Committee, "Russia's Strategic Interests and Intentions in Europe," Feb. 14, 1947, 28.

19. Discussions of Zhdanov with Leino, Kuusinen, and Pessi, May 10, 1945, RGASPI, f. 77, op. 3, d. 63, l. 33.

20. Nevakivi, "A Decisive Armistice," 95.

21. "Interview between Marshal Stalin and Molotov and Finnish Cultural Delegation on 10th Oct. [1945], Report by Mme. Hertta Kuusinen," Enclosure from Shepherd to Bevin, Oct. 19, 1945, in *British Documents on Foreign Affairs: Reports and Papers from the Foreign Office*, Confidential Print, Part III. From 1940–1945, vol. 6, series A, Soviet Union and Finland, ed. Anita Prazmowska (Bethesda, MD: University Publications of America, 1999), 195. Diullen, "Gde prokhodit granitsa?," 117–118. Polvinen, *Between East and West*, 166.

22. Alfred J. Rieber, *Zhdanov in Finland* (Pittsburgh, PA: Carl Beck Papers in Russian and East European Studies, 1995), 18.

23. Zhdanov to Stalin and Molotov about visit with Mannerheim, Jan. 18, 1945, RGASPI, f. 77, op. 3, d. 54, ll. 2–3.

24. Molotov to Zhdanov, Jan. 20, 1945, RGASPI, f. 77, op. 3, d. 54, l. 5.

25. Polvinen, *Between East and West: Finland in International Politics 1944–1947*, 61. See George Maude, *Aspects of the Governing of the Finns* (New York: Peter Lang, 2010), 162.

26. Marvin Rintala, *Four Finns* (Berkeley: University of California Press, 1969), 94.

27. See Efraim Karsh, "Finland: adaptation and conflict," *International Affairs* 62, no. 2 (1986): 267.

28. Cited in Risto E. J. Penttilä, *Finland's Search for Security through Defence, 1944–89* (Basingstoke: Macmillan, 1991), 12.

29. Maude, *Aspects of the Governing of the Finns,* 168.

30. That policy—sometimes called the "Paasikivi-Kekkonen line" was continued by Urho Kekkonen, the leader of the Agrarian Party and long-time president of Finland from 1956–1982. Kekkonen moderated his anti-Soviet stance by the end of the war, and in Stockholm in Dec. 1943, spoke out in favor of a policy of "good neighborliness" toward the Soviet Union. Singleton, *Short History,* 137.

31. Thorsten V. Kalijarvi, "Finland since 1939," *The Review of Politics* 10, no. 2 (1948): 219.

32. Sir Clark Kerr, Moscow to Foreign Office, Sept. 8, 1944. Finnish Armistice Terms. . . . TNA, WO/06/4333.

33. Kerr, Moscow to Foreign Office, TNA, WO/06/4333.

34. Diullin, "Gde prokhodit granitsa?," 111. Penttilä, *Finland's Search for Security,* 8.

35. Sir V. Mallett, Stockholm to Foreign Office, Sept. 18, 1944. TNA, WO/06/4333.

36. Osmo Jussila, Seppo Hentilä, Jukka Nevakivi, *From Grand Duchy to a Modern State: A Political History of Finland since 1809,* trans. David and Eva-Kaia Arter (London: Hurst and Company), 219.

37. Penttilä, *Finland's Search for Security,* 5, 14.

38. "Finland: Political Review, 1945," in Shepherd to Bevin, Mar. 12, 1946, *British Documents on Foreign Affairs,* vol. 1, *Northern Affairs, January 1946–June 1946,* 234. Karsh, "Finland: Adaptation and Conflict," 174.

39. Rieber, *Zhdanov in Finland,* 18.

40. Shepherd to Bevin, Oct. 10, 1945, *British Documents on Foreign Affairs,* vol. 6, series A, Soviet Union and Finland, 182.

41. Sir A. Clark Kerr, Moscow to Foreign Office, Sept. 18, 1944. TNA, WO/0614333, "Finnish Armistice terms, Mar. 44–Dec. 44." This phrase describes Molotov's attitude.

42. Rintala, *Four Finns,* 97–105.

43. Jussila, Hentilä, Nevakivi, *From Grand Duchy to a Modern State,* 225.

44. Rieber, *Zhdanov in Finland,* 15. Polvinen, *Between East and West,* 29.

45. Nevakivi, "A Decisive Armistice 1944–1947," 19.

46. Milovan Djilas, *Conversations with Stalin,* trans. Michael Petrovich (New York: Harcourt Brace Jovanovich, 1962), 155.

47. Rieber writes that Zhdanov "arrived in Finland determined to efface the impression of him as a hard, ruthless, uncompromising, ideological fanatic." Rieber, *Zhdanov in Finland,* 14.

48. The U.S. Representative in Finland (Hamilton), to the Secretary of State, Apr. 28, 1945, FRUS, 1945, vol. 6, 613–614.

49. RGASPI, f. 77, op. 1, d. 975, l. 124.

50. Zhdanov on "The International Situation," *Soveshchaniia Kominforma 1947, 1948, 1949: Dokumenty i materialy*, ed. G. M. Adibekov, A. Di B'iadzho, et al. (Moscow: ROSSPEN, 1998), 158.

51. James Ford Cooper, *On the Finland Watch: An American Diplomat in Finland During the Cold War* (Claremont, CA: Regina Books, 2000), 38.

52. Shepherd to Eden, Feb. 6, 1945, *British Documents on Foreign Affairs: Reports and Papers from the Foreign Office*, vol. 6, *Soviet Union and Finland*, 24.

53. Cited in Nevakivi, "A Decisive Armistice," 104.

54. Zhdanov speech at election campaign in Leningrad, Feb. 6, 1946," RGASPI, f. 77, op. 1, d. 975, l. 123.

55. Cited in: The Minister in Finland (Hamilton) to the Secretary of State, Mar. 15, 1945, FRUS, 1945, vol. 4, 608.

56. Rintala, *Four Finns*, 97, 106.

57. Talks between Zhdanov and Pessi, Aptonen, and Kuusinen, Jan. 23, 1945, RGASPI, f. 77, op. 3, dd. 53–58, l. 11.

58. Talks between Zhdanov and Leino, Kuusinen, and Pessi, Mar. 28, 1945, RGASPI, f. 77, op. 3, d. 63, ll. 1–2.

59. Maude, *Aspects of Governing*, 168.

60. See Nevakivi, "A Decisive Armistice 1944–1947," 101–102.

61. The Secretary of Mission in Finland (Higgs) to the Secretary of State, Jan. 25, 1945, FRUS, 1945, vol. 6, 600.

62. Rentola, "The Finnish Communists and the Winter War," 600.

63. Nevakivi, "A Decisive Armistice," 105.

64. Rentola, "Great Britain and the Soviet Threat in Finland," 176.

65. RGASPI, f. 77, op. 3, d. 74, l. 1.

66. RGASPI, f. 77, op. 3, dd. 53–58, l. 9.

67. RGASPI, f. 77 op. 3, dd. 53–58, l. 13.

68. Cited in Rieber, *Zhdanov in Finland*, 24.

69. There was some modest aid from the British Labor Party to the Finnish Social Democratic party, but the British in general were careful not to encourage the Finns to oppose Soviet wishes because there was no way they were going to bail the Finns out of potential trouble. Rentola, "Great Britain and the Soviet Threat in Finland," 174.

70. The U.S. Representative in Finland (Hamilton) to the Secretary of State, Mar. 23, 1945, FRUS, 1945, vol. 6, 611.

71. Penttilä, *Finland's Search for Security*, 18.

72. Karsh, *Finland: adaptation and conflict*, 174.

73. Shepherd to Eden, July 4, 1945, *British Documents on Foreign Affairs*, vol. 6, Soviet Union and Finland Jan. 1945–Dec. 1945, 21.

74. "Finland: Political Review, 1945," in Shepherd to Bevin, Mar. 12, 1946, *British Documents on Foreign Affairs,* vol. 1, *Northern Affairs,* Jan. 1946–June 1946, 234–235.

75. Iu. Komissarov, *'Liniia Paasikivi—Kekkonena': istoriia, sovremennost', perspektivy* (Moscow: Mezhdunar. Otnosheniia, 1985), 19. Pentillä, *Finland's Search for Security,* 19.

76. ACC Helsinki to War Office, June 30, 1945. TNA, WO 106 / 4334B.

77. Secretary of Mission in Finland (Higgs) to the Secretary of State, Jan. 25, 1945. FRUS, 1945, vol. 6, 599.

78. Shepherd to Bevin, Nov. 22, 1945, in *British Documents on Foreign Affairs,* vol. 6, 196.

79. Maude, *Aspects of Governing,* 183–185.

80. Zhdanov to Stalin and Molotov, Oct. 10, 1945, RGASPI, f. 77, op. 3, d. 56, l. 58.

81. Karsh, *Finland: adaptation and conflict,* 181–182.

82. Zhdanov to Molotov, Jan. 29, 1946, RGASPI, f. 77, op. 3, d. 73, l. 36. Zhdanov told Mannerheim that he personally guaranteed that the Marshal would not be tried after he signed the armistice.

83. The United States Representative in Finland (Hamilton) to the Secretary of State, Apr. 25, 1945. FRUS, 1945, vol. 6, 612.

84. Discussions of Zhdanov with Leino and Kuusinen, Aug. 21, 1945, RGASPI, f. 77, op. 3, d. 70, l. 3.

85. Zhdanov to Stalin and Molotov, Oct. 10, 1945, RGASPI, f. 77, op. 3, d. 56, l. 61. On Oct. 16, 1945, Molotov answered Zhdanov that it should not be surprising that the Finns resisted trying their war criminals, and that Zhdanov should make a firm recommendation in this matter, since he was the one on the ground in Finland (l. 101). Zhdanov then recommended calling in the members of the court to the ACC and reminding them of Finland's obligations to try war criminals. Molotov answered in the negative, stating that the Soviets then could be accused of interfering in the independence of the judiciary. Zhdanov to Stalin and Molotov, Nov. 20, 1945, and Molotov to Zhdanov, Nov. 24, 1945, RGASPI, f. 77, op. 3, d. 78, ll. 47, 50.

86. Zhdanov and Paasikivi, Dec. 12, 1945, RGASPI, f. 77, op. 3, d. 77, ll. 40–44.

87. Zhdanov to Stalin and Molotov, Nov. 20, 1945, RGASPI, f. 77, op. 3, d. 78, l. 48.

88. Zhdanov with Leino and Kuusinen, Dec. 11, 1945, RGASPI, f. 77. op. 3, d. 80, l. 140.

89. See Jussila, Hentilä, Nevakivi, *From a Grand Duchy to a Modern State,* 227. Zhdanov noted about the possibility of not trying Tanner: "A judicial process against the war criminals without Tanner: this would absolutely be without the person who sat in the driver's seat [*bez shofera*]." Zhdanov and Kekkonen, Oct. 15, 1945, RGASPI, f. 77, op. 3, d 73, l. 26.

90. Chargé in Finland (Hulley) to Secretary of State, Dec. 14, 1945, FRUS, 1945, vol. 6, 623.

91. Maude, *Aspects of Governing*, 185.

92. Cited in Anatole G. Mazour, *Finland Between East and West* (Princeton, NJ: Van Nostrand, 1956), 175. For a fuller history, see Mikko Majander, "The Limits of Sovereignty: Finland and the Question of the Marshall Plan in 1947," *Scandinavian Journal of History* 19, no. 4 (1994): 309–326.

93. Zhdanov with Pessi, Kuusinen, Leino, Mal'berg, and Miakinen, Feb. 7, 1947, RGASPI, f. 77, op. 3, d. 84, l. 82.

94. Zhdanov and representatives of Seim factions, Feb. 8, 1947, RGASPI, f. 77, op. 3, d. 86, ll. 1–2.

95. Majander, "Post-Cold War Historiography," 47.

96. Rentola, "Great Britain and the Soviet Threat in Finland," 176.

97. Zhdanov and Leino, Sept. 29, 1945, RGASPI, f. 77, op. 3, d. 73, l. 2.

98. Maude, *Aspects of Governing*, 204n184.

99. Maude, *Aspects of Governing*, 203.

100. *New York Times*, Feb. 14, 1947. Cited in Karsh, "Finland: adaptation and conflict," 268.

101. Singleton, *Short History*, 144.

102. See Karsh, "Finland: Adaptation and Conflict," 269.

103. Cited in Penttilä, *Finland's Search for Security*, 30.

104. Penttillä, *Finland's Search for Security*, 31.

105. Cited in Djilas, *Conversations with Stalin*, 155.

106. Maude, *Aspects of Governing*, 200.

107. J. A. S. Grenville and Bernard Wasserstein, eds. *The Major International Treaties, 1914–1973: A History and Guide with Texts* (London: Methuen, 1974), 146–147.

108. Cited in T. V. Androsova, "Finliandiia v planakh SSSR kontsa 1940-kh—serediny 1950-kh godov: Politiko-ekonomicheskii aspekt," *Otechestvennaia istoriia*, no. 6 (Nov.–Dec. 1999): 51. Penttilä, *Finland's Search for Security*, 31.

109. Maude, *Aspects of Governing*, 205.

110. Singleton, *Short History*, 145.

111. Cited in Maude, *Aspects of Governing*, 208.

112. Cited in Jussila, Hentilä, Nevakivi, *From a Grand Duchy to a Modern State*, 248.

113. Cited in Jussila, Hentilä, Nevakivi, *From a Grand Duchy to a Modern State*, 248.

114. Penttilä, *Finland's Search for Security*, 34.

115. Androsova, "Finliandiia v planakh SSSR," 50.

116. Nevakivi, "A Decisive Armistice," 113.

117. Maude, *Aspects of Governing*, 196.

118. Allan A. Kuusisto "The Paasikivi Line in Finland's Foreign Policy," *The Western Political Quarterly* 12, no. 1, part 1 (Mar. 1959): 43n25.

119. Rieber, *Zhdanov in Finland*, 16.

4. THE ITALIAN ELECTIONS

1. William C. Bullitt, "The World from Rome," *Life*, Sept. 4, 1944, 100.

2. Memorandum of Deputy Foreign Minister I. M. Maiskii to Molotov, Jan. 11, 1944, *SSSR i Germanskii Vopros, 22 iiunia 1941 g.–8 maia 1945 g.*, vol. 1, ed. G. P. Kynin and l. Laufer (Moscow: Mezhdunarodnye Otnosheniia, 1996), 340.

3. Salvatore Sechi, "Die neutralistische Versuchung: Italien und die Sowjetunion 1943–1948," *Italien und die Großmächte 1943–1949*, ed. Hans Woller (Munich: R. Oldenbourg Verlag, 1988), 95.

4. Silvio Pons, "Stalin, Togliatti, and the Origins of the Cold War in Europe," *Journal of Cold War Studies* 3 (2001): 4. *Dagli Archivi di Mosca: L'URSS, il Cominform e il PCI (1943–1951)*, ed. Francesca Gori and Silvio Pons (Rome: Carocci editore, 1998), 31–32.

5. *The Diary of Georgi Dimitrov, 1933–1939*, ed. Ivo Banac (New Haven, CT: Yale University Press, 2003), Mar. 5, 1994, 304. Emphasis in the original.

6. Silvio Pons, "A Challenge Let Drop: Soviet Foreign Policy, the Cominform and the Italian Communist Party," *The Soviet Union and Europe in the Cold War, 1943–53*, ed. Francesca Gori and Silvio Pons (London: Palgrave Macmillan, 1996), 255.

7. Elena Aga-Rossi and Victor Zaslavsky, "The Soviet Union and the Italian Communist Party, 1944–8," *The Soviet Union and Europe*, ed. Gori and Pons, 164.

8. Robert Service, *Comrades: A History of World Communism* (Cambridge, MA: Harvard University Press, 2010), 265–266; Aga-Rossi and Zaslavsky, "The Soviet Union and the Italian Communist Party," 164.

9. *New York Times*, Sept. 8, 1947, 5. There is some question whether this was actually the case.

10. For example, Aleksandr Bogomolov, who was Soviet representative in the Allied Advisory Council in Italy, attacked Togliatti's moderate policies and his lack of preparation for what he believed was the inevitable social revolution. Pons, "Stalin, Togliatti, and the Origins of the Cold War," 10.

11. Remo Roncati, *Verso la giustizia sociale: le ragioni di Alcide De Gasperi* (Chieti: Solfanelli, 2015), 179.

12. Piero Craveri, *De Gasperi* (Bologna: Societa editrice il Mulino, 2006), 152–153.

13. Ian Kershaw, *To Hell and Back: Europe 1914–1949* (New York: Penguin, 2015), 495.

14. "The Tasks of the Party in the Current Situation: Speech at Florence," Oct. 3, 1944, Palmiro Togliatti, *On Gramsci, and Other Writings* (London: Lawrence and Wishart, 1979), 86.

15. De Gasperi to Togliatti, Sept. 12, 1944, in *De Gasperi scrive: Corrispondenza con capi di Stato, cardinali, uomini politici, giornalisti, diplomacy*, vol. 2 (Brescia: Morcelliana, 1974), 207–209.

16. See Giovanni De Luna, *La Repubblica inquieta: L'Italia della Costituzione, 1946–1948* (Milan: Feltrinelli, 2017), 185.

17. Cited in Craveri, *De Gasperi*, 269.

18. Speech to the Cadres of the Communist Organization of Naples, Apr. 11, 1944," (trans. Derek Boothman), in Palmiro Togliatti, *On Gramsci*, 42.

19. Fond Instituto Gramsci (hereafter FIG), Direzione Verbale (1944–1958), Fonda Mosca, Section 12, Meetings of the Party Directorate, PCI, Jan. 21, 1948, Feb. 11, 1948, Togliatti to Regional Secretaries, Feb. 23, 1946.

20. See De Luna, *La Repubblica inquieta*, 228–229.

21. Michael Straight, "Italy: Talks of Peace and Civil War," *New Republic*, Nov. 24, 1947, 9.

22. Sechi, "Die neutralistische Versuchung," 107–108.

23. For De Gasperi's trip to the United States, see Craveri, *De Gasperi*, 271–277.

24. Cited in Robert A. Ventresca, *From Fascism to Democracy: Culture and Politics in the Italian Elections of 1948* (Toronto: University of Toronto Press, 2004), 139.

25. Ventresca, *From Fascism to Democracy*, 75.

26. Craveri, *De Gasperi*, 157.

27. Craveri, *De Gasperi*, 322.

28. Craveri, *De Gasperi*, 267.

29. Donald Sassoon, *Contemporary Italy: Politics, Economy and Society since 1945* (London and New York: Routledge, 1997), 61, 71n3.

30. Pons, "Stalin, Togliatti, and the Origins of the Cold War," 16.

31. *Diary of Georgi Dimitrov*, Aug. 8, 1947, 422.

32. Cited in Pons, *Stalin and the Inevitable War 1936–1941*, 219–220.

33. On Stalin's role in the establishment of the Cominform and in the meeting itself, which he closely followed from Moscow, see the analytical articles in: *The Cominform: Minutes of the Three Conferences 1947/1948/1949*, ed. G. Procacci (Milan: Fondazione Giangiacomo Feltrinelli, 1994): Grant Adibekov, "How the First Conference of the Cominform Came About," 3–11; Anna Di Biagio, "The Establishment of the Cominform," 11–35. *Dagli Archivi di Mosca*, 31–32.

34. Eugenio Reale, *Nascita del Cominform* (Milan: Mondadori, 1958), 17. Translation from HIA, Eugenio Reale Collection, box 1. Eugenio Reale, "The Whole Truth," 2.

35. *The Cominform: Minutes of the Three Conferences 1947/1948/1949*, 37–423. Zhdanov, for example, responded to Longo's speech by asking "Has the party a plan of attack, or does it intend to go on keeping to the defensive, waiting for

the reaction to bar the Party and force it underground." He states, additionally: "You want to be greater parliamentarians than the parliamentarians." 195, 197.

36. Longo in "Summary Report" on the Cominform meeting, in FIG, Directorate of PCI, Oct. 7–10, 1947, 1.

37. On Terracini's statement, see *New York Times*, Oct. 23, 1947, on Longo's criticism of Terracini's interview see *L'Unità*, Oct. 24, 1947.

38. Claire Neikind, "The Communist Show of Strength," *New Republic*, Dec. 1, 1947, 8.

39. Craveri, *De Gasperi*, 323.

40. Report on the discussion between Secchia and Stalin, Dec. 14, 1947, *Dagli Archivi di Mosca*, 289.

41. Cited in Sechi, "Die neutralistische Versuchung," 127.

42. I. V. Stalin i Moris Torez: Zapis' besedy v Kremle, 1947g.," *Istoricheskii arkhiv*, no. 1 (1996): 14.

43. Zhdanov and Secchia, Dec. 12, 1947, in *Dagli Archivi di Mosca*, 279. See also Sassoon, *Contemporary Italy*, 279.

44. Zhdanov and Secchia, Dec. 12, 1947, in *Dagli Archivi di Mosca*, 277. Robert Conquest writes that these funds were delivered to Secchia just two days later on Dec. 14. Robert Conquest, *Dragons of Expectation: Reality and Delusion in the Course of History* (New York: W. W. Norton, 2004), 98.

45. Dunn to Secretary of State, Mar. 1, 1948, FRUS, 1948, vol. 3, 837.

46. See Valerio Riva, *Oro da Mosca: I Finanziamenti Sovietici al PCI dalla Rivoluzione d'Ottobre al Crollo dell'URSS* (Milan: Arnoldo Mondadori Editore, 1999). See also Aga-Rossi and Zaslavsky, "The Soviet Union and the Italian Communist Party," 122–124.

47. *Dagli Archivi di Mosca*, 289.

48. Silvio Pons, "A Challenge Let Drop: Soviet Foreign Policy, the Cominform, and the Italian Communist Party," in *The Soviet Union and Europe*, 259.

49. Partito Socialista dei Lavoratori Italiani, Newsletter on the first national conference of the P.S.L.I., Sept. 18, 1947, in HIA, Jay Lovestone Papers, box 244, folder 244.5.

50. Cited in Claire Neikind, "Italy's Dark April," *New Republic*, Mar. 29, 1948, 12.

51. Dunn to Secretary of State, Mar. 10, 1948, FRUS, vol. 3, 846.

52. Alfredo Canavero, Pier Luigi Ballini, Francesco Malgeri, *Alcide De Gasperi*, vol. 3 (Rome: Fondazione De Gasperi, 2009), 13.

53. Tony Judt, *Postwar: A History of Europe Since 1945* (New York: Penguin, 2005), 208.

54. The Director of Policy Planning Staff (Kennan) to the Secretary of State, Mar. 15, 1948, *FRUS* (1948), vol. 3, 849.

55. Dunn to Secretary of State, Jan. 29, 1948. FRUS, 1948, vol. 3, 824.

56. "Consequences of Communist Accession to Power in Italy by Legal Means," Mar. 5, 1948, CIA, FOA, CREST, 4.

57. Cited in Vladislav Zubok, *A Failed Empire: The Soviet Union in the Cold War from Stalin to Gorbachev* (Chapel Hill, NC: University of North Carolina Press, 2007), 49.

58. NSA, NSC 1 / 1, Nov. 14, 1947.

59. NSC 1 / 2, FRUS, 1948, vol. 3, 767.

60. "The Position of the United States with Respect to Italy," Feb. 10, 1948, NSA, NSC 1 / 2, 2, 7.

61. NSC 1 / 3, FRUS, 1948, vol. 3, 775.

62. H. Woller, "Amerikanische Intervention oder kommunistischen Umsturz: Die Entscheidungswahlen von April 1948," *Italien und die Großmächte 1943–1949,* ed. Hans Woller (Munich: Oldenbourg Verlag, 1988), 79.

63. Dunn to Sec. of State, Jan. 12, 1948, FRUS, 1948, vol. 3, 818.

64. Campaign Funding sources. . . . NSA, Interview with Mark Wyatt, Feb. 15, 1996, 44. Wyatt, who served with the CIA in Italy, considers the four months of activity leading up to the Italian elections in April 1948 as marking the first serious CIA covert operation in its young history, setting precedents for decades to come. See also Dunn to Secretary of State, Feb. 21, 1948, FRUS, 1948, vol. 3, 833.

65. Ventresca, *From Fascism to Democracy,* 79.

66. "Position of the U.S. in Respect to Italy," NSA, NSC 1 / 3, Mar. 8, 1948, 7.

67. Cited in De Luna, *La Repubblica inquieta,* 192.

68. Dunn to Secretary of State, Apr. 1948, FRUS, 1948, vol. 3, 881.

69. The United States even went so far as to support the writing of circular letters to approximately five thousand U.S. Veterans Administration beneficiaries in Italy warning that they could lose their remittances if a communist government were elected. Dunn to Secretary of State, June 16, 1948, FRUS, 1948, vol. 3, 881. See "Communists Worried," *New York Times,* Apr. 11, 1948, E2, and, "Millions in Italy at Party Rallies," *New York Times,* Apr. 12, 1948, 4. See C. Edda Martinez and Edward A. Suchman, "Letters from America and the 1948 Elections in Italy," *Public Opinion Quarterly* 14, no. 1, 111–125.

70. CIA, "Evaluation of Psychological Effect of U.S. Effort in Italy," Jan. 6, 1953, CIA, FOIA, CREST, 5.

71. See "Twenty-nine ships restituted to Italy from the U.S.," *Corriere della Sera,* Mar. 17, 1948.

72. See J. A. Miller, "Taking Off the Gloves: The United States and the Italian Elections of 1948," *Diplomatic History,* no. 7 (1983): 49–55, and H. Woller, "Amerikanische Intervention oder kommunistischer Umsturz," *Italien und die Großmächte 1943–1949),* 86–94.

73. Dunn to Secretary of State, Mar. 20, 1948, FRUS, 1948, vol. 3, 857. "Mr. Marshall's Call for U.S. Leadership," *The Times of London*, Mar. 20, 1948.

74. *Corriere della Sera*, Mar. 20, 1948.

75. *Corriere della Sera*, Apr. 17, 1948.

76. Secchia and Stalin, Dec. 14, 1947, in *Dagli Archivi di Mosca*, 292.

77. Secchia and Zhdanov, Dec. 16, 1947, in *Dagli Archivi di Mosca*, 309.

78. "Stenographic Record of a speech by Comrade J. V. Stalin at a Special Section of the Politburo, Mar. 14, 1948," Woodrow Wilson Center Digital Archive, doc. 117823, 2.

79. Mario Einaudi, "The Italian Election of 1948," *The Review of Politics*, no. 3 (vol. 10):351.

80. *Corriere della Sera*, Apr. 4, 1948.

81. Stalin withdrew his support for giving Italy the colonies when it became clear that the Christian Democrats might win the election and turn over use of the colonies to the Americans for military bases. See Manlio Brosio, *Diari di Mosca 1947 / 1951*, ed. Fausto Bacchetti (Bologna: Società Editrice Il Mulino, 1986), 220–221. See also "L'URSS vuole lasciarci Libia, Eritrea e Somalia," *L'Unità*, Feb. 17, 1948.

82. On the *foibe* killings and their contemporary meaning, see Arnold Suppan, *Hitler-Beneš-Tito: Konflikt, Krieg und Völkermord*, part 2 (Vienna: Verlag der ÖAW, 2014), 1343–1347, 1691–1698. See also Glenda Sluga, "The Risiera di San Sabbe: Fascism, Anti-Fascism and Italian Nationalism," *Journal of Modern Italian Studies*, no. 1 (1996): 401–412.

83. "Italian Red Defeat Seen in Soviet Act," *New York Times*, Apr. 15, 1948, 8. "Western Powers' Proposals for Trieste," *The Times of London*, Mar. 22, 1948, 4.

84. CIA, "An Evaluation of Psychological effect of U.S. Effort in Italy," Jan. 6, 1953, NSA, CIA, FOIA, CREST, 10, 22. Norman Kogan also thinks that the Trieste issue was a huge setback for the communists and was "the one foreign policy issue really felt by large numbers of Italians, even those in small villages and remote rural areas." Norman Kogan, *A Political History of Italy: The Postwar Years* (New York: Praeger, 1983), 5–6.

85. Brosio, *Diari di Mosca*, 251.

86. Notes from Secchia's manuscript on the Cominform meeting (June 21, 1948) (PCI representatives Togliatti and Secchia), 2–5. FIG, Perro 2, 14 (MF 1010). For the minutes of the Second Conference of the Cominform, June 19–23, 1948, see *Cominform 1947/1948/1949*, 507–605. Togliatti played an active role in the deliberations; Secchia did not.

87. See, for example, the comments from party members, Arturo Columbi and Fedeli, FIG, Meeting of Apr. 26, 1948, 8–9, 18.

88. Eugenio Reale writes of Togliatti's critique of the Marshall Plan: it was "only because of his supine acquiescence to his master's orders." HIA, Eugenio Reale Papers, "The Whole Truth and the Cominform," transl. of first part of *Nascita del Cominform* (Milan: Arnoldo Mondadori Editore, 1958).

89. "Pope, U.S envoy, Study Elections," *New York Times*, Apr. 14, 1948, 3. See E. Di Nolfo, "Von der Konfrontation zur Partnerschaft: Italien und der Vatikan 1943–1948," in *Italien und die Großmächte*, 194–200.

90. "An Archbishop's Letter," *The Times of London*, Feb. 24, 1948.

91. See FIG, Direzione Verbale (1944–1958), Fond Mosca, (MF 199) I, Meeting of the Party Directorate, Apr. 26, 1948, Pellegrini from Venice, 1–2.

92. Woller, "Amerikanische Intervention," 93.

93. "An Archbishop's Letter," *The Times of London*, Feb. 24, 1948.

94. De Luna, *La Repubblica inquieta*, 191.

95. Donald Sassoon, *The Strategy of the Italian Communist Party: From the Resistance to the Historic Compromise* (London: Francis Pinter, 1981) 64.

96. Einaudi, "The Italian Elections of 1948," 347.

97. NSA, CIA, "Diminished Communist Capabilities in Italy," Apr. 9, 1948, 1.

98. See, for example, "Violent clashes in Florence between demonstrators and public forces," *Corriere della Sera*, Jan. 23, 1948, or "Bloody Conflict in San Ferdinando di Puglia," *Corriera della Sera*, Feb. 10, 1948.

99. Craveri, *De Gasperi*, 326–327, 330.

100. There is some disagreement about whether an actual uprising was planned or whether armed communist groups simply increased their activities and secret military exercises in the winter of 1947–48 in order to put pressure on the Italian government and society. (There has been a similar argument about the larger purposes of the communist inspired strike movement in France in Nov. and Dec. 1947.) A Dec. 1947 report from the Italian Ministry of the Interior stated: "It has become clear that the PCI has strengthened its paramilitary organizations and pays ever more attention to them." Woller, "Amerikanische Intervention," 81. Silvio Pons suggests that the communists "prepared themselves for a post-election uprising in the case of a coup d'état by the conservative forces, supported by the U.S.," as a way to counter the predicted Popular Front victory in the elections. Silvio Pons, private communication, Sept. 2018. This is consistent with Moscow's general thinking about the use of communist uprisings in western Europe to protect the respective parties and their institutions from the counter-revolution.

101. Pons, "A Challenge Let Drop," 259. Aga-Rossi and Zaslavsky, "The Soviet Union and the Italian Communist Party," 75–82.

102. Dunn to Secretary of State, Dec. 7, 1947, in FRUS, vol. 3, 1948, 736–737.

103. Pier Luigi Ballini, *Alcide de Gasperi*, vol. 3, 7.

104. Woller, "Amerikanische Intervention," 82–83.
105. On weapons, see Dunn to Secretary of State, Mar. 12, 1948, FRUS, 1948, vol. 3, 784–785. See also Dunn's further communiques of Mar. 18 and Apr. 16 on the same issue. Washington found a way to siphon off supplies and weapons from their forces in Germany to be distributed to the Italian government.
106. *New York Times*, Sept. 8, 1947. The American embassy came up with similar estimates, stating that in June 1947 there were some 10,000 armed communist partisan "elements" in the north, which, in the case of a PCI-led insurrection, could be supplemented by 40,000 men who had been organized in the Garibaldi partisan brigades during the war. Dunn to Secretary of State, June 18, 1947, FRUS, vol. 3, 923–924. See intelligence estimates of the relative strength of the government and communists, NSA, CIA, "Diminished Communist Capabilities in Italy," 2.
107. "Kominform: vzgliad iz Parizha," *Istoricheskii arkhiv,* no. 1 (1996): 138–139. This is a French counter-espionage document, dated Jan. 1948, that draws on Cominform sources in Switzerland.
108. FIG, Directive of the C.C., May 4, 5, 6, 1948, 1–3.
109. FIG, Meeting of Party Directorate, Apr. 26, 1948, 25–26.
110. Craveri, *De Gasperi,* 325.
111. Giorgio Bocca, *Togliatti* (Milan: Feltrinelli, 2014), 432–433. *L'Unità* (Milan, Special Edition), "Vile attentato a Togliatti," July 14, 1948.
112. *New York Times,* July 15, 1948, 18.
113. "Togliatti Shot," *The Times of London,* July 15, 1948.
114. Sassoon, *Strategy of the Italian Communist Party,* 65.
115. FIG, Meeting of the Directorate of the PCI, Aug. 1948, 22.
116. *Alcide de Gasperi, scrivi,* vol. 2, 218.
117. "L'Appello della Direzione del partito Comunista Italiano," July 14, 1948, in Pietro Secchia, *Lo sciopero del 14 luglio* (Roma: Educazione comunista, 1948), 53.
118. On the meeting between Di Vittorio and De Gasperi in the account of the Republican Party member and CGIL leader, Enrico Parri, see Craveri, *De Gasperi,* 361.
119. There is a remarkably well-informed CIA report on the general strike, which emphasizes the tension between Secchia, who was in favor, and PCI member Ruggero Grieco, who was against. According to the document, both took their cases to the Soviet embassy. "Soviet Disapproval of Communist Action Following the Attempted Assassination Attempt of Togliatti," August 18, 1948, CREST, CIA FOIA, 1–3. Silvio Pons writes: "Secchia told the Soviet ambassador that according to the PCI leadership, as well as recent assessments by

friends of the Italian Communists [meaning in Moscow], it was not yet time for an armed uprising." Pons, "Stalin, Togliatti, and the Origins of the Cold War," 22.

120. See Craveri, *De Gasperi*, 325, 347–348n65.

121. *Times of London*, July 17, 1948. De Luna states that eleven strikers and six policemen were killed and altogether two hundred people injured. De Luna, *La Repubblica inquieta*, 203, 216.

122. Craveri, *De Gasperi*, 361.

123. Cited in Service, *Comrades*, 265.

124. FIG, Stalin to Gottwald and Togliatti, July 4, 1948 (in original Russian). Iudin to Luigi Longo, Aug. 3, 1948.

125. Wilson Center, Digital Archive, Collection "Stalin and the Cold War," "Soviet Plan to Assassinate Tito," Jan. 1, 1953. Pavel Sudoplatov and Anatoli Sudoplatov with Jerrold L. and Leona P. Schechter, *Special Tasks: The Memoirs of an Unwanted Witness—A Soviet Spymaster* (Boston: Little Brown & Co., 1994, 335–339. Dimitri Volkogonov also published material from the archives about the assassination plans. *Los Angeles Times*, June 12, 1993.

126. Bocca, *Togliatti*, 461–462. Sassoon, *Strategy of the Italian Communist Party*, 84.

127. *Dagli Archivi di Mosca*, Togliatti to Stalin, Jan. 4, 1951, 417–420.

128. NSA, National Security Council 67 / 2 (Dec. 29, 1950) and 67 / 3 (Jan. 5, 1951), both entitled "The Position of the United States with Respect to the Communist Threat to Italy."

129. Allen W. Dulles, Deputy Director to the Director of Central Intelligence, Chairman of the Psychological Strategy Board, Sept. 15, 1951, CIA, FOI, CREST.

5. THE BERLIN BLOCKADE

1. The operation's name originated with General Walter Bedell "Beetle" Smith. "Hell's Fire," he supposed declared. "We're hauling grub. Call it Operation Vittles." The British called it Operation Plainfare. Thomas Parrish, *Berlin in the Balance 1945–1949: The Blockade, the Airlift, The First Major Battle of the Cold War* (Reading, MA: Addison-Wesley, 1998), 202–203. The famous candy dropping was called "Operation Little Vittles," first using small parachutes and then just emptying candy over western Berlin from the cargo doors. Barry Turner, *The Berlin Airlift: The Relief Operation That Defined the Cold War* (London: Icon Books, 2017), 198.

2. General Curtis E. LeMay (with MacKinlay Kantor), *Mission LeMay: My Story* (Garden City, NY: Doubleday & Company, 1965), 401–402.

3. Memo Policy Planning Staff, no. 23. George Kennan, Feb. 28, 1948. FRUS, vol. 1, 1948, 516.

4. *The OMGUS Surveys*, Report no. 105 (Mar. 27, 1948), 218.

5. Cited in Ian Kershaw, *To Hell and Back: Europe 1914–1949* (New York: Penguin, 2016), 481.

6. On Stalin's goals in Germany in general, see Norman M. Naimark, *The Russians in Germany: A History of the Soviet Zone of Occupation, 1945–1949* (Cambridge, MA: Harvard University Press, 1995), 465–466.

7. V. M. Gobarev, "Soviet Military Plans and Activities during the Berlin Crisis, 1948–1949," *Journal of Slavic Military Studies* 10, no. 3 (1997): 6.

8. David E. Murphy, Sergei A. Kondrashev and George Bailey, *Battleground Berlin: CIA vs. KGB in the Cold War* (New Haven, CT: Yale University Press, 1997), 61. In response to Truman's decision to base "nuclear-capable" U.S. bombers in Britain as part of the U.S. build-up in response to the blockade, the Soviets did boost their anti-aircraft defenses. Matthew A. Evangelista, "Stalin's Postwar Army Reappraised," *International Security* 7, no. 3 (1982–83): 132–133.

9. Vojtech Mastny, "NATO in the Beholder's Eye: Soviet Perceptions and Policies, 1949–56," Cold War International History Project, Woodrow Wilson Center, Working Paper no. 35, 17, 27–29.

10. On the desire for peace on both sides, see Marc Trachtenberg, *A Constructed Peace: The Making of the European Settlement 1945–1963* (Princeton, NJ: Princeton University Press, 1999), 86–91.

11. A. M. Filitov, *Germanskii vopros: ot raskola k obedineniiu* (Moscow: Mezhd. Otnosheniia, 1993), 104. Hannes Adomeit makes a similar argument, noting that there was "little evidence indeed to show that Stalin was aware of the dynamism which the first East-West crisis would unleash, or that he had a clearly mapped-out plan for the future of Germany." *Imperial Overstretch: Germany in Soviet Policy from Stalin to Gorbachev* (Baden-Baden: Nomos, 1998), 67.

12. This view is generally accepted by post-Soviet Russian historians, as well as Western ones. See E. P. Timoshenkova, *The German Issue in Soviet Foreign Policy (1945–1955)*, Reports of the Institute of Europe, no. 217 (Moscow: Izd. "Russkii suvernir"), 28. See Melvyn Leffler, *For the Soul of Mankind: The United States, The Soviet Union and the Cold War* (New York: Farrar, Straus and Giroux, 2008), 77–79.

13. Naimark, *Russians in Germany*, 167–168; Melvyn P. Leffler, *A Preponderance of Power: National Security, the Truman Administration, and the Cold War* (Stanford, CA: Stanford University Press, 1992), 67.

14. See, for example, Jochen Laufer, *Pax Sovietica: Stalin, die Westmächte und die deutsche Frage 1941–1945* (Köln: Böhlau Verlag, 2009), 559–562.

15. On the issue of "socialism," see Aleksej M. Filitov, "Die sowjetische Deutschlandpolitik 1948–1949: Einführung zu den Dokumenten," in *Die UdSSR und*

die deutsche Frage 1941–1949: 18. Juni 1948 bis 5. November 1949: Dokumente aus russischen Archiven, vol. 4, ed. Jochen P. Laufer and Georgij P. Kynin (Berlin: Duncker & Humbolt, 2012), 88–89. The Laufer and Kynin documents, which are cited throughout this chapter, are also available in Russian in: *SSSR i germanskoi vopros: Dokumenty iz arkhivov Rossiiiskoi Federatsii* (Moscow: Ist.-dok. depart. MID, Inst. vseob. ist. RAN, Tsentr izuch. noveish. ist. v Potsdame, 2012).

16. Cited in Melvyn P. Leffler, "The Struggle for Germany and the Origins of the Cold War," The Alois Mertes Memorial Lecture, German Historical Institute Washington, D.C., Occasional Papers no. 16 (1996), 64–65.

17. Molotov to Stalin, June 18, 1948," in *Die UdSSR und die deutsche Frage,* vol. 4, 5.

18. M. M. Narinskii, "Berlinskii krizis 1948–1949 gg.: Novye Dokumenty iz rossiskikh Arkhivov," *Novaia i noveishaia istoriia,* no. 3 (1995): 18. See also the English version of Narinskii's important article, "The Soviet Union and Berlin Crisis, 1948–49," in *The Soviet Union and Europe in the Cold War, 1943–53,* ed. Francesca Gori and Silvio Pons (New York: St. Martin's Press, 1996), 57–76.

19. Laufer, "'Reingeschlittert?', Die UdSSR und die Ursprünge der Berliner Blockade 1944–1948," *Sterben für Berlin? Die Berliner Krisen 1948: 1958,* ed. Burghard Ciesla, Michael Lemke, and Thomas Lindenberger (Berlin: Metropol, 2000), 44.

20. Leffler, "The Struggle for Germany," 51.

21. Dratvin and Semenov to Molotov and Bulganin (Apr. 17, 1948), cited in Narinskii, "Berlinskii krizis," 20.

22. Elke Scherstjanoi, "Die Berlin-Blockade 1948 / 49 im sowjetischen Kalkül," *Zeitschrift für Geschichtswissenschaft,* 46 (1996): 497.

23. Clay to Lt. Gen. Stephen J. Chamberlin, Director of Intelligence, Army General Staff, in Jean Edward Smith, *The Papers of General Lucius D. Clay,* vol. 2, *Germany 1945–1949* (Bloomington: Indiana University Press, 1974), 568.

24. Wilson D. Miscamble, "Harry S. Truman, the Berlin Blockade and the 1948 Election," *Presidential Studies Quarterly* 10, no. 3 (Summer 1980): 307–308.

25. Scherstjanoi, "Die Berlin-Blockade," 499.

26. Gobarev, "Soviet Military Plans," 11, estimates the number of troops in the Group of Soviet Forces in Germany as wavering between 500,000 and one million in the period from the late 1940s to the early 1980s. He tallies the total Allied strength at the time of the blockade at 398,000. NSA, C.I.A, "Soviet Control Mechanism in Germany," ORE 51–49, May 26, 1949, 3, estimates that there were only 350,000 Soviet troops in the Soviet zone.

27. Murphy to Secretary of State, Mar. 1, 1948, FRUS, 1948, vol. 2, 155. By the summer, Murphy was much more supportive of Clay's policies.

28. Cited in Miscamble, "Harry S. Truman," 312.

29. NSA, James V. Forrestal, Memorandum for the National Security Council, July 26, 1948, "U.S. Military Courses of Action with respect to the Situation in Berlin," Record Number 83–80.

30. NSA, CIA, "Consequences of a Breakdown in Four-Power Negotiations on Germany," ORE 57–48, 2.

31. According to a draft State Department analysis from the Foreign Policy Studies Branch, "The Berlin Crisis," Research Project no. 171, these informal agreements formed the basis for the American right of access "by land, air and water to Berlin," Truman Library, Documents, 2, 6. The State Department Legal Advisor concluded that any action which interfered with such free access was "a direct violation of an international agreement." The Soviets argued in response that since the three Western powers "by their separate actions in the western zones of Germany destroyed the system of the four-power administration of Germany," they abrogated the legal basis for the Berlin occupation. Robert Murphy worked from different premises. Unlike the land access routes to Berlin, the three air corridors to the city were agreed upon in writing by the Four Powers in the Allied Control Council (Nov. 30, 1945), and updated by a convention of Oct. 22, 1946. He writes in his memoirs that the legal availability of air corridors was "down in black and white," while the agreements about access to Berlin by ground were "less certain." Robert Murphy, *Diplomat Among Warriors: The Unique World of a Foreign Service Expert* (Garden City, NY: Doubleday, 1964), 315–316. See also, Peter Auer, *Ihr Völker der Welt: Ernst Reuter und die Blockade von Berlin* (Berlin: Jaron Verlag, 1998), 217.

32. Telegram from Clay to Army Security Agency, Mar. 1948. HIA, Albert C. Wedemeyer Papers, box 106, folder 1.

33. In response to a Mar. 31, 1948 teleconference between Clay and Generals Bradley and Wedemeyer, in *The Papers of General Lucius D. Clay*, vol. 2, *Germany 1945–1949*, ed. Jean Edward Smith (Bloomington: Indiana University Press, 1974), 604–606; Omar Bradley and Clay Blair, *A General's Life* (New York: Simon and Schuster, 1983), 478.

34. Clay to Bradley, Apr. 1, 1948, in *The Papers of General Lucius D. Clay*, vol. 2:607. My emphasis.

35. Wedemeyer writes that Clay's idea of taking on the Soviets would not work given Soviet military supremacy on the ground and that he recommended to William Draper, the Under Secretary of the Army, that an airlift, as in China, be employed. Wedemeyer convinced the British that it was a good idea and Clay agreed, even though he still wanted to send in an armed convoy. Later, Wedemeyer wrote that the Joint Chiefs made the recommendation of an airlift to President Truman, who gave the final approval. He also recommended that Air Force General William H. Tunner, who had overseen his air

operations in China, be appointed head of the airlift, as he eventually was, replacing General Curtis Le May. See Wedemeyer to William Tunner, Nov. 23, 1960; Wedemeyer to Mr. Arnold Foster, Jan. 30, 1978. HIA, Albert C. Wedemeyer Papers, box 106, folder 1.

36. Avi Shlaim calls it a "mini-blockade." Avi Shlaim, *The United States and the Berlin Blockade, 1948–1949: A Study in Crisis Decision-Making* (Berkeley: University of California Press, 1983), 43.

37. Clay to the Department of the Army, Mar. 17, 1948, *The Papers of Lucius D. Clay*, vol. 2:349.

38. Clay to Brig. Gen. Charles K. Bailey, June 13, 1948, in *The Papers of Lucius D. Clay*, vol. 2:677.

39. Teleconference Bradley and Clay, Apr. 10, 1948, in *The Papers of Lucius D. Clay*, vol. 2:622.

40. (Pro Quest) U.S. Central Intelligence Agency, "Reaction of the West German Political Parties of the decisions of the Tripartite London conference 1948," Aug. 5, 1948, ORE 37–48.

41. Cited in V. K. Volkov, "Germanskii vopros glazami Stalina (1947–1952)," in *Uzlovye problemy noveishei istorii stran tsentral'noi i iugo-vostochnoi Evropy* (Moscow: "Indik," 2000), 129–131.

42. General Clay noted "the immediate benefits of currency reform have been unbelievable." Clay to Byrnes, Sept. 18, 1948, *The Papers of Lucius D. Clay*, vol. 2, 858. One contemporary scholar wrote: "the immediate effect of the reform was startling. On June 19th, a Saturday, not a single article could be seen or had in retail shops, on June 21st the shops were full of goods." The currency reform, the Marshall Plan, and the free market "did wonders for the West German economy." F. A. Lutz, "The German Currency Reform and the Revival of the German Economy," *Economica*, n.s., 16, no. 62 (1949): 131–132.

43. Cited in Laufer, "'Reingeschlittert'?," 44.

44. Murphy to Secretary of State, June 23, 1948, FRUS, 1948, vol. 2, 914.

45. Shlaim, *United States and the Berlin Blockade*, 178–179. The British and the Americans, Washington and London, worked exceptionally well together during the Berlin crisis. State Department Summary of Telegrams, June 28, 1948, Truman Library (online), Truman Papers. Naval Aide Files, May–Aug. 1948.

46. Michael W. Wolff, *Die Währungsreform in Berlin 1948 / 1949* (Berlin: Walter de Gruyter, 1991), 2.

47. George F. Kennan, *Memoirs 1925–1950* (Boston: Little Brown and Company, 1967), 421.

48. *Die UdSSR und die deutsche Frage*, vol. 4, 41–44.

49. See especially Paul Steege, *Black Market, Cold War: Everyday Life in Berlin, 1946–1949* (Cambridge: Cambridge University Press, 2007), 211. Steege argues that

the Soviet intention behind the blockade was not to reverse the decisions of the London Conference by starving Berliners but to bring order to stabilize the economy of the Soviet zone. See also William Stivers, "The Incomplete Blockade: Soviet Zone Supply of West Berlin, 1948–49," *Diplomatic History* 21, no. 4 (1997): 569–572.

50. Steege, *Black Market, Cold War,* 210–211.

51. Heinrich Rau, SAPMO-BARCH, DY 30 IV 2 / 1 48 "11(25) Tagung des Parteivorstands der SED, June 29–30, 1948, p. 66. See also Steege, *Black Market,* 249.

52. Cited in Narinskii, "Berlinskii krizis," 23.

53. Cited in Laufer, "'Reingeschlittert,'" 41. See also Murphy, et al., *Battleground Berlin:* 57.

54. Lucius D. Clay, *Decision in Germany* (Garden City, NY: Doubleday, 1950), 368.

55. Clay to Bradley, Sept. 6, 1948, in *The Papers of Lucius D. Clay,* vol. 2, 828.

56. See Arnold A. Offner, *Another Such Victory: President Truman and the Cold War, 1945–1953* (Stanford, CA: Stanford University Press, 2002), 258.

57. Frank Howley, *Berlin Command* (New York: G. P. Putnam's Sons, 1949), 174.

58. The meetings of the commandants had already been very testy in the summer and fall of 1947. See minutes in HIA, GTUAO, Box 32. Murphy notes that from the end of Jan. 1948, the Soviets contested every statement by the Western delegations "no matter how simple, how friendly or innocent, to launch violent propaganda attacks. . . ." Murphy to Sec. of State, Mar. 3, 1948, FRUS, 1948, vol. 2, 878. See also Sec. of State to Sov. Ambassador Paniushkin, July 6, 1948, FRUS, 1948, vol. 2, 951–952.

59. Kennan, *Memoirs,* 427–428.

60. Report on Negotiations with Soviets (circa July / Aug. 1948), Truman Library (online), Truman Papers, PSF.

61. For the Russian transcriptions of the talks, which occurred episodically from Aug. 2 until Aug. 30, 1948, and the resulting communiqués, see *Sovetsko-Amerikanskie otnosheniia 1945–1948,* ed. G. N. Sevost'ianov (Moscow: Mezhdunarodnyi Fond "Demokratiia", 2004), 600–674.

62. The Ambassador in the Soviet Union (Smith) to the Secretary of State, Aug. 3, 1948, FRUS, 1948, vol. 2, 1006. Smith himself worried that the Soviets held the better poker hand; he was not convinced that the airlift could supply Berlin or that "the mood of the German people would stand the strain." Walter Bedell Smith, *Moscow Mission, 1946–1949* (London: William Heinemann Ltd., 1950), 233. FRUS, 1948, vol. 2, 1007–1008.

63. FRUS, 1948, vol. 2, 1003.

64. FRUS, 1948, vol. 2, 1004.

65. Naimark, *Russians in Germany,* 55–59.

66. Parrish, *Berlin in the Balance,* 165; FRUS, 1948, vol. 2, 1004.

67. FRUS, 1948, vol. 2, 1004.

68. The Ambassador in the Soviet Union (Smith) to the Secretary of State, Aug. 5, 1948, and Aug. 24, 1948, FRUS, 1948, vol. 2, 1017, 1066.

69. Truman Library (online), State Department, Foreign Policy Studies Branch, "Berlin Crisis," 16–17.

70. Smith, *Moscow Mission*, 243.

71. Sokolovskii and Semenov to Molotov, Aug. 30, 1948, *Die UdSSR und die deutsche Frage*, vol. 4, 112–113.

72. Molotov to Sokolovskii, Aug.31, 1948, *Die UdSSR und die deutsche Frage*, vol. 4, 113.

73. Marshall to Smith, Aug. 3, 1948, in FRUS, 1948, vol. 2, 1008–09. Also quoted in Shlaim, *United States and the Berlin Blockade*, 316.

74. Hannes Adomeit writes that Sokolovskii was on a "very tight leash" in Germany, especially when it came to the Berlin question. Adomeit, *Imperial Overstretch*, 152.

75. Murphy to Secretary of State, Sept. 7, 1948, FRUS, 1948, vol. 2, 1134.

76. An O.S.S. report of Sept. 1945 describes the ease of movement between the eastern zone and the western sectors, especially in the largely rural and forested area surrounding the American sector. NACP, RG 226, O.S.S. Miss. for Germany (Sept. 1, 1945), L-722, box, 60, folder 117.

77. HIA, Margarita Gaertner, "The Siege of Berlin," folder XX514-10.V, 11.

78. Soviet Measures to Further Tighten the Sector Blockade in Berlin, Central Intelligence Agency Information Report, Dec. 30, 1948 (facsimile), in Murphy et al., *Battleground Berlin*, 60.

79. HIA, Elizabeth S. Selden Papers, Blockade 1948, box 2, folder 3 (to Elizabeth Selden from a museum worker in Berlin-Friedenau, Jan. 16, 1949).

80. Ruth Andreas-Friedrich, *Battleground Berlin: Diaries 1945–1948*, trans. Anna Boerresen (New York: Paragon House, 1990), 240–241.

81. Alexandra Richie, *Faust's Metropolis: A History of Berlin* (London: HarperCollins, 1998), 662.

82. Curtis E. LeMay, MacKinlay Kantor, *Mission with LeMay: My Story* (New York: Doubleday, 1965), 417.

83. Russkikh to Suslov and Shatilov, Sept. 20, 1948, "Zur Lage in Berlin," *Die UdSSR und die deutsche Frage*, vol. 4, 129.

84. Howley, *Berlin Command*, 212.

85. "Polozhenie v Berline," *Krasnaia zvezda*, Aug.14, 1948.

86. Interview with Sokolovskii in *Krasnaia zvezda*, Oct. 3, 1948. See also *Sovetskoe slovo*, the occupation newspaper for Soviet soldiers in Germany, Aug. 23, 1948, Mar. 3, 1949.

87. Shlaim, *United States and the Berlin Blockade*, 211n38.

88. *Tägliche Rundschau*, July 20, 1948.

89. See V. Semenov and A. Russkikh to Sokolovskii, Program for Berlin, Aug. 13, 1948, in *Die UdSSR und die deutsche Frage 1941–1949*, vol. 4, 85–86.

90. Volker Koop, *Kein Kampf um Berlin? Deutsche Politik zur Zeit der Berlin-Blockade 1948 / 1949* (Bonn: Bouvier Verlag, 1998), 174–175.

91. Russkikh to Suslov and Shatilov, Sept. 20, 1948, *Die UdSSR und die deutsche Frage*, vol 4, 129–130. Murphy et al. *Battleground Berlin*, 63. Steege, *Black Market*, 212–213.

92. *Public Opinion: OMGUS Surveys*, Report no. 132 (Aug. 10, 1948), 251.

93. Russkikh to Suslov and Shatilov, Sept. 20, 1948, *Die UdSSR und die deutsche Frage*, vol. 4, 130.

94. *Die UdSSR und die deutsche Frage*, vol. 4, 566–569n113.

95. Russkikh to Suslov and Shatilov, Sept. 20, 1948, in *Die UdSSR und die deutsche Frage*, vol. 4, 129.

96. Russkikh to Ponomarev and Shikin, Dec. 13, 1948, in *Die UdSSR und die deutsche Frage*, vol. 4, 207–208.

97. Russkikh to Tereshkin and Kuznetsov, Mar. 16, 1949, in *Die UdSSR und die deutsche Frage*, vol. 4, "Zur Lage in Berlin," 271.

98. Willy Brandt and Richard Löwenthal, *Ernst Reuter: Ein Leben für die Freiheit. Eine politische Biographie* (Munich: Kindler, 1957) 459.

99. Beschluss des ZK der VKP(b), Nov. 12, 1948, with Anlage, *Die UdSSR und die deutsche Frage*, vol. 4, 179–182.

100. Semenov to the MID of the UdSSR, Nov. 14, 1948, in Beschluss des ZK der VKP(b), Nov. 12, 1948, with Anlage, *Die UdSSR und die deutsche Frage*, vol. 4, 183–185.

101. See *Die UdSSR und die deutsche Frage*, vol. 4, 543n51.

102. The Western commanders, though unhappy about dividing the city, supported the West Berlin politicians' case for setting up a separate provisional government in the West. TNA, CAB 129 / 31.27: "Currency Situation in Berlin," Dec. 7, 1948.

103. These observations did not change much between the fall of 1948 and the spring of 1949. Russkikh to Tereshkin and Kuznetsov, Mar. 16, 1949, 276–277, Russkikh to Suslov and Shatilov, Sept. 20, 1948, 128–129. *Die UdSSR und die deutsche Frage*, vol. 4, 130–131.

104. Discussion between Kotikov and Matern, July 30, 1948, *Die UdSSR und die deutsche Frage*, vol. 4, 49–50.

105. SAPMO-BArch, NY 4076, Matern, 16.

106. SAPMO-BArch, NY 4076, Matern, Matern Draft Speech, Bilanz der Bankrotts," 58.

107. SAPMO-BArch, NY 4090, Grotewohl, 304, Oct. 1948.

108. David E. Barclay, *Schaut auf diese Stadt: Der unbekannte Ernst Reuter* (Munich: Siedler, 2000), 212–213.

109. HIA, Ernst Reuter Papers, 1917–1953. Copy of Ernst Reuter in Nordwestdeutschen Rundfunk, Aug.12, 1948, 312 / 2.

110. See Shlaim, *United States and the Berlin Blockade*, 203n19.

111. Auer, *Ihr Völker der Welt*, 218.

112. Richie, *Faust's Metropolis*, 671.

113. Auer, *Ihr Völker der Welt*, 7–8.

114. *The Papers of Lucius D. Clay*, vol. 2, Clay to Col. Gerhardt, May 5, 1949, Teleconference, 936. See also 1169.

115. Cited in Brandt and Löwenthal, *Ernst Reuter*, 426.

116. Public Opinion, Occupied Germany, The OMGUS Surveys, Report no. 130 (July 23, 1948), 248–240.

117. The army newspaper, *Krasnaia zvezda*, (Sept. 21, 1948, Sept. 26, 1948) was predictably incensed by the events ("fascist disorders"), attacking Reuter by name for his "fascist-militarist" propaganda.

118. Howley, *Berlin Command*, 217–218.

119. Russkikh to Suslov and Shatilov, Sept. 20, 1948, *Die UdSSR und die deutsche Frage*, vol. 4, 132.

120. Clay to Draper, Sept. 11, 1948, *The Papers of Lucius D. Clay*, vol. 2, 857.

121. Teleconference, Clay, Secretary of the Army Royall, and General J. W. Collins, June 25, 1948, *The Papers of Lucius D. Clay*, vol. 2, 700. For ongoing pessimism about militarily defending Berlin, see NSA, The Secretary of Defense, "A Report to the National Security Council," Possible U.S. Courses of Action in the Event the USSR reimposes the Berlin Blockade, June 1, 1949, 5.

122. Molotov to Stalin, Nov. 30, 1948, *Die UdSSR und die deutsche Frage*, vol. 4, 195. On the CFM, see Truman Archives (online), State Department Report, Foreign Policy Studies Branch, "Berlin Crisis," 29.

123. See question 3 about Berlin and Stalin's answer in, "Editorial Notes," FRUS, 1949, vol. 3, 666.

124. Malik's long telegrams to the Ministry of Foreign Affairs (MID) about his talks with Jessup are in Malik to MID, Feb. 16, 1949, 261–262. Malik to MID, Mar. 16, 1949, 280–282; Malik to MID, Mar. 22, 1949, 283–285; Malik to MID, Apr. 6, 1949, 291–295; Malik to MID, Apr. 11, 1949, 297–301; Malik to MID, Apr. 27, 1949, 306–312; Malik to MID, Apr. 30, 1949, 314–319; Malik to MID, May 4, 1949; 321–322; Malik to MID, May 5, 1949, 328–332, in *Die UdSSR und die deutsche Frage*, vol. 4. Page numbers as indicated.

125. Yoram Gorlizki and Oleg Khlevniuk, *Cold Peace: Stalin and the Soviet Ruling Circle, 1945–1953* (New York: Oxford, 2004), 76–77.

126. Memorandum of Conversation (Jessup), FRUS, 1949, vol. 3, 695.

127. *Die UdSSR und die deutsche Frage,* vol. 4, 623n268.

128. Wolff, *Die Währungsreform in Berlin 1948 / 49,* 3.

129. In addition, the CIA was deeply concerned about losing its intelligence networks due to Soviet countermeasures associated with the blockade. NACP, CIA. "Effect of Soviet Restrictions on the U.S. position in Berlin," ORE 41–48, June 14, 1948.

130. HIA, Robert Daniel Murphy Papers, box 59, folder 50–19, letter of Mar. 10, 1949. British foreign minister Ernest Bevin similarly worried about subjecting the formation of the West German state to negotiations about currency and blockade. TNA, CAB 195/7/27) Notebook (of conversations), May 2, 1949.

131. *Die UdSSR und die deutsche Frage,* vol. 4, 637, n. 299. Gorbaev, "Soviet Military Plans," 21.

132. NSA, The Secretary of Defense, A Report to the National Security Council, "Phase-out of the Berlin Blockade," July 25, 1949.

133. NSA, The Secretary of Defense, A Report to the National Security Council, "Possible U.S. Courses of Action in the Event the USSR reimposes the Berlin Blockade," June 1, 1949. TNA, CAB 129/36/4, Memorandum by the Secretary of State for Foreign Affairs, July 15, 1949.

134. Gorbaev, "Soviet Military Plans," 21.

135. Turner, *Berlin Airlift,* 266.

136. HIA, Murphy, box 68-2, OMGUS to USMA Paris, June 3, 1949.

137. Dean Acheson, *The Pattern of Responsibility,* ed. by McGeorge Bundy, (Cambridge, MA: Riverside Press, 1951), 111.

138. NSA, CIA Report: "The Soviet Position in Approaching the CFM," May 18, 1949, 9. The report concludes that the Soviets would most likely turn to a "conciliatory" policy on Germany seeking unification, the withdrawal of occupation forces, and detente in Europe. The Intelligence Organization of the State Department submitted its "dissent", suggesting instead that the Soviets would not be willing to sacrifice its controlling position in the eastern zone.

139. Brandt and Löwenthal, *Ernst Reuter,* 431.

140. Trachtenberg, *Constructed Peace,* 72.

141. General Clay noted that except for sometimes important issues having to do with "the difference in economic ideologies," the British and Americans had a relatively harmonious relationship. Clay to Draper, Oct. 4, 1948, *The Papers of Lucius D. Clay,* vol. 2, 889.

142. Gerhard Wettig writes that "as a result of the blockade a feeling of threat from the East and a resultant awareness of the need for joint resistance were spreading. . . . The perception that Moscow as a source of mortal danger to 'freedom' extended [even] to the neutral countries of Europe." Gerhard

Wettig, *Stalin and the Cold War in Europe: The Emergence and Development of East-West Conflict, 1939–1953* (Lanham, MD: Rowman & Littlefield, 2008), 173–174.

143. Discussion between Stalin, Pieck, Grotewohl and Ulbricht, Dec. 18, 1948, *Die UdSSR und die deutsche Frage*, vol. 4, 209–231.

144. Otto Grotewohl, "Entschliessung des Landesvorstandes der SED Gross-Berlin zur Lage in Berlin und zu den Aufgaben der Partei," Special Enclosure of *Vorwärts*, Oct. 19, 1948, SAPMO-BArch, NY 4090, 304. Mark Kramer, "The Soviet Union and the Founding of the German Democratic Republic: 50 Years Later—A Review Article," *Europe-Asia Studies* 51, no. 6 (1999): 1100. Naimark, *Russians in Germany*, 308–312. On Soviet ideas of the "new democracy," see E. Varga, "Demokratiia novogo tipa," *Mirovoe khoziaistvo i mirovaia politika*, no. 3 (1947): 3.

145. Naimark, *Russians in Germany*, 57–60.

146. Cited in Brandt and Löwenthal, *Ernst Reuter*, 514.

147. NSA, CIA, "The Soviet Position in Approaching the CFM, ORE 48–49, May 18, 1949, 4.

148. Harry S. Truman, *Years of Trial and Hope: Memoirs*, vol. 2 (Garden City: Doubleday, 1956), 130.

149. See NSA, CIA, "Effect of Soviet Restrictions on the U.S. Position in Berlin," June 14, 1948. ORE 41–48.

6. GOMUŁKA VERSUS STALIN

1. "Report of Comrade V. M. Molotov . . . at Sitting of Supreme Soviet of USSR, Oct. 31, 1939," *Moscow News*, Nov. 6, 1939.

2. These included the priest and prominent Polish-American Catholic leader Stanisław Orlemański, whose discussions with Stalin on Apr. 28 and May 4, 1944, are in *Vostochnaia Evropa v dokumentakh rossiiskikh arkhivov, 1944–1953*, ed. T. V. Volokitina et al. (Moscow: "Sibirskii khronograf," 1997), vol. 1, 36–42 and in *Sovetskii faktor v vostochnoi Evrope 1944–1953*, ed. T. V. Volokitina et al. (Moscow: ROSSPEN, 1999), vol. 1, 58–62, as well as Oskar Lange, a Polish leftist and distinguished academic economist, who returned to Poland from the United States after the war and became Warsaw's first ambassador to the United States. Lange's conversation with Stalin on May 17, 1944 is in: "Stalin i Pol'sha, 1943–1944 gody," *Novaia i noveishaia istoriia*, no. 3 (2008): 123–137. He told Lange, for example, that the London Polish government-in-exile's concerns about "Sovietization" were a "stupidity," and that a hybrid government including politicians from London would be highly desirable. Ibid., 126–131.

3. TNA, JIC (46) 1 (o), Chief of Staff Committee, Joint Intelligence Sub-Committee, "Russia's Strategic Interests and Intentions," Jan.–Apr. 1946, 19.

4. See, for example, Stephen Kotkin, *Stalin*, vol. 2: *Waiting for Hitler, 1929–1941* (New York: Penguin, 2017), 102.

5. Sarah Meiklejohn Terry, *Poland's Place in Europe: General Sikorski and the Origin of the Oder Neisse Line, 1939–1943* (Princeton, NJ: Princeton University Press, 1983); Norman M. Naimark, *Fires of Hatred: Ethnic Cleansing in 20th Century Europe* (Cambridge, MA: Harvard University Press, 2001), 108–120.

6. There is some controversy about the relative responsibility of the government versus the AK in starting the uprising. The reasons for the uprising are described by AK General Leopold Okulicki in his Apr. 1945 deposition to the NKVD. Norman Davies, *Rising '44: The Battle for Warsaw* (New York: Viking, 2003), appendix 31, 680–681; see also 210–211; Halik Kochanski, *The Eagle Unbowed: Poland and the Poles in the Second World War* (Cambridge, MA Harvard University Press, 2009), 400.

7. The Soviet war plans did not call for the crossing of the Vistula and liberation of Warsaw at this time. Many historians will also argue that the London government should not have called for an uprising at this time, especially without any coordination with the Soviet forces. Stalin nevertheless contributed to the tragic outcome by refusing to come to the aid of the insurrection.

8. Kochanski, *Eagle Unbowed*, 424–425.

9. Ivan Serov, *Zapiski iz chemodana: Tainye dnevniki predsedatelia KGB, naidennye cherez 25 let posle ego smerti (Proekt Aleksandra Khinshteina)* (Moscow: "Prosveshchenie," 2017), 229, 233.

10. Beria to Stalin, June 17, 1945, *NKVD i Pol'skoe Podpol'e 1944–1945 (Po "Osobym papkam" I. V. Stalina)*, ed. A. F. Noskina (Moscow: Rossiiskaia Akademiia Nauk; Institut Slavianovedeniia i Balkanistiki, 1994), 199.

11. Serov to Beria, Mar. 23, 1945, *NKVD i Pol'skoe Podpol'e*, 105–106.

12. Serov, *Zapiski*, 250.

13. Robert Spałek, *Komuniści przeciwko komunistom: poszukiwanie wroga wewnętrznego w kierownictwie partii komunistycznej w Polsce w latach 1948–1956* (Warsaw, Instytut Pamięci Narodowej, 2014), 597.

14. See Norman M. Naimark, "Revolution and Counterrevolution in Eastern Europe," in *The Crisis of Socialism in Europe*, ed. Gary Marks and Christiane Lemke (Durham, NC: Duke University Press, 1993), 70. Zygmunt Berling, the commander of the Polish First Army formed in the Soviet Union, complained about these unpatriotic Poles, as he did about the communist leaders Berman, Minc, and Zambrowski, whom he did not distinguish from Gomułka. Zygmunt Berling, *Wspomnienia. Przeciw siedemnastej republice*, vol. 1 (Warsaw: Polski Dom Wydawniczy, 1991), 26–27, 313.

15. Inessa Iazhborovskaia, "The Gomułka Alternative: The Untravelled Road," trans. Anna M. Cienciala), in *The Establishment of Communist Regimes in Eastern*

Europe, ed. Norman M. Naimark and Leonid Gibianskii (Boulder, CO: Westview, 1997), 125–126. *Pol'sha v XX veke: Ocherkii politicheskoi istorii,* ed. A. F. Noskova (Moscow: "Indrik," 2012), 344.

16. Władysław Gomułka, *Pamiętniki,* vol. 2, ed. Andrzej Werblan (Warsaw: Polska Oficyna Wydawnictwa, 1994), 360–363. The entries to Dimitrov's diary on Jan. 7 and Jan. 9, 1943, which describe the murder of Nowotko and the ascension of Finder and Fornalska, however, mention Gomułka, along with the others as "unquestionably honest and devoted comrades." *The Diary of Georgi Dimitrov,* ed., Ivo Banac (New Haven, CT: Yale University Press, 2003), 253.

17. Serov, *Zapiski,* 250. Except for attending a year-long course in a KPP school in Kraskov near Moscow, Gomulka was completely self-taught. Krystyna Kersten, *The Establishment of Communist Rule in Poland, 1943–1948,* trans. John Micgiel and Michael H. Bernhard (Berkeley: University of California Press, 1991), 12.

18. Ryszard Strzelecki-Gomułka, with Eleonora Salwa-Syzdek, *Między realizmem a utopią: Władysław Gomułka we wspomnieniach syna* (Warsaw: Studio Emka, 2003), 27.

19. Gomułka, *Pamiętniki,* vol. 2, 422–423.

20. Gomułka, *Pamiętniki,* vol. 2, 475.

21. Piotr Skwieciński, "'Ta narodowa zaściankowość . . . Stalin do Gomułki: 'Dlaczego patrzycie na mnie tak, jakbyście chcieli mnie zabić?'" *wSieci Historii,* Feb. 17, 2015, https://wpolityce.pl/historia/234091-ta-narodowa-zasciankowosc-stalin-do-gomulki-dlaczego-patrzycie-na-mnie-tak-jakbyscie-chcieli-mnie-zabic; Anita Prazmowska, *Wladyslaw Gomulka: a Biography* (London: I. B. Taurus, 2016), 60–61.

22. Spałek, *Komuniści przeciwko komunistom,* 609–610, 609n53.

23. Gomułka, *Pamiętniki,* vol. 2, 397.

24. Gomułka, *Pamiętniki,* vol. 2, 465–66, 515. See also Strzelecki-Gomułka, *Między realizmem a utopią,* 32.

25. In the Kremlin's visitors' book, Gomułka was listed nineteen times between 1944 and 1948, which does not include the many visits to Stalin at his dacha in Kuntsevo. Strzelecki-Gomułka, *Między realizmem a utopiąą,* 123.

26. For Gomułka's rendition of this meeting, see Gomułka, *Pamiętniki,* vol. 2, 476–477; 515–517.

27. Stanisław Mikołajczyk later complained, incorrectly, "that no one from the new Polish government had intervened on behalf of the 'sixteen.'" Stanisław Mikołajczyk, "Poland in Chains: My Experiences in the Post-war Government," Soundings (Aug. 1948), 42. HIA, Stanisław Mikołajczyk Collection, box 20.

28. Gomułka, *Pamiętniki,* vol. 2, 515.

29. Andrzej Werblan, "Gomułka i Stalin," *Polityka,* no. 10 (Mar. 6, 2010), 78. *NKVD i pol'skie podpol'e,* 21.

30. Gomułka, *Pamiętniki*, vol. 2, 517. Serov states in his diary that once Poland was cleared of the Wehrmacht, he was ready to move on with the troops to Berlin. Serov, *Zapiski*, 249. Following this version, historian Andrzej Paczkowski thinks that Serov's move to Germany should not be understood as a response to Gomułka's complaint. Spałek, *Komuniści przeciwko komunistom*, 779n648.

31. Andrei Ivanov, "Narodnaia demokratiia: cherez koalitsionnye formy vlasti k sotsialisticheskim preobrazovaniiam (iz opyta Narodnoi Pol'shi)," *Sovetskoe slavianovedenie* 2 (1989): 10.

32. Stalin made this statement at the founding meeting of the Government of National Unity in Moscow (June 23, 1945). "Szkic pamięciowy z przemówienia Stalina 23 czerwca 1945 roku," HIA, Władysław Gomułka, folder 3 / 4.

33. Gomułka, *Pamiętniki*, vol. 2, 479.

34. Cited in *Pol'sha v XX veke*, 508.

35. Kersten, *Establishment of Communist Rule in Poland*, 173–176.

36. This well-known story is told in Stanisław Mikołajczyk, *The Rape of Poland: Pattern of Soviet Aggression* (New York: Whittlesey House, 1948) and in Arthur Bliss Lane, *I Saw Poland Betrayed* (Belmont, MA: American Opinion, 1961).

37. The Ambassador to Poland (Lane) to the Secretary of State, Jan. 18, 1947, FRUS, 1947, vol. 6, 409n3; Ambassador to State Department, Feb. 25, 1946, FRUS, 1946, vol. 6, 418.

38. Naimark, *Fires of Hatred*, 108–138.

39. Cited in Antony Polonsky and Bolesław Drukier, eds., *The Beginnings of Communist Rule in Poland* (London: Routledge and Keegan Paul, 1990), 425.

40. Iazhborovskaia, "The Gomułka Alternative," 135.

41. Andrzej Garlicki, *Z tajnych archiwów* (Warsaw: Polska oficyna Wydawnicza "BGW", 1993), 34.

42. "III kw. 45 (adnotacja na rękopisie): Wypowiedź Stalina," quoted in Strzelecki-Gomułka, *Między realizmem a utopią*," 139.

43. Prazmowska, *Wladyslaw Gomulka*, 147–148. Spałek, *Komuniści przeciwko komunistom*, 777n638.

44. Andrzej Werblan, "Dlaczego Gomułka przegrał ze Stalinem," Feb. 13, 2005, http://www.tygodnikprzeglad.pl/dlaczego-Gomułka-przegral-ze-Stalinem/.

45. Gomułka, *Pamiętniki*, vol. 2, 476.

46. Cited in *Pol'sha v XX veke*, 434, 448.

47. L. Ia. Gibianskii, "Dolgii put' k tainam: istoriografiia Kominforma," in *Soveshchaniia Kominforma 1947, 1948, 1949: Dokumenty i Materialy* (Moscow: ROSSPEN, 1998), 39–40.

48. HIA, Berman, box 1, folder 20. "Wstępne Rozmowy w sprawie zwołania Narody Europejskich Partii Komunistycznych w 1947 r.," 3.

49. Strzelecki-Gomułka, *Między realizmem a utopią*, 33.

50. See Gibianskii, "Dolgii put'," 40.

51. See Zhdanov's speech "On the international situation" in *Soveshchaniia Kominforma*, 297–302.

52. See Peter Raina, *Gomułka. Politische Biographie* (Köln: Verlag Wissenschaft und Politik, 1970), 70. Raina notes here that the Yugoslav representative, Milovan Djilas, stated that Gomułka "spoke carefully but unmistakably about the Polish road to socialism." Kersten writes that Gomułka thought about resigning as a demonstration against the Cominform meeting, but that his comrades did not support his idea. Kersten, *Establishment of Communist Rule in Poland*, 407.

53. Cited in Strzelecki-Gomułka, *Między realizmem a utopią*, 34.

54. *Pol'sha v XX veke*, 546.

55. Spałek, *Komuniści przeciwko komunistom*, 618.

56. See Ivo Banac, *With Stalin Against Tito: Cominformist Splits in Yugoslav Communism* (Ithaca, NY: Cornell University Press, 1988), 117ff.

57. T. V. Volokitina, G. P. Murashko, A. F. Noskova, T. A. Pokivailova, *Moskva i vostochnaia Evropa. Stanovlenie politicheskikh rezhimov sovetskogo tipa: 1949–1953: Ocherki istorii* (Moscow: ROSSPEN, 2002), 499.

58. Werblan, "Dlaczego Gomułka przegrał ze Stalinem," 79.

59. Leonid Gibianskii, "The Beginning of the Soviet-Yugoslav Conflict and the Cominform," *The Cominform: Minutes of the Three Conferences, 1947/1948/1949* (Milan: Feltrenelli, 1994), 480; see also Leonid Gibianskii, "The Soviet-Yugoslav Split and the Cominform," in *The Establishment of Communist Regimes in Eastern Europe, 1944–1949*, ed. Norman Naimark and Leonid Gibianskii (Boulder, CO: Westview, 1997), 302.

60. *Pol'sha v XX veke*, 556.

61. Berman in Teresa Torańska, *"Them": Stalin's Polish Puppets* (New York: Harper & Row, 1987), 281–284.

62. For the involvement of Polish Jews in the communist movement, see Marci Shore, *Caviar and Ashes: A Warsaw Generation's Life and Death in Marxism, 1918–1968* (New Haven, CT: Yale University Press, 2006). For an earlier version of this section, see Norman M. Naimark, "The Anti-Semitic Factor in Postwar Polish Politics," in Murray Baumgarten et al., eds., *Varieties of Anti-Semitism: History, Ideology, Discourse* (Newark: University of Delaware Press, 2000), 237–251.

63. Norman M. Naimark, *The Russians in Germany: A History of the Soviet Zone of Occupation 1945–1949* (Cambridge, MA: Harvard University Press, 1995), 338.

64. Yuri Slezkine, *The Jewish Century* (Princeton, NJ: Princeton University Press, 2006), 289–290.

65. Lebedev to Molotov, Mar. 10, 1948, in *Sovetskii faktor*, vol. 1, 561.

66. See Andrzej Albert [Wojciech Roszkowski], *Najnowsza historia Polski 1914–1993*, vol. 2 (London: Puls, 1993), 133. *Pol'sha v XX veke*, 555.

67. Krzysztof Persak, "Stalin and the Polish Leaders; The Soviet Dictator's Mediation between the Polish Communist and Socialist Parties, 1946," unpublished manuscript, Sept. 1999.

68. John Coutouvidis and Jaime Reynolds, *Poland 1939–1947* (Leicester: Leicester University Press, 1986), 309.

69. The PPR politburo's reaction to the June 3 speech is contained in Paczkowski, ed., *Dokumenty do dziejów PRL*, 224–228, and Jakub Andrzejewski, ed., *Gomułka i inni: dokumenty z archiwum KC 1948–1982*(London: Aneks, 1987), 13–16.

70. Berman speech, July 21, 1948, *Soveshchaniia Kominforma*, 420–421.

71. HIA, Berman, box 2, folder 11, "Stenogram przemówienia z Plenarnego Posiedzenia KC PZPR," Aug. 31–Sept. 3, 1948, 7, 9, 10. See also *Gomułka i inni*, 13–16.

72. *Gomułka i inni, 36*. (July 28, 1948).

73. Cited in *Pol'sha v XX veke*, 554.

74. HIA, Bierut, "Oświadczenia t. W. [Gomułka]," Aug. 18, 1948. See also Iazhborovskaia, "The Gomułka Alternative," 135.

75. Cited in Volokitina et al., *Moskva i vostochnaia Evropa*, 510.

76. Gomułka letter, July 4, 1948, to KC PPR, *Gomułka i inni*, 28–29.

77. See Iazhborovskaia, "The Gomułka Alternative," 135.

78. Norman Davies, "Poland," in *Communist Power in Europe 1944–1949*, ed. Martin McCauley (London: Macmillian Press Ltd. 1977), 51–52. Davies rightly notes here that divisions in the Polish party were much more complicated than simply between the "home" communists of Gomułka and the "Muscovites."

79. HIA, Bierut, "Tomasz [Bierut] to Dimitrov, June 10, 1944. See *Pol'sha v XX veke*, 557.

80. Raina, *Gomułka, 83*. "American Embassy Warsaw to Secretary of State, 1181, Sept. 6, 1948. Summary of Resolution of Aug.–Sept. Plenum." Confidential U.S. State Department Central Files. Poland, 1945–1949 [microform], internal affairs decimal number 86c and foreign affairs decimal numbers 760c and 711.60.c.

81. HIA, Bierut, Suslov (?) to Bierut (n.d.).

82. For documents on the attack on Gomułka, see *Dokumenty do dziejów PRL*. For descriptions of Gomułka's struggle in this period, see Paweł Machcewicz, *Władysław Gomułka* (Warsaw: Wydawnictwa Szkolne i Pedagogiczne, 1995), 24–33. See also Confidential U.S. State Department Central Files, "Warsaw to Secretary of State, 1192, Sept. 7, 1948.

83. Józef Światło, "Behind the Scene of the Party and Bezpieka," 5. "Literal" translation of Światło's *Za kulisami bezpieki i partii* (Warsaw: BIS, 1990).

84. Raina, *Gomułka*, 75. Bierut, for example, was known to have lived in luxurious circumstances.

85. Yosef Litwak, "Polish Jewish Refugees Repatriated from the Soviet Union at the End of the Second World War and Afterwards," in *Jews in Eastern Poland and the USSR, 1939–46*, ed. Norman Davies and Anthony Polonsky (New York, St. Martin's, 1991), 229; Bożena Szaynok, "Komuniści w Polsce (PPR / PZPR) wobec ludności żydowskiej (1945–1953)," *Pamięć i Sprawiedliwość* 3 / 2, no. 6, 193.

86. See Berman's reflections on this issue in Torańska, *"Them,"* 51–52.

87. Spałek, *Komuniści przeciwko komunistom*, 662.

88. Roman Werfel, "Ostatni spór Gomulki ze Stalinem: Nieznana korespondencja z 1948 r.," *Dziś: Przegląd Społeczny*, no. 6 (33) (1993): 103.

89. Spałek, *Komuniści przeciwko komunistom*, 663.

90. Gomułka to Stalin, Dec. 14, 1948, in *SSSR—Pol'sha: Mekhanizmy Podchineniia, 1944–1949 gg.: Sbornik Dokumentov*, ed. Gennadii Bordiugov et al. (Moscow: "Airo—XX," 1995), 274–275.

91. Gomułka to Stalin, Dec. 14, 1948, in *SSSR—Pol'sha*, 275.

92. August Grabski, cited in Szaynok, "Komuniści w Polsce," 193.

93. Dariusz Stola writes that Gomułka should not be considered an anti-Semite because of the lack of an ongoing and consistent prejudicial attitude against the Jews. Private communication, Jan. 2019.

94. See Berman's description of the Gomułka issue in Torańska, *"Them,"* 281–284.

95. See Volokitina et al., *Moskva i vostochnaia Evropa*, 510.

96. Spałek, *Komuniści przeciwko komunistom*, 782.

97. *Pol'sha v XX veke*, 561. See also the *Trybuna Ludu* report of Gomułka's speech at the Congress, translated in "Warsaw to Secretary of State, Dec. 17, 1948."

98. According to Spałek, by the spring of 1949 Lebedev's position as plenipotentiary in Warsaw was so strong that his reports went directly to Stalin. Spałek, *Komuniści*, 672.

99. Lebedev to Vyshinskii, July 10, 1949, *Vostochnaia Evropa*, vol. 2, 173.

100. Spałek, *Komuniści*, 676–677.

101. Wolski was particularly critical of Zambrowski, because as a member of the "Jewish Triumvirate" he was in charge of cadre policy. At the fourth plenum of the PZPR in 1950, he charged that Zambrowski only drew from experienced cadres, many of whom had Trotskyite backgrounds (a shorthand for Jews), and that he demonstrated a "lack of confidence in new people from the working class," which resembled Gomułka's criticism. Cited in Andrzej Werblan, *Stalinizm w Polsce* (Warsaw, Wydawnictwo FAKT, 1991), 47.

102. Lebedev to Vyshinskii, July 10, 1949, *Vostochnaia Evropa*, vol. 2, 176.

103. Lebedev to Vyshinskii, *Vostochnaia Evropa*, 176. This charge was also leveled— apparently with some justification—at Ana Pauker, a leading Romanian

communist, whose brother lived in Israel and returned periodically to Romania to meet with her on behalf of potential Jewish emigrants. See Robert Levy, *Ana Pauker: The Rise and Fall of a Jewish Communist* (Berkeley: University of California Press, 2001), 167–183.

104. Lebedev to Vyshinskii, July 10, 1949, *Vostochnaia Evropa*, vol. 2, 177.

105. Torańska, *"Them,"* 235.

106. HIA, Bierut 1944–1950. Bierut to Stalin, May 1950.

107. HIA, Bierut 1944–1950, Stalin to Bierut, May 22, 1950.

108. Torańska, *"Them,"* 265.

109. Ogol'tsov to Molotov, May 13, 1950, with a telegram from the MGB advisor Bezborodov about the expulsion of W. Wolski from the PZPR, *Sovetskii faktor,* vol. 2, 322.

110. Volokitina et al. believe that Lebedev's removal on Mar. 16, 1951, had nothing to do with the Wolski affair. This seems unlikely to me. Volokitina et al., *Moskva i vostochnaia Evropa,* 551.

111. Volokitina et al., *Moskva i vostochnaia Evropa,* 549.

112. [Władysław Gomułka], "Przygotowania do procesu o odchylenie prawicowo-nacjonalistyczne," "Fragmenty notatek Władysława Gomułki," in Strzelecki-Gomułka, *Między realizmem a utopią,* 180. In the "Generals Trial," which took place between July 31 and Aug. 13, 1952, General Stanisław Tatar and eight other high-ranking officers were accused and convicted of various crimes associated with undermining the socialist state. At the trial, Spychalski, who was not a defendant but still under arrest and investigation at that time, was forced to testify against them. See Andrew Michta, *Red Eagle: The Army in Polish Politics, 1944–1988* (Stanford, CA: Hoover Institution Press, 1990): 45–49. Bierut linked the alleged military conspiracy, at work since 1945, to the "Spychalski-Gomułka group" in a letter to Stalin. HIA, Boleslaw Bierut, 1944–1950, Bierut to Stalin, 1950, 5.

113. V. I. Ovcharov (a Cominform official) on the Polish party, Dec. 15, 1949, in *Sovetskii faktor,* vol. 2, 233–234n2, 235. The American architect Hermann Field, in search of his missing brother Noel Field, the alleged CIA agent and organizer at the center of various East European anti-communist conspiracies, was arrested in Poland in Aug. 1949 and interrogated in the hopes of constructing a case against Gomułka. Meanwhile, Noel was imprisoned and tortured by the Hungarian secret police in conjunction with the László Rajk trial in Hungary. Hermann Field and Kate Field, *Trapped in the Cold War: The Ordeal of an American Family* (Stanford, CA: Stanford University Press, 1999).

114. Col. Zaitsev on the Polish military-judicial system, Jan. 8, 1951, in *Sovetskii faktor,* vol. 2, 434–435.

115. Some of the letters are in HIA, Władysław Gomułka, folder 3:2: Gomułka to Bierut, (July 24, 1950); Bierut to Gomułka (July 27, 1950); Gomułka to Berman (July 28, 1950); Gomułka to Bierut (Aug. 14, 1950).

116. Spałek, *Komuniści*, 724–725.

117. Andrzej Paczkowski, *Trzy twarze Józefa Światły* (Warsaw: Prószyński i S-ka, 2009), 113.

118. HIA, Władysław Gomułka, box, 3, folder 1. Gomułka to Central Committee, June 28, 1952, 7.

119. The Hoover Institution Archives hold copies of the originals of many of the interrogation protocols. HIA, Władysław Gomułka, box 3, folder 1.

120. "Notes from the interrogation of GOMUŁKA, May 4, 1953," in HIA, Władysław Gomułka, box 3.

121. Protocol of Interrogation, Oct. 6, 1953, HIA, Władysław Gomułka, box 3, folder 1. This was a repeated theme in his responses. See Protocol of Interrogation, Feb. 19, 1953, HIA, Władysław Gomułka, box 3, folder 1.

122. Andrzej Werblan, ed. "The Conversation between Władysław Gomułka and Josef Stalin on 14 November 1945," *Cold War International History Project Bulletin* 11 (Winter 1998): 138.

123. L. W. Głuchowski, "The Defection of Józef Światło and the Search for Jewish Scapegoats in the Polish United Workers' Party, 1953–1954," https://www .marxiso.org/subject/jewish.Głuchowski.pdf., 14.

124. Paczkowski, *Trzy twarze*, 147.

125. Andrzej Paczkowski, "Poland, the 'Enemy Nation'," in *The Black Book of Communism: Crimes, Terror, Repression*, ed. Stephane Courtois et al., trans. Jonathan Murphy and Mark Kramer (Cambridge, MA: Harvard University Press, 1999), 381–382. See Andrzej Werblan, *Stalinizm w Polsce* (Warsaw: Wydawnictwo FAKT, 1991), 21.

126. R. T. Davies, "Comrade Gomułka in Coventry," July 19, 1948, 4, in Confidential U.S. State Department Central Files. Warsaw to Secretary of State, July 23, 1948.

127. Volokitina et al., *Moskva i vostochnaia Evropa*, 527.

128. Józef Światło, *Za kulisami bezpieki i partii* (Warsaw: BIS, 1990), 16–22.

129. Spałek, *Komuniści*, 711. Machcewicz agrees with this argument in *Władysław Gomułka*, 32. See also Bolesław Szydek in his edited collection, *Władysław Gomułka we wspomnieniach* (Lublin: Wydawnictwa Lubelskie, 1989), 25. Prazmowska, *Wladyslaw Gomulka*, 174.

130. "'Moje czternaście lat' . . . 'Zwierzenia Władysława Gomułki'" opracował Leo Dan, from Israeli daily "Nowiny Kurier," June–July 1973, HIA, Ryszard Gontarz, box 1.

131. Torańska, *"Them,"* 327.

132. One of Gomułka's earliest biographers, Peter Raina, suggests that Bierut had a conscience, knew that Gomułka was not guilty, and therefore resisted pressure to put him on trial. Raina, *Gomułka*, 88. Andrzej Werblan notes that Bierut did "prolong the process," but whether he did this to save Gomułka, says Werblan, is hard to determine. "Maybe he did it out of pedantry, for which he was known." Paweł Dybicz, "Naród nie może zginąć—rozmowa z prof. Andrzejem Werblanem," Oct. 2014, http://www.tygodnikprzeglad.pl/narod-nie -moze-zginac-rozmowa-prof-andrzejem-werblanem.

133. "Moje czternaście lat . . . ," 1. HIA, Ryszard Gontarz, box 1, 2.

134. See G. P. Murashko, ed., "Delo Slanskogo," *Voprosy istorii*, no. 3 (1997), 8.

135. Cited in Volokitina et al., *Moskva i vostochnaia Evropa*, 551.

136. Anat Plocker, "Homelands: Poles and Jews under Communism," manuscript, 2019, chapter 3, 36–37.

137. HIA, Władysław Gomułka, folder 3 / 6. Interviews after Gomułka's death. Stanisław Trepczyński (Dec. 1983).

138. Dariusz Stola, *Kampania antysyjonistyczna w Polsce 1967–1968* (Warsaw: ISP PAN, 2000), 213.

7. AUSTRIAN TANGLES

1. "Moskovskaia Deklaratsiia," Oct. 30, 1943, in *Die Rote Armee in Österreich: Sowjetische Besatzung 1945–1955 / Krasnaia Armiia v Avstrii: Sovetskaia okkupatsiia 1945– 1955*, ed. Stefan Karner, Barbara Stelzl-Marx, and Alexander Tschubarjan (Vienna: Oldenbourg, 2005), 38 (hereafter *RAÖ / KAA*.) The collection includes both German and Russian translations. I use the page numbers for the original language of the document. See Guenter Bischof, *Austria in the First Cold War, 1945–55* (New York: St. Martin's Press, 1999), 25–26. Gerald Stourzh and Wolfgang Mueller, *A Cold War over Austria: The Struggle for the State Treaty, Neutrality, and the End of East-West Occupation* (Lanham, MD: Rowman & Littlefield, 2018), 1–10.

2. *The Diary of Georgi Dimitrov*, ed. Ivo Banac (New Haven, CT: Yale University Press, 2003), 365.

3. Deputy Foreign Minister Solomon Lozovskii to Stalin, Jan. 23, 1945, AVPRF, "Ob Avstrii," no. 3797-g., ll. 6–7.

4. "K Avstriiskomu Narodu!" in AVPRF, "Ob Avstrii," no. 3797-g.

5. *Understanding Austria: The Political Reports and Analysis of Martin F. Herz, Political Officer of the U.S. Legation in Vienna 1945–1948* (Vienna: Neugebauer, 1984), 132.

6. Wolfgang Mueller, *Die sowjetische Besatzung in Österreich 1945–1955 und ihre politische Mission* (Vienna: Böhlau Verlag, 2005), 140–141.

7. Ukrainian Front, Military Council, "On the provision of products for the people of the city of Vienna," Apr. 21, 1945, in *SSSR i Avstrii na puti k*

gosudarstvennomu dogovoru: Stranitsy dokumental'noi istorii 1945–1955, ed. V. I. Iakunin (Moscow: ROSSPEN, 2015), 40.

8. *Understanding Austria*, "Compendium of Austrian Politics," Dec. 2, 1948, 559. Mueller, in *Die sowjetische Besatzung*, 112, writes that contemporary estimates of the incidence of rape ranged between 70,000 and 100,000 in Vienna and Lower Austria, and between 5,000 to 10,000 in the Steiermark.

9. Stenogram of a report on the domestic situation in Austria, ZK VKP(b), Aug. 7 (probably Aug. 18), 1945, in *Sowjetische Politik in Österreich 1945–1955: Dokumente aus russischen Archiven. Sovetskaia politika v Avstrii 1945–1955gg. Dokumenty iz Rossiiskikh arkhivov*, ed. Wolfgang Mueller, Arnold Suppan, Norman M. Naimark, Gennadii Bordiugov (Vienna: Verlag der Österreichischen Akademie der Wissenschaft, 2005), 190. (Hereafter *SPÖ / SPA*). The documents are in Russian and German on facing pages. I cite the original language version of the document.

10. Smirnov to Kiselev, Sept. 7, 1945, in *RAÖ / KAA*, 418.

11. HIA, Austria: Territory under Allied Occupation, 1945–1955, box 6. "Military Government in Austria," July 31, 1946, 1–3.

12. The many problems with the "Four in a Jeep" patrols in Vienna are explored in Ralph W. Brown III, "Making the Third Man Look Pale: American-Soviet Conflict in Vienna during the Early Cold War in Austria, 1945–1950," *Journal of Slavic Military Studies* 14, no. 4 (Dec. 2001): 87–88.

13. ÖS, NL Renner E 1731: 307.

14. For Renner and the Soviets, see Robert Knight, "The Renner State Government and Austrian Sovereignty," in *Austria 1945–95: Fifty Years of the Second Republic*, ed. Kurt Richard Luther and Peter Pulzer (Aldershot: Ashgate, 1998), 30–36; and Wilfried Aichinger, "Die Sowjetunion und Österreich 1945–1949," in *Die bevormundete Nation: Österreich und die Alliierten 1945–1949*, ed. Günther Bischof and Josef Leidenfrost (Innsbruck: Haymon, 1988), 275–279. The Renner-Stalin documents are also published in *SSSR i Avstriia*, 33–39, 43–51.

15. David J. Dallin, "Stalin, Renner und Tito: Österreich zwischen drohender Sowjetisierung und den jugoslawischen Gebietsansprüchen im Frühjahr 1945," *Europa-Archiv*, July–Dec., 1958, 11.030. S. M. Shtemenko, *Generalnyi shtab v gody voiny*, kn. 2 (Moscow, 1973) 356–358. Renner's recent biographer, Siegfried Nasko, reviews the evidence at some length. Siegfried Nasko, *Karl Renner: Zu Unrecht umstritten? Eine Wahrheitssuche* (Salzburg, Vienna: Residenz Verlag, 2016), 358–366. Nasko cites a newspaper interview with Andrei Sorokin, Director of RGASPI in Moscow: "We have no documents that Stalin sought out Renner. . . . In my view, he reacted operationally to Renner's offer and used the opportunity." Nasko, *Karl Renner*, 362. See Mueller, *Die sowjetische Besatzung*, 75–77.

16. Tolbukhin and Zheltov to Stalin about Renner, Apr. 4, 1945, *SPÖ / SPA*, 110.

17. Dallin, "Stalin, Renner and Tito," 11.031. Like the issue of Stalin seeking out Renner, this too may be conjecture.

18. General Staff (Stalin and Antonov) to Third Ukrainian Front (Tolbukhin) on Renner, Apr. 4, 1945, in SPÖ / SPA, 112. See Dallin, "Stalin, Renner und Tito," 11.031.

19. Report of M. Koptelov, Political Advisor of the Third Ukrainian Front. Meeting of Renner, Marshal Tolbukhin, and Col.-General Zheltov, June 6, 1945, in AVPRF, no. 3797-g. "Ob Avstrii," ll. 27–28.

20. *Protokolle des Kabinettsrates der provisorischen Regierung Karl Renner 1945*, Band I, ed. Gertrude Enderle-Burcel et al. (Vienna: Verlag Berger, 1995), 37 (May 10, 1945).

21. AVPRF, f. 060, op. 25, papka 119, d. 10, ll. 3–4.

22. Renner wrote to Stalin (Apr. 15, 1945): "With Trotsky, I had ongoing contacts in the year he spent in Vienna." AVPRF, f. 066, op. 25, papka 119, d. 10, l. 2. Dallin, "Stalin, Renner und Tito," 11.031–11.032. RAÖ / KAA, Letter of K. Renner to Stalin, Apr. 15, 1945, 103. Some historians doubt that Renner was as naïve as it seems by employing this reference to Trotsky. See Nasko, *Karl Renner,* 372.

23. Tolbukhin on the formation of the Austrian Provisional Government, Apr. 17, 1945, SPÖ / SPA, 126–128.

24. Cited in Ol'ga Pavlenko, "Österreich im Kraftfeld der sowjetischen Diplomatie," *Die Rote Armee in Österreich: Beiträge,* ed. Stefan Karner and Barbara Stelzl-Marx (Vienna: Oldenbourg, 2005), 572.

25. *Protokolle des Kabinettsrates,* vol. 2 (Vienna: Böhlau, 1999), Aug. 7, 1947, Aug. 22, 1947, 211, 217, 292–293.

26. Nasko, *Karl Renner,* 378.

27. ÖS, NL Renner E / 1731, 306–309, box 51. See also AVPRF, f. 066, op. 25, papka 118a, d. 7. l. 64.

28. Nasko, *Karl Renner,* 380.

29. Politburo decision of October 19, 1945, in SPÖ / SPA, 220.

30. Richard Saage, *Der erste Präsident: Karl Renner—eine politische Biografie* (Vienna: Paul Zsolnay Verlage, 2006), 310–311.

31. Cited in Bischof, *Austria in the First Cold War,* 51.

32. *Protokolle des Kabinettsrates,* vol. 1, 55 (May 10, 1945).

33. Koptelov to Dekanozov on his discussion with Renner, Apr. 19, 1945, RAÖ / KAA, 110.

34. HIA, ZZ146, "Karl Renner interview transcript," With Herr Dalauney ("Quotidiens provinciaux"), Feb. 12, 1947, 2.

35. ÖS, NL Renner, E / 173 / :309. Zheltov-Renner Conference Aug. 28, 1945.

36. Vyshinskii diary, Aug. 3, 1946, AVPRF, f. 066, op. 25, d. 9, papka 119, l. 30.

37. Hexmann, "Einschätzung der Wahlergebnisse in Österreich," Dec. 8 1945, RGASPI, f. 17, op. 128, d. 781, l. 264.

38. Cited in James J. Carafano, *Waltzing into the Cold War: The Struggle for Occupied Austria* (College Station: Texas A&M Press, 2002), 91.

39. Fürnberg at Sitzung of the Wiener Landesausschuß, Sept. 27, 1946. RGASPI, f. 17, op. 128, d. 108, l. 35.

40. ÖS, NL Renner, Renner Oct. 22, 1945, E / 1731, 313–321 box 53.

41. Anthony Eden later wrote to the Prime Minister about Figl: "I know Dr Figl well. He is a courageous man who spent many years in a German concentration camp where he was brutally treated. He is nonetheless a cheerful soul who likes his glass of wine." TNA, FO 800 / 7511, Secretary of State's File, Private Papers of Anthony Eden, 16.

42. Helmut Wohnout, *Leopold Figl und das Jahr 1945: von der Todeszelle auf den Ballhausplatz* (St. Pölten, Salzburg, Vienna: Residenz Verlag, 2015), 145.

43. General I. V. Shikin to G. F. Aleksandrov in the Central Committee, Jan. 15, 1946, *SPÖ / SPA*, 244.

44. On the initial promises to close down the Allied Council, see Wolfgang Mueller, "Stalin and Austria: New Evidence on Soviet Policy in a Secondary Theatre of the Cold War, 1938–53 / 55," *Cold War History* 6, no. 1 (Feb. 2006): 68–69.

45. See Pavlenko, "Österreich im Kraftfeld," 586.

46. FRUS, vol. 5, 1946, 364.

47. RGASPI, f. 17, op. 128, d. 909, ll. 11, 22.

48. *Understanding Austria* (Dec. 2, 1948), 591.

49. *SPÖ / SPA*, Dimitrov to Stalin, Apr. 3, 1945, 108.

50. See Oliver Rathkolb, "Historische Fragmente und die 'unendliche Geschichte' von den sowjetischen Absichten in Österreich 1945," in *Österreich unter alliierter Besatzung 1945–1955*, ed. Alfred Ableitinger, Siegfried Beer, and Eduard G. Staudinger (Vienna: Böhlau, 1998), 147.

51. Franz Marek, *Beruf und Berufung Kommunist: Lebenserinnerungen und Schlüsseltexte*, ed. Maximilian Graf and Sarah Knoll (Vienna: Mandelbaum Kritik & Utopie, 2017), 172–173, 184. Thanks to Maximilian Graf for pointing out this source.

52. Marek, *Beruf und Berufung Kommunist*, 170.

53. See Minutes from the meeting between General Kurasov and the leaders of the Central Committee of the KPÖ where Fürnberg told Kurasov that the party had "insignificant" influence in the countryside and was simply "too weak" to carry out work there. *SPÖ / SPA*, 318.

54. Report of the Foreign Affairs Section of the Central Committee, Oct. 23, 1946, and "Report of G. F. Aleksandrov and M. A. Suslov to the Secretary of the Central Committee, A. A. Zhdanov, on the Situation of Soviet Propaganda

in Austria," Feb. 1947, SPÖ / SPA, 1945–1955, 334, 360. The latter document contains particularly critical views of the propaganda section of the Soviet element in the Allied Commission.

55. See the stenogram of the discussion in the Central Committee on the work of the Sovinformburo, June 28, 1946, and, B. Sapozhnikov, "Report of the Foreign Policy Section of the Central Committee," Oct. 23, 1946, SPÖ / SPA, 272–276, 334–340.

56. HIA, Allied Commission for Austria, box 1, Annex A, Minutes (July 10, 1947), Statement by Col. Gen Kurasov, 1.

57. Rolf Steininger, Austria, Germany, and the Cold War: From the Anschluss to the State Treaty, 1938–1955 (New York: Berghahn, 2008), 52.

58. Minutes of the discussions between G. Korotkevich and the leaders of the KPÖ, Apr. 16, 1947, SPÖ / SPA, 378.

59. Minutes of the discussions between G. Korotkevich and the leaders of the KPÖ, Apr. 16, 1947, SPÖ / SPA, 378.

60. Korotkevich to Suslov, Nov. 19, 1946, RGASPI, f. 17, op. 128, d. 910, l. 234.

61. Report of the Propaganda Section of the Soviet Element of the Control Commission about the Elections of Oct. 27, 1949, 622, and, From the Diary of the Soviet Political Representative in Austria, M. E. Koptelov about a Discussion with F. Fürnberg, Aug. 17, 1950, SPÖ / SPA, 680.

62. In response to Fürnberg's statement that the Yugoslavs had suggested partition as a solution to the Austrian question, Zhdanov responded: "this is fundamentally incorrect advice." Protocol of the Discussion between Zhdanov and Koplenig and Fürnberg, Feb. 13, 1948, SPÖ / SPA, 462 (Zhdanov's emphasis). From his reading of foreign ministry documents, Oliver Rathkolb concludes: "The division of the country or an occupation ad infinitum seemed—as far as the documents that we now have show—never to have been taken very seriously." Rathkolb, "Historische Fragmente," 157.

63. See Wolfgang Mueller, "Stalin and Austria: New Evidence on Soviet Policy in a Secondary Theater in the Cold War, 1938–53 / 55," Journal of Cold War History 6, no. 1 (2006): 70–71.

64. Suslov to Molotov and Zhdanov, June 11, 1946, SPÖ / SPA, 1945–1955, 268.

65. Marek, Beruf und Berufung, 168.

66. From the political report of the Propaganda Section of the Soviet Element in Austria, Aug. 6, 1946, SPÖ / SPA, 292. See also Rathkolb, "Historische Fragmente," 149–150.

67. Letter from Koplenig and Fürnberg to Stalin on the economic and political situation in Austria, Mar. 31, 1947, SPÖ / SPA, 362–368.

68. Korotkevich to Suslov, Nov. 1946, SPÖ / SPA, 340.

69. According to the Americans, some 286 Austrians were seized in 1948 alone; 152 of these were not released. Erhardt to Sec. of State, Nov. 2, 1948, FRUS, 1948, vol. 2, 1442. See also *Stalins letzte Opfer: Verschleppte und erschossene Österreicher in Moskau, 1950–1953*, ed. Stefan Karner and Barbara Stelzl-Marx (Vienna: Böhlau / Oldenbourg, 2009).

70. HIA, Allied Commission for Austria, Allied Council, June 25, 1948, Statement by British Member.

71. Giles MacDonough, *After the Reich: The Brutal History of the Allied Occupation* (New York: Basic, 2007), 514.

72. Stenogram of Central Committee meeting on Sovinformburo, June 28, 1946, *SPÖ / SPA*, 274.

73. Report of the Central Committee Commission on Soviet Propaganda in Austria, to Suslov, June 12, 1948, *SPÖ / SPA*, 504. On Zheltov's failings, see 502. For a similar purge of Jews from the propaganda organs of the Soviet Military Administration in Germany, see Naimark, *The Russians in Germany: A History of the Soviet Zone of Occupation 1945–1949* (Cambridge, MA: Harvard University Press, 1997), 338, 416.

74. Report of the Central Committee Commission on Soviet Propaganda in Austria to Suslov, *SPÖ / SPA*, June 12, 1948, 502.

75. On financial support, see Korotkevich to Suslov, Nov. 19, 1946, RGASPI, f. 17, op. 128, d. 910, l. 234. Mueller, *Die sowjetische Besatzung*, 171–173.

76. Report of the Soviet Element of the Allied Council in Austria on the July Plenum of the Central Committee of the KPÖ, Aug. 19, 1949, *SPÖ / SPA*, 592–598.

77. From the Report of the Section on Internal Affairs of the Soviet Element of the Allied Council in August for the year 1949, Jan. 26, 1950, in Report of the Soviet Element of the Allied Council in Austria on the July Plenum of the Central Committee of the KPÖ, Aug. 19, 1949, *SPÖ / SPA*, 640.

78. From the Diary of the Political Representative of the USSR in Austria, M. E. Koptelov, about a Discussion of F. Fürnberg, Aug. 1950, in Report of the Soviet Element of the Allied Council in Austria on the July Plenum of the Central Committee of the KPÖ, 680–681. See Heinz Gärtner, *Zwischen Moskau und Österreich: Analyse einer sowjetabhängigen KP* (Wien: Braumiller, 1977), 116.

79. See Bevin's observations in TNA FO 800 / 439. Secretary of State (Ernest Bevin), Telegram, Sept. 17, 1949.

80. *Understanding Austria* (Feb. 10, 1947), 330.

81. FRUS, 1947, vol 2, 1169.

82. *Protokolle des Kabinettsrates*, vol. 2, Aug. 24 1945, 353.

83. ÖS, NL Renner, E / 1731: 332. Sten. Protokol, Erste Länderkonferenz, Wien, Sept. 24–26, 1945, 2. Emphasis in the original.

84. Renner to Stalin, Oct. 17, 1945, AVPRF, f. 066, op. 25, papka 119, d. 10, l. 132. *RAÖ / KAA*, Renner to Stalin, Oct. 17, 1945, 243.

85. The agreement was initially concluded on May 24 for approval of the respective governments. *SSSR i Avstriia*, 96–97.

86. AVPRF, no. 3797-g. "Ob Avstrii," l. 25.

87. AVPRF, f. 06, op. 8, papka 22, d. 311. Molotov to Stalin, June 12, 1946. See Wolfgang Mueller, "Gab es eine 'verpasste Chance'? Die sowjetische Haltung zum Staatsvertrag 1946–1952," *Der Österreichische Staatsvertrag: Internationale Strategie, rechtliche Relevanz, nationale Identität*, ed. Arnold Suppan, Gerald Stourzh, and Wolfgang Mueller (Vienna: Österreichische Akademie der Wissenschaften, 2005), 93.

88. For Yugoslav claims, see Arnold Suppan, *Hitler-Beneš-Tito: Konflikt, Krieg, und Völkermord in Ostmittel- und Sudösteuropa*, part 2 (Vienna: Verlag der ÖAW, 2014), 1625–1631.

89. See Stourzh and Mueller, *Cold War over Austria*, 75.

90. TNA FO 800 / 439, UK Delegation to CFM to Foreign Office, Apr. 23, 1947.

91. Barulin to Smirnov, Final Report of the Soviet Element of the Allied Commission for the 1947, Apr. 1948, *RAÖ / KAA*, 344.

92. TNA FO 800 / 439, Statement of Secretary of State at CFM, Dec. 4, 1947.

93. Keyes to Secretary of State, Mar. 4, 1948, FRUS, 1948, vol. 2, 1384.

94. In its reporting on the possibility of a "Czech coup" scenario in Austria, the CIA noted that the Austrian communists "will remain no more than a nuisance factor" and "only physical force" on the part of the USSR could integrate Austria into the eastern bloc. CREST, CIA FOIA, "Intelligence Memorandum no. 219 (Revised), "Soviet Intentions in Austria," Sept. 22, 1949, 1–4. Still, the State Department worried about serious Soviet political influence even after the withdrawal of Soviet troops. Dept. of State Policy Statement on Austria, Sept. 20, 1948, FRUS, 1948, vol. 2, 1350.

95. HIA, Allied Commission for Austria, box 1, Statement by French High Commissioner, Jan. 28, 1949.

96. NSA, Secret Intelligence Estimate, "The Current Situation in Austria," Apr. 28, 1948, ORE 13–48, 2.

97. Already in Nov. 1947 General Keyes worried about an Allied withdrawal from Austria without "reasonable assurance that [the] south flank of our occupation forces in Germany is not being exposed by creation of another potential Soviet satellite." Keyes also argued—like those who opposed withdrawal from Berlin—that leaving Austria would deprive the United States of "valuable

facilities for gaining intelligence relative to [the] USSR and Balkan States."
Keyes to European Command, Nov. 10, 1947, FRUS, 1947, vol. 2, 1201.

98. CREST, CIA FOIA, Department of the Army, General Staff Memorandum to the Assistant Director, R&E, CIA, Jan. 18, 1949, "Possible Developments in Soviet Policy Towards Austria."

99. See Mueller, "Gab es eine 'verpasste Chance,'?" 96.

100. See Audrey Cronin, *Great Power Politics and the Struggle over Austria, 1945–1955* (Ithaca, NY: Cornell University Press, 1986), 68–94. See also Mueller, "Gab es eine 'verpasste Chance,'" 100–103.

101. TNA FO 800 / 439, Record of meeting of Bevin and Schumann in Paris, Oct. 2, 1948.

102. Vyshinskii's Diary, May 4, 1949, in AVPRF, f. 066, op. 29, papki 136, d. 10, l. 8. Reprinted in *SSSR i Avstriia*, 159–160.

103. Vyshinskii's Diary, June 9, 1949, in AVPRF, f. 066, op. 29, papki 136, d. 10, l. 11. Reprinted in *SSSR i Avstriia*, 161–165.

104. See Reber (U.S. Deputy for Austria at the CFM) to the Secretary of State, Apr. 16, 1949, FRUS, 1949, vol. 3, 1088.

105. AVPRF, f. 023, Molotov to Stalin, Feb. 9, 1949, ll. 1, 5.

106. CREST, CIA FOIA, Partial Agreement on Austrian Treaty," June 17, 1949. Bevin notes, however, that Gruber had private doubts about a treaty, though he was prepared to take the risk "so long as they could get the Russians out of the country." TNA FO 800 / 439, Secretary of State telegram, Sept. 16, 1949. See also Bevin's rendition of Gruber's concerns at the Paris meeting of U.S., French, and British Foreign Ministers, Oct. 4, 1948 in TNA FO 800 / 439.

107. See Mueller, "Gab es eine 'verpasste Chance,'?" 102.

108. Michael Gehler, *Österreichs Aussenpolitik der Zweiten Republic: Von der alliierter Besatzung zum Europa des 21.Jahrhunderts*, vol. 1 (Innsbruck, Vienna: Studien-Verlag, 2005), 65.

109. Coburn Kidd to Williamson, July 29, 1949, FRUS, 1949, vol. 3, 1111.

110. Reber to Sec. of State, July 14, 1949, FRUS, 1949, vol. 3, 1106.

111. *The Department of State Bulletin,* July 4, 1949, 86–861.

112. TNA FO 800 / 439, Secretary of State to Prime Minister, Sept. 29, 1949.

113. TNA FO 800 / 439, Record of a Conversation between Bevin and Vyshinskii at Lake Success, Sept. 30, 1949.

114. Cited in Cronin, *Great Power Politics,* 87. Mueller, "Gab es eine 'verpasste Chance,'" 105.

115. Extract from telegram from Mr. Bevin, Aug. 26, 1949, FRUS, 1949, vol. 3, 1126. The French were also ready to sign the treaty. Reber to Acting Secretary of State, FRUS, 1949, vol. 3, 1159.

116. TNA FO 800 / 439. Extract from letter, Secretary of State to Prime Minister, Sept. 29, 1949.

117. It should be noted that even the State Department was not completely convinced about signing the treaty. Acheson himself wavered, while his acting Secretary of State, James E. Webb, warned that the Soviet Union would only agree to a treaty "that would subsequently permit Soviet penetration and repossession of all of Austria." Webb also noted that signing a treaty after the dropping of the Soviet atom bomb, announced by President Truman on Sept. 23, might give Moscow "the mistaken impression" that this affected U.S. concessions in connection with Austria. On Acheson's concerns (and his dismissal of Gruber's), see Secretary of State to U.S. Deputy (Reber), Aug. 23, 1949, FRUS, 1949, vol. 3, 1123. See also Secretary of State to U.S. Deputy (Reber), Aug. 20, FRUS, 1949, vol. 3, 1130. James. E Webb to Acheson, Sept. 28, 1949, FRUS, 1949, vol. 3 1161.

118. Gale Group. U.S. Declassified Documents Online, NSC 38 / 3, Nov. 8, 1949, Report to the National Security Council, "Future Courses of U.S. Action with Respect to Austria," 1, 10. To assuage the Pentagon's concerns, the NSC report confirmed that the Western powers were training and equipping a gendarmerie regiment in the western zones and engaging in covert military planning with the Austrian government.

119. Vojtech Mastny, The Cold War and Soviet Insecurity: The Stalin Years (New York: Oxford University Press, 1996), 67.

120. Gale Group. U.S. Declassified Documents Online. Harry S. Truman Library (online), Papers of Harry S. Truman, President's Secretary's Files. Bradley to Secretary of Defense, "Future Course of U.S. Action with Respect to Austria," Nov. 14, 1949, 1–2.

121. Jenny Thompson and Sherry Thompson, The Kremlinologist: Llewellyn E. Thompson, America's Man in Cold War Moscow (Baltimore, MD: Johns Hopkins University Press, 2018), 99.

122. CREST, CIA FOIA, Europe / Austria, Nov. 30, 1949. BA FO 800 / 751. "Use of Austrian Manpower in the Event of War." Memorandum by the Secretaries of State for Foreign Affairs and War. NSA, CIA, Secret Intelligence Estimate, Aug. 31, 1949, "The Current Situation in Austria," ORE 56–49.

123. Secretary of State to U.S. Deputy (Reber), Aug. 23, 1949, FRUS, 1949, vol. 3. 1123.

124. Gribanov to Vyshinskii, Dec. 17, 1949, AVPRF, f. 066, op. 30, papka 141, ll. 176–177.

125. Gromyko to Stalin, Oct. 22, 1949, in RAÖ / KAA, 740.

126. Politburo Rescript, Oct. 24, 1949, in RAÖ / KAA, 744. See Mueller, "Stalin and Austria," 75.

127. Gerald Stourzh, *Um Einheit und Freiheit*, 177. Mueller, "Gab es eine 'verpasste Chance,'?" 110.

128. *Khrushchev Remembers: The Glasnost Tapes* (Boston: Little, Brown, 1990), 72. See the somewhat fuller Russian version of the Austrian story, "Memuary Nikity Sergeevicha Khrushcheva," *Voprosy istorii*, 8 (1993): 73–88.

129. *Khrushchev Remembers: The Glasnost Tapes*, 72. There were fundamental differences between the Yugoslavs and the Soviets on the Austrian issue. Tito urged the Austrian communists to seek a division of Austria.

130. See Audrey Kurth Cronin, "Eine verpasste Chance? Die Grossmächte und die Verhandlungen über den Staatsvertrag im Jahre 1949," *Die Bevormundete Nation: Österreich und die Alliierten, 1945–1949*, ed. Günter Bischof and Josef Leidenfrost (Innsbruck: Hayman, 1988), 347.

131. Discussion between Zhdanov and Koplenig and Fürnberg, Feb. 13, 1948, in RGASPI, fond 77, op. 3s, d. 100, ll. 9–16. See also *RAÖ / KAA*, 726–732.

132. *Understanding Austria* (June 4, 1948), 403.

133. Gehler, *Österreichs Aussenpolitik*, vol. 1, 69–70. A weakened and ailing Ottilinger was released in 1955 after the state treaty was signed.

134. Tsinev to Smirnov, RGASPI, f. 17, op. 137, d. 108, ll. 7–68.

135. Stourzh and Mueller, *Cold War over Austria*, 173.

136. On the Stalin note and its effects on the Austrian negotiations, see Stourzh and Mueller, *Cold War over Austria*, 174–175; Rolf Steininger, *Austria, Germany and the Cold War: From the Anschluss to the State Treaty, 1938–1955* (New York: Berghahn Books, 2008), 98–100. Michael Gehler, "Österreichs aussenpolitische Emanzipation und die deutsche Frage," *Österreich unter alliierter Besatzung 1945–1955*, ed. Alfred Ableitinger, Siegfried Beer, and Eduard Staudinger (Vienna: Böhlau, 1998), 257 ff.

137. Vladislav M. Zubok, *A Failed Empire: The Soviet Union in the Cold War from Stalin to Gorbachev* (Chapel Hill: University of North Carolina Press, 2007), 82–83. Mark Trachtenberg, *A Constructed Peace: The Making of the European Settlement, 1945–1963* (Princeton, NJ: Princeton University Press, 1999), 129–130. The EDC was signed on May 27, 1952, but failed to be ratified by the French parliament. Western Germany was then admitted to the Western European Union (WEU), as well as to NATO.

138. U.S. High Commissioner for Austria (Keyes) to Dept. of Army, Nov. 10, 1949, FRUS, 1949, vol. 3, 1289.

139. See Carafano, *Waltzing into the Cold War*, 172–192.

140. For the complicated relationship between the German question and the final phases of concluding the Austrian State Treaty, see Michael Gehler, "Österreich, die Bundesrepublik und die deutsche Frage, 1945 / 49–1955: Zur Geschichte der gegenseitige Wahrnehmungen zwischen Abhängigkeit und

gemeinsamen Interessen," *Ungleiche Partner? Österreich und Deutschland in ihrer gegenseitigen Wahrnehmungen,* ed. Michael Gehler et al. (Stuttgart: Franz Steiner Verlag, 1996), 531–581.

141. Jonathan Haslam, *Russia's Cold War: From the October Revolution to the Fall of the Wall* (New Haven, CT: Yale University Press, 2011), 156–159. Stourzh, *Um Einheit und Freiheit,* 524–525.

142. Mueller, "Stalin and the Austrians," 75.

143. Oliver Rathkolb, "Österreich als Teil der U.S.-Geopolitik, 1950–1970," *Mit anderen Augen gesehen: Internationale Perzeptionen Österreichs 1955–1990,* ed. Oliver Rathkolb, Otto M. Maschke, and Stefan August Lütgenau (Vienna: Böhlau, 2002), 25–26. Gerald Stourzh, *Geschichte des Staatsvertrages 1945–1955: Österreichs Weg zur Neutralität* (Graz: Styria, 1985), 99.

ACKNOWLEDGMENTS

I have been working on this project on and off for more than twenty years and have been interested in the immediate postwar period in Europe, including the Soviet Union and east central Europe, since the mid-1980s, when I started the research for *The Russians in Germany* (Harvard University Press, 1995), a book about the Soviet occupation zone of Germany. This makes the important task of thanking those colleagues and institutions that have helped me at various times over those decades very difficult indeed. Relying on memory, as historians understand all too well, can be treacherous and leave important gaps. I recognize at the outset that I will omit some important people and institutions, while trying, as best I can, to give proper credit to individual members of the collegium of historical scholarship for their important help and support.

Let me start with Stanford University, which has been the primary home for this work since I was hired in 1988. My colleagues in and the staff of the Department of History could not have been more supportive of my teaching and scholarship. The Center for International Security and Cooperation (CISAC), housed at the Freeman-Spogli Institute (FSI), has provided a wonderfully conducive environment for research, writing, and scholarly interchange. Thanks to Tracy Hill of CISAC for her ineffably gracious help. I also owe a deep debt of gratitude to the Hoover Institution and especially the Library and Archives, now superbly directed by Eric Wakin, for decades of interest in and support of my research. Archivists at Hoover, too many to name, have been critical advisors on this project, as have archivists in many locations in Russia, Europe, and the United States. My ongoing associations with Stanford's Center for Russian, East European, and Eurasian Studies (CREEES) and the Europe Center (TEC) have also redounded to the benefit of this book.

My close friend and colleague David Holloway introduced me to CISAC, shared his ideas about my subject, and has put up with my laments over the years about the problems of "finishing" this book. My History Department colleague, friend, and long-time interlocutor, Amir Weiner, discussed this work with me dozens of times and maybe more. I was fortunate to spend a total of two-and-a-half years of sabbatical time at Stanford's Center for Advanced Study in the Behavioral Sciences (CASBS), working episodically on this study, as well as on projects in the field of genocide studies. In residence himself at CASBS for a year, Ronald G. Suny of the University of Michigan has been a long-time intellectual and emotional compadre. The bulk of the manuscript was finished up during a blissful year, 2016–17, at the Stanford Humanities Center, skillfully led by my colleague Caroline Winterer. At all of these Stanford institutions, I have had priceless opportunities to discuss my work in both formal and informal settings.

The American Academy in Berlin was home to this work and my family for an unusually comfortable and stimulating six months, as was, for shorter periods, the Potsdam Zentrum für zeithistorische Forschung, and the Vienna Institut für die Wissenschaften vom Menschen. I value and miss the close academic partnership over many years with Jochen Laufer of the Potsdam center. He unexpectedly died on March 16, 2016, having finished the fourth and final volume of his superbly edited and annotated document collection on Soviet-German relations. Both the Department of East European History of the University of Vienna and the Austrian Academy of Sciences, of which I am now a foreign corresponding member, also provided welcome support and collegial input into the project. Here I am particularly grateful for the ongoing friendship of and discussions about postwar European and especially Austrian history with Arnold Suppan and Wolfgang Mueller. I would also like to thank my Italian friend and colleague, Silvio Pons, for his help and his interest in this project, including, but not limited to, sponsoring my visit to the Gramsci Institute Archives, of which he is the Director.

My Moscow home, more than any other, has been the apartment of Nina Petrova and Leonid Gibianskii of the Institute for Slavic and Balkan Studies of the Russian Academy of Sciences. My friendship and collegial relationship with Gibianskii go back to the early 1990s, when we organized a conference together at the Academy on the establishment of communist regimes in postwar eastern Europe, and subsequently co-edited a book on the subject. Since that time, at Stanford, in Moscow, and at various locations in Europe, including the Rockefeller Center at Bellagio, where we held a joint grant, we have talked and argued about Soviet policy in Europe in the postwar period. Perhaps more than any other single scholar, Gibianskii's work and thinking, which are not at all confined to his academic specialty, Yugoslav history and the Balkans, have influenced my own. But in his case, like the other scholars I mention in these acknowledgments, there are many points where he would disagree with my rendition of postwar European developments. Gennadii Bordiugov, another Moscow historian, has also been an important part of this long-term project, and I owe him and his wife Ira a great debt for their friendship and help over the years.

These and other friends and colleagues took their precious time and made the effort to read and comment on the manuscript in part or in whole. Those who read individual chapters include: Leonid Gibianskii, Erik Kulavig, Wolfgang Mueller, Daniel Perez, Silvio Pons, and Anita Prazmowska. Alfred J. Rieber and Ronald G. Suny read and commented on the entire manuscript, as did my Stanford History Department colleague and friend, James J. Sheehan. Both of the readers for Harvard University Press were also very helpful in this connection. Especially Mark Kramer's incisive criticisms were extremely important in sharpening my approach to several conceptual issues in the manuscript. Many of the readers above responded willingly to the questions and issues I placed before them in response to their suggestions and critiques. I trust the book is better as a result. Many thanks also go to Kathleen McDermott, Executive Editor at Harvard University Press, who—from the time she received the manuscript—has been an enthusiastic and engaged partner in this endeavor.

Over the years I have had numerous student research assistants, both graduate and undergraduate, who have contributed to this project. The undergraduates usually worked with me on the Soviet Union and postwar Europe as part of the International Relations Summer Research College. I thank the Director of Stanford's International Relations Program and Summer Research College over the past several years, Michael Tomz, as a way to express my gratitude both to him for the opportunity to participate in the program, but also to the many summer college students who contributed to this book. The undergraduates in my spring 2016 freshman seminar on Stalin and Europe helped me re-gear my thinking about the project. Let me also express my gratitude to present and past Stanford Ph.D. students in East European and Soviet History who have contributed in various ways to the completion of this work: Jelena Batinic, Lukas Dovern, Kristo Nurmis, Daniel Perez, and Beata Szymkow. I am beholden in particular to Simon Ertz, a former Ph.D. student, who did yeoman work in reading, editing, and commenting extensively on the entire manuscript. Natalia Reshetova of the Hoover Institution provided important research assistance on various issues. These younger Stanford scholars and others, whom I have undoubtedly left out, took this work seriously, collected materials, asked thought-provoking questions, and participated in its execution.

Two document collections and one compendium that I co-edited with Austrian, German, and Russian colleagues make their appearance in the footnotes of this study. I also authored several articles and dictionary and encyclopedia pieces that articulate some of the ideas and use some of the material that make up parts of the book. Perhaps most centrally, I wrote a general article on Stalin and Europe an embarrassingly long time ago that set out some of the ideas and the case study approach I follow in this book: Norman M. Naimark, "Stalin and Europe in the Postwar Period, 1945–53: Issues and Problems," *Journal of Modern European History,* vol. 2, no. 1 (2004): 28–57. I thank the editors and publisher of that journal for their interest in that piece. Since the early 1990s, my thinking about early postwar Europe has been nurtured by the conferences and publications of The Cold War International History Project at the Woodrow Wilson International Center for Scholars in Washington, DC. I am indebted to the Center, to the National Security Archive located at George Washington University, as well as to the community of Cold War historians—John Gaddis, Mark Kramer, Melvyn Leffler, Vojtech Mastny, Christian Ostermann, Silvio Pons, Arne Westad, and Vlad Zubok, among others—for including me in their endeavors.

Finally, I would like to thank my wife and fellow historian Katherine Jolluck and my son Ben, for putting up with the frequent absences from home on research trips and the long weekend hours in my office on campus. Katherine has followed this work almost from the beginning, read much of it in draft, and contributed to the completion of the manuscript in countless ways. I have been extremely fortunate in having such supportive friends and family, including my now adult daughters, Sarah and Anna. No one has been more important in my life and work than my spectacularly loving mother, Selma Carra, who died on September 5, 2017, at the age of ninety-six, when I was teaching and finishing up the Italian chapter in Florence. This book is dedicated to her memory.

Index